THE TEXT
AND THE VOICE

THE TEXT AND THE VOICE

Writing, Speaking, and Democracy in American Literature

ALESSANDRO PORTELLI

COLUMBIA UNIVERSITY PRESS
New York

Columbia University Press
New York Chichester, West Sussex

Library of Congress Catalog-in-Publication Data

Portelli, Alessandro.
[Testo e la voce. English]
The text and the voice : writing, speaking, and democracy in American literture / Alessandro Portelli.
p. cm.
Includes bibliographical references and index.
ISBN 0-231-08498-6
1. American—literature—History and criticism. 2. National characteristics, American, in literature. 3. Politics and literature—United States—History. 4. Written communication—United States—History. 5. Oral communication—United States—History. 6. Demcracy—United States—History. 7. Democracy in literature. I. Title.
PS169.N35P6713 1994 93-38926
810.9—dc20

CIP

Casebound editions of Columbia University Press books are printed on permanent and durable acid-free paper.

Printed in the United States of America

c 10 9 8 7 6 5 4 3 2 1

Contents

Acknowledgments

Gracias a la vida
que me ha dado tanto
me ha dado el sonido
y el abecedario.

Violeta Parra

This book was made possible by the encouragement, advice, and critical conversation of a number of people. Agostino Lombardo, always more than a teacher to me, announced twenty years ago that I would one day write a book like this; I didn't believe I would, but he did, and I thank him for it. Like him, Biancamaria Pisapia, Myra Jehlen, and Werner Sollors read different versions of the manuscript and helped with criticism and suggestions. Annalucia Accardo, Bruno Cartosio, Riccardo Duranti, Gurney Norman, Maria Antonietta Saracino, Anna Scacchi, Anna Scannavini, and Michael Staub are only a few of the friends and colleagues with whom I shared dialogues and conversations that influenced the writing of the book. Franco Moretti provided the first occasion in which the general outline was put together and tested in public. The project grew and took shape in the classroom, under the eyes and ears of hundreds of students. Their reactions, misreadings included, were precious to me. And then, Mariella, Matteo, and Stefano Portelli: they endured.

This book is the result of research and thinking that goes back to the beginnings of my career and therefore incorporates both ideas, passages, and analyses that have appeared in different form elsewhere and the germs of many future projects. Wherever appropriate, I have indicated these earlier formulations in the notes; in all cases, what appears here is so thoroughly revised and thought over as to be unrecognizable. The same applies to the Italian edition, *Il testo e la voce* (Rome 1992). I see the present book not as a translation but as a different text. In the first place, the fact of addressing a U.S. rather than an Italian audience changed my approach, subtly at times, radically always. In the second place, I have been able to benefit from reviews and public discussions, and thus to identify strengths and weaknesses and to recognize at least some of the points that needed revision and clarification: I owe a great deal to a very kind and perceptive review by Remo Ceserani, as well as to Laura Coltelli, Guido Fink, Nadia Fusini, Domenico Starnone, Carole Beebe Tarantelli, and, once again, Agostino Lombardo. In the third place, the passing of time allowed me to do more research and more thinking.

Fellowships at the W. E. B. DuBois Institute at Harvard University and at the Appalachian Center of the University of Kentucky allowed me to concentrate on research and to have access to the sources. On the other hand, the book was conceived and written almost entirely in Italy, where bibliographic resources can be very spotty. Therefore, the editions used are essentially those available to me at the different stages of research and writing: not always the very best but, I hope, always adequate. I received precious cooperation from Giovanna Marrone and Tiziana Buonfiglio, of the Foreign Languages library at Villa Mirafiori, and from Alessandra Surdi and the staff of the library of the Centro Italiano di Studi Americani in Rome. Gianni Grazioli made thousands of photocopies. Francesca Battisti did what she could to verify continuity and coherence in the Italian text and to put some order in the chaos of footnotes and references. Julia Hairston carefully read the first draft of my English version and improved it immensely.

Of course, errors and imperfections are bound to crop up, and they are my responsibility alone. I hope, however, that they may be matters of detail. "What I contend for," as Hawthorne said, "is the authenticity of the outline."

Introduction: The Torn-Up Letter and the Headless Ghost

I will take as my text a passage from Washington Irving's "The Legend of Sleepy Hollow." This is one of the stories in which Irving lays the foundations of a national imagination by importing and inventing legends for a nation that believed it had none. As is to be expected in a foundation text, "Sleepy Hollow" opens on the explanation of names:

> This name [Tarrytown] was given, we are told, in former days, by the good housewives of the adjacent country, from the inveterate propensity of their husbands to linger about the village tavern on market days. Be that as it may, I do not vouch for the fact, but merely advert to it, for the sake of being precise and authentic.[1]

However, how can a narrator who cannot vouch for his facts, who only has access to legends and gossip, be "precise and authentic"? Diedrich Knickerbocker, Irving's imaginary historian among whose "papers" this story is said to have been found, prefers in fact to conduct his "historical researches . . . not so much among books as among men," and women: only among "the old burghers, and . . . their wives" does he find stores of "that legendary lore so invaluable to true history."[2] The "scrupulous accuracy" and the "unquestionable authority" of precise and authentic written history float, therefore, on a ghost sea of orality.

The legend of Sleepy Hollow is about a ghost, who lost his head in "a nameless battle in the Revolutionary war." While drawing our attention to the naming of the place, Irving hints of the fact that he cannot name the events on which the country is founded. Nameless and headless, the "revolutionary war" evokes that symbol of all revolutions, from Cromwell to Robespierre: the beheading of the king; the "headless ghost" is the unburied memory of a violent national origin. But the headless ghost also designates the revolution's consequences: an apparently formless republican democracy, a state without a center and without a head, in which authority is elusive and yet inescapable, and where the outlines of identity fade in equality and mobility. As we will see, the cluster of symbols centered on the connection of orality, the headless ghost, and the foundations and form of American democracy reappears throughout the history of American literature.

Let us now take another text, also endowed with a founding status, since it has been said that "all modern American literature comes"[3] from it: Mark Twain's *The Adventures of Huckleberry Finn.* Its most crucial scene is the one in which Huck faces the conflict between his "conscience," which prompts him to return the slave Jim to his legal owner, and his "heart," which tells him to help Jim run away.[4]

"[S]omething inside of me kept saying . . . ": Huck's conflict is also a contrast between orality and writing. Conscience is always a "voice" of some kind, but an inner one, a voice that cannot issue into sound: Huck attempts to pray, "But the words wouldn't come." "You can't pray a lie," he concludes—but you can write it: "I'll go and write a letter . . . So I got a piece of paper and a pencil, all glad and excited, and set down and wrote."

Writing defers language away from the subject enough for Huck to be able to put down words other than those of his own deeper, inner self. But this will not be denied: "And [I] got to thinking . . . and I see Jim before me . . . and we a-floating along, talking and singing, and laughing." Memory and voice, the stuff of oral culture, rise up to defeat the power of writing. At this point, with a reversed sort of prayer, " 'All right, then, I'll go to hell,'' Huck destroys the letter.

Irving's legendary orality is an incorporeal presence that destabilizes the concrete matter of facts and the authority of history; in Mark Twain, the voice appears instead as the vehicle of a higher, further authenticity and concreteness, expressed in the material presence of the body, the spontaneity of the "heart," the supposed naturalness of Huck's vernacular. Huck's and Jim's voices "a-floating" on the river in laughter and song are Mark Twain's response to the "floating facts" of Irving's historians. Floating and flowing no longer stand for the threat of ghostly formlessness, but for the liberating possibilities of mutability and movement.

And yet, if we look and listen again, we realize that the scene of Huck's conflict is all but silent. Huck's voice will not come, Jim's laughter and talking and singing are only remembered, and after all Huck is writing a book: the authentic presence of the voice is deferred, remembered, transcribed. The voice of the heart does not materialize as an alternative presence to replace the scripture dissolved by the headless ghost. "I was double," says Huck—and so is language, doubled into an orality (immaterial sound) seeking to become permanent without freezing and a writing (soundless matter) that seeks to achieve movement and voice without dissolving—an incorporeal ghost seeking a body, and a material body seeking a voice.

This book is an attempt to interpret the foundations of American culture through literature and to interpret literature through the interplay of the written and oral foundations of language. It is a search for the complex and shifting relationships between language and imagination on the one hand and American cultural and political history on the other. The perception and recollection of origins in discovery and revolution, the anxieties of the democratic experiment, the multiple stratifications of race, ethnicity, gender, and class—all these elements are shaped in unstable representations, founded in concepts of authenticity and authority identified from time to time either with the textualized documents of writing or with the elusive presence of the voice.

My thesis is that democracy, orality, and writing are all mobile signifiers, not anchored once and for all to fixed paradigms of meaning. Orality and writing are forever exchanging roles, functions, and meanings in a mutual relationship of seeking and desire rather than exclusion and polarization. Both orality and writing are capable of standing either for absence or for presence, for society and for the individual, for certainty and for doubt, for the spirit and for the body, for life and for death, according to which facet these pairs happen to present and to the connecting matter that holds them together. Democracy, in turn, stands at the shifting center of a polarity between delegation and participation (that is, from deferment to presence, from writing to voice); between the order of achieved democracy and the disorder of the revolution from which it originates (and the revolutions that it fears); between the impersonal language of institutions and the fusional immersion of mass society; between the equality of citizenship rights and difference imposed, claimed, sought for.

Between these two axes of shifting signifiers, the relationship can only be one of elusive and contradictory change. Writing appears to found national identity and institutions, only to be undermined and called into question by orality; orality attempts to establish itself as a satisfactory alternative foundation, only to be frustrated by the ironic deferment of writing; and the interplay of textualized discourse and aural shape in the artificial voices of the electronic age delineates the foundations of a new power, permanent and always new, incorporeal and inescapable.

Part 1, "Foundation: The Voice Below the Text," shows how the unacknowledged shadow of orality haunts and shakes the stability and certainty of texts and institutions. The first chapter discusses theories of orality, and their impact on the practice and theory of literature. (Given the theoretical and methodological character of this introductory chapter, some readers may want to start from chapter 2, and go back to this later). The next two chapters explore the symbolic tensions that identify orality with disorder and formlessness in literary texts and in political discourse, both in the post-Revolutionary generations and in certain contemporary ethnic and postmodern texts.

Part 2, "The Voice in the Text," studies the ways in which the relationship of voice and time influences the creation and form of the literary text in terms of composition, reproduction, and symbolism. Chapter 4 explores the relationship of orality, writing, and time as it materializes in the devices of improvisation, repetition, open and multiple endings, intertextuality, and digression; chapter 5 is concerned with the spatial representation of a multiplicity of voices in dialogue and in narration; chapter 6 analyzes the sound symbolism of creation, birth, and death.

Finally, part 3, "Second Foundation: The Text upon the Voice," follows the ways in which, from the age of realism to the Depression to the mass culture of the electronic age, the technologizing of the word has attempted to control and possess language by appropriating the voice and textualizing its sound. Chapters 7 and 8 are devoted to the questions of dialect, folklore, and regionalism in literature. Chapter 9 explores the distinct Native American and African-American ways of dealing with the interplay of orality and writing and suggests that American literature is the weaving of interacting but distinct traditions rather than a unitary phenomenon. Chapter 10 analyzes the silencing and recovering of the voice of working people in the industrial age, and the final chapter is dedicated to the transition of public orality from political and religious oratory to the secondary orality of mass media, both in popular music and in the projections of a technological voice in science fiction.

The book's manner of presentation is determined both by its subject matter and by its methodological approach. Contemporary critical practice has made us aware that while some distance must be maintained at all times, yet one can not discuss a subject in a language and logic entirely alien to it. In the case of this book, the study of orality highlights the importance of process and performance rather than product and result; therefore, establishing definitive conclusions may at times be less important than illuminating—and involving the reader in—the process of working toward them. For this reason, I tend in most cases to lay my "texts" before the reader, and then proceed to "open" them in interpretation, inviting the reader to accompany and challenge me in the sort of (ideal) antiphonal dialogue that structures conversational exchanges as well as sermons. I am aware that this means expecting my implied reader to do a great deal of work rather than just chiming in amens from the Amen Corner; it is my hope that actual readers may find that this work does not go altogether unrewarded. As has been said, "In este libro, we wish to stretch la imaginación."[5]

Earlier, I described the theme of the book as the analysis of the elusive relationship between two shifting sets of signifiers. This means that the manner of presentation cannot be linearly descriptive and syntagmatic but must be methodological and paradigmatic. Consequently, the discussion is organized less on chronology or lines of theme and genre than on the associative, allusive unfolding of ideas in the course of discussion. Paula Gunn Allen speaks of the "achronic" and "accretive" traits that modern Native American novels derive from their oral sources; in the same fashion, this book, steeped in the experience of oral discourse, grows and builds accretively upon itself rather than on a preconceived outline or an objective chronology.[6]

Thus while I do follow a broadly historical drift (from early national literature to contemporary mass culture), what interests me are the lines and links of analogy and difference over space and time, across genres and identities. The procedures, devices, and symbols I am looking for are not to be found in isolation in individual authors, texts, or historical periods: rather, they are shared by widely diverse texts and authors, and in turn coexist with their opposites within the same texts. Injecting Pynchon, DeLillo, and Vizenor in a discussion of Hawthorne, Melville, and Poe (and juxtaposing Hank Williams to Emerson) may seem quite a leap, until it can be seen that the connection illuminates both sides in ways in which a series of distinct chronological presentations might not.

In the same manner, although the book includes a number of detailed treatments of specific texts (from Poe's "William Wilson" to Morrison's *Beloved*, from Momaday's "Man Made of Words" to Jack London's *The Iron Heel*), the order of treatment is organized around the technical, symbolic, political forms of the voice's impact over the text. Now, most complex texts involve more than just one paradigm and one set of devices and symbols: for instance, in *The Scarlet Letter* the voice appears both as a threat to textual authentication and authority and as the possible foundation of a higher sort of authority and authenticity; the text is both threatened by the voice and built upon it. It will be found, therefore, that the discussion of certain texts and authors—Washington Irving and Toni Morrison, N. Scott Momaday and Herman Melville, Leslie Silko and William Faulkner—is not exhausted in one place only but is picked up again and again at different points, according to the methodological aspect under consideration. Indeed, the fact that one has to return again to certain texts and authors is evidence of their canonic dimension: it means that their internal dialectics and contradictions confer to their treatment of the relationship between voice and text a complexity and an intensity not found elsewhere and not to be exhausted in one approach.

Now that I have mentioned the concept of canonicity, a few words are in order about canon, inclusions, and exclusions.

Although the coverage of the book may appear to be quite extensive, inclusiveness per se is not a goal. Authors and texts have not been chosen on the basis of a desire to cover everything but according to their aptness in illuminating specific methodological and theoretical aspects (and if examples abound and sometimes duplicate, it is in order to show that we are not dealing with exceptional or unique cases). The aim is to create a grid in which other, perhaps equally important texts, may be located, compared, and re-interpreted. Thus an African-American paradigm that includes Frederick Douglass, Charles Chesnutt, Zora Neale Hurston, Ralph Ellison, and Toni Morrison leaves out—to name only a few—Jean Toomer, Langston Hughes, Sterling Brown, James Baldwin, John Wideman, Paule Marshall, Toni Cade Bambara. The sequence of Rebecca Harding Davis, Jack London, F. Scott Fitzgerald, John Steinbeck, Erskine Caldwell, James Agee, and Woody Guthrie far from exhausts all representations of the voices of the industrial age and of working people but sketches an interpretive hypothesis and method that can be checked against other texts. My emphasis on Momaday, Silko, Vizenor, and Welch does not adequately recognize Linda Hogan or Louise Erdrich. While Native American and African-American ethnic orality is discussed in detail, the treatment of the Hispanic tradition focuses on one Puerto Rican exemplary author, the Jewish tradition is only referred to in passing, and there is no reference to Asian American writing. This is not intended to diminish the importance of these cultural traditions and literary expressions; rather, these limits of the text indicate the limitations of the author. "Oh, Time, Strength, Cash, and Patience!" My feeling, however, is that while much is left out yet the grid provides the reader with the means to fill out the gaps. Still, I wish I had had more time and space to give Ring Lardner and Maxine Hong Kingston their due.

With very few exceptions (most notably Dickinson and Whitman), this book is about prose. This has to do with the limits of the author's competence, but also with a theoretical consideration. One of the fundamental assumptions of the book is that literariness consists to a large extent in language's effort to go against its own grain. Sound—rhythm, breath, and, to some extent, voice and performance—is, however, the very grain of poetry.[7] Therefore, an analysis of the poetic voice would go "against the grain" of the text much less than an analysis of sound and voice in narrative prose, to which they are supposedly less intrinsic (the same consideration shapes the emphasis on writing and literacy in the discussion of Native American and African-American authors, whose grounding in orality is much more explicit than, say, Hawthorne's and has already received ample and competent treatment).

The same reason lies behind the exclusion of the analyses of oral genres (from ballads to blues) that were part of my original project and early drafts. On the other hand, the direct experience of orality through fieldwork in folklore and oral history impregnates the entire approach of the book and its specific readings of literary texts.

This book does not wish to involve itself in the moot point of canon expansion and revision. Too often, opening the canon has meant either assimilating the new inclusions under the old paradigms (proving that Zitkala-Sa is "as good as" Henry James, or vice versa) or skipping the question of paradigms altogether (whereby Zitkala-Sa and Henry James may be included in the same book, but for different and often unanalyzed reasons, and remain ultimately uncommunicating). It seems to me that if we are really looking for new canons we must also look for paradigms that may account both for comparability and difference, and that the paradigm of the voice—the interplay, the mutual search of orality and writing—offers great possibilities in this regard. The paradigm of the voice is, on the one hand, universal enough to be relevant to a variety of texts; on the other hand, it is specific (culture-specific, gender-specific, class-specific) enough to protect us from the risk of assimilating this variety into an enforced unity and implicit hierarchy. One further advantage is that, while allowing for the recognition and analysis of the social difference that is one primary motive for canon revision, the paradigm of the voice remains firmly grounded in the foundations of literary study, i.e., the meanings and uses of language.

Male and female; whites, blacks, Native Americans, Hispanics; intellectuals and workers; the literary mainstream and mass culture—all of these, and others, must necessarily face the question of writing the voice and voicing the text; but they approach this problem from different backgrounds with different points of view and go about it in different ways. Thus the common terrain of comparability becomes the background that allows communication and enhances difference: the paradigm of the voice allows us to talk about Herman Melville and Dolly Parton in the same book, but it also allows them to talk to each other without having to be measured by each other's standards.

Canons traditionally imply hierarchies, and a consolidated hierarchy in our culture (grounded on a linear concept of history and progress) has implied the superiority of writing over orality. So intrinsic is a hierarchic, value-laden approach that, in discussing the ideas in this book, I have found that listeners often assumed that when I was arguing that writing is not "better" than orality I was automatically (and romantically) claiming that orality is better than writing. It is a fact that the tendency has often been to replace the vision of orality as "impoverished" with respect to writing with one of orality as "exemplary" and somewhat more virtuous.[8] This book, however, is not about vertical hierarchies but about horizontal differences; the recognition that both orality and writing possess qualities and perform functions that the other lacks is what makes the voice invaluable to the writer and the text invaluable to the singer and storyteller. The moving force in this dialectic of difference is desire; the ultimate impossibility for text and voice of possessing each other in perfect reproduction and representation is what keeps both of them alive and moving. The mutual search of voice and text goes on forever.

The dialectical tension and mutual search of orality and writing, which I have attempted to reconstruct in this book, are also a version of a larger dilemma. After a meeting with Melville, Nathaniel Hawthorne noted in his diary that his friend could "neither believe, nor be comfortable in his unbelief."[9] In our times, it is easy to feel comfortable in unbelief and to cultivate doubt as an arrogant basis of certainty. Melville has provided text for critical approaches founded on a euphoric sense of the dissolution of meaning, infinite semiosis, and vanishing referents. Yet, if Melville's "erections" are unfinished, it is not only because he does not wish to complete them but also because, though wishing it, he finds it impossible. "Would that a man could do something & then say—It is finished.—not that thing only, but all others—that he has reached his uttermost, & can never excel it," he wrote.[10] Just as there is a "political realism" that adapts to the world as it is and rejects all efforts to find meanings in it, there is also a "realism" that insists in asking for the impossible.

This is what the impossible reciprocal search of voice and text is about. At the most naive level, orality stands for the desire of all that is "authentic," for lived experience, for the people; it stands for the body, the breath, the spirit. As we will see, all this disappears when we reach out to touch it, and the only thing left is the "difference" of writing. On the other hand, the textual, rational, documentary, and material certainties of writing slip through our fingers when we begin to listen for the voices inside and underneath the written page.

Yet, as we contemplate dissolution, we ought not to forget that if we have chosen to listen and to look, it was for the sake of something that we could hold on to. And if we have chosen to speak and to write, it was in the attempt to create it.

Part One

Foundation: The Voice Beneath the Text

CHAPTER ONE

Houses of Dawn

In *True Stories*, David Byrne's 1986 movie, the workers of an electronics assembly plant are shown talking to one other as the pieces move forward on the assembly line. Thus in the very place where the modern high-tech machinery of communication is created and assembled, the human voice still seems to be the ordinary tool of communication and exchange. Our contemporary world is "as much an oral as a literate [we might add, and electronic] culture."[1] The word *orality*, however, still retains connotations of archaism, tradition, and folklore. Both in common and academic usage, the ordinary, ephemeral uses of the voice in our everyday experience are often overlooked, in favor of the more durable and elaborate forms of oral expression associated with "oral" and "primitive" cultures. The very mechanics of scholarly work promote this approach. Scientific study seems to require a permanent object that will not slip through our fingers as we are attempting to understand it. The movement of spoken discourse must be turned into the stability of a "preserved lasting form," a text (memorized, transcribed, or recorded), before we are ready to consider it.[2] The fact that writing is of more recent origin than orality also helps create a false sense that orality belongs to the past history of human communication, to epochs and societies antecedent to the advent of writing. These attitudes, however, derive less from the nature of orality than from the mentality of observers steeped in the reified and linear world of writing and print.

It is a fact, however, that, while orality is a universal trait, reading and writing are "secondary attainments in human life."[3] Some cultures do not write, but all cultures speak; and, even in societies endowed with writing, literacy and access to means of written communication are unevenly distributed. Thus "oral" and folk cultures still perform orally functions that other cultures entrust to writing or to other means of communication. In order to do so, "oral" cultures are forced to create sophisticated forms of textualization of the voice and elaborate oral aesthetics. What makes "oral" cultures different, however, is not that they speak more but that they write less or not at all: not just the continuity of a nexus but the violence of an exclusion as well. The nostalgia and fantasies about "primitive orality," generated from the very core of the hegemonic cultures of literacy, often serve the function of hiding the fact that exclusive orality can also be the result of an imposition, of cultural violence.

The relationship of orality and literacy is ultimately shaped by the interaction of three factors: the universal practice of orality; its intense and formalized use in social environments with limited or no access to writing; and the ideological aura of orality within literate societies. In this chapter, we will review the theories of the relationship of orality and writing with the formation of mentality and the forms of knowledge. We will discuss the limitations of a binary opposition of orality and literacy as opposed to a dialogic interaction, and explore the relationship of voice and presence, as imagined by literate culture (e. g., in deconstruction) and as represented by artists steeped in cultures of orality. Literature is the ground where the separation and hierarchy between orality and writing is blurred and subverted, where language goes against its own grain to seek dynamic writing and stable voice. This is why, to a great extent, contemporary literary theory and modernist literary experiment are grounded (often unawares) in terms, precedents, and models generated by orality.

THEORIES: ORALITY, WRITING, KNOWLEDGE, PRESENCE

When I tell these stories, do you picture it, or do you just write it down?

—Joseph Peynetsa

As the hunter looks upon the snow and says, Here but yesterday there passed a rabbit . . . so . . . doest thou, too, look upon the paper and say thus."

—Jack London, "The League of the Old Men"

According to Jack Goody, the emergence of writing (especially in its alphabetic and, later, typographic forms) freed the human mind from the problem of "memory storage" and allowed humanity to "stand back" from language and "examine it in a more abstract, generalized, and 'rational' way." Writing helps objectify language and thus develop rational and critical thinking as well as impersonal authority: "criticism and commentary on the one hand and the orthodoxy of the book on the other."[4]

The process Goody describes is gradual and multicausal: alphabetic writing does not create rationality and scientific objectivity but rather—along with other factors—increases, facilitates, or foregrounds functions that already existed, albeit in embryonic forms, in the human mind.[5] These developments, however, are still represented as basically linear, minimizing both the elements of reciprocity (the contributions of orality to the diffusion of writing) and the prices paid. In the dualistic approach, diachrony has an irresistible tendency to turn into dichotomy.

For instance, although Walter J. Ong has done more than anyone else to clarify the importance of orality, both in the past and in the contemporary world, he finally adopts a binary approach in which the oral and the literate mind are characterized by sharp dualistic, and implicitly hierarchic, oppositions: aggregative vs. analytic, redundant vs. essential, conservative vs. innovative, agonistic and empathetic vs. objectively distanced, situational vs. abstract. These pairs are laid out in a linear historical series, so that writing seems at times to replace orality altogether.[6]

"We have to die to continue living," writes Ong. Orality dies to make way for writing and rationality and only reappears in our time and world as a "secondary" phenomenon, "revived" or resuscitated by the aural dimension of electronic media, like some kind of revenant.[7] This is a metaphor we will find over and over in the literary record, in which orality often appears as a ghost or an unburied corpse that refuses to stay dead while writing functions as a sort of tombstone that keeps in place the agonistic subjectivity evoked by the voice.

This diachronic hierarchy, describing our very speech as a "residual" form of expression overcome and replaced by a more recent and advanced one, is itself the product of a typographic (linear and hypotactic) vision of history. An "oral" approach, additive and paratactic, would help us realize instead that each new mode of language does not replace and abolish earlier ones but adds to and modifies them, expanding possibilities and restructuring the whole field of communication. "You Americans have a strange way of thinking about time," says a Mexican character in Sandra Cisneros's *Woman Hollering Creek* (but he could be talking about any typographic culture): "You think old ages end, but that's not so. It's ridiculous to think one age has overcome another. American time is running alongside the calendar of the sun even if your world doesn't know it."[8] Thus the advantage of our literate (and electronic) cultures over exclusively oral ones does not lie in the fact that we possess better tools of communication but that we possess more of them, "alongside" one another.[9] We are able to both read and write (and to transmit and receive) and to speak and hear; we can select, for each situation and function, the more appropriate medium; we can experiment with different modes and technologies of the word, specialize them, mirror them, weave them together, and mix them in ever-changing syntheses and dialogues.

This, of course, is an abstract model, which becomes more complicated when we take into account the relationships of language and power. Of course, especially in exclusively oral cultures in which other means were not available, orality has historically been used as a tool of power and social control; and this function is by no means abolished by the advent of literacy[10] (one need only think of Ahab's speech to the crew of the Pequod in *Moby-Dick*). It is a fact, however, that the voice is materially accessible to all, while the technologizing of the world implies, if nothing else, materials and knowledge that can be owned and restricted. As Goody shows, the advent of writing is also a watershed in the formation of the state, from Hammurabi to the modern nation-states of Africa (a key step in the process, of course, is the first modern written constitution, that of the United States). The hegemony of writing, in other words, depreciates all those functions that do not require alphabetic competence or writing-generated knowledge.[11]

Hence the insistence on the prices paid, on what was lost for the progress that writing made possible. As the Egyptian king Thamus says in Plato's *Phaedrus*, writing plants forgetfulness in the hearts of men, who will lose the art of memory and only be able to recall things from external signs rather than from their own interior. Claude Lévi-Strauss notes that, with the advent of writing, we no longer relate to others in terms of concrete, direct mutual understanding but increasingly depend on mediated, written reconstructions. A dangerous gap seems to open between language and knowledge and experience, between outside and inside.[12] In the words of Joseph Peynetsa, Zuni oral storyteller and poet, we know how to write things and forget how to imagine them.[13]

Writing frees the mind from the anxiety of losing what it cannot contain; but it atrophies individual memory and makes collective memory (to lift a word from Melville) "ungraspable." Modern literate individuals have potential access to such a surplus of stored information that no one is able to perceive culture as a meaningful whole or even to master entirely a single field of knowledge.[14] Orality then remains the imagined location of what Lévi-Strauss called "authenticity," and others call "presence." Gianni Bosio saw in the advent of the tape recorder the possibility of giving recognizable permanence to the oral culture of the popular classes, to build "the critical awareness and the antagonistic presence of the popular and proletarian world."[15] Walter J. Ong notes the link between immaterial, oral "word" and spiritual, divine "Word"; to him, the passage from orality to writing also implies a loss of the presence of the sacred, which may be recovered in the "aural" environment of contemporary media.[16] The "presence of the voice" in oral poetry has also been linked to the awareness of space and context, and to the material, erotic impact of the body; in the "grain" of the voice, Roland Barthes feels "the materiality of the body speaking its native tongue."[17]

There are obvious dangers of romantic reductionism in the identification of voice and "presence." This explains the insistence, especially in poststructuralist thinking, on reversing the logical, chronological, metaphoric order of orality and writing. Roland Barthes appreciates the bodily "grain" of the voice but rushes to clarify that it is but another form of writing, a singing writing of the tongue, generated by the "friction" of music and language. Together with Eric Marty, Barthes claims in a deliberate paradox that "man knew how to read before he knew how to speak": the first traces and inscriptions mankind saw were animal tracks on the snow—like the rabbit tracks in Jack London's story or the traces of the bear deciphered by the hunter ("I know the signs so well") in Thomas Bangs Thorpe's "The Big Bear of Arkansas."[18]

But these acts of interpretation can only be described as "reading" metaphorically, if at all. As a linguistic act, reading (like writing) implies a degree of convention (and intention) not to be found in the animal tracks on the snow or in atmospheric signs. Otherwise we could say that early human instinctive vocal responses to the environment were already "speech," and reverse chronology once more. Barthes's and Marty's paradox is an intriguing statement of the autonomy of writing as a distinctive realm of language and signs rather than as a mere reproduction of speech and sound; but to assign chronological priority to writing is only another ideological depreciation of the functions and subjects of speech in favor of writing and its depositaries.

The most radical and definitive criticism of the voice as "presence" is Jacques Derrida's attack on "logocentrism" and "phonocentrism." Derrida deconstructs the metaphysics of presence (origins and truth, and their connection with the logos) to prove that distance, the chasm of difference/deferment, is embodied in the very constitution of linguistic signs. This lack, this absence, is found in both writing and speech; therefore, "oral language already belongs to this writing."[19]

In this way Derrida makes a clean sweep of all residues of presence implied in the idea of orality and the voice: all language, all symbolic production hinge on the absence that constitutes writing. In this process, however, rather than demythicizing orality, Derrida erases it completely (and needlessly) as a dimension of, and difference in, language: "writing" designates all linguistic functions, and language is language only in so far as it pertains to this "writing."[20] This creates an unnecessary, implicit hierarchy, and a need for acrobatic and embarassed distinctions and specifications. Thus when Derrida asks "When and where does the trace, writing in general, common root of speech and writing, narrow itself down in 'writing' in the colloquial sense"[21], he oscillates between at least three overlapping meanings of "writing":

- a general "grammatological" one ("writing" as "the trace," "common root")
- a "colloquial" one (writing as opposed to speech)
- an intermediate one, which includes all nonlinguistic forms of graphic expression, as well as the universal ability to "defer" and "program" absence.

Between these three meanings, slidings and confusions are frequent. In so far as writing is said to be constitutive of humanity, Derrida cannot deny that it is possessed by those humans who do not write language. He is forced therefore to widen or tighten the definition according to circumstances and context. Thus when he criticizes Lévi-Strauss's statement that the Nambikwara do not possess "writing," he shifts from Lévi-Strauss's "colloquial" meaning (the Nambikwara do not write language) to the intermediate one (like most human societies, the Nambikwara trace some kind of graphic sign) and then to the "grammatological" meaning (like all human beings, the Nambikwara possess a language, and their language is constituted by an absence).

This kind of undeclared shift in meaning recurs frequently in criticism influenced by deconstruction. Discussing the figures of the voice in Whitman, Régis Durand writes that "speech in its 'articulated' form [is] already of the nature of writing," as if all articulation belonged to writing.[22] Even Henry Louis Gates, Jr., in his reading of the Yoruba myths of Esu Elegbara (mediator between men and gods, and therefore guardian of language), writes of "a complex notion of writing, a notion that accounts for a vocal writing and a graphic writing." The intense interaction of voice and script, "the tension between the oral and the written modes of narration," which Gates uncovers and discusses differs from the Derridean orthodoxy of the primacy or exclusivity of writing; this difference, however, is somewhat obfuscated by the use of the Derridean paradox "vocal writing."[23] What would we lose if we were to write "a complex notion of language, one that accounts for a vocal mode and a written one"? Perhaps we would lose the notion of writing as the only true language, of which speech is a secondary manifestation. On the other hand, we would perhaps gain the vision of a system with no center, or with a multiple, movable one: the play of mirrors of an endless reciprocal figuration. After all, as Gates points out, Esu-Elegbara has two mouths.

In all his discussion of writing and speech, Derrida rarely analyzes actual examples of oral discourse, as practiced by performing speakers rather than as imagined by writers. The couple writer-reader is seldom complemented by the system of speaker-hearer-respondant; in the Derridean universe, one hardly ever listens to the voice of another but only hears\understands one's own, in the process of "*s'entendre parler*." Derrida's definition of our culture as "phonocentric," then, is to be read as a deliberate paradox. Only cultures centered on writing delegate the myth of presence to an imaginary orality: alphabetic societies are not dominated by the voice but haunted by its ghost. As Ong notes, Plato's phonocentric passages in the *Phaedrus* can only be conceived and formulated in and through writing (in fact, Plato carries out a deliberate attack on orality in the *Republic*).[24] Though Saussure claims that writing only exists to represent speech, modern linguistics in the very process of establishing itself as a science (i.e., a cognitive mode only made possible by writing) assumes writing as the datum and derives from textualized and printed language its postulates of isochrony and segmentation.[25] The voice deconstructed by Derrida is not the phonetic voice of human utterance but the phonologic voice imagined by alphabetic linguistics.[26] To deconstruct this voice is not so much to subvert the supposed hegemony of sound and speech, as to liberate ourselves from the phonocentric nostalgia generated by the hegemony of writing as a memory of its lost other side and a symptom of the uneasy awareness of its limitations.

OF AIR AND BRICKS: HOLDING THE VOICE, FREEING THE TEXT

So I grab the air and sing my song
But the air can not stand my singing long.

—Etheridge Knight, "The Violent Space"

And then they were commanded to make
bricks out of nothing.

Margaret Walker, *Jubilee*

If we turn from the ambivalent self-perception of writing to the self-awareness of oral cultures, we can see that these, far from being uncritically "phonocentric," are constantly reexamining the relationship between voice and presence.

If there is a place where the deferment has "always already" taken place, this is indeed the voice: "Listening to speech is a sequential process dealing with just-vanished sounds," note Roman Jakobson and Linda Waugh; "the idea you have once spoken," Carlyle wrote, "is no longer yours; it is gone from you, so much life and virtue is gone."[27] Oral cultures are, as the South-African writer Bessie Head says, "precariously oral," intensely aware of living not so much in the fullness of presence as on the edge of disappearance—"one generation from extinction," as the Kiowa author N. Scott Momaday puts it.[28] Maxine Hong Kingston's Chinese ancestors knew that "Every word that falls from the mouth is a coin lost"; Louise Erdrich's Chippewa characters always speak "carefully, without letting . . . names loose in the wind"; and Leslie Marmon Silko's Pueblo storytellers and medicine men "never threw away words" because, when all you have is the voice, "the world is fragile."[29]

"It seemed to me," Momaday writes, "that the singers—and especially the old men among them—bore everything up on the strength of their voices, the valley, the mountains, and the grey November sky; that if suddenly they should fall silent, the whole of Creation would collapse in a moment."[30] The power of the voice is not founded on a reassuring presence but on its ambiguous and dangerous precariousness; it is "cherished and revered"—rare, precious, and holy—because it can both create the world and make it disappear. Silko's *Ceremony* opens with the story of Thought-Woman, who "named things/ and as she named them/they appeared"; precisely because it is made of the immaterial substance of voice and thought, the world is fragile and tenuous, like a song that the air barely manages to sustain.[31]

In literature, this spoken word giving birth to itself is consolidated in the tangible substance of writing and yet struggles to preserve its original motion. Those writers who retain a more direct and intense link with oral cultures represent the process of stabilizing orality in durable writing and of injecting into writing the movement, lightness, and the ungraspable airiness of the voice by means of synthetic metaphors of dissolution and consolidation, of melting and freezing. Leslie Silko is fascinated by images of lace and spider-webs: immaterial and indestructible textures capable of catching and holding sunlight in the fragile chain of language. Momaday develops the Navajo image of the universe—a *House Made of Dawn*—as a metaphor of his own writing, and perhaps of all literature; to make bricks out of the impalpable dawn is both to make orality permanent in writing and to dissolve in light the weight of the written word.[32]

African-American literature, as the epigraphs from Etheridge Knight and Margaret Walker demonstrate, is also quite familiar with the task of creating, with nothing but air, a building strong enough to sustain a song. W. E. B. DuBois depicts this dilemma in a similar image, one of song turning into bricks and bricks making music:

> To me Jubilee Hall seemed ever made of the songs themselves, and its bricks were red with the blood and dust of toil. Out of them rose for me morning, noon, and night, bursts of wonderful melody, full of the voices of my brothers and sisters, full of the voices of the past.[33]

From another oral culture and genre, the Appalachian folk sermon, James Still derives another metaphor of flow and consolidation, the *River of Earth* after which he names his 1940 novel. The mountains, Still's preacher says, are frozen waves, in which the planet preserves the memory of when it was made of fluid magma; likewise, the formulas, sayings, and proverbs of folk memory preserve the linguistic forms generated in the everlasting motion of orality.[34]

J. D. Salinger's classic image of the ducks and the pond in Central Park is yet another vision of frozen flight and suspended motion growing out of the influences of generational and ethnic orality. It is a figure of the immobility of writing and entropy,[35] but also of ironic salvation; stopping the flight, catching the children before they fall over the cliff, is one way of making time stand still, of frustrating death by anticipating it, of preventing words from melting and disappearing. Holden Caulfield knows one may lose the world by throwing words away: "don't ever tell anybody nothing: if you do, you start missing everybody" ("You'll lose it if you talk about it," says his laconic ancestor, Hemingway's Jake Barnes).[36]

Holden's fear of losing what you talk about is geared to the relationship between adolescence and time; like time (and like the river in *Huckleberry Finn*), the voice only moves in one direction, and its unilinear flow becomes an image of irreversible mutability, precariousness, even danger. What the voice says cannot be unsaid; what the voice creates cannot be undone. The words that created white people in *Ceremony* "cannot be called back"; they can only be partially and temporarily repaired, modified, or controlled by more words. Both the precariousness and the power of the voice, then, call for the same strategy: endeavoring to stop the motion of the voice in order to preserve and control it; making bricks out of air by means of ritual, form, and memory.

Memory is often represented as a form of writing, spatial and durable yet transient and changeable, like a wax tablet (or a computer disk).[37] Formalization, ritual, and repetition are necessary in order to inscribe words into memory. Zora Neale Hurston's folk audiences encourage storytellers by saying, "Yeah we done heard it, Joe, but Ah kin hear it some 'gin"; and the medicine man in *Ceremony* speaks as if "all had beed said before and he was only there to repeat it." Yet each repetition is a re-writing, one that injects time and individual modulation into the transmitted communal forms.[38] To repeat, then, is less a display of banality or redundancy than an active contribution to the survival of precarious cultures that retain the sense of their own presence only as long as they renew contact with themselves.

INTERACTION AND CONTRADICTION: ORALITY, WRITING, LITERATURE

An approach to the relationship of orality and writing that avoids some of the pratfalls of hierarchic binary oppositions can be found in conversation theory and discourse analysis. Here, orality and writing are viewed as distinct but coexistent sociolinguistic registers, which share the tasks of communication according to goals and circumstances. Orality and writing are not assigned to separate mentalities or historical periods but interact within one global sphere of communication. The difference is more of emphasis along a continuum than of inherent contrast; orality is more apt to focus on interpersonal involvement rather than message content, shared experience and knowledge rather than abstract logical coherence, synthetic understanding and recollection of themes rather than details of verbal form, and interaction with context and the nonverbal layers of exchange rather than the search for self-sufficient verbalization.[39]

A written text, therefore, is not the supplementary transcription of a preexistent oral utterance, nor is oral discourse incomplete writing or the mere actualization of preexistent text. Autonomous and interrelated, orality and writing "are always communicating with each other, by means of ambassadors and messengers" in terms of "painstaking or ironic" mutual representations.[40] Both, after all, share the same living space and general laws of language, refer to a common semantic universe, and are used by societies in which all writers are also speakers and many speakers are also writers.

The most immediate difference is that only writing (and recording, which, under many aspects, is another form of writing) preserves words after they are separated from the subject and context of enunciation. For this reason, writing is usually identified with the lasting, the tangible, the "certain, well-defined, durable," while orality is described as incorporeal, ephemeral, mutable, irreproducible, and continuous.[41] These differences, on the other hand, enable either mode of language to perform tasks that the other cannot: flowing with time or resisting it; interacting in real time with an actual hearer or projecting toward future and possible ideal or empirical readers; adapting to circumstances or adapting circumstances to itself. Because of this complementarity and tension, beyond mutual representations, each conscious speech act, written or oral, carries within itself the trace of its unfinishedness and the yearning for its missing half.

"More rational, more exact, more precise, more clear," writes Derrida, with reference to Rousseau, "the writing of the voice corresponds to a more efficient civil order."[42] In the age of writing, Giorgio R. Cardona noted, "the written form stands as the necessary, definitive ideal model of all expression, including oral utterance. Orality is no longer the same, even to its practitioners; it will always appear as somewhat lacking, less finished, less accomplished, less exquisite." The meaning of this perception, however, depends on whether we believe that complete is better than incomplete, that definitive, accomplished, certain, efficient are to be preferred to aleatory, indefinite, ephemeral. Good sociohistorical reasons support these preferences, but they are neither automatic nor universal nor entirely satisfying.

Literature is one of the areas in which this hierarchy of values is questioned and often subverted. "God keep me from ever completing anything," Melville cries out, as he leaves his cetology "unfinished" like the "uncompleted" cathedral of Cologne: "For small erections may be finished by their first architects; grand ones, true ones, ever leave the copestone for posterity."[43] Literature, of course, has an inherent tendency to erect itself into a monument more lasting than bronze; but it also knows that monumental durability could be its death. If all that is written can be preserved, soon there will be nothing new to write. The "anxiety of influence" haunts "a tradition grown too wealthy to need anything more," which may ultimately be "murdered by its own past strength."[44] Even as it erects its bronze monuments, literature endeavors to melt them; as it builds houses and cathedrals, it carefully leaves the copestone unplaced and dissolves the walls into the light of dawn and the air of sound.

In Grace Paley's story "Friends," a group of mothers get together to help the Spanish-speaking students in a New York public school. The principal, however, refuses to admit them into the building. His decision is transmitted "in written communication," and he also talks and looks like a book—motionless, authoritarian, and impersonal. His lips are "pressed" ("printed"?), and his voice has no intonation. The mothers, however, don't give up. Faith, the narrator, sneaks into the school to do her work: "I'd take Robert Figueroa to the end of the hall, and we'd work away at storytelling for about twenty minutes. Then we would write the beautiful letters of the alphabet invented by smart foreigners long ago to fool time and distance." Oral storytelling, maternal and secret (and rich with the great history of the Jewish and Latino spoken word), defies power and creates an emotional relationship, a starting point from which to go further, to seize absence and otherness by appropriating the alphabet's power over time and space. Perhaps, when Faith and Robert Figueroa begin to write, their grounding in orality and storytelling will allow them to invent a writing less violent, less authoritarian, less ethnocentric, and less aggressively male.[45]

DIALOGUE, VOICE, PERFORMANCE, TEXT: ORALITY AND MODERNISM

The last verse of the ballad of "Jesse James" announces that "This song was made up by Billy Gashade/As soon as the news did arrive." The authorial figure is inherently weak in oral forms; while writing permanently identifies the author in ad hoc paratextual apparatuses, orality can only do so by including the signature in the "text" and repeating it in the performance, as if to prevent the appropriation by others. Like Billy Gashade, Walt Whitman names himself and his own mythic genealogy in "Song of Myself" ("Walt Whitman, a kosmos, of Manhattan the son"), as an explicit mark of the orality of his "song." In fact, the first edition carried no paratextual designation of the author's name on the cover but included his photograph, as if to suggest his bodily performing presence.[46]

The example of orality thus helps break down the concept of authorship and the self-sufficient closure of the finished artistic work. As W. J. Ong points out, orality is in fact also incapable of producing "texts."[47] Anonymous and polymorphous, orality shatters the identity of the author and explodes the very idea of "text" into a multiplicity of discourses engaged in a perpetual, hopeless search for one another, and into a myriad of equally "authentic" variants. It is no wonder, then, that contemporary literary theory, endeavoring to shake the static closure attributed to texts, should resort—often unawares—to terms and concepts derived from the practice and theory of orality.

Such terms as *folk laughter, Carnival, voice, polyphony*, and, most of all, *dialogue*, which have become current in critical practice and theory through the work of Michail Bakhtin, are all rooted in orality and sound. Language, Bakhtin believes, is a social and intertextual reality, constantly recreated and transmitted in numberless dialogues between individual speakers. Dialogue is also embedded in the trace that previous usage by others leaves on the very words we use, as well as in the gap between speakers' intention and listeners' decodification. Bakhtin, however, does not identify this dialogic principle of language with dialogue per se. Only spoken dialogue in the literal sense, oral face-to-face communication and exchange, retains two essential features of dialogicity: intonation ("the subtlest, most sensitive signifier of social relationships"), and the role reversal between speakers and hearers that takes place when an utterance is followed and replaced by another.[48] Only in oral exchanges does an utterance "go away" so that its place can be taken by another; when dialogue is conducted in writing, an utterance does not cease to exist when it is completed, and the response does not replace it (as Bakhtin seems to imply) but merely follows it and lies alongside it.

In other words: language is always a dialogue, always a social event; but dialogue in the strict sense (the conversationalist's "dyad") is a microsociety in action. The distinction must be carefully kept in mind, lest we lose all meaning of the very idea of "dialogue." If every utterance is already dialogue, there is in fact no way of telling a dialogue from a monologue; if "you" and the "other" are already included in the dialogism of my discourse, all I need in order to converse is myself. Indeed, in literature, intense inner or dyadic-fusional dialogues (such as those in Saul Bellows's *Dangling Man* or Toni Morrison's *Beloved*) are the prelude to stories of intense, solipsistic isolation.

These notions also apply to the dialogic relationship between author and reader, narrator and narratee. Gerald Prince writes: "All narration, whether oral or written, presupposes not only (at least) one narrator but also (at least) one narratee," between whom "a dialogue is established."[49] Dialogue, however, is not the same in oral or in written discourse: true dialogue, in fact, can only exist when the subjects involved are in a position to exchange roles and alternate as speakers and hearers.[50] In writing, such an exchange may take place between textual narrators and narratees but is virtually impossible between narrator (or author) and reader (whether implied or "real"). "The writer's audience is always a fiction," insists W. J. Ong; written texts are "one-way movements," but "oral storytelling is a two-way street."[51]

Conversation is also a two-way street, which implies several interactive, simultaneous processes. Speakers monitor their own speech; hearers participate with responses; the emission source is frequently reversed; and all subjects involved strive toward some sort of joint conclusion, agreement, or action.[52] Only the first of these processes, self-monitoring, can be duplicated in writing. Whatever agreement may exist between writer and reader(s) is not of the same nature as that established in oral conversation. In conversation, agreement implies a reciprocal influence of two (or more) discourses and two (or more) subjects; in writing, readers may agree (or believe they agree) with a text (or with other absent readers) but have no way of interfering with the verbal form of the text as found, which will remain exactly as it was before it was answered.

The idea of agreement between text and reader, however, paves the way for the literary use of yet another concept imported from orality and folklore: "community." Stanley Fish has spoken of "interpretive communities" that include those readers who share interpretive strategies not so much to "read" texts as to "write" them—that is, to define their properties and determine their existence.[53]

The idea of the text as a "communal creation" of some kind has a long history of gradual progression. Romantic folklorists placed communal creation at the source, at the moment of composition by the primitive "dancing throng."[54] Later, Roman Jakobson and Pëtr Bogatirev moved the community's intervention one step forward: folkloric texts are originally created by individuals, but their existence depends on the "collective censorship" of a community that filters, selects, and reworks them in the process of transmission.[55] What Fish does is to take another step down this path by placing the community's intervention at the final stage of the creative process, that of interpretation: texts only "exist" if an interpretive community defines them as such. If we wish, we may start the spiral all over again with Bakhtin's dialogic principle: if all language is social, each text or utterance is ultimately a "communal" creation.

What remains undefined, and somewhat dubious, is the concept of community itself. Folklorists and sociologists have learned to be wary of the association between "community" and "homogeneity"; after all, actual oral audiences are, if anything, "very little concerned with interpretive uniformity." Yet, this association is implicit in Fish's use of the term: community is established precisely on the basis of consent and uniformity. "The only 'proof' of membership [in an interpretive community] is fellowship, the nod of recognition from someone in the same community, someone who says to you what neither of us could ever prove to a third party: 'we know.' "[56]

The tension between communal uniformity and individual utterance evokes another literary term derived from the realm of orality: *voice*. As a recent college writing textbook defines it, "Voice is the sum effect of all the stylistic choices a writer makes to communicate not only information about a subject but also information about himself or herself to a particular audience." Behind this definition is Bakhtin's concept of "style" as the linguistic expression of individuality. Style, Bakthin argues, is best conveyed by complex, literary genres of discourse; yet the oral actualization of even the most standardized genres (such as military commands) inevitably retains traces of what he calls "the more superficial, almost biological aspects of individuality," which may indeed be the deepest and most ineradicable. The material grain of the voice is the irreducible core of individuality and style; no two human voices are exactly alike. Thus, in critical usage, *voice* designates a stylistic idiolect, a perceptible and personal authorial involvement, a gap between story and discourse, signs and referents. Ultimately, *voice* becomes another synonym for *person* (as our textbook phrases it, "the person behind the information"), either in the biographical or grammatical sense: a universal signifier of expressive difference and of its implications in terms of political individuality—"an ideological speaking presence in the text."[57]

There is nothing wrong with this, of course, as long as we recognize that *voice*, like other critical terms derived from orality, is being used metaphorically. In most cases, however, literary terms borrowed from orality to literature are taken literally, appropriating the interactive mobility of the voice into the static written text and losing sight of their original source in speech and sound. The clause *as if* appears occasionally, only to be quickly forgotten: "the text must, *as it were*, perform" (my italics); "many . . .

written narratives offer themselves to us on the page *as if* they were performances before an audience " (italics in the text).[58]

Performance is another term shared, with different meanings, by literary theory and by the theory of orality. As we have seen, Jack Goody has noted that with the advent of writing "the human mind was *freed* to study static 'text' rather than be limited by participation in the *dynamic utterance*" (my italics). In literary theory, the evaluation is reversed: dynamic utterance liberates, and static text imprisons. Agostino Lombardo describes performance (from the theater to the reader's involvement in the play of textual variants and historical or personal perspectives) as a creative dynamic principle expressly associated with orality; Richard Poirier also insists that the literary work should be looked at not as finished product but as performance, "another dimension of action" endowed with a "beautiful liberating instability."[59]

However, while literary theorists see in performance the play of openness and mutability, anthropologists and ethnographers of writing also recognize some of its socially stabilizing functions.[60] Returning to Momaday's metaphor, we might say that, while literary theory sees the dawn, anthropology also sees the bricks. According to Dell Hymes and Richard Bauman, performance is "cultural behaviour for which a person assumes responsibility to an audience"; it is a personal and creative "display of communicative competence" that emerges against a background of shared cultural materials, formalized codes, and recognized spaces and roles. In literary performance, autonomy prevails over "responsibility"; the social and physical context and the empirical audience are, at best, implicit. The artist and the reader are alone, in a singularly disembodied relationship to the text; the "static text" is the still trace of an already past artistic performance and the motionless (Goody would say: fortunately motionless) object of the reader's active performance to be.

In order to enhance performance, then, literary theory must appropriate for writing another trait of orality: the absence of the "text." In orality, words have no existence outside the moment of utterance and the persons of the speaker and hearer; in literature, the nonexistence of the text is predicated on the fact that each reader and reading create a different "text." The text, Stanley Fish explains, is "a changing object—and therefore no 'object' at all"—as if in order to exist an object has to be totally static, and as though changing objects (such as the human body, for one) have no existence at all. "Literature is a kinetic art," Fish continues, "but the form it assumes prevents us from seeing its essential nature, even though we experience it." But is it possible, in literature, for the form of an object to be other than its nature?[61]

Let us take the classic incipit, "Call me Ishmael." Whether this is a text, what it means, through what conventions we perceive and understand it, and how differently we experience it in different circumstances, is all debatable. But there is no doubt that whenever we open *Moby-Dick* the first words of the first chapter will always be "Call me Ishmael." On the other hand, a folk song in the oral tradition is always itself, but the eleven variants of "Gypsy Laddie" published in Francis J. Child's collection present eleven different first lines. Each of them poses the same general questions as the first line of *Moby-Dick*; but beyond that, when we prepare to hear a performance of "Gypsy Laddie," we do not know what the first words will be. We may even create our own brand new incipit and legitimately attempt to float it on the current of tradition.[62]

In writing, "interpretation" is downstream from "text"; in orality, it is intrinsic to the performance. The theatrical and hermeneutic meanings of the term merge. "We are in the presence of a *performing art*, all right," writes Dennis Tedlock, "but we are getting the *criticism* at the same time and from the same person."[63] Performers of "Gypsy Laddie" change the text (and the tune) according to how they "interpret" past performances (their own or other people's), and these changes will in turn dialogically influence future performances. An oral performer's "rereading," as opposed to a reader's (but not unlike a critic's) is also a re-writing (or a re-telling)that leaves its mark on the text on the wax tablet of memory.

The movement that allows the reader of literature to "create" the text is guaranteed by the stability of the text's material substance. The audience of an oral or theatrical performance must accept the performers' timing and sequence; but, because the text does not move, readers are free to move any way they want (Fish's first recommendation is to slow down the tempo of reading).[64] One implicit decision we are constantly making as we read is whether to follow the conventional linear form of the printed page or to skip to the last page, find out how it all turns out, and then perhaps go back and read the whole thing as a flashback. But there is no way we can do this when we listen to a song or to a folk tale: we must wait patiently for the teller to proceed from "Once upon a time" to "happily ever after" in her or his own good time. Unless, of course, we interrupt and seize the floor ourselves.

Alberto Asor Rosa has written that "classic-romantic art, that is, traditional art, places *the work in time*; vanguard art, or contemporary art which breaks away from tradition, places *time in the work*. . . . vanguard art is the art which, for the first time in history, endeavors to *incorporate* time *directly into the materials* of which the work is made."[65] In fact, the arts of orality have been doing this since time immemorial; their ephemeral, immaterial substance has forced them to invent a sophisticated aesthetics of immediacy and improvisation as well as of formalization and repetition. The inevitably open and *in fieri* composition of oral discourse is perhaps precisely what "contemporary écriture—shaken by the new orality [of electronic media]—attempts to imitate by creating open works, works in progress, books that are read by reshuffling the pages, stories with no beginning and no endings, metanarrative reflexivity."[66]

Hence, the sense of modernity that radiates from writings influenced by orality and folk cultures. Highly figurative and allusive oral discourse—such as the metaphor-studded language of the visionary Sioux storyteller Black Elk, or the many nuances of African-American signifying—blur the distinction between poetic and everyday language; the texts of "ethnic" modernism, such as Jean Toomer's *Cane*, Leslie Silko's *Ceremony*, Maxine Hong Kingston's *The Woman Warrior*, and the works of Ishmael Reed and Gerald Vizenor break the barriers of genre, force the spatial form of writing into a temporality of rhythm, and abolish or attenuate beginnings and endings, in order to recover some of the oscillation and flow of ordinary and ritual speech. It is no wonder that a manifesto of modernist narrative, Gertrude Stein's "Melanctha," is also a creative stylizing of black (and female) orality.

There is no word for "poet" in Black Elk's language.[67] But the metaphor he uses—"word sender"—is akin to Charles Olson's "projective" verse: "What we have suffered from, is manuscript, press, the removal of verse from its producer and its reproducer the voice, a removal by one, by two removes from its place of origin and its destination." "With visible breath I am walking," Black Elk's vision sings, and Olson insists that "breath allows all the speech force of language in (breath is the 'solid' of verse, the secret of a poem's energy." The traditional Sioux word sender and the white experimental poet and critic share the projective, kinetic, and material power of breathing. And a modernist Indian poet, N. Scott Momaday, merges the two visions in the allegory of the poet as "arrow-maker."[68]

The modernist awareness of orality, however, is no recent development. The Imagist generation discovered in translation the "thinking in images" and the articulation of voice in Indian poetry. Olson sees the experimental typography of e. e. cummings and others as a way of using the substance and space of writing like the voice uses the substance of sound—the white spaces between characters replace the pauses of breathing. Brian Swann and Jerome Rothenberg use analogic typography to represent or recreate the multimediality and physicality of Indian poetry; "ethnopoetics" returns poetry to the performing voice, and a "re-oralizing" trend can be detected throughout postmodern poetics.[69] At the same time, a linguist-anthropologist familiar with ethnopoetics, Dennis Tedlock, develops ways of transcribing oral narrative poetry that on the page look very much like modernist experiments.[70]

Perhaps then, we can suggest a hypothesis: that one constituent of "literariness" may be the intensity with which language turns against its own grain and substance. Before the invention of printing, when the ordinary shape of the language was oral, the very act of writing stopped its natural flow, and all writing was therefore "literature." In the age of the printing press, ordinary and instrumental writings stabilize and objectify language, and *literature* takes on a more specialized meaning, designating all writing that goes against the resistance of the text to become fluid, pliable, dynamic, and interactive. Written literature, then, achieves at great effort what orality has been doing all along, naturally and spontaneously but also under the inescapable coercion of its physical form. On the other hand, striving against its own fluidity and precariousness, orality achieves its own "literary" forms by creating oral expressions endowed with the autonomy, the detachment, the monologic stability of writing.[71]

CHAPTER TWO

Foundations: Orality, Origins, and the Democratic Revolution

Beneath the cement foundations
of the motel, the ancient spirits
of the people conspire sacred tricks
They tell stories and jokes and laugh
and laugh

The American passersby . . .
haven't noticed that the cement
foundations of the motel
are crumbling, bit by bit.

—Simon Ortíz, "Washyuna Motor Hotel"

From the beginning, America behaves as a literate society, ostensibly unencumbered by the memories of ancestral origins and the illiterate darkness associated with orality and folklore. "An American who cannot read and write," wrote one of the Founders, "is as rare as a comet or an earthquake." These words should not be taken literally; when John Adams wrote them, at least half the population could not read or write (including a majority of women and almost all blacks, not counting Native Americans). Yet his claim had an unquestionable relative credibility.[1] More than any other modern nation, America traces its own foundations to written documents and scriptures: the Mayflower Compact, the Declaration of Independence, the

Constitution, and, of course, the Bible. "We began as a nation," Ralph Ellison wrote, " when a group of men . . . put down, upon what we now recognize as being quite sacred papers, their conception of the nation which they intended to establish on these shores." [2]

But, between the lines of these writings of origins, we glimpse the headless ghost of orality. It evokes darker, violent, and repressed origins and undermines the historical, political, and narrative authority of records and texts. Giorgio Cardona notes that, in Italy, the "collision" between literature and orality occurs first in modern, innovative texts (Gadda, Moravia, Pasolini), not as archaic and rural nostalgia but as a contemporary, urban "linguistic infringement," an "unlawful entry" of orality into the realm of writing.[3] In the United States this linguistic burglary happens at the very beginning: the constant, problematic interaction with orality is one of the reasons for the intriguing modernity of American literature. It indicates a literary and cultural foundation based on an infringement and a violation, an authority founded on subversion. This explains why the same ghosts that haunted the early foundations of national identity return—in certain postmodern literary fabulations, in ethnic writing, and in science fiction—to question the foundations of language and knowledge and to undermine our sense of the future.

THE INVISIBILITY OF AMERICAN FOLKLORE

At the time when romantic Europe was discovering in folklore the popular sources of national legitimation, the United States had already been a constitutional state for one or two generations. The people were not evoked through ancestral folklore, but in the first words— "We, the People"—of constitutional writing. As Sacvan Bercovitch has noted, in America "revolutionary genealogy" takes the place held by "folk culture" in European nationalism.[4]

"Actually a *folk* does not exist in the United States in the Old World sense of a rooted, tightly knit, traditionally minded community," says folklorist Richard Dorson. "American history," he continues, "begins in the seventeenth century. It looks back to no ancient racial stock, no medieval heritage, no lineage of tradition shrouded in a dim and remote past."[5] Shortly after landing in New York, Alexis de Tocqueville wrote: "As for what we generally intend for *beliefs*, that is, ancient customs, ancient traditions, and the power of memories, I have seen no trace of them so far." Americans, he later wrote, came to the continent already "in a state of civilization," so that "the ignorance of more remote ages, the simplicity of rural life, and the rusticity of the villages have not been preserved among them." The American lexicon, he noted, has no use for the key word of European romanticism: *peasant*.[6] One of Charles Brockden Brown's characters also claimed that "The ideas annexed to the word *peasant* are wholly inapplicable to the tillers of the soil in America"; yet they were received by an American culture that imported from Europe, with its books, the "notions" and "the prejudices which infect us."[7]

America, then, lacks the idea of a "folk substratum" and an originary organic community. The "commonwealth" is not founded on hereditary homogeneity but on separation and secession, on emigration and revolution, and on contractual ties among individuals and each individual's own relationship to God. The American version of economic utopia does not look forward to collective solidarity but to the self-sufficiency of the Jeffersonian yeoman. The only exceptions are the involuntary Americans, both Native and African. As Arnold Krupat notes, they can be used to great advantage as substitutes for America's "missing feudal past"; but they also present serious ideological risks. As Washington Irving teaches, if one digs too deep into the roots and soil of New England, one is likely to unearth the devilish specter of Native American massacres and the slave trade, seeping from below the ground like the voice of Simon Ortíz's trickster spirits beneath the cement.[8]

America's supposed lack of ancestral folk heritage is to some extent an ideological projection. Each generation of immigrants, from the Pilgrim Fathers on, carried a cultural baggage with them, even when they ignored or rejected it. A specifically *American* folklore, however, emerges most of all as a response to new conditions in a new land, weaving together old and new oral traditions with a vivid popular culture that is expressed both in oral forms and in the popular press and the theater.[9] Rather than as a cohesive, self-enclosed, and uncontaminated community, the democratic people appear therefore as an indistinct mass that contaminates as it legitimates; they are seen as a mob that cannot be dealt with through the detached "pietas" of the educated elites because it unceremoniously invades the precincts and institutions of cultural and political life.[10] This is how Washington Irving, founder of American literary folklore, describes popular democracy: "I have seen, in short, that awful despot, the People, in the moment of unlimited power, wielding newspapers in one hand and with the other scattering mud and filth about like some desperate lunatic relieved from the restraints of his strait waistcoat. I have seen beggars on horseback, ragamuffins riding in coaches, and swine seated in places of honor; I have seen liberty; I have seen equality; I have seen fraternity! I have seen that great political puppet show: AN ELECTION." And Mark Twain, not the least democratic of writers: "Low foreheads and heavy faces they all had; some had a look of animal cunning, while the most were only stupid. The entire panel formed that boasted heritage commonly described as the 'bulwark of our liberties.' "[11]

To speak of orality in the United States, then, is to break the romantic nexus between the voice, the people, and national identity; it is to deal not with archaic relics but with modern democracy and its promises and fears. Orality gives voice to democracy but also secretly undermines national institutions by feeding memories, rituals, aggregations, and passions, which escape the controls and certainties of written reason and law. If puritanism and capitalism establish the supremacy of the rational will and of controlled behavior, then orality represents an antinomian challenge of immediacy, mutability, and "spirit." Perhaps John Adams's association of American illiterates with the unpredictability and upheaval of comets and earthquakes was more than an innocent figure of speech.

POSTHUMOUS PAPERS OF A DECAPITATED SURVEYOR: *THE SCARLET LETTER* AND OTHER BEHEADINGS

King Louis was the king of France
Before the revolution
But then he got his head cut off
Which spoiled his constitution.

—American sailors' song

In "The Custom House," Nathaniel Hawthorne narrates how he found, among the papers abandoned by the English after the Revolution, the A in scarlet cloth with a document written by his predecessor, Surveyor Pue. This manuscript, he claims, is the factual basis of *The Scarlet Letter*: "the main facts of the story are authorized and authenticated by the document." Yet, like Diedrich Knickerbocker's "precise" and "authentic" history in "Sleepy Hollow," the facts in *The Scarlet Letter* are authorized and authenticated only in dubious irony, since the document is in turn based upon the shifting and unverifiable "oral testimony" of "aged persons" whose names we don't even know.[12]

Hawthorne regularly uses oral sources and the presence of the voice to create, and immediately destroy, the illusion of direct testimony and lived experience. In "Howe's Masquerade," the narrator hears a revolutionary legend from an "elderly gentleman" who "professed to have received it, at one or two removes, from an eye-witness." The "removes" are more important than the "eye"; the lapse of time and the many links in the narrative chain generate so many variations that, "despairing of literal and absolute truth," the narrator himself feels authorized to make "further changes" of his own.[13]

In *The Scarlet Letter*, again, the eruption of the voice systematically scatters "literal" truth and documentary authority, historical certainty and narrative credibility. Each appearance of the scarlet letter, alphabetic sign and matrix of indelible writing, dissolves into a cloud of contradictory rumors and discordant voices. Immediately after the last revelation of the scarlet letter, "there was more than one account"; "most of the spectators testified . . . some affirmed . . . others contended . . . others again . . . whispered." The rhythmic repetitions of this "multiple choice" among "alternative possibilities" couch the presence of mystery and the eruption of the supernatural in the protean multiplicity of orality. The ending repeats symmetrically the ironic formula of the beginning: "The *authority* which we have chiefly followed—a *manuscript* of old date, drawn up from the *verbal testimony* of individuals . . . fully confirms the view taken in the foregoing pages"(italics mine). The foregoing pages, on the other hand, carefully abstain from identifying with *any* univocal view.[14]

By invoking the "authority" of "verbal testimony" both at the beginning and at the end of his tale, Hawthorne seems to suggest that orality stands both upstream and downstream from the text. It functions as a dubious source and an ambivalent interpretation, as a missing yet haunting origin and as an ambiguous and uncertain future. Once again, orality ("*a*nonymous" and "*a*cephalous") is, like Irving's headless horseman, the metaphor of a repressed, unknowable beginning, and of a present without a center or a definite outline. In its own way, the scarlet A is also a severed head: the beginning of a suspended alphabet, the pictographic image of an animal's head,[15] an indeterminate article, a mark of absence (the Greeks' privative *alpha*), an indefinite, blurred "shwa sound."

No wonder, then, that headless ghosts haunt "The Custom House." The ghost of Surveyor Pue hands Hawthorne the scarlet symbol and the manuscript "with his own ghostly hand" and urges him to write "with his own ghostly voice." In doing so, Pue's ghost emphatically nods his imposing head; but his corpse—recently unearthed in Boston's cemetery—retains only a magnificent and perfectly preserved wig, while "the head that it used to adorn" is gone, somehow lost in the time between the past and the present. The essay concludes with Hawthorne's own transformation into a headless ghost: his head is (metaphorically) axed after his party's electoral defeat, so that, he says, the whole book might be described as the "Posthumous Papers of a Decapitated Surveyor." As the newspapers discuss his case, Hawthorne goes "careering through the public prints, in my decapitated state, like Irving's Headless Horseman; ghastly and grim, and longing to be buried."[16]

The decapitated dead, however, will not stay buried but emerge from the grave like the ghost at Sleepy Hollow or the corpse of Surveyor Pue. In the Salem custom house, a transparent metaphor of memory, "Prior to the Revolution there is a dearth of records"—and yet, "the past was not dead." Prior to the beginnings of written memory, we can hear the hum of a past that entrusts to the voice its refusal to stay dead.[17]

As we know, "The founders of a new colony, whatever Utopia of human virtue and happiness they might originally project, have invariably recognized it among their earliest practical necessities to allot a portion of the virgin soil as a cemetery, and another portion as the site of a prison."[18] A new beginning on virgin soil (but *was* it "virgin"?) represents the hope—albeit in vain—of escaping evil and death. In the same fashion, a new, revolutionary nation will, later, endeavor in vain to forget the violence and war that accompanied its birth. This is what Irving's "Rip Van Winkle" is about: the impossibility of forgetting these dual origins—the time preceding colonization and the trauma of revolution. Rip exorcises the revolution by sleeping through it, but in his sleep he encounters the living dead of the Dutch past, hidden unburied in the Kaatskill Mountains, an America that had already vanished before "America" began.[19]

Beyond the unknowable origin, the headless ghost also evokes the violence of acknowledged origins. Revolution is always a ghost haunting something somewhere, and the act of beheading the king, from Cromwell to Robespierre, is its symbolic climax. " 'For violating the people's rights," preached the Reverend Isaac Skillman of Boston's Second Baptist Church during the Revolution, "Charles Stewart, King of England, lost his head, and if another king, who is more solemnly bound than ever Charles Stewart was, should tread in the same way, what can he expect?"[20]

In 1793 Hugh Henry Brackenridge was elated that "Louis Capet lost his caput"; but a few years later he complained that "the sovereign people never had a good head upon their shoulders." James Fenimore Cooper also lamented that "the French, since they beheaded their king, have done nothing but fight," having fallen prey to discord and licentiousness.[21] To some contemporaries, the American revolution also seemed to threaten a drift "from revolution through democracy into anarchy and finally into despotism," and many misgivings were entertained, as Michael Kammen writes, about "how far the dogs of anti-authoritarianism should be unleashed." This concern is represented in Edgar Allan Poe's "The System of Doctor Tarr and Professor Fether"; though the story is set in a "madhouse" in revolutionary France, when the inmates rebel, seize power, and break out into a screaming orgy of subversion, the tune they play is not the "Marseillaise," but "Yankee Doodle."[22]

Cooper's and Poe's references to licentiousness and madness suggest that revolution not only beheads political authority but also decapitates reason and morals. In Irving's "The Adventure of the German Student," the political and the sexual revolutions are linked by yet another decapitated ghost: the guillotined girl, dead but walking and alluring, who again loses her precariously restored head after an illicit sexual encounter in revolutionary Paris. The story is filtered through a chain of unreliable oral narrators; narrative authority is one more sovereign decapitated by orality and revolution.[23]

Orality's headless ghost, however, haunts not only the sources of writing but its results as well; it designates both repressed origins and present ambiguities and fears. Charles Baudelaire imagines Poe's democratic America as a "headless monster," not worthy of being called "a State" because it lacks "a center of motion that is its Sun and its brain." Later, Henry James finds in America "No State, in the European sense of the word, and indeed barely a national name."[24] Like revolution, democracy is another headless ghost: a state with no center, a society with no visible hierarchies or well-defined boundaries ("No sovereign, no court," declares James), and an agglomeration of individuals with no tangible ties ("no personal loyalty," says James) or stable identities. In the United States, as Karl Marx noted, "though classes already exist, they have not yet become fixed, but continually change and interchange their elements in constant flux."[25]

Flow and flux, air and light, designate democracy as an unlimited possibility of mobility and equality and as a frightening, undifferentiated magmatic conglomeration. Tocqueville was awed by "the extreme instability of all things, the absolute lack of a sense of continuity and duration" in the emerging democracy.[26] In more recent times, Ralph Ellison's *Invisible Man* (he, too, "invisible and without substance, a disembodied voice," "like the bodiless heads you see sometimes in circus sideshows") perceived in the American experience both "the recognition of possibility" and the "real chaos" of emptiness and absurdity.[27] The world he was looking at was the mature mass society in which Tocqueville's insights about early democracy were coming to fruition; in post-World War II America, as David Riesman points out, the indeterminacy and formlessness of power were a source of widespread anxiety and fear.[28]

Democratic power is elusive and therefore inescapable; as Tocqueville says, "it often changes hands and assumes a new direction," yet "whichever way it turns, its force is almost irresistible."[29] "The tyrant majority," shouted a Congressman in the Jacksonian age, banging his fist on the table, "has no ears, no eyes, no form," and is "deaf, sightless, inexorable." But if democracy has no head it is also because—like Princess Langwidere in the Oz books, or Woody Allen's Zelig—it has many interchangeable ones: Henry James described the electoral body as a "many-headed monster."[30] As a Roman emperor complained, one cannot cut off the people's head—it has none, and it has too many, and no one knows which is the real, essential one. No ceremony of beheading will rid us of this new sovereign.

The multiple headlessness of democracy adds a new dimension to the "beheading" of Hawthorne by the impersonal and inexorable mechanisms of the party system. In a republic, individuals are as headless as the government; no identity is safely estabished, no head is secure on its own neck. In absolute governments, writes Thomas Paine, "if the people suffer, they know the head from which their suffering springs." But in democracy this consolation is impossible: as Bob Dylan says, "the executioner's face is always well hidden."[31]

We understand this better if we compare the democratically decapitated Hawthorne to the narrator in *The Arabian Nights*. An oral storyteller in an absolute monarchical state, Scheherazade speaks in order to keep her head from being cut off; in contrast, Hawthorne's writing is set in motion precisely by his democratically decapitated condition. Scheherazade's interactive orality heals a temporary aberration and restores sanity to an organic state; Hawthorne's deferred writing is a response to the elusiveness of power and the precariousness of identity in an incipient mass society.

In an earlier story, "My Kinsman, Major Molineux," Hawthorne describes how young Robin encounters "the spectre of his kinsman," the last representative of an authority swept away by the crowd, and confronts the faceless red and black mask of the new age. When his guide tells him he "may rise in the world, without the help of [his] kinsman," Robin Molineux must have felt elated but also, at least for a moment, very much alone.[32]

"Henceforth be masterless" is D. H. Lawrence's version of the American imperative. "Whoso would be a man must be a nonconformist," Emerson enjoined. These proclamations of freedom take the ironic form of sharp, authoritarian commands. While these aphorisms express the euphoria of public optimism, they also convey an undercurrent of "enormous private anxiety."[33] The new, masterless individuals must create the features of their own face; and when they look in the mirror, chances are they see nothing, or—like Laura Palmer's father in David Lynch's *Twin Peaks*—the face of a ghost.

Or, perhaps, they disclose, behind their own mirrored image, the red "spectral image . . . untenanted by any tangible form" that haunts prince Prospero's mansion surrounded by the mob announcing the end of his reign.[34] Democracy is a ghost threatened by ghosts; it has not buried the ghosts of the revolution behind it and is already haunted by the red masks of revolutions to come.

THE ANCESTOR, THE SLAVE, AND THE INDIAN: "BENITO CERENO," *THE ALGERINE CAPTIVE*, "THE DEVIL AND TOM WALKER"

Between Independence and the Civil War, revolutionary or dubious origins and contemporary revolutionary stirrings are often connected in American literature. For instance, in James Fenimore Cooper's distopic *The Crater*, written in the crucial year 1848, the republican island created by an earthquake is finally swallowed by another one.[35] In *The Scarlet Letter*, the scaffold evokes both the Puritan New England of the seventeenth century and the revolutionary France of 1793 and of 1848— the period of hardly accomplished evolution, and still seething turmoil, in which the story shaped itself." From another scaffold, in Melville's "Benito Cereno," the severed head of the slave Babo casts a shadow of subversion and death on the central square of the city of Lima. The year is 1856, only five years before the Civil War; Babo's head is both a reminder of how American democracy is founded on slavery and an anticipation of the approaching violent collapse of this foundation.[36]

Shortly after the revolution, one of the earliest American novels, Royall Tyler's *The Algerine Captive* (1797), had already explored the relationship between slavery and national origins. It is not an accident that *The Algerine Captive* and "Benito Cereno" should both be haunted by images of beheading and headlessness. In both texts, written documents and histories are undermined by oral narratives; and both combine the images of beheading and the theme of orality in complex metaphors of the crisis of political, historical, and textual authority.

The Algerine Captive opens with an attack on historical and legal stories of origins. First comes the suggestion that the truth about colonial origins is to be sought less in the Puritan founders' histories and records than in less edifying, orally transmitted family stories. In these narratives the hero's first ancestor did not come to America in search of religious freedom but to get away from some lowly court intrigue. Next comes the legal truth: the ancestor is expelled from Boston after a trial that is recalled in so many different versions as to make them all unreliable.

Later the novel attacks another of America's written foundations: the Bible. Enslaved in Algeria, the hero is asked by a *mullah* how he knows that the Bible is divinely inspired, and the only answer he can come up with is that it was handed down by his ancestors. America's scriptural history is thus dissolved into the relativistic orality of unreliable family narratives.[37]

The tension between orality and judicial and historical writing is also crucial to "Benito Cereno." Melville's story culminates in an "official document," the transcript of the Spanish captain's courtroom testimony on the voyage of the *San Dominick*. At first the court finds his oral testimony "dubious for both learned and natural reasons," but it is finally persuaded by the fact that this testimony is in agreement with that of other witnesses: "subsequent depositions of the surviving sailors, bearing out the revelations of their captain in several of the strangest particulars, gave credence to the rest."[38]

This is standard judicial and historical procedure: if we cannot rely on a concordance of testimony, what can we rely on? Yet, another such agreement of oral narratives had already occurred and proved deceptive. When Amasa Delano first boards the *San Dominick*, he finds Benito Cereno's story hard to believe but casts his doubts aside because it is "corroborated" by "the wailing ejaculations of the indiscriminate multitude" of sailors and slaves who greeted him "as with one voice" and made him, indeed, "the mark of all eager tongues." If Don Benito's narrative is "an invention," Delano muses, "then every soul on board . . . was his carefully drilled recruit in the plot: an incredible inference." Yet, as we also suspect and as is later shown, the story is indeed an invention—a collective one.[39]

One of the hidden snares in "Benito Cereno" is that an oral narrative, no matter how "corroborated," does not carry the same authority to the reader as a written one—especially when the reader forgets that the written document is based on oral narratives to begin with. As a result, we are prepared to suspect Benito Cereno's oral narrative, but we accept it as truth when it is transcribed as judicial testimony. This attitude is reinforced by the circumstances of the performance and reception of Benito Cereno's first tale; at first Delano is disturbed by the "gloomy hesitancy and subterfuge" in the Spaniard's manner; later, however, he reassures himself that the story is confirmed "by the very expression and place of every human feature." This double contradiction—between Cereno's words and the expression on his face, and between the two stages in Delano's reception, casts doubt over the entire story. However, when we read the judicial transcript, that is, when we pass from performance to text, Cereno's voice and face are out of sight, and all we have is the impersonal objectivity of the document.

Formally, Don José de Abos and Padilla, His Majesty's Notary, as well as Notary Public of the Holy Crusade of this Bishopric, can only "certify and declare" that this is what Benito Cereno said; but anything bearing an official seal is assumed to be not only truly said but also said in truth. The official document, however, is credible not because it contains more information but because it contains less; by excluding tone of voice and facial expression, it decreases the level of ambiguity. On this dubious certification, the court "rested its capital sentences" and proceeded to cut the rebels' heads off.

Severed heads haunt "Benito Cereno," warning readers of authority's weakness and excess. Babo's head planted in the plaza is less a warning to the slaves than a threat to the masters. Earlier, he had appeared in the act of beheading the master while shaving him. In this story, power is either empty (like Cereno's scabbard) or illegitimate and/or violent (like Babo's razor, the American sailors' guns, and the mass beheadings of the survivors). The tension between the weaknesses and excesses of power returns in text after text, as an expression of the central contradiction of a democracy generated by a revolution.

The Algerine Captive also includes an apologue of the weakness and excess of authority. Employed as a country schoolmaster, the hero uses the whip so freely that his students rebel and burn the school; he then becomes so lenient that the pupils get out of hand, and burn the school again. The burning of a school also appears, with similar metaphorical implications, in Hugh Henry Brackenridge's *Modern Chivalry*.[40] Brackenridge and Tyler were involved, as magistrates, in the two most relevant challenges to authority in early republican America, the whiskey rebellion in Pennsylvania and the Shays rebellion in New England; the mobbing of schools and the burning of books by illiterate masses (comets and earthquakes?) are their metaphors for a familiar democratic nightmare, the dilemma between fear of despotism, fear of the masses, and fear of the despotism of the masses.

Another nightmare of beheaded identity and authority, evoking the guilty origins of America in the invasion of the continent and the expropriation of its original inhabitants, occurs in *The Algerine Captive*, when the protagonist's mother dreams that Indians are playing football with his head.[41] Later, the document that reveals the true history of the hero's ancestor is discovered hidden on the back of "an old Indian deed"; history and property are the two sides of a writing that legalizes and hides the expropriation of the Indians. More indirectly, "Benito Cereno" alludes to the theme of discovery and conquest by another beheading; the skeleton of Don Aranda (*vuestro jefe* [your chief, your head]) replaces the ship's missing "figurehead," a carved image of Christopher Columbus. In this way, Melville and Tyler link the guilty past of Indian conquest with their main subject, the guilty present of African slavery.[42]

Washington Irving weaves oral and written narratives to explore this double nightmare in his perhaps most haunting tale. "The Devil and Tom Walker" asks the question: what would happen to America if the expropriated Indian and the enslaved African returned to take control of their life and lands?

In a swamp near Boston, digging "unconsciously" among the buried ruins of an old colonial fort, the Puritan Tom Walker uncovers a cloven skull with an Indian tomahawk buried in it. As in the dream of the Algerine captive's mother, what is buried in the unconscious coincides with what is buried in history; the fort had been the site of a battle and massacre during King Philip's War, the most traumatic encounter of Puritan New England with Indian resistance and warfare, at the end of which the rebel Indian chief was torn to pieces and beheaded by the conquerors.[43]

The buried skull stands for a violence that has impregnated the land and of which Indians are both perpetrators and victims, like the blacks on the *San Dominick*. Looking up from the ground, Tom Walker's eyes meet a double, ambiguous figure, who is neither black nor Indian because he is, ultimately, both: the black-faced and red-sashed Devil in person. This apparition is a synthesis of all ghostly images of foundations; it embodies both the Indians (like them, he claims "prior possession" to the land) and the "white savages" who exterminated them (he persecuted Anabaptists and Quakers, protected slave merchants, and was the master of the Salem witches). In this guilt-ridden land, the Devil, then, is both persecutor, victim, and avenger; he is the Puritan and the Indian, the slave and the slave trader, the witch and the witch-hunter.[44]

Tom Walker sells his soul to the Devil, finds a treasure, and makes money in the slave trade. His wealth, however, is ephemeral; when the Devil comes back to claim his soul, neither the biblical scripture nor his account books can save him. Tom Walker disappears, and his coffers, on being opened, are found to contain nothing but sand. If the Indians come back to claim their own, America disappears; or, conversely, as in Vizenor's apocalyptic *Bearheart* or in the millennial myths on the return of the buffalo, when America disappears, then the Indians will retrieve their heritage.

The truth of Irving's story is certified by two "tangible" pieces of evidence: a "hole" (that in which the treasure was found) and a ghost, Tom Walker himself, haunting the scene of his encounter with the Devil. In this ironic "most authentic old story," narrative authority fades, like authority in democracy, because it is spread too thin; what really happened, "nobody knows, in consequence of so many pretending to know." This story contains so many Chinese boxes of embedded written and oral narrators that, as in "Benito Cereno" and *The Scarlet Letter*, the facts "become confounded by a variety of historians."[45]

HOODED PHANTOMS: MELVILLE AND POE

Like "The Devil and Tom Walker," Edgar Allan Poe's "The Gold Bug" is a story of buried treasure and buried meaning; like *The Scarlet Letter*, it is the story of a manuscript lost and found, and of its multiple readings. The hero, Legrand, discovers a parchment that, upon being exposed to the fire, reveals the map of a treasure. Through a spectacular deductive process, Legrand deciphers the map and goes on to retrieve the hidden gold. The story, therefore, is ostensibly about the power of ratiocination and the permanence of writing, invisible but undestructible. These themes are set in sharper relief by the contrast between Legrand and the illiterate slave Jupiter; as Legrand's English is opposed to Jupiter's dialect, writing becomes opposed to orality, science to folklore, and solution to mystery.

An easily overlooked detail, however, spoils Legrand's wonderful logical sequence: though writing can give him a text, he needs orality to find his way around the context. His parchment informs him that he must seek "the bishop's hostel in the devil's seat" (where he will look through the eyes of another severed skull); but it does not tell him *what* the bishop's hostel is or *where* to find it. For that information, Legrand must rely on the memory and oral testimony of the likes of Jupiter; only after "inquiries among the older negroes," does he find an old woman who "had heard of such a place."[46] The old woman is never mentioned again; alphabetic, white, male reason cannot recognize its dependency on oral, black, female memory and experience.

Poe encourages the reader likewise to ignore the contribution of oral sources to the solution of the mystery. Not only does he make Legrand's ratiocination the most memorable passage of his text, he frames Legrand's very words so as to create the illusion that he is writing rather than speaking. Legrand's spoken explanation, for instance, includes no less than two charts: a form of verbal expression that, as Jack Goody tells us, can only be written, never spoken.[47] The severed skull and the old woman's recollected gossip are to Legrand's document and to Poe's text what the "oral testimony" is to Surveyor Pue's roll of parchment, and what the sailors' multiple narratives are to Benito Cereno's transcript: oral foundations of authority, denied and repressed in the name of writing but ever destined to return.

What makes Poe different is that he uses this symbolic cluster less to attack America's particular foundations and identity than to stage a broader and more radical demolition of the foundations of all writing, knowledge, and language. A similar shift can be recognized in Herman Melville's *Pierre or, The Ambiguities* (1852), a novel in which the dissolution of reality is always accompanied by the presence of sound, music, and voice. The inexplicable "shriek" that reveals to Pierre the destabilizing nearness of Isabel evokes in the protagonist images of the discovery of America—again, as a ghostly eruption of disorder rather than as a foundation and advance of civilization:

> [Pierre] felt that what he had always before considered the solid land of veritable reality, was now being audaciously encroached upon by bannered armies of hooded phantoms, disembarking in his soul, as from flotillas of specter-boats.[48]

We have already encountered a "grand hooded phantom" in Melville's work: the vision of the white whale at the close of the first chapter of *Moby-Dick.* In the chapter that bears his name, Moby-Dick is described as the object of "wild," "fabulous," "strange" oral narrations, "rumors," and "tales." The pervasiveness and formlessness of this anonymous orality concerning Moby-Dick anticipate the "indefiniteness" and the "elusive quality" conveyed by the whiteness of the whale and the "nameless terror" it generates. Like the voice, whiteness is absence and presence together, a concrete immateriality; no wonder, then, that the chapter on the whiteness of the whale is a catalogue of legendary ghosts. Voice, whiteness, and ghosts together evoke "a peculiar apparition of the soul"; we do not know whether, beneath the hood, the whale hides a face or only a "pasteboard mask." But it is a fact that every whale, once caught, skinned, and processed, is nothing but a "vast white headless phantom."[49]

THE TRICKSTER IN MANUSCRIPT: HAWTHORNE AND POE HEARD THROUGH GERALD VIZENOR AND OTHER POSTMODERNS

Poe and Melville thus anticipate the functions and forms with which the symbolic cluster of orality, foundations, and the headless ghost returns in the fabulations of the postmodern imagination. For instance, the narrator of Kurt Vonnegut's *Galapagos* (a tale of the demise and refoundation of the human species), is a beheaded ghost who writes "words on air . . . with the tip of my index finger of my left hand; which is also air." Like the vibrations of the voice, this writing of "air on air" is destined to disappear without any trace.[50]

In Thomas Pynchon's *The Crying of Lot 49*, another official writing seems to certify a historical event, only to dissolve into a series of texts at the end of which gapes the abyss of orality. The protagonist inquires at the California state archives about a historical marker concerning a battle between Indians and pioneers; but he already expects that he will be referred back to a "source book" that in turn will say something about " 'old timers remember the yarn about' whatever happened. Old timers. Real good documentation." Indeed, just as good as the "oral testimony" of Hawthorne's "aged persons"; once again, the anonymous, hopelessly vague halo of oral sources behind the apparent solidity of the marker and the book confirms the impossibility of reaching the "central truth." The chapter ends with more symbols related to our by now familiar cluster; a graveyard, bones, memory, a ghost, a past not dead. The dandelion wine, made with flowers picked in a lost cemetery, clouds over each year in the flowering season: "As if they remembered . . . As if . . . bones still could rest in peace, nourishing ghosts of dandelions, no one to plow them up. As if the dead really do persist, even in a bottle of wine."[51] Wine, as we will see, is also an Emersonian metaphor for the voice.

Don DeLillo's *Libra* examines writings and voices concerning the murder of John Fitzgerald Kennedy, the beginning of the postmodern era, "the seven seconds that broke the back of the American century." Again, history is reconstructed in an official document, the Warren report, "with its twenty-six accompanying volumes of testimony and exhibits, its millions of words." The document is surrounded by a constellation of public writings ("baptismal records, report cards, divorce petitions"), but consists mainly of transcribed oral testimony: "thousands of pages of testimony, of voices droning in hearing rooms." The written record is only the frozen trace of this "incredible haul of human utterance" that "lies so flat upon the page, hangs so still in the lazy air, that it resembles a kind of mind spatter, a poetry of lives muddied and dripped in form of language." The historical truth, which the Warren report finally fails to deliver, is replaced by a truth of imagination. The report becomes "the Joycean book of America," "a document of human heartbreak" (like *The Scarlet Letter*, "a story of human frailty and sorrow"). The novel forsakes a narrative of factual documentary for one of hypothesis and fantasy, a house made of dawn, of voices in the air: "The stories hang in time, spare, perfect in their way, unfinished."[52]

In another government archive, a deposit of Indian "heirship records" filed away in miles and miles of shelves (very similar to Hawthorne's custom house), sits and writes the Native American narrator of the prologue of Gerald Vizenor's *Bearheart* (1978, 1990). As he sits at his government desk like Hawthorne or De Lillo's historian, the narrator feels that the voice of his totemic bear ancestor is rising inside him. On the wings of this voice, he soars to tell a story and write a manuscript that is later discovered buried in the archive's files like the scarlet letter in the custom house, like the voice beneath the written text, or like Indian history beneath the artificial heritage.[53]

Steeped in ritual and mythic knowledge, and bursting with freewheeling postmodern literary play, *Bearheart* is the comic, obscene, holy story of thirteen crossblood pilgrims, seven "clown ravens," and two bastard shaman dogs traveling across a postapocalyptic America, out of time and in our immediate future. Once more it all begins with a beheading: Proude Cedarfair, founder of an Indian family-nation that refuses to give up its sovereignty, is murdered by a corrupt tribal leader, and his head is thrown into the river. The metaphor of beheading, which was used by Irving and Hawthorne to question the certainties of national identity, serves in Vizenor to undermine the consolations and stereotypes of ethnic identity.

In many traditions of pre-Columbian America, the buried head of a decapitated founder-hero strikes roots in the earth and generates new fertility and rebirth. Proude Cedarfair's head, however, is not buried in the earth but in water, where no roots can take hold. On the other hand, this water is itself an origin and a beginning: the sources of the Mississippi, the father of the waters. If roots do exist, then, they are not fixed for all time but shifting and liquid. "The power of the human spirit," his successor Fourth Proude explains, "is carried in the heart, not in histories and materials." Another traveler, Inawa Biwide ("the one who resembles a stranger"), later warns, however, that "Even the heart has prisons."[54] Only these two, Fourth Proud (whose heart carries roots ineradicable because they are fluid) and Inawa Biwide (who doubts even of the heart because he has no roots at all) will complete the journey and enter the "fourth world" of origins and the future.

Vizenor, then, does not negate the origins of Indian identity. Rather, he denies that they can be incorporated in any given place or text. "Terminal creeds," ossified beliefs, and textualized certainties are the deadliest disease in Vizenor's world, and the most lethal terminal creed is the artificial idea of the Indian and of Indian-ness. The pilgrim Belladonna is put to death for mouthing conventional (and therefore false) clichés about "tribal values."

In the course of their journey, the pilgrims come to a Federal Word Hospital, in which words are "cured" of their destabilizing ambiguity. Chronically hospitalized words are reduced by machines to meanings without equivocation, complexity, or dialogic creativity.[55] In contrast, words flow free and alive in the oral narratives told in the pilgrim camps along the motorless highways:

> Oral traditions were honored. Families welcomed the good tellers of stories, the wandering historians of follies and

> tragedies. Readers and writers were seldom praised but the traveling raconteurs were one form of the new shaman on the interstates. Facts and the need for facts had died with newspapers and politics. Nonfacts were more believable. The listeners traveled with the tellers through the same frames of time and place. The telling was in the listening. Stories were told about fools and tricksters and human animals. Myths became the center of meaning again.[56]

The trickster is the nemesis of terminal creeds and plastered words, "an erotic shimmer, a burn that sunders dioramas and terminal creeds; an enchanter, comic liberator, and word healer," careering through the public prints like a figure of creative disorder and change.[57] If we look back at the American literary canon through the filter of Vizenor's postmodern Native American imagination, we can detect early manifestations of such a trickster, often in the form of a voice that haunts and disrupts writings and texts: Hawthorne's ghostly "decapitated surveyor" careering through the public prints; or Poe's "imp of the perverse," whose career is inaugurated by the killing of a reader of books and culminates in "a maddening desire to shriek aloud."[58]

Hawthorne's "Devil in Manuscript" is another such trickster of sound, animating and disrupting the written text. In this story an author throws his work into the fire, and the flames melt the chilling silence of the manuscript, liberating a demon that shrieks and roars like Vizenor's bear, amid a tumult of sounds (the "air full of voices," "the iron tongues" of bells, and the "roar and thunder of the multitude"). Finally, the writer is himself overwhelmed and possessed: "I will cry out in the loudest of the uproar, and mingle my spirit with the wildest confusion."[59]

Therefore the roar of Vizenor's totemic bear assimilates and interprets many earlier sounds of insurgent disruption, of suppressed natural forces straining against the authority of reason and writing: Hawthorne's roaring fire and crowd, the oceanic "roar" of Jack London's "people of the abyss," and, most of all, the roaring orangutan in Poe's rue Morgue. The American imagination often embodies this upheaval of suppressed forces in the figure of the Indian. It is no accident, perhaps, that the murderer of the rue Morgue comes from the *Indian* Ocean.

ORAL HISTORIES: FROM COTTON MATHER TO URSULA LEGUIN.

The historians of Sleepy Hollow hanker in vain after "the floating facts concerning [the] spectre." On the other hand, how else but "floating" can facts about a specter be? Yet facts revealed by specters were recognized as credible testimony in one of the founding crises of American identity, the Salem witch trials. The most important theorist of "spectral evidence," and a major force behind the trial, was Cotton Mather. No wonder he appears both in *The Algerine Captive* (as a juror in the ancestor's trial), and in "Sleepy Hollow," as the author of the book that Ichabod Crane reads voraciously until evening dusk "made the printed page a mere mist before his eyes," turning writing into its own ghost.[60]

Cotton Mather's work may be described as another text that establishes America's foundations by means of a writing based on orality. Many of the episodes included in his histories, such as that of the ghost ship sighted in Boston harbor or of Ann Hutchinson's monstrous childbirth, came from oral sources. Mather collates and retells them with the skill of a storyteller offering his listeners pleasure as well as truth in "the entertainment of two or three well-attested stories."[61] Collector and retailer of legends, interrogator of ghosts and hunter of witches, Cotton Mather himself becomes something of a folk character. He appears as such in the works of Irving and Hawthorne, merging at times with his father Increase who—like many a future folklorist—enlisted the help of his fellow-ministers to gather tales of prodigies, wonders, and other remarkable providences.[62]

In Cotton Mather's work, however, these oral tales are the building blocks for the first massive and organic American historical work, *Magnalia Christi Americana*. Generations of later historians followed his example, making ample use of oral sources. Especially after the War of Independence, interviews, revolutionary folklore, and veterans' memoirs were widely used as historical sources.[63] For generations, the Revolution was the subject of endless, ubiquitous narration. According to Richard Dorson, the veterans' stories and memoirs mark "the departure of American from English prose, as they too mark the founding of the Republic."[64]

Literature was quick to avail itself of this extraordinary narrative resource. A typical character is the "old Revolutionary pensioner telling stories at a tavern over mugs of cider with the help of the villagers, who know the stories all by heart," in George Handel Hill's New England sketches. Irving's Rip Van Winkle, who repeats the story of the long sleep with which he skipped the Revolution, is an early parody of this type. Hawthorne transcribed revolutionary legends (*True Stories from History and Biography*, 1841) and invented his own ("Legends of the Province House"). Later, George Lippard published a successful series of revolutionary legends that he had originally heard from his aunt. Walt Whitman heard from his grandmother, an accomplished storyteller, the story of the battle between the Bonhomme Richard and the Serapis, which he retells in "Song of Myself." And Emerson collected oral testimony in preparation for the Concord bicentennial.[65]

Until the Civil War, American historians "relied heavily on interviews," without worrying too much about their reliability. Yet William Gilmore Simms, while recognizing that oral tradition is more interesting than the "certified chronicles of the historian," complained of the "inaccuracy of local lore and oral traditions." Between the decline of romantic historiography and the rise of local-color nostalgia, an obscure Vermont historian coined the expression "oral history."[66] By then, however, historians were relying increasingly on documents and archival sources. It was the artists and the poets who preserved and increased the awareness of the implicit truth and power of oral historical narratives. In 1855 Walt Whitman had written: "Did you *read* in the *seabooks* of the old-fashioned frigate fight?" In later versions of *Leaves of Grass*, he changed it to: "Would you *hear* of an old-time sea-fight? . . . *Listen* to the *yarn*, as my grandmother's father the sailor told it to me "(italics mine). While witnessing the Civil War, he already imagined himself as its future oral narrator, an "old man" telling history to the young: "Now be witness again . . . What saw you to tell us?" [67]

The junction of historical memory and imagination is at the core of Melville's *Israel Potter.* The book is based on a veteran's memoir, probably dictated orally to a scribe and editor. Melville uses it to debunk the bourgeois myth of the revolution (embodied here by Benjamin Franklin) through an appeal to the apparent authenticity of direct folk experience. The story, however, is not written by Potter himself but "taken down from his lips by another," transcribed, forgotten, rewritten. This process turns this supposedly authentic testimony into an explicit metaphor for the expropriation of memory and for the separation of memory from writing. Melville sarcastically dedicates the book to His Highness the Bunker Hill obelisk, a monument to public and official memory, which looks like a pen ("the Great Biographer") and is made of marble like a gravestone. Indeed, the book itself is "a dilapidated old tombstone retouched"; the authenticity of the Revolution, "promoted to a still deeper privacy under the ground," is finally stilled, buried in a graveyard from which only the imagination can evoke its ghost not as history but as fiction.[68]

Oral history was rediscovered in another time of crisis—the Great Depression—mainly by the writers employed in the Federal Writers' Project. In a somewhat ironic reversal from the situation described in "The Custom House," the federal archives turned to the very "oral testimony" that haunted them, in order to fill the "dearth of records" concerning the lives of the common people, the sharecroppers, and the slaves. Oral history, however, influenced literature as readily as it did history. The thousands of pages of testimony collected in those years are one source and model for the so-called "neo-slave narratives," novels of African-American history based on family memories (Margaret Walker's *Jubilee*) or on the mimesis of the ethnographic dialogue of the field interview (Ernest J. Gaines's *The Autobiography of Miss Jane Pittman*).[69]

One stimulus for the rediscovery of oral history was the belief that it would reveal the immediate authenticity of experience and direct testimony. Like Hawthorne in the custom house, however, historians and writers were soon to realize that there is much more to oral sources than a purely referential function.

What allows oral history not only to enrich standard, documentary, and archival historiography but also to change and even to disrupt it is that, in oral sources, factual recollection merges with symbolic imagination to an extent unequaled by other sources. Therefore, oral history approaches truth as much when it departs from "facts" as when it records them carefully, because the errors and even the lies reveal, under scrutiny, the creative processes of memory, imagination, symbolism, and interpretation that endow events with cultural significance. This liberating and intriguing power of oral history makes positivistic historians uneasy, but is bound to attract novelists, poets, and historians of the imagination.[70]

Thousands of years into the future, a space envoy returns from "the left hand of darkness":

I'll make my report as if I told a story, for I was taught as a child on my homeworld that Truth is a matter of the imagination . . . Facts are no more solid, coherent, round, and real than pearls are. But both are sensitive.

The story is not all mine, nor told by me alone. Indeed I am not sure whose story it is; you can judge better. But it is all one, and if at moments the facts seem to alter with an altered voice, why then you can choose the fact you like best, yet none of them are false, and it is all one story.[71]

Ursula LeGuin (whose *The Left Hand of Darkness* opens with this passage) describes her other major novel, *The Dispossessed*, as "an ambiguous Utopia," a definition that would also apply nicely to *The Scarlet Letter.* Science fiction, in fact, is a history of the future that mirrors the same stages—origin, revolution, utopia—as the history of the past. In Isaac Asimov's *Foundation* series, between the collapse of a Galactic Empire and the foundation of another, the mathematician and historian Hari Seldon establishes at the opposite ends of the Galaxy two Foundations to guide the course of history. The first Foundation specializes in physical sciences; it develops industry and nuclear energy and undertakes the writing of a huge Encyclopaedia Galactica. The Second Foundation is invisible and immaterial; it deals with psychology and sciences of the mind. Its leaders are called "Speakers" and communicate with each other in insubstantial ways: "To us they are merely voices."[72]

Isaac Asimov's *Foundation* cycle partly provided the structure of this book: the double foundation, written and oral, positive and immaterial, of language and of the state (the most important difference being that for Asimov the contact between material and immaterial communication is mathematics; here, it is literature). Orality and writing stand at the far ends of language (the Gutenberg Galaxy?) like the two Foundations at the opposite ends of the universe. These ends, as Asimov reveals, turn out to be, finally, in the same place like the "opposite" ends of a circle, or one on top of the other like the ends of a spiral in which the poles touch and center and margin coincide.[73]

In the history of the future, our time becomes the lost, negated, blurred time of origins, only remembered through faded oral traditions. The more recent novels in the *Foundation* cycle are obsessed by the so-called Origin Question—that is, with what there was before the worlds were "founded," and where the founders came from. Even in the electronic future the search for humanity's lost home planet has to be based on oral sources. "Records don't last forever . . . Memory banks can be destroyed or defaced" and eventually drown "in accumulated noise."[74]

What remains is myth, legend, and folklore. Repeating almost verbatim Diedrich Knickerbocker's formula in "Sleepy Hollow," one of Asimov's Galactic historians admits, "We have a tale about that—a fable perhaps. I cannot vouch for its authenticity." And the Founder, Hari Seldon, learns the true story of the planet Earth from a most peculiar oral source: the artificial, yet unreliable voice of an android robot.[75]

CHAPTER THREE

Checks and Balances: The State, The Mob, and The Voices of the Heart

Every book that the public library circulates helps to make . . . railroad rioters impossible.

—*Library Journal*, 1877

According to Harvey J. Graff, "A strong place for the oral, as well as the printed, must be accorded to the culture of eighteenth-century America."[1] The printing press was a central agent of revolutionary change; yet orality also shaped the perception and memory of national origins and played a central role in the unresolved tension between revolution and institutions, between subversion and control.

"May not a man have several voices, Robin, as well as two complexions?" asks young Robin Molineux's guide in Hawthorne's tale, as the roaring revolutionary carnival approaches them. While the king reigns, authority speaks with one voice; but when sovereignty is embodied in the numberless heads and mouths of the people, voices become helplessly confused. The question then is, how can the tumult of a "democracy" be channeled into the order of a "republic"?[2] The written Constitution puts an end to the revolution by establishing the authority of a state with its system of "checks and balances." The question then becomes: Can an order born of revolution and open (in theory, at least) to the presence of the multitude avoid the contamination of disorder and excess? Can a textuality accessible to the mob still guarantee the necessary rule of law and order?

Armando Petrucci has pointed out that "the religious schools for the lower classes in Counter-Reformation Italy stressed the teaching of reading over that of writing" purposefully, in order to "enforce and retain some form of social and ideological control." That literacy can be a means of control was also in the minds of reformers in the United States, especially during the industrial revolution. As Graff notes, the teaching of literacy, with its implicit "links to morality," was often part of educational programs intended "to control the lower class, not to assist their advancement." "Gradually," Graff continues, "more children were instructed in the moral bases of literacy, in the dominant culture's behavioral and attitudinal standards, as immigrant and lower-class-children were assimilated to the social order." The purpose of literacy, then, was to a great extent that of making these newcomers accessible to hegemonic discourse, rather than enabling them to express themselves.[3]

No wonder, then, that the spectacle of *writing* masses, seizing literacy from below as a means of active emancipation rather than receiving it from above as a vehicle of passive moralization, can appear to conservative observers as a democratic nightmare. Rather than accessing the orderly rationality of writing, democratic mobs and politics taint and "carnivalize" writing itself. Irving's demagogue in "Rip Van Winkle," harangues the crowd and deals out leaflets, and in the "confusion" of election day, Irving's New York appears to be "given up to the tongue *and* the pen" (my italics).[4] Rather than keeping literacy and orality each in its appointed place of rational authority and folk purity, "the puffers, the bawlers, the babblers, and the slang-whangers" contaminate both in democratic synchretism.

Even aside from the more extreme forms of the popular press, the ambiguous interaction between literacy and the people in the revolutionary era and the early republic fosters forms of writing originating in orality or meant to be actualized by the voice, as well as genres of orality impregnated with writing. The postrevolutionary age is a golden age of the cheap newspaper, of political and judicial oratory, and of the rising hegemony of another hybrid form: the novel, with its popular characters, vernacular speech, and mass readership. And, on the lower frequencies, the mixing and doubling of writing and voice becomes a central metaphoric link between the public political dynamics of authority and subversion and the private inner struggle between passion and control.

THE VOICE OF THE PEOPLE AND THE CONSTITUTION OF WRITING.

> The House was pretty full. I had prepared a Number of printed Copies, and provided Pens and Ink dispers'd all over the Room. I harangu'd them a little on the Subject, read the Paper & explain'd it, and then distributed the Copies which were eagerly signed.
>
> —Benjamin Franklin, *Autobiography*

On the evening of March 4, 1770, Samuel Adams had the walls of Boston carpeted with posters announcing that the English troops quartered in town were preparing to fire on the people. The next day an English platoon faced a crowd in the street. "The multitude was shouting and huzzing," Adams later recalled; "the mob [was] whistling, screaming, and rending like an Indian yell." The soldiers fired and killed five men. This event was destined to be remembered as the Boston Massacre, a prelude to the revolution. The next day, in an impassioned speech at Faneuil Hall, Adams incited the crowd to rebel.[5] Until the Fourth of July took its place in 1783, the Boston Massacre was celebrated as a national holiday, with memorable orations and eloquent pamphlets.[6]

Orality and writing converge in the Boston Massacre and in its memory and celebration. The printed poster, the shouting crowd, the political oratory, and the printed pamphlets all play their part. This balance, however, is a precarious one. In the revolution both orality and writing have their own different functions to perform; but the establishing of the new state formalizes the hegemony of writing and the printing press.[7]

The generation that fought the revolution and wrote the Constitution was faced with two contrasting tasks: tearing down an order, and erecting another one. The screaming "mob," whose disorderly rebellion had made separation from England possible, was to be reshaped into a republican "people" that would make it legal. The multiple identities, religious fervor, social insurgency, and radical tendencies conveyed by the voice of the crowd were to be encouraged but also to be restrained until they could be channeled into the Constitutional text.[8]

Vox populi, vox Dei was, of course, one of the slogans raised by the crowd in Boston during the Stamp Act riots.[9] A few years earlier the relationship between voice and God had been restated by the Great Awakening, which was to some extent a direct challenge of the oral culture of the people against the alphabetic culture of the gentry.[10] Both the written and the oral expressions of the revolution were steeped in the immediacy of direct communication, aimed at performance, and bound to time and context. In his history of the literature of the revolution, Moses Coit Tyler would later point out the pervasive presence of an aggressive, strident, "rasping" polemical sound, which displays precisely the agonistic, participatory, personal, and situation-oriented traits that W. J. Ong attributes to the oral mentality. The literary genres of the revolution are interactive and ephemeral (letters, pamphlets), agonistic (satire), personal (autobiography, memoir), and often eminently oral ("speeches, formal oration, and political sermons," songs, "the actual play of popular humor"). Later, the veterans' writings create, as Richard Dorson writes, a new "people's literature, rude and sturdy," forged "from oral rather than literary expressions," "shaped by plain speech and sharpened by powerful emotion."[11] These characteristics would continue in the democratic popular press of the republic; but even the most solemn writings of the revolution make abundant use of devices based on sound—such as rhythm or alliteration—and possess the immediacy of time and place: "When in the course of human events," or "These are the times that try men's souls."[12]

The immediacy of the voice is checked by the deferment of writing. The purpose of the Constitution (an etymological metaphor for stability) is to restore order to the confusion of the early republican period. The Constitution thus *sanctions* the revolution. It recognizes it and terminates it; it absorbs and replaces the revolution in the national political imagination, and in the process it obliterates the revolution's uneasy connotations of movement and disruption.

The new order is to be founded "on a written constitution emanating directly from the people";[13] but it remains to be seen in what way *writing* can emanate *directly* from a plural subject. In other words: how can the people found and legitimate their own sovereignty? As Michael Warner has shown, the answer to both questions lies in the hegemony of the printed word. "The indifferentiated universality of print" depersonalizes and diffuses the authority of the invisible subject of written law. Printed and distributed in thousands of identical, equally authentic copies, the Constitution stands for an impersonal sovereignty that emanates from no one in particular and therefore from everyone.[14] The republican ideology of print so puts the general ahead of the personal that, as the typographer Benjamin Franklin realizes, anonymity itself becomes a virtue.[15]

Franklin is an emblem and a protagonist of the process that constitutes writing as the sanction of this new authority. As

Larzer Ziff has noted, during Franklin's time books no longer function as a transcription of the community' shared values, but rather as a vehicle of social mobility and the badge of an elite: "Prose writing," Franklin recalls, "was a principal Means of my Advancement."[16] From this vantage point, the writing of the *Autobiography* is itself the constitution of a place of authority, an example and a lesson.

Franklin also reiterates the power of writing by developing an elaborate parallelism between printing and living:

> Were it offer'd my Choice, I should have no Objection to a Repetition of the same Life from its Beginning, only asking the Advantage Authors have in a second Edition to correct some Faults of the first . . . However, since such a Repetition is not to expected, the Thing most like living one's Life over again, seems to be a *Recollection* of that Life, and to make that Recollection as durable as possible, the putting it down in Writing.[17]

Writing becomes the place of memory; indeed, it actually corrects memory by allowing revision and control. In the ironic epitaph composed and printed for himself, Franklin compares himself to a book, and the afterlife to a "new & more perfect Edition,/ Corrected and amended/ by the Author."[18] Here the author is God; later Franklin will play the part himself. What remains unchanged is the relationship between writing and perfectibility that is embodied in the processes of proofreading and reprinting. Franklin always assimilates his mistakes to typographical "errata," which he amends as opportunity arises. If writing an autobiography is one way of reliving one's life, then perhaps one way of amending one's life's "errata" is to print a corrected and amended version of them in the text.

The controlling function of writing develops in the exercises of composition, imitation, and rewriting with which Franklin improves his style and—through that style—his character and public image. This process culminates in the famous chart of virtues: "I made a little Book in which I allotted a Page for each of the Virtues. I rul'd each Page with red Ink so as to have seven Columns, one for each Day of the Week, marking each Column with a Letter."[19] As we know, and as Franklin confirms in his foregrounding of ink and paper, charts are the distillation of the rationalizing powers of writing over language and thought. By means of the chart, Franklin identifies the rationality of writing with the supreme virtue of control over passions and instincts.

It was Franklin, of course, who inspired both the graphic and ideological solution that sanctioned the impersonality, and thus the universality, of the Constitution: that it should be signed by all the members of the convention. This would make it more impersonal and a-temporal, by making it impossible to distinguish those who had approved it from those who had not. This strategy of depersonalization and control is reinforced and sanctioned by the decision not to publish the convention's debates. Once the discord and uncertainties of the oral discussion have been suppressed, as R. A. Ferguson notes, "the published word that follows inevitably claims for itself the realm of simplicity, clarity, moderation, and, thereby, universality."[20] In the Constitution, again, the nation's written foundations rest on a basis of negated orality.

By replacing the "empirical verbalization of the people," the press becomes "the hinge" between a revolution that tears down a government and the constitution of a new one.[21] The deferment of writing, in fact, also implies a deferment of sovereignty. As writing sanctions the separation between language and presence, so representative democracy is based on a separation of the people from their elected representatives. This form has been dubbed as "government by fiction": the people are sovereign, but they are present in government only in figure.[22] Vox populi can again be recognized as *vox Dei* only when it is amended, rationalized, and spoken by someone else, or—to use James Madison's words in *The Federalist*—when it is "refined" and "enlarged" in the machinery of representative government.

Madison explains this process in a classic text on the control of popular emotions and passions. A "democracy," he says, allows all to express themselves indiscriminately; but a republic puts the government in the hands of "a small number of citizens." The people's voice is still the basis of legitimacy, but it is now separated from its source. "The public voice, pronounced by the representatives of the people, will be more consonant to the public good than if pronounced by the people themselves."[23]

USING THE VOICE: FREE SPEECH AND SPEECHMAKING

In a democracy, explains the narrator in Hugh Henry Brackenridge's *Modern Chivalry*, "every man is equally protected by the laws, and has equally a voice in making them. But I do not say an equal voice": some have "stronger lungs," others speak more eloquently or sensibly. Yet, "the right being equal, what great harm if it is unequally exercised?"[24]

Voice interferes with the checks and balances of the republican ideology of print, by pointing out the unequal enjoyment of supposedly equal rights. In fact, the voice is often associated with subjects not included in the Constitutional writing—blacks, women, Native Americans, domestics. In the early days of the republic, therefore, the most representative genres of discourse were those that conveyed the political tension and duplicity of writing and voice: law, oratory, and the novel.

In the shift from common law to history's first written Constitution, the principle of legality replaces that of authority.

Lawyers, judges, magistrates, and legal scholars become the "natural guardians" of the new political entity and the protagonists of public discourse.[25] Almost half the signers of the Declaration of Independence are lawyers or judges; so are more than half of the signers of the Constitution, thirteen out of the first sixteen Presidents, and all the most important writers of the first generations: the judges Brackenridge and Tyler, the reluctant lawyers Charles Brockden Brown, Washington Irving, and William Cullen Bryant.

But an unresolved ambiguity haunts legal discourse. On the one hand, its power rests increasingly on books; the law's technicalities, its arcane terminologies, and its formalistic procedures make it suspect in the eyes of common people. On the other, this literate machinery is actualized orally in courtroom oratory, with high eloquence as well as with specious quibbling and manipulation of passions and interests. While writing is supposed to guarantee a stable, impersonal text of the law, it is also subjected to the vagaries of interpretation and debate. As Madison admits, even when laws are "penned with the greatest technical skill," they are not exempted from the "unavoidable inaccuracy" of all language, which can only be "liquidated and ascertained by a series of particular discussions and adjudications."[26] Lawyers, then, appear to be both the guardians of neutral juridical reason and the bearers of multiple particular interests. They are the agents both of the certainty of the law and of its manipulation.

Ultimately, the suspicion toward lawyers, expressed by folklore and popular culture, is motivated by the fact that they hold both the authority of writing and the power of the voice. As an "honest German" says in *Modern Chivalry*, "de lawyers are de tyvil; wid deir pook, and deir talks in de courts."[27] In fact, they can be worse: in Stephen Vincent Benét's popular story, "The Devil and Daniel Webster," the great nineteenth-century lawyer and orator manipulates the writing of contracts and the speech of persuasion so well that he fools the devil himself.

Daniel Webster, along with such great public speakers as John C. Calhoun, Henry Clay, Frederick Douglass, Wendell Phillips—to name a few—is a protagonist of the so-called golden age of American oratory, between independence and the Civil War. The orator evolves from revolutionary hero (as demonstrated in the exhortations of Samuel Adams and Samuel Otis or in Patrick Henry's classic "Give me liberty or give me death") to verbal artist and ceremonial voice of national consensus. America becomes a "nation of orators"; oratory is "the chief source of political information, inspiration, and entertainment" and an integral part of the national literature. Writing the history of the age of Jackson, Arthur J. Schlesinger makes a point of always describing the voice of the protagonists: Daniel Webster's "deep booming voice" or Henry Clay's "rich and musical voice" accompanied by gestures and expressions that "made the emotion visible as well as audible."[28]

That it makes emotions audible and visible (entertaining audiences in the process) is also what makes oratory suspect. Through persuasion and the "aesthetics of cohesion,"[29] the orator molds the discordant *vox populi* of the crowd into the harmonious *vox Dei* of national ideology. Yet, in the very act of manipulating and controlling the sources of disorder—the crowd, the heart, the emotions—the orator is contaminated and tainted by them. To use Madison's metaphor, rather than "refining" the popular voice, orators are suspected of merely "enlarging" and amplifying it. As the title character says in Gore Vidal's historical novel *Burr*, while the speakers of the revolutionary age were concise, dry, and almost inaudible, those of the Jacksonian era "deal with a much larger electorate" and therefore "must thrill the multitude with brass and cymbal."[30]

"Cymbal" sounds like "symbol," and the pun may be intentional. As democracy expands, oratory spills out of the restricted chambers and considered deliberations of the literate elites, and takes to the streets and to the rostrums in a loud, often bombastic appeal to the sentiments and to the imagination of the masses. Yet the type of oratory typified by Fourth of July speeches has ritualistic rather than political functions, for decisions and deals are still made elsewhere. The great popular orators leave their mark on the national imagination, but none of them ever became President.

In the latter part of the nineteenth century, a novel bearing the sarcastic title *Democracy* denounces the perverse link between the theatrical rhetorics of Senate orations and the inaudible deals of the spoils system. To one of the characters, "the Senate was a place where people went to recite speeches," not unlike the church and the opera, always reminiscent of "performance of some kind." Ironically, the author, Henry Adams, was a direct descendant of the revolutionary orator of the Boston Massacre.[31]

THE REPUBLIC OF LETTERS: BRACKENRIDGE AND BROCKDEN BROWN

The novel takes its place among these contaminations of writing and voice. Though written, the novel is pervaded by the voice of the crowd in the use of dialogue, in the prevalence of ordinary language, in the mimesis of everyday action, and in the crowd as implied reader and intended audience. Early American novels, Cathy Davidson writes, "spoke to those not included in the established power structures of the early Republic and welcomed into the republic of letters citizens who had previously been invited, implicitly or explicitly, to stay out." Anticipating Bakhtin's theory of genres, Ralph Waldo Emerson identifies the American dialectics between social mobility and literary discourse: "The same movement which affected the elevation of what was called the lowest class in the states" is the source of the specific themes and moods of the national literature—the "meaning of the household life," the "near," the "low," the "common."[32]

In the "republic of letters" (a phrase that alone was enough to frighten the conservative imagination), readers do not recognize hierarchies and canons of taste; they resent authority even in novels. Artists, on the other hand, express in a free play of subjectivity their disappointment at finding themselves powerless and marginal in a society in which they expected to be recognized as figures of authority and prestige. The result is a decentered, digressive, multivoiced writing, "dominated by voices in ideological conflict and mutual misapprehension."[33]

In *Modern Chivalry*, the plurality of empirical voices contrasts with the univocality of constitutional discourse. The meandering loose narrative and the incipient heteroglossia of its dialects (quite unreliable, at times obscenely stereotyped, but—what counts here—different from one another) reveal a chaotic, opaque, muddled America that can hardly be contained in the Founders' clear and rational design.[34] Vernacular and popular voices speak out of turn: the Irish servant Teague turns orator and actor; a black slave delivers a scientific lecture; and a false preacher's emotional and demagogic sermon is more successful than the rational arguments of a real one. Captain Farrago, a modern Don Quixote, endeavours to silence these subjects, who not only have a voice but insist on using it. His authority, however, is not founded on reason but on deceit and coercion. It does not foster the general interest but his personal and class advantage: a "desperate desire" to retain Teague's services, and to keep him "ignorant of his republican rights for as long as possible."[35] In a democracy, it seems, servants will no longer serve but have not yet learned how to do anything else; and masters speak about the law but use force and deceit to keep servants in their place.

Another metaphor for the subversive multiplicity of the popular voice is the "biloquism" of the obscure criminal hero of Charles Brockden Brown's *Wieland*, a novel published in 1798 but set on the eve of the Revolutionary War. Rootless, marginal, and ambiguously subversive, Carwin sends out disincarnated voices of "phantoms" and "phantasms,"[36] compromising conversations, and "mellifluous" sounds that unchain "an emotion altogether involuntary and incontrollable." Ultimately, these voices destroy Clara's reputation and push her brother Wieland's religious mania over the brink of murderous insanity—which Clara calls "revolution."[37]

Voice and writing pursue each other throughout the text. Wieland uses ventriloquism to avoid being caught while reading someone else's correspondence, and imitates Clara's voice while she is at home leafing through "the Della Crusca dictionary." Brown, a lawyer himself, also represents the duality of voice and writing through the ambiguity of legal discourse. At the beginning of the novel, Wieland is at work trying to reconstruct the correct pronunciation of Cicero's Latin orations; at its end, the text reports his oral courtroom confession as "faithfully recorded" and transcribed by "one of the hearers."[38] These are the two poles of an impossible search: a scientifically controlled orality (the correct enunciation of a language that only survives in written form) and an emotionally authentic writing (turning a personal oral confession into a public document).

These short circuits between writing and voice anticipate and represent the deathly encounter of madness and reason. "Mysterious voices had always a share in producing the catastrophe; but they were always to be explained on some known principles." Explanation is a form of transcription, and the rational explanations of the mysterious voices are always supplied by Carwin himself; the voice of scientific reason coincides with that of emotional disorder. Carwin first drives Wieland to madness and then enjoins him to be "rational and human." "Be lunatic no longer"; in this version of the American imperative, the voice of madness demands reason. Of course, when Wieland's mind clears and he realizes what he has done, his recovered reason brings him to his death.[39]

"WILLIAM WILSON": THE VOICE AND ITS DOUBLE

> At twenty minutes past five in the afternoon, precisely, the huge minute-hand had proceeded sufficiently far on its terrible revolution to sever the small remainder of my neck.
>
> —Edgar Allan Poe, "A Predicament"

Signora Psyche Zenobia's ironic beheading by the clock's "terrible revolution" invests with subtle but intense political implications Poe's theme of the separation of mind and body. If madness is a metaphor for revolution, then revolution (and democracy) is a metaphor for madness, another way of losing one's head.[40] This is the case in Poe's "The System of Doctor Tarr and Professor Fether," a satire of the revolutionary utopia of popular self-government, and in "The Haunted Palace," which represents loss of reason as the collapse of the reign of Monarch Thought in a palace shaped like a head.[41]

Democracy, then, is one form of the dissociation of sensibility, of the disorder provoked by the unstable separation of mind and body, and passion and reason, and by their yearning for reunion. In "William Wilson," these metaphors of mental and political dissociation are further articulated by the dialectics of writing and voice.

> I grew self-willed, addicted to the wildest caprices and the most ungovernable passions. Weak-minded, and beset with constitutional infirmities akin to my own, my parents could do

> but little to check the evil propensities which distinguished me . . . Thenceforward my voice was a household law.[42]

Words such as *law*, *ungovernable*, *check*, and *constitutional* have the unmistakable ring of political allusions. The authority of family, reason, and state, is disrupted by the eruption of a passionate un-"refined" voice, free from controls, checks and balances. Unlike "The Haunted Palace," however, "William Wilson" is not about a monarchy but about a republic. It is not about the overthrow of an enlightened autocracy but about the rise of a new power itself tainted with subversion.

In fact, the "constitutional infirmities" of the narrator's parents designate both the frailty of a state that lacks a central authority and the congenital ambiguity of an authority generated by a revolution. The text underlines this political weakness by reminding us that "the mob" is at the origin of everything. In spite of his "noble descent," the narrator's "real appellation," his true identity, is in fact "the common property of the mob" and must not sully "the fair page now lying before me." Born out of the democratic mob, "William Wilson" is as nameless as the revolutionary battle that created Irving's headless ghost.[43]

In a democracy, however, the "mob" ("*demos*") is included in the written "constitution." The constitutional infirmity consists in the fact that, as in the system of Doctor Tarr and Professor Fether, control is placed in the hands of those who ought to be controlled. The instances of order are infected by the disorder that has founded them; the narrator's parents also bear his mob-tainted name, and their infirmities are akin to, and perhaps the cause of, his own.

Throughout the story the narrator is haunted by a double, who acts as the very incarnation of conscience and control. This second William Wilson, however, is also tainted. Not only does he look like the narrator and wear the same contaminated name, he also suffers from a revealing "constitutional disease": he has no voice. The double is described as a copyist and portrait painter, and thus identified with graphic representation and with the soundless trace of writing. This, however, no longer guarantees anything. In spite of his "majestic wisdom" and "control," there is too much anger in the way the double pursues his prey, too much sarcasm, deceit, and disguise for him to be recognized as a representative of wisdom and balance. Rather, the uncontrolled utterance of the voice and the controlled trace of writing pursue and mirror each other while they are engaged in deathly struggle. During a Carnival season in Rome, the narrator finally confronts and kills his double. By setting the end of the story in a time and a place identified with the release of irrational behavior, popular voices, and dark passions, Poe reiterates the political metaphor: the power born of the democratic revolution is irrational and vulnerable to future subversion.

This double, so closely associated with writing, "presumed . . . to interfere with my arbitrary dictation." "Dictation" is a crucial metaphor, one that links political power to the speaking voice. In democracy, the "arbitrary dictation" of the multitude (Tocqueville's "dictatorship" of the majority) requires representative institutions faithfully to reproduce the will of the people (or the "mob"); in language, the dictating voice expects writing to be merely a passive, subordinate double, an exact copy or portrait. William Wilson's double, however, is a copyist with a will of his own. "Disdaining the letter," the double seeks and achieves an identical difference, an alienated resemblance; although he recognizes the double as a perfect copy of himself, the narrator admits that, unaccountably, "the imitation, apparently, was noticed by myself alone."[44]

This invisible likeness is the space of absence and deferment that constitutes the life of the language: the space between face and mirror, voice and recording, recording and transcript, signifier and signified, original and copy, the people and their representatives, and "mob" and "government." After the final collision between the two, this vital distance is crushed; the voiceless double speaks, the narrator begins to write. For both of them, however, as for Brown's Wieland, the elision of the distance between writing and voice, passion and reason, and mob and government coincides not with life but with death.

"In me thou didst exist." If voice catches writing, it also kills itself, and vice versa. It is as if writing were the life of the voice, as if the fate of writing were furiously to pursue this ungraspable voice, only to be finally nailed to death by it. The antagonistic mirroring of the two modalities of language reverberates into a pessimistic metaphor for political control. As Ralph Ellison's invisible man cannot free himself from the machine that imprisons him without destroying himself in the process, so the instance of disorder—the mob, the voice—cannot seize control of the "constitution" that contains it, without either destroying it or silencing itself.

THE SCARLET LETTER AND THE VOICES OF THE HEART

Let us now go back to Hawthorne:

> Before Mr. Dimmesdale reached home, his inner man gave him other evidences of a revolution in the sphere of thought and feeling. In truth, nothing short of a total change in dynasty and moral code, in that interior kingdom, was adequate to account for the impulses now communicated to the unfortunate and startled minister.[45]

Once again, political and legal metaphors (revolution, dynasty, kingdom) represent a conflict between control and passion articulated in an eruption of the voice: Dimmesdale's fear that "his tongue should wag itself." In Hawthorne, however, passion has "a consecration of its own," and the "office" of orality in *The Scarlet Letter* is both to desecrate textual authority and to consecrate it again on other grounds.[46] Oral sources undermine the authority and authenticity of the original document; but the voice also evokes a further, deeper authenticity, "a tongue native to the human heart" promising liberation and threatening destruction. The pages of Dimmesdale's inner conflict and his final sermon articulate this tension in one of the most effective descriptions of orality in American literature.

When he reaches his study after painfully controlling his tongue, Dimmesdale's eyes fall on the scene of writing: "There, on the table, with the inky pen beside it, was an unfinished sermon, with a sentence broken in the midst, where his thoughts had ceased to gush upon the page two days before." This writing, however, is already turning into something else; the unfinished sentences, the gush of inspiration, even the liquidity of ink, suggest a process of melting under way. Like the author in "The Devil in Manuscript," Dimmesdale throws his manuscript into the fire and rewrites everything in "an impulsive flow of thought and emotion." In metaphors of flow, air, and sound Hawthorne suggests that Dimmesdale's impulsive writing approaches the forms of oral composition: "he only wondered that Heaven should see it fit to transmit the grand and solemn music of its oracles through so foul an organ-pipe as he."[47]

The next day Dimmesdale's oral delivery of his written sermon soon grows into improvisation and prophecy: "inspiration" (itself a metonymy of the breath) "could be seen . . . lifting him out of the written discourse" and even beyond language and articulation.[48] Standing outside the church, Hester cannot make out his words, but understands the meanings of the "indistinct, but varied murmur and flow of the minister's very peculiar voice":

> This vocal organ was in itself a rich endowment; insomuch that a listener, comprehending nothing of the language in which the preacher spoke, might still have been swayed to and fro by the mere tone and cadence. Like all other music, it breathed passion and pathos, and emotions high or tender, in a tongue native to the human heart, wherever educated . . . Hester Prynne listened with such intentness, and sympathized so intimately, that the sermon had throughout a meaning for her, entirely apart from its undistinguishable words. These, perhaps, if more distinctly heard, might have been only a grosser medium, and have clogged the spiritual sense.[49]

The higher authenticity of the voice is announced in the very first lines of "The Custom House." Here Hawthorne complains that the autobiographical "impulse" (a revealing word, in view of its later uses) hardly agrees with the impersonality of the book-reading public: "thoughts are frozen and utterance benumbed, unless the speaker stand in some true relation with his audience." The autobiographical "revelation," indecent in the public sphere of writing, can only be countenanced in a face-to-face relationship of "perfect sympathy." He thus proposes that we should pretend to be about to not read a book but listen to a conversation, in which "a friend, a kind and apprehensive, though not the closest friend, is listening to our talk."[50] Only on this condition may *The Scarlet Letter* be "revealed."

The tension between the authenticity of feeling in dialogue and the referential authenticity of documents is symmetrical to Hawthorne's distinction between the novel and the romance. The former is anchored to "minute fidelity" and likened to the solidity of "the actual soil," while the latter is bound only to the "truth of the human heart" and is likened to the insubstantial air and vapor of the "clouds overhead."[51] In *The Scarlet Letter*, orality contributes to the shifts between romance and novel; the voice is the vehicle of the marvelous and the supernatural, which introduces into the midst of factual fidelity the ambiguity of the "human heart."

As Nina Baym has noted, "not one reference to books and learning in *The Scarlet Letter* is favorable." The oppositions of book to voice and eyes to mouth structure the presentation of Chillingworth and Dimmesdale. Chillingworth is "the bookworm of great libraries" and derives his knowledge entirely from reading. The freezing connotations of the name by which he has chosen to call himself extend from his moral character to the world of books with which he is identified. Dimmesdale's knowledge, on the other hand, comes from the personal teaching of great masters and takes second place to his "eloquence and religious fervor." Hester remembers Chillingworth's eyes, "dim and bleared" by poring over "ponderous books." The first thing we see of Dimmesdale, instead, is his mouth: "a mouth which, unless he forcibly compressed it, was apt to be tremulous, expressing both nervous sensibility and a vast power of self-restraint."[52]

Chillingworth's eyes possess "a strange and penetrating power" to "read the human soul," yet he fails to foresee and understand Hester's fall. A man of science, he said, "should have learned this too in his books." But this is the point: the human heart is not a book, nor will it allow itself to be read as one. Chillingworth persists in his error ("I shall seek this man, as I have sought truth in books"), and his error grows into a sin. To violate the "sanctity of a human heart" is to approach it as a book, like the "lines and figures of a geometrical problem."[53]

Yet things are not so simple. The part of Dimmesdale that Chillingworth penetrates and manipulates is precisely that of his feelings, passions, desires. The "interior of the heart" finds in the voice its direct and uncontrolled expression; both authenticity and danger originate there. Hawthorne insists in reminding us that not all that comes from the heart is necessarily desirable and good. Dimmesdale's trembling mouth and compressed lips, like his hand pressed on the heart as if to hold it still, reveal a dramatic battle between "sensibility" and "self-restraint" that results in the frustrating stalemate of voices unspoken or unheard: words not said, reticent self-denunciations, the inarticulate cry from the scaffold, and those calculated conversations with Chillingworth in which neither truly speaks.

The fact is that when we reach deep enough, near enough to the origin of everything—to birth, to sex—we find that the immateriality of feelings is filtered and obstructed by the opacity of the body, like the rays of "moral life" reaching Pearl through her mother's "impassioned state." In this tangle of spirit and matter, passion is an "intervening substance," which interferes between soul and grace, obscuring the crystalline transparence of the Oversoul.[54] The revelation of the voice in Dimmesdale's last sermon is not a new breath of life but rather the exhalation of his soul, as if by releasing the voice Dimmesdale had loosened the self-restraint that kept body and soul together.

The symmetric contrast of voice and book associated to Dimmesdale and Chillingworth seems straightforward enough. It is complicated, however, by two motifs associated with Hester: silence, and the scarlet letter. Both concern the relationship of writing and voice, and both are related to the heart; Hester's silence on the scaffold reveals the "wondrous strength and generosity of a woman's heart"; and "in her heart" is where every stitch of her gorgeously embroidered scarlet letter is felt.[55] But what they tell us about the content and expression of the heart is complex and ambiguous.

The scarlet letter is never "written," but always "branded," "scorched," "stitched," "seared," or "engraved." Its place is not in books. It is "imprinted" not "printed." The letter is an exposed epigraph, a public scripture, and also the most private and secret of writings. Dimmesdale exhibits it like stigmata, externalizing the inner signs. Hester wears it as a hieroglyph—a public writing exposed on monuments, a hidden writing buried in tombs—and like a seal, Authentic and Authorized, sanctioning a document's source and guaranteeing its inviolability.[56]

The writing impressed on the heart performs a dual office of external protection and internalized control. When Hester takes off her letter in the woods, she "regains her pagan sexuality," and Pearl makes her put it on again. The letter is visible and indecipherable, and thus protects the interior of Hester's heart from interference and scrutiny. Its textual fixity guarantees constancy, the highest Puritan virtue of the heart, which supports Hester as she preserves her secret and her love. Finally, the letter controls the tongue; Hester refrains from praying for her enemies lest her tongue should wag itself and "the words of the blessing should stubbornly twist themselves into a curse." In the same fashion, the letter's double, Pearl, keeps Hester from voicing her secret thoughts as an orator, a preacher, an agitator, and a prophet.[57]

It is only right, then, that the last manifestation of the scarlet letter should be in a form that would have pleased Benjamin Franklin: an epitaph on a tombstone. A petrification of the flow of voice and passion, the scarlet letter is also its organic concretion, its materialization and transcription. This is the meaning of the letter's revelation on Dimmesdale's chest, but also the reason why Hester displays it so proudly and compulsively: "a mode of expressing, and therefore soothing, the passion of her life."[58] Writing *of* the heart and *on* the heart, the scarlet A inscribes control over feeling but also publishes the feeling's power and form. It sanctions feeling, as its punishment and as its recognition.

In the "inner kingdom," then, the scarlet letter performs the same office that the Constitution performs in America's "infant Commonwealth." It controls and limits democracy but makes it permanent; it recognizes the revolution and terminates it. This is why, trying to recover the original "consecration" of her transgression, Hester attempts to rid herself of the scarlet letter—and finds that she can't.

Part Two

The Voice in the Text

CHAPTER FOUR

Philosophies of Composition

Everything is the same except composition and time.

—Gertrude Stein, "Composition as Explanation"

Grace Paley describes the letters of the alphabet as devices created to "fool time and distance."[1] We will discuss in the next chapter some of the implications of the relationship between orality and space, and its effects on writing. The present chapter, however, starts with a consideration of time.

Writing is indeed a way of controlling time. It generates texts that can be read at any time and in any sequence; at the stage of composition, it requires and allows design, planning, and the shaping of discourse toward a distant end. Orality, on the other hand, is largely controlled by time; it lives and dies with the time of enunciation, and is bound by time's unilinear sequence. Thus, one of the most important consequences of the impact of the voice on the text is the reshaping of the text's relationship with time.

Writing, in fact, tends to become estranged from time precisely because of its relative power over it. The liberating possibilities of abstraction, objectification, and impersonality that writing derives from its relative timelessness can turn into the dry lifelessness of an utterance with no immediate subject, context, listener, or place. One of the functions of literature, then, is to rescue writing from this danger, by going against its grain to recover "the time of the composition and the time in the composition."[2]

To this end, writing appropriates the devices of oral composition, doing by choice what oral discourse does from necessity. As a result of this encounter, the time and circumstances of composition are foregrounded, textual beginnings and endings are attenuated, and the separation of text and context is blurred. The use of repetition, variation, digression, combination, and montage imitates the ways in which orality manages to retain some control over time while being carried along by its wake.

None of these devices are exclusive to American literature; most of them are already fully and consciously developed, for example, in Laurence Sterne's *Tristram Shandy*. What seems to be specifically American, however, is the extent to which these devices are perceived as political metaphors, and the intensity of meaning they derive from their associations with the social and political environment. America's fluid frontiers, its composite, mobile, egalitarian democracy, the degree to which it seems, more than any other nation, to live in the present: all these traits are intentionally evoked in American literary writing by the improvisational, digressive, expansive, fluid and time-bound mark of the voice.

STRATEGY AND TACTICS: WRITING, ORALITY, AND TIME

First place, I don't write. I create everything that I do, you know: I never actually sit down and write before, but I'll *ad lib* things on the floor, and then they'll become bits . . . But the fact that I've created it in an *ad lib* seems to give it a complete feeling of free form.

—Lenny Bruce

"Nothing is more clear," writes Poe, "than that every plot, worth the name, must be elaborated to its denouement before anything be attempted with the pen. It is only with the denouement constantly in view that we can give a plot its indispensable air of consequence, of causation."[3] Composition "with the pen" is ideally related to strategy, to design and intention, to keeping in mind at every step a pre-fixed end, and to terminating only after careful revision and correction. The model, as M. Dupin teaches us, is the theorem.

Let us now listen to an artist who is an oral poet before he is a writer—Woody Guthrie. Writing, he says (in vernacular spelling), is no problem: "Just deecide what you want to write about. Then you deecide why you want to write about it. Then you climb gently and sweetly up to your paper and with pen, pencil or typewriter thoroughly cocked and primed . . . just go ahead an' WRITE IT."[4] Rather than Poe's final destination, Guthrie thinks in terms of initial motivation. While Poe suggests the advantages of composing "backwards," Guthrie pushes urgently forward. Rather than a strategy, his philosophy of composition is a tactics, a guerrilla whose only aim is to gain time and stay alive. The method is improvisation, fabulation, conversation; the model is the experiment.

Of course, there is design in Guthrie, and there are forms of improvisation in Poe. But their statements do outline two different programs of composition, related respectively to the spatialized horizon of writing and to the sequential deployment of the voice. Poe's strategic approach prevails in the critical norm, but literary praxis follows "oral" tactics akin to Guthrie's at least as often as it does Poe's strategy. In fact, Poe himself complained that most American writers "seem to begin their stories without knowing how they are to end; and their ends, generally . . . appear to have forgotten their beginnings."[5]

Poe never knew Mark Twain, but he could have been talking about the controversial ending of *Huckleberry Finn*, or the catastrophic conclusion of *Connecticut Yankee,* which shatters the optimistic assumptions of the beginning. As William Dean Howells said, Mark Twain's way was to "use in extended writing the fashion we all use in thinking, and to set down the thing that comes into his mind without fear or favor of the thing that went before or the thing that may be about to follow." This improvisational bricolage generates contradictory or implausible denouments, but, as becomes an experiment, allows Mark Twain to make ever new discoveries as he pushes ahead.[6]

By imitating the linear perspective and the explorative, cumulative movement of oral discourse, literary writing emphasizes performance over text, process over results. As Gertrude Stein explained, "creation must take place between the pen and the paper, not before"; in what we may call "improvisational" writing, as in orality, enunciation and composition coincide. And then, "without thinking of the result in terms of the result," composition becomes "discovery," "explanation." Composition is the act, not the end, of composing.[7]

Since its very beginnings, Constance Rourke wrote, American literature has possessed the unfinished features of an adventurous exploration. Improvisation, she explains, "had been abundant on popular levels," injecting in the products of mass literacy and the popular press the imprint of the oral forms of creation.[8] But this is also true for much more recent and more literary writings. "The only way I could finish a book and get a plot," said Nelson Algren, "was just to keep making it longer and longer until something happened." And Raymond Carver:

> "I once sat down to write what turned out to be a pretty good story, though only the first sentence of the story had offered itself to me when I began it . . . I sat down in the morning and wrote the first sentence, and other sentences began to attach themselves . . . one line and then the next, and the next."[9]

The improvisation of unplanned oral discourse merges with modernist experimentation in a variety of ways. The most easily recognizable point of contact, of course, is the influence of jazz: Allen Ginsberg's "spontaneous bop prosody" or Kerouac's programmatically unrevised spontaneity ("By not revising," Ted Berrigan explained, "you simply give the reader the actual workings of your mind during the writing itself"). Paula Gunn Allen, a Laguna Pueblo writer and critic, suggests another, more unexpected way of short-circuiting the separation between traditional oral storytelling and the modern technologies of the word in the name of unplanned discourse: "I sit down at the word processor and off we go."[10]

The imperceptible interval between pen and paper, or the even more imperceptible fraction between keyboard and screen, leave perceptible marks on the text. "Let me begin by saying" (Raymond Carver again) "that I'm writing this at a place called Yaddo which is just outside of Saratoga Springs, New York. It's afternoon, Sunday, early August." One of Henry Roth's partly autobiographical characters copies "today, this February 4th, 1985" an earlier text that also started with another date: "Today is Tuesday, April 13, 1979." Emphasizing the moment of composition indicates an effort to shed the aloofness of writing and return it to the "rude stream" of time.[11]

Elsewhere, the foregrounding of the time of composition suggests the reappropriation of time by subjects who are not guaranteed the right to writing time: the proletarian time of the early Roth and Carver, the proletarian and feminine time of Rebecca Harding Davis and her ideal heir, Tillie Olsen: "I stand here ironing." But it may also evoke the effort to create a writing as ephemeral and insubstantial as a voice; thus, Melville records "this blessed minute (fifteen and a quarter minutes past one o'clock P.M. of this sixteenth day of December, A.D. 1850)" to tell us that we can never really know whether the whale's spout is water or "nothing but vapor."[12]

"This is hardly the scientific way to compose," Perry Miller complained, "nor is it apt to produce symmetrical or controlled form," at least, not without "thorough revision." Actually, integrating the oral philosophy of composition into writing does not necessarily imply abdicating revision and control. Whitman, for instance, applies extensive revision and rewriting to the intuitive, improvisational nucleus of discovery. Both Grace Paley and Paula Gunn Allen describe an initial, spontaneous, forward impulse, followed by considerable rereading and correction. Yet these revisions take place on the body of texts that an oral philosophy of composition has, as it were, branded at birth, at the moment of ideation. In these texts, the impulse to escape scientific ways, symmetry, and control, is at least as powerful as the effort to achieve them.[13]

Revision, then, takes the form of additional variants and "twice-told tales," visibly stratified within the finished text, as if each rewriting, each phase of composition, were a new performance. An aura of unfinishedness is retained in the text even after it has been printed and published. For instance, a creditable critical tradition detects not one, but at least two *Moby-Dick*s: the sea adventure Melville set out to write, and the intellectual adventure generated by his encounter, in mid-composition, with Hawthorne and Shakespeare. Both *Moby-Dick*s, however, coexist within one book. As in the oral tradition, the new version does not replace the earlier ones, but aligns itself alongside or on top of them, creating a "formless" text that has bewildered generations of conventional critics.[14]

Earlier, Brackenridge published *Modern Chivalry* cumulatively, with frequent references to the moment of composition, in a public improvisation largely unconcerned with revision: "I have an impression of having treated upon these particulars in the preceding pages, and that I may seem to repeat."[15] And, like oral fabulators in the manner of Rip Van Winkle, who spend their whole life telling and amplifying the same tale, Walt Whitman republishes and expands through his life always the same book, implicitly abolishing all requirements of uniqueness, stability, and closure of the printed text.

In Brackenridge, Melville, and Whitman, the stratification of variants takes place as accumulation and expansion. In the oral tradition, however, variation also takes the form of elision, selection, and subtraction—especially of endings. For instance, narrative ballads may have totally different conclusions (and, therefore, meanings) in different versions, as the last verses are dropped, replaced, dropped again, or modified. This formal aspect also has its literary equivalents. The elision of the ending in Raymond Carver's "So Much Water So Close to Home," for instance, confers contrasting meanings on the two versions of the story.[16]

The highest articulation of the relationship of time and variant is to be found in the work of Emily Dickinson. Closely identified with the physical act of writing, Emily Dickinson is also steeped in the orality of hymns, nursery rhymes, sermons, ballads, riddles, and of the daily family reading of the Bible and Shakespeare. Her poems are always in the process of becoming, constantly revisited with additional variants and alternative versions, and with "candidate words" lining up to be chosen or replaced according to the interactive relationship with the hearer or the empirical reader.[17]

In orality, variation depends on the urgency of time. In Emily Dickinson, the plurality of variants instead seems to depend on her sense of having all the time in the world to go back to text, to improve, polish, and adapt it at will. This inexhaustible possibility of finishing defers the necessity of ending; the striving toward perfection generates a practice of the temporary.

In the end, the critical edition of the poems of Emily Dickinson looks very much like the critical edition of a corpus of folk songs, where the only "authentic" text is the total of all variants, each as final and authoritative as any other. W. J. Ong remarks that the "new orality" of the electronic age is what authorized

Dickinson's editor to print poems that exist only as "a set of alternatives."[18] True—but it was not the electronic age that authorized Emily Dickinson to write them that way.

SENSE OF AN ENDING (OR; TOMORROW IS ANOTHER DAY)

Yes, that's the trouble with writing," I said
"You can't go on and on the way we do
When we tell stories around here.
People who aren't used to it get tired.

—Leslie Marmon Silko, *Storyteller*

The voice is both a unilinear flow of discourse and a circular irradiation of sound waves. The sense of formlessness associated with orality depends, to a large extent, on the indefiniteness of its circumference. Oral discourse merges imperceptibly with the surrounding space and expands in all directions according to the multiple and open shape of improvisation, the oscillating interactivity of dialogue, and the blurring of textual markers of beginning and end.

Deliberately weak endings occur in many American literary classics.[19] This trait is often clearly associated with the influence of orality either in the linguistic register or in the identity and status of the narrator. This applies to the ending of *Huckleberry Finn* as well as to the ambiguous double ending of "The Legend of Sleepy Hollow."[20] In *The Scarlet Letter*, the double ending (Dimmesdale's theatrical demise and Hester's return) is associated with the orality of alternative possibilities and multiple choice. In *Moby-Dick*, the different destinies of Ahab and Ishmael are also necessitated by the latter's function as the narrator who must survive "to tell" the tale.

Dialogue is another oral form that fosters open literary endings. Multiple or open endings are implicitly dialogic, as they defer the task of making ultimate decisions to the readers. Explicit final appeals to the reader express a desire that discourse be continued outside the text itself, by subjects other than the author. The last word in *Leaves of Grass* is a dialogic *you* (symmetrical to the opening *I*); in the first edition, the dialogic openness was enhanced by the lack of a typographic full stop mark. Mirroring Whitman's device, Ralph Ellison also opens and ends *Invisible Man* with *I* and *you*, weaving the cyclical form of prologue and epilogue into the formal and thematic openness of the story toward an undefined new beginning.

The formal implications of the dialogic openness of oral discourse frequently merge with its thematic and symbolic suggestions. Whitman's blurring of textual boundaries becomes a figure of the manifest destiny of a boundless, democratic, imperialistic America with movable borders in fluid and perennial expansion. The unfinished continuity of oral discourse suggests metaphors of the nation's weak and thus inexorable form. *Huckleberry Finn*'s open conclusion, or the double ending to Cooper's *The Pioneers* (the closure of the young people's wedding and the opening of Leatherstocking's departure toward the Western "setting sun") designate, and reproduce, the open "territories" of the frontier. On the other hand, a reluctance to end a story may suggest a resistance to the ethics of productivity and progress, which require "conclusion" at all costs. This is the case with the desultory and derisory ending of Irving's "The Stout Gentleman," the unproductive narrative of an irrelevant and therefore unresolved mystery.[21]

Eventually the telling must come to an end, but the story goes on. Narrative and geographical openness may be a message of optimism; it is also a safety valve against tensions that do not dissolve when the book is closed. The stories go on, both because America is an open country and because its contradictions stay open, its conflicts unresolved. Thus, the weak endings in Cooper and Twain suggest that the questions of racism toward blacks and Indians or the ambiguous relationship between nature and society continue after the formal conclusion of the tale. For the same reason, the great African-American biographies of "emersion," from Frederick Douglass's *Narrative* to Richard Wright's *Black Boy*, frequently end on new beginnings; they are journeys that end not with an arrival but with a departure. Even the "proletarian novel," an ideologically closed form, is narratively open because of the implications of its main themes. The revolution, in fact, is expected to take place in an undefined future, while the "raising of consciousness" is not an end but a beginning. "O great beginning" is, in fact, the invocation to the revolution that concludes Michael Gold's *Jews without Money*.[22] In Leslie Silko's *Ceremony* the ending reiterates the sentence "It is dead for now," as if to signify that not even the circular shape of text and ritual can really put an end to "witchery."

Continuing to weave words is also one way of deferring and exploring what Henry James called the "terror" of the "vast expanse" of the "canvas of life." With all due respect, and for more complex reasons, tomorrow is as much of another day for Isabel Archer as it is for Scarlett O'Hara. Contemporary reviewers, in fact, remarked upon "Mr James's reluctance, or rather his positive refusal, to complete a book in the ordinary sense of the word," which makes "Mr James's denouements so unsatisfactory" in their eyes. "Really, universally, relations stop nowhere." The artist can only trace "the circle within which they shall happily *appear* to do so" and thus face "the cruel crisis from the very moment one sees it grimly loom"—like the white figure of ice in the most cryptic suspended ending ("or rather double-ending," as one critic puts it) of American literature, that of *Gordon Pym*, written by the theorist of denouement, Edgar Allan Poe.[23]

James seeks a temporary security and boundary in the artistic form. Whitman and Poe, on the other hand, prefer to explore what lies beyond the boundaries of form, even at the risk of dissolving form altogether. Yet their explorations take different routes. Whitman travels the horizontal expanse of the "open road" and of the great American land, following a promise of unlimited expansion. In the interrupted ending of *Gordon Pym*, Poe instead gazes into the vertical darkness of the abyss, hopelessly seeking ultimate origins and meanings. These missing endings weave together a sense of emptiness and a sense of expansion, of possibility and chaos—"the deeper opposition that lies at the heart of the American dream—the opposition between endless optimism and ultimate desperation."[24] Ultimately, however, the distinction fails, and the dizziness of infinite possibilities turns into the annihilation of all possibility. No territory is more open than a desert.

In a famous debate in the early twentieth century, the socialist Morris Hillquit asked Samuel Gompers what was the "end," that is, the ultimate goal, of the American Federation of Labor's merely pragmatic unionism. Gompers's reply made history: we will just go on and on, day by day, he said, without an end—"You have an end. We do not."[25] It was the proud announcement of a history without limits and closures; but it was also the depiction of a serially cumulative history, a history ever changing and ever the same. As in *Gordon Pym*, Samuel Gompers's missing end denies stable meanings and prefixed goals; infinite semiosis and infinite marketing meet where everything can be exchanged, where all is sign and nothing is referent.

A story without end, then, is a story that has already ended. There will be no catastrophe, either nuclear or revolutionary, because the future will be only an infinite present where everything has always already happened. In the 1950s Daniel Bell and Leslie Fiedler proclaimed "the end of ideologies" and "the end of innocence." Today Francis Fukuyama brings glad tidings of

"The End of History." As Mario Savio pointed out during the Berkeley movement in 1964, "the conception that bureaucrats have is that history has in fact come to an end." The student movement was a reaction to the end of history, an effort to start it anew by recovering the word in a struggle for "free speech." The new history of radicalism in the 1960s and after was also the history of the antagonistic reinvention of forms and places of orality: rallies, slogans, meetings, "rap groups," and music.[26]

While Bell and Fiedler were putting an end to innocence and ideology, Isaac Asimov was writing about *The End of Eternity*. In the novel's future, "time travel" is an everyday experience, and the possibility of moving up and down in time turns the stream of time into something akin to a text; history becomes a book that can be perused forward and backward, and also revised and rewritten according to the plans of all-powerful authorities/authors. Time travel is, then, the metaphor for a stifling planned society; by the end of the novel it is replaced by the forward movement of space travel, a metaphor for the mobility of the frontier and the unpredictable denouements of venture capitalism. Asimov's hero finally chooses the temporary evil of the atom bomb over the deathly oppression of social planning. Ironically, however, this utopia of innovation is an exact reproduction of the present, a projection of eternal, individualistic capitalism. Asimov's recovered history is as end-less as Gompers's, the eternal unchanging history of free-market economy and ideology. [27]

As an alternative to Asimov's present-as-utopia, science fiction offers Kurt Vonnegut's desert of hopelessness. Here, the refrain of infinite openness—"So it goes"—always accompanies death, and the ultimate voice is the interrogation of total nonsense—"*Poo-tee-weet*?"[28]

ON REPETITION: STEIN, HEMINGWAY, TWAIN, JAMES, FAULKNER . . .

"Out of the dimness opposite equals advance, always substance and increase." In one line, Whitman sets forth a cosmogony, an expansive vision of egalitarian democracy, and a verse form rooted in orality. Paratactic balance and parallelism ("opposite equals") and incremental repetition ("always increase") are, in fact, necessary devices of oral discourse. In order to control the narrower horizon and the peculiar movement of the voice, orality tends to break down discourse into paratactic, linear, fragmentary, and self-sufficient units, with a high occurrence of repetition and osmotic redundancy. Writing, instead, tends to organize discourse along broader and discrete units that are ranked along a vertical hypotactic hierarchy.[29]

According to Deborah Tannen, repetition "is a fundamental, pervasive and infinitely useful linguistic strategy." It helps composition by enabling speakers "to produce fluent speech while formulating what to say next," either by repeating themselves or by resorting to preexisting formulas and patterns. Also, repetition helps comprehension by supplying the time necessary to elaborate the message. More subtly, the rhythmic oscillation of repetition between alternating speakers and hearers orchestrates the "ensemble" of conversation and the group's cohesion. In this way, as Paula Gunn Allen also notes, repetition paves the way from dialogue to ritual, creating the hypnotic, "entrancing" effect of accumulated power in the accumulation of words.[30]

While Whitman's balanced parallelism becomes a political metaphor of equality, in the modernist stylizations of Gertrude Stein or Ernest Hemingway the linear fragmentation of paratactic discourse is functional to the implicit characterization of the narrator. Sequences of equalized clauses without syntactic subordination, connected by the neutrality of polysyndeton, establish an ostensibly pure narration, a mask of exasperated objectivity[31]:

> I said, "Who killed him?" and he said, "I don't know who killed him but he's dead all right," and it was dark and there was water standing in the street and no lights and windows broke and boats all up in the town and trees blown down and everything all blown and I got a skiff and went out and found my boat where I had her inside of Mango Key and she was all right only she was full of water.[32]

One reason for the use of cumulative iteration and incremental repetition in orality is the unilinear direction of discourse.Once uttered, words cannot be called back or erased but only amended by additional words, in the form of variation, specification, or repair.[33] Oral discourse is a work in progress that includes its own drafts and revisions. Literature, in turn, adopts repetition and repair to stage a discourse steeped in the forms and timing of orality. In the first paragraph of *Huckleberry Finn*, each clause includes conversational corrections ("that ain't no matter," "mainly," and so forth), which are often also corrected in turn. For instance, "He told the truth, mainly" is repeated as "mainly he told the truth." The adverb is first introduced as an improvised repair to modify the assertiveness of the principal clause; but when the clause is repeated the order of words is regularized, as if the earlier, tentative phrasing had been set in fair copy. Through these osmotic transformations, composition becomes performance, and text becomes process.

In this way repetition becomes not only "equal" but also "incremental." Even word-by-word repetitions include difference and change against a background of sameness: "In many ways, the ceremonies have always been changing," says Betonie, the medicine man in *Ceremony*, "if only in the aging of the yellow gourd rattle if only in the different voices from generation to generation, singing the chants."[34] In this sense, repetition is the ultimate test of unrepeatability, in which the equal sets out the new in discernible relief. Gertrude Stein insists on the intrinsic connection between repetition and variation by showing, like a video advancing frame by frame, the microvariations through which a phrase evolves into the next:

> Jane began to explain how eager Melanctha always had been for that kind of learning. Jane Harden began to tell how they had wandered. Jane began to tell how Melanctha once had loved her. Jane began to tell Jeff of all the bad ways Melanctha had used with her. Jane began to tell all she knew of the way Melanctha had gone on, after she had left her.[35]

The repetition of the proper name, instead of the personal pronoun or other alternative designations, is a stylization of the anaphoric devices typical of oral discourse. Slower than reading and faster than writing, orality can only rely on a limited span of attention and memory; it cannot rely on pronominal references to possibly already faded and forgotten antecedents but must constantly renew the memory both of the topic and of the characters of discourse. In "Melanctha," anaphoric sequences include up to twenty consecutive paragraphs in which the heroine is rhythmically, hypnotically named in the first word or clause. This is one of the elements that contribute to the creation of Stein's "continuous present." It produces a text with no memory nor anticipation of itself and feigns a time-bound reader, one incapable of either connecting a pronoun to a name mentioned earlier or of returning to reread the text.[36]

The emphasis on discourse as process also helps project a fluid image of reality. Stein, Hemingway, and Twain make ample use of the so-called "run-on sentence": a borderline construct, formally hypotactic but semantically paratactic, which evolves osmotically from a starting point toward a conclusion that seems to have all but forgotten it. The run-on sentence reproduces at the level of the phrase both the experimental uncertainty of incomplete endings and language's progressive adaptation to mutable reality.[37] In the dawn scene on the river, in *Huckleberry Finn*, the development of the run-on sentence is functional to the osmotic change from night to day and to the gradual revelation of sky and river. An interminable sentence carries us, through a series of coordinated clauses and polysyndeta, from the initial cosmic silence ("Not a sound anywheres") to the final explosion of natural sounds ("And the song birds just going it!"). In Hemingway's "A Natural History of the Dead," the process instead takes place in the mind of the narrator. At first the neutral, paratactic clauses seem to imitate the neutrality of scientific description, but the horror reveals itself in the loose sentence structure that reproduces the dissolution of reason and language in the face of the massacres of war.[38]

By means of osmotic repetition-variation, then, the text imitates orality's ability and need to change along with time without being swallowed by it. The extreme form of this function, of course, is identical repetition: an (always frustrated) attempt to control time by stopping it altogether. As a story without an end is a story already ended, so a discourse that repeats itself unchanged is a virtually endless discourse, and thus the most open of all possible discourses. Let us take an example, an entire small chapter from William Faulkner's *As I Lay Dying*. This is Cash Bundren's voice speaking:

> "It wont balance. If you want it to tote and ride on a balance, we will have—"
>
> "Pick up. Pick up goddamn you, pick up."
>
> "I'm telling you it wont tote and it wont ride on a balance unless—"
>
> "Pick up! Pick up, goddamn your thick-nosed soul to hell, pick up!"
>
> It wont balance. If they want it to tote and ride on a balance, they will have[39]

As the lack of punctuation indicates, this discourse is literally without end; Cash could go on indefinitely saying the same thing (which he does, in fact, sixty pages later), and the others could go on interrupting him always in the same way. Repetition stages a dialogue among the deaf, in which each person utters and ruminates over always the same words, without being influenced in the least by what the others say, and without influencing them in turn; a conversation of garrulous ghosts whose history was interrupted at, and keeps coming back to, some indefinite moment in the past.

The opposite is the case with Henry James's dialogues. Here, repetition is not monologic but interrogatively bounced from one character to the other, in a wary, dialogic interrogation of the different meanings the same words have for each speaker. To take an almost random example from an early story, "The Patagonia":

> "How do you reconcile her laying a trap for Jasper with her going to Liverpool on an errand of love?"[. . .]
>
> "I don't for an instant suppose she laid a trap [. . .] She's going out on an errand of marriage; that's not necessarily the same thing as an errand of love."[40]

In the final lines of *The Wings of the Dove*, verbal repetition expresses the unrepeatability of life: " 'As we were?' 'As we were.' 'We shall never be again as we were.' " The problem here is no longer the past but the future.[41] Thus, repetition is not only a way of stalling time, it is also an anxious exploration of what lies ahead. In Faulkner, we may say, the "equals" are so "opposite" that they never meet, and immobility guarantees endlessness; in James, the revelation of the "opposite" dialogically embedded in the "equal" establishes language as the arena of endless movement and conflict.

INTERTEXTUAL NETWORKS: FROM LEATHERSTOCKING TO YELLOW WOMAN

Nathaniel Hawthorne's son Julian once wrote that if American life is "nothing but a series of episodes, of experiments," then it will be best expressed by an aggregation of short stories rather than by an organic novel of the European type.[42] American literature is indeed fond of agglutinative forms, from the montage of thematically connected stories to picaresque novels that expand the cumulative, egalitarian principle of parataxis from the single phrase to the text as a whole. Among such combinatory texts, we may include Sherwood Anderson's *Winesburg, Ohio* and William Faulkner's *Go Down, Moses*, Hemingway's Nick Adams stories and Salinger's Glass family tales, the framed narratives of frontier humor and ethnic and regional realism, and the reckless patchwork digressions of the "American Subversive Style" of early popular literature.[43] These open, freely digressive sequences or networks of episodes or tales are held together, like the clauses in paratactic syntax, only by the identity of the narrator or the hero, or by setting and locale.

Their free form makes them an explicit metaphor for America's self-perception as a heterogeneous, unfinished entity in montage, patchwork, and bricolage. *Leaves of Grass*, an agglutinative mosaic of interchangeable blocks, shares the formulaic and combinational composition of oral poetry, and is at the same time isomorphic to Whitman's image of America as a "teeming Nation of nations," an "unfinished vast and varied collation," with its syncretic language ("the accretion and growth of every dialect, race, and range of time").[44] The same may be said of the "composite style" of Judge Temple's residence in Cooper's *The Pioneers* (which Edwin Fussell recognizes as a "commanding emblem for American civilization in its formative stages"), or the absurd bricolage of landscapes and architectural styles of Nathanael West's Hollywood in *The Day of the Locust*.[45]

Parataxis, agglutination, montage, and repetition dominate the potentially endless seriality and myth-making power of the great national sagas throughout the spectrum of genres and cultural levels, from Leatherstocking to Yoknapatawpha, from *Dynasty* to *Dallas.* Faulkner's Quentin Compson shares with a comic-book hero like Superman not only the ambiguous relationship with a double but also their multitextual and infratextual existences. Quentin inhabits not only the texts in which he appears (*The Sound and the Fury, Absalom, Absalom!*, "That Evening Sun") but also "that imaginative space that the novels create *in between* themselves by their interaction."[46]

This space is not unlike the space of myth, where characters do not exist as functions of the stories, but stories exist to articulate the characters' potential existence. The characters in Keres Pueblo myths on Yellow Woman exist, as Paula Gunn Allen writes, "in the minds of the audience as much as in the minds of the storyteller," independent of their textual or performative actualizations. In the same fashion, according to Janice A. Radway, the mythic narratives of popular fiction "resemble the myths of oral cultures in the sense that they exist to relate a story already familiar to the people who choose to read them" (and are so independent of linguistic actualization that, as Leslie Fiedler notes, they suffer very little in being transferred from one medium to another).[47]

This infratextual space, between and before all stories, is largely coincident and isomorphous with memory. Memory, in fact, may be viewed as an active matrix of text and performance, like "the mind of the storyteller" and the "mind of the audience" that generate myths and popular fictions. In this space, mythic oral imagination, written literary imagination, and visual filmed imagination merge with and incessantly turn into one another. As Gunn Allen notes, if the Yellow Woman stories were to be written down in typographical order, they would form a narrative cycle comparable in size to any novel. This fact is reflected in the shape of the picaresque saga that is so common in much fiction written by Native American women. Anthropologist Donald M. Bahro brings the circle to a close by remarking that, inasmuch as both genres are fascinated by the endless study of complicated family and kinship relationships, "myths.. are cosmic soap operas."[48]

Introducing Leatherstocking's fatidic duel with the Indian in *The Deerslayer*, the narrator comments: "Such was the commencement of a career in forest exploits, that afterwards rendered this man . . . as renowned as many a hero whose name did adorn the pages of works more celebrated than legends simple as ours can ever become."[49] The opposition between "pages" and "legends" parallels in its ironic hierarchy the polarity of writing and orality, and that between characters restricted to the pages and characters who—like Leatherstocking's mythic progeny of Western heroes—inhabit the composite and expansive imagination of folklore and popular culture.

DIGRESSIONS: TWIN PEAKS AND YOKNAPATAWPHA

By my rambling Digressions, I perceive my self to be grown old. I us'd to write more methodically.

—Benjamin Franklin, *Autobiography*

Holden Caulfield, hero and narrator of J. D. Salinger's *The Catcher in the Rye*, tells how his schoolmate Richard Kinsella kept failing Speech on account of his inability to stick to the assigned topic of discourse.

They kept yelling "Digression!" at him the whole time . . . What he did was, Richard Kinsella, he'd *start* telling you all

> about that stuff—then all of a sudden, he'd start telling you about this letter his mother got from his uncle, and how his uncle got polio and all when he was forty-two years old, and how he wouldn't let anybody come to see him in the hospital because he didn't want anybody to see him with a brace on. It didn't have anything to do with the farm—I admit it—but it was *nice*.[50]

Digression is a consequence of the limited horizon and low cohesiveness of oral discourse. For Holden and Kinsella, it is a source of oral associative possibility; to Benjamin Franklin, it appears as a lapse from written method and discipline. Indeed, the most apparent cause of digression is lack of control; we shall never know what happened in the story of "Grandfather's Ram" (in Mark Twain's *Roughing It*), because the narrator insists on taking the wrong turn at each of the infinite intersections that deviate from the course of every narrative, thus digressing from each digression in spiraling progression.[51]

Yet at the roots of his uncontrolled digressing is an obsessive need for control; digressions are also an effort to reproduce in the linear associations of diachronic discourse all the simultaneous connections of the synchronic web of memory. As the medicine man Ku'oosh explains in *Ceremony*, the world is interconnected in fragile and complex ways. "No word exists alone" and all must be explained by means of histories made of words that will have to be explained in turn; in order to say anything, one must say everything.[52] In the same way, the narrator of "Grandfather's Ram" recalls everything and insists on saying everything about everyone, on rehearsing the life and kinship of each person he names, thus naming other persons who will have to be correlated in turn. From the very first paradigmatic digressive text, Sterne's *Tristram Shandy*, digression is the sign of the impossible effort to contain all the world within one text; it is "the complete description of everything" and "the complete description of anything" that induces Gertrude Stein to "enlarge [her] paragraphs so as to include everything."[53]

Digression is also a form of control in another, more profound way. In narrative, every decision hastens the end; digressions, then, are ways of keeping discourse alive, of pushing the end further and further back. As a classic digressive text, *The Arabian Nights*, makes clear, digression postpones death by keeping all options open, exploring all possible byways, extending the pleasure of performance, and retaining the phatic control of discourse in the hands of the speaker.

The interaction between digression as lack of control and digression as total control is at the core of the American style of humorous storytelling as described by Mark Twain. The American humorous story, Mark Twain explains, may "string incongruities and absurdities in a wandering and sometimes purposeless way, and seem innocently unaware that they are absurdities." The unawareness is simulated, but the absurdities are real: the relaxation of control must be closely controlled. This is why Mark Twain sees the conscious digressions of the humorous story as an artistic virtue but lists Cooper's uncontrolled digressive style, which "accomplishes nothing and arrives in the air," among Cooper's offenses to literature.[54]

The ambition of total control is frustrated, in oral performance, by the fact that each narrator and each narrative are only one among the many that are possible and cover only a part of what could be told. There are as many potential narratives as there are narrators; each is central in his/her own story and marginal and digressive in those of others, and vice versa. Besides, oral narrative must make special efforts in order to establish itself as a self-sufficient discoursive microcosm, because the borders of text, no-text, and context are weaker than in writing; the very presence of formulas for openings and closings in formalized oral genres signifies the need to stake artificial borders in what is otherwise a continuum of discourse. Whatever one tells does not eliminate the presence and awareness of what is not told.

The visible partiality of both narrator and narrative influence the literary forms of digression. The partiality of the oral narrator is rendered through the "distributional" paradigm of multiple narrators and mobile points of view. In *The Sound and the Fury*, the stories of Benjy and Quentin are as "digressive" to Jason's as Hamlet's is to Rosencrantz and Guildenstern's. The partiality of the tale, on the other hand, is absorbed by the weakening of beginnings and ends and in the digressive expansion of saga and myth. In theory, for instance, we might think of *Absalom, Absalom!* as nothing but a huge digression from the second section of *The Sound and the Fury* and from the infinite number of possible stories that might be told about Quentin Compson.

A corollary to the double face of digression as endless rambling and as obsessive description is the law according to which the potentially endless saga is always contained in a finite unit: a character (Leatherstocking or Superman), or a space, either social (the Compson family or The Jeffersons) or geographical (Yoknapatawpha County or the town of Twin Peaks). In this way the story offers both the dizzy prospects of boundlessness and the reassuring, though deferred, promise of a boundary. Like memory, these stories are finite and yet inexhaustible, because we can never finish examining all that they contain. The more we dig into the partial, the more we find the infinite.

Digression as discussed thus far may be described as "expansive": a progressive broadening of the text due either to lack of control or to the effort to control all information. There is, how ever, another modality, which we may call "concentric"; here the object of control is meaning rather than information, and uncontrolled ramblings are drawn back in obsessive repetition rather than allowed to go forward in aimless rambling. As Eudora Welty puts it, events succeed one another in time, but meanings follow a different chronology.[55] Discourse deviates from chronological and logical sequence because it constantly swerves aside or back in search of meaning—especially when meaning is hidden in a traumatic event in the past, such as Caddie's fall for Quentin or Rocky's death for Tayo. The narrative deviations grow sharper and more obsessive in direct proportion to the darkness and danger at the center of meaning. Rather than dissolving the ending, concentric regressive digressions search for an unsayable beginning—"beginning again and again and again," says Gertrude Stein.[56] Psychoanalytic narration is a model of concentric digression, an emblematic form of contemporary orality exemplified by some of J. D. Salinger's novels and stories as well as by Philip Roth's *Portnoy's Complaint.*

At the level of the sentence, the expansive modality takes the form of run-on sentences, adapting to shifts and changes that lead toward an unforeseeable conclusion. The concentric mode generates, instead, hypotactic spirals, phrases "involuted with the explanation of their own origins," like those of Silko's medicine men, or "trying to put all mankind's history in one sentence,"[57] like some of Faulkner's narrators:

> Not responsibility for the evil to which he held himself for no other reason than that of having spent the afternoon with her while it was happening, having been chosen by circumstance to represent Jefferson to her who had come afoot and without money for thirty days in order to reach there.[58]

Both modalities, however, share the same function: staging a loss of control and a failed attempt at recovery. The expansive multi plication and distribution of stories and narrators, then, is also a way of returning from all possible angles to an ungraspable center—Caddie's fall, Sutpen's ascent, Joe Christmas's identity—that is the origin of all.

CHAPTER FIVE

Conversations

> Honest John [Bunyan] was the first that I know of who mix'd Narration and Dialogue, a Method of Writing very engaging to the Reader, who in the most interesting Parts finds himself as it were brought into the Company, and present at the Discourse. Defoe in his Cruso, his Moll Flanders . . . has imitated it with success. And Richardson has done the same in his Pamela, etc.
>
> —Benjamin Franklin, *Autobiography*

"Casual everyday conversation is the most common, frequent, and pervasive way in which speech is organized." This statement holds true whether we refer to oral verbal exchanges, or to their literary representations. "Conversation" writes Franco Moretti, is "the chosen linguistic medium of the novel"; indeed, conversations—open, interactive, sensitive, and, as Franklin recognizes, intensely involving—"accompany most novelistic events, or constitute them."[1] Dialogue incorporates into the detached and monologic space of writing the spatial dimension of orality, in which two or more subjects speak not only at the same time but in the same place, and therefore to, at, or against each other; a space in which words can only exist in the same place as the body of the speakers.

Together with the registers of ordinary language, dialogue injects into the novel (the intrinsic form of the age of print) the incessant movement and blurred outlines of everyday conversation, and thereby tests the very limits of the novel's mimetic ambitions. As Ralph Ellison has noted, dialogue is one of the "shining achievements" of modern American fiction, yet "the rich babel of idiomatic expression," the "imagery and gesture of rhetorical canniness" of everyday conversation are still to be rendered in all of their richness and power.[2]

In this chapter, I will explore some of the ways in which the text attempts to represent and regulate orality in conversation and narrative. In order to do so, I will treat literary dialogue and "natural conversation" as related but distinct concepts, differing in the simultaneity and alternation of voices and codes, in the interaction of discourse and pause, and in the role assigned to silence.

Oral narration is always face-to-face communication, hence always to some extent dialogue. The example of oral narration contributes, therefore, to the dialogic dimension of the literary text. On the one hand, the individual partiality and precarious authority of the oral storyteller are an important precedent for the self-reflexive narrations and personalized narrators of modern fiction. On the other, inasmuch as both oral and written narratives recognize the limitations of discoursive authority, they attempt to establish on these very limitations another type of authority. And once again, this process evokes unmistakable political metaphors and implications.

DIALOGUE AND MANNERS: DAISY MILLER VS. BIGGER THOMAS

Alas! The phonograph was invented three quarters of a century too late. If type could entrap one-half the pretty oddities of Aurora's speech—the arch, the pathetic, the grave, the earnest, the matter-of-fact, the ecstatic tones of her voice—nay, could it but reproduce the movement of her hands, the eloquence of her eyes, or the shapings of her mouth,—ah

but type—even the phonograph—is such an inadequate
thing!

—George Washington Cable, *The Grandissimes*

According to Gérard Genette, direct speech in literature goes beyond the boundaries of mimesis and representation. Contrary to classical definitions, he argues, true mimesis is found in narrative rather than in dialogue. "The verbal equivalent of nonverbal events" (and only occasionally of verbal ones), narrative is a necessarily imperfect "imitation" or "representation," requiring choices "which are evidently not there when all that the poet or the historian does is transcribe speech." Direct speech, on the other hand, is not an imitation at all but the reproduction by verbal means of verbal events. Rather than an equivalent or representation, in Genette's view direct speech is "the thing itself," reproduced by means of "mechanical transcription."[3]

Transcribing speech, however, happens to be one of the very few things that still cannot be done "mechanically." Indeed, even a recording is a special type of "reported speech," created by a process of selection and choice: "You can't record a concert in an artistic way without exercising artistic judgment," Evan Eisenberg points out.[4] Even videotaping a normal conversation implies a sequence of decisions: the choice and placement of camera and microphone, camera movements, inclusion or exclusion of the observer, and so on.[5] As George Washington Cable realized at the dawning of the recording age, the more inclusive the technology becomes, the broader grows the gap between the range of events that might be technically recordable and the events that can actually be included in the record. And when we pass from recording to transcribing, conventions become increasingly sophisticated and complex, and increasingly aware of their own inadequacy. Each comma, each spelling solution is an act of interpretation bristling with ambiguities.

Though literary dialogue and natural conversation share many common traits, they are regulated by different conventions and are not mimetically transparent to each other. A natural conversation, as opposed to a literary dialogue, is not purely verbal behavior. "*Verbal* exchanges may be the natural unit of plays, novels, audiotapes," writes Ervin Goffman, "wherein words can be transcribed much more effectively than actions can be described. Natural conversation, however, is . . . not subject to systematic transformation into words." Conversation blurs "the boundary between language and nonlanguage" by including as its constituent parts such behaviour as gestures and gaze, produced simultaneously with words, and regulating the interchangeable relationship of speakers and hearers.[6] No such simultaneous, interactive plurality of codes is possible in writing: gesture and gaze can only be included in description, interrupting rather than accompanying and regulating direct speech.

Furthermore, the fictional text does not "transcribe" or "repeat" speech but *imagines* it. Direct speech in literature is not "tidied up"[7] oral discourse but written discourse imagined according to the conventions of literary writing and imagination. In most cases the conventions of literary dialogue coincide with those of a code of manners: uniform volume, constant speed, balanced intonation, still hands, and eyes on the hearer. An excessive mobility of voice, eyes, and hands violates social and literary etiquette and makes speech unreportable. "He smiled and bowed and showed his white teeth"—this is Giovanelli, "the handsome native" of Henry James's *Daisy Miller.* "He curled his moustaches and rolled his eyes, and performed all the proper functions of a handsome Italian at an evening party"—thus proving himself to be outside his proper social sphere, and exempting the narrator from telling what he says. Giovannelli's conversation will be reported only in the last scene, when he displays an "imperturbable" urbanity and his only gesture is a lowering of the eyes.[8]

Turn-taking, another anxious problem in conversation, is also solved in fiction by the code of etiquette. Articulate, symmetric "replies" prevail over instinctive, uncontrolled "responses."[9] Most important, no one interrupts; interruptions, like gestures, can not be imitated in writing, only described. This is why the social groups more at home in the novel are those that have established the codes of manners—often, indeed, shaping conversation to imitate books. In the Renaissance, for instance, Baldassare Castiglione and Giovanni Della Casa recommended to the complete courtier "the beautiful way of speaking which resembles beautiful books." And Henry James, complaining of the faulty, blurred diction of American young ladies, suggested that they speak like books, imitating the distinct isochrony of print.[10]

When the code of social interaction changes, so does the form of literary dialogue. In Henry James's *The Ambassadors*, characters take long and very articulate conversational turns; in Richard Wright's *Native Son*, for pages and pages no one—certainly no one black—speaks uninterrupted for more than one typographical line. The point is not that James's characters are articulate and Wright's are not, but that they are staging different codes of articulation. In James, where attention and respect are conveyed by the hearer's silence, conversational turns are more monologic and self-sufficient; Wright's dialogues, on the other hand, place more emphasis on the participatory rhythmic support of antiphonal call-and-response. The ghetto street code ritualizes in verbal virtuosity the aggression and hostility that James's characters learn to stifle or mask underneath the rules of polite conversation—another, subtle way of playing the dozens. Indeed, Bigger Thomas only becomes "inarticulate" when he steps out of his environment and can no longer count on the participatory and antiphonal antagonistic cooperation of his peers.[11]

Wright's characters, we know without being told, speak sharper, louder, and faster than James's—except when they ritually imitate them, "playing whites."[12] They also speak faster and louder than Hemingway's, though the latter's characters also prefer short pointed utterances and turns. As opposed to Bigger Thomas's, however, Hemingway's code of conversation includes intervals of silence between utterances and minimizes vocal and gestural display of emotion. The "hard-boiled stance and monosyllabic utterance" that Ellison admires in American literary dialogue are not the same thing in Chicago's South Side and on the streets of Montmartre.[13]

Intonation, volume, and gestures are, therefore, implicit in the social context and the speech styles that accompany them. For this reason Toni Morrison is able to claim that she does not need to describe her characters' voice or intonation ("getting the sound without some mechanics that would direct the reader's attention to the sound," such as adverbs), because they are implicit in the creation of their personal, social, and cultural context. Readers, however, can reconstruct a character's voice or the intonation of a sentence on this basis only if the context is familiar and the code is shared or, at least, acknowledged. When the perception and application of the code is precisely what is being questioned, things are more complicated.[14]

"I was always fond of conversation," says Daisy Miller. This story is a veritable grammar of the possibilities and limitations of literary dialogue; at its center, in fact, lies a complex play of superimpositions and confusions between conversational etiquette and moral codes. Winterbourne's first meeting with Daisy is deployed mainly on the plane of nonverbal exchange, as he attempts to secure "the benefit of her glance"—that is, to constitute her in the role of hearer in conversation. But when her glance arrives "perfectly direct and unshrinking," revealing that "she was much disposed toward conversation," he interprets it as a lapse of modesty rather than as unaffected openness. In fact, Winterbourne is the one who is violating etiquette, by addressing, unrequested, a young lady to whom he has not been properly introduced. But he covers this transgression by affecting a "tone of great respect" in his voice.[15]

The same "glance," then, conveys different meanings in Daisy's and Winterbourne's codes. The same applies to voices; there are too many codes for readers to be able to imagine them without descriptive support. When Daisy addresses sharp words to her mother, the narrator remarks that her intonation lacks "that harshness of accent which her choice of words may imply."[16] Unable to guarantee automatic associations between words and intonation, James renders dialogue by quick-paced combinations of brief units of direct and indirect speech, in which quoted utterances alternate with narrative clauses, descriptions, and summaries, in ways that have very little to do with a "mechanical transcription" of the "thing itself."

Readers have first-hand access to Daisy's "choice of words," but must take the narrator's word for what concerns her "tone" and her "unshrinking" eye. "Show, don't tell," James teaches us; yet he can show the words but he is forced to "tell" the tone and the glance. We thus perceive adjacent clauses through different cognitive modes, and are requested to shift modes very rapidly. The interpretation of the scene depends on our ability to operate this shift: for instance, on whether we think that the contrast between Daisy's words and her tone is objective, or whether we attribute it to Winterbourne's reverberating consciousness.

One way of obviating the irreproducibility of tone is to work analogically through the graphic substance. Thus, James weaves typographic emphasis, punctuation, and proxemic description, as in the conversation of Daisy Miller's little brother: " 'I told *you*!' Randolph exclaimed. 'I tell *you*, sir,' he added jocosely, giving Winterbourne a thump on the knee. 'It *is* bigger, too!"[17]

James, however, does not for a moment believe that this is a solution. "Transcribed here the speech sounds harmless enough," he writes of little Miles in "The Turn of the Screw," who "threw off intonations as if he were tossing wild roses." He has no delusions about "mechanical transcription"; the synaesthesic simile is infinitely more suggestive than the flat description of tone in "Daisy Miller." Yet, when he wishes to convey the impression of sound, James can only resort to an analogic use of typography and punctuation: "You know, my dear, that for a fellow to be with a lady *always*—"[18]

WRITING SILENCE: JAMES, MOMADAY, AND WHARTON

In "Daisy Miller," a novel of manners, sentences are usually complete, and there is a remarkable correspondence between conversational, grammatical, and semantic units. Speakers avoid repetitions and false starts; the oscillating, reciprocal "glance" prevails. In "The Turn of the Screw," glance is replaced by a fixed and silent "gaze" ("the dead silence of our long gaze"), and dialogue is made up of sentences suspended on the brink of silence, hesitations, soundings, and false starts, and punctuated with dashes and ellipses ("Look here, my dear, you know . . . when in the world, please, am I going to school?").[19]

Ellipses have been identified as evidence of the fact that "Writing, too, has silence." Yet silence is absence of sound, while ellipses and dashes are manifestations of writing, not its absence. Through them, writing signifies the cessation of sound but does not itself cease. Also, they have more than one use: they may stand for silence, for the beginning of a new sound (when a conversational turn overlaps with another), and even for mere continuity of sound, mere background noise.[20]

In Poe's "Silence—A Fable," the advent of silence is designated by the appearance of the word *silence* written on a stone; between two lines of dialogue in "Daisy Miller," we are told that "for some time there was silence." The stone and the character are silent, but the text must continue to speak. It can describe and name silence but not reproduce it.[21] "The worst thing about written prose," notes Dennis Tedlock, "is that there is no SILENCE in it," for "the spoken word is never delivered in the gray masses we call prose."[22] The pauses of writing, the skipped line or the blank page (a widespread metaphor of young America), connotate a challenge or a possibility more than an absence or an impediment. The purely spatial form of the blank page does not include duration, the source of agony in silence (James: "it was a deep soundless minute"). Silence is, then, the extreme challenge to writing; it can be described but never transcribed, because, as Tillie Olsen teaches us, the only writing of silence is the writing that is not there at all.[23]

This is the reason why typographic cultures tend to mistake absence of sound with absence of communication, charging silence with higher anxiety than cultures more centered on orality. Writing, N. Scott Momaday remarks, makes us insensitive to silence, whereas in oral cultures "silence too is powerful. It is the dimension in which ordinary and extraordinary events take their proper place. In the Indian world a word is spoken or a song is sung, not against, but within silence." If the world is created and sustained by the word, then there is no such thing as the absence of word in the world, and silence appears as an aspect of speech rather than a lack of it. "He would pause to let you get a feeling for the words," writes Leslie Silko of a Pueblo storyteller, "and even silence was alive in his stories." This different attitude toward silence shapes the white stereotype of the dumb and asocial Indian; Native Americans, on the other hand, may perceive the rapid verbal flow of white speech as a form of aggression.[24]

Different modes of silence define the phases and forms of Abel's cultural and personal conflicts in Momaday's *House Made of Dawn*. On the one hand, he rediscovers Indian silence as an articulation of speech, "the older and better part of custom." In the end, he can sing without even sending out his new-found voice: "There was no sound, and he had no voice; he had only the words of a song. And he went running on the rise of the song." On the other hand, in his encounters with whites, Abel experiences the white meaning of silence as an inability to communicate or as enforced powerlessness, as in his speechless appearance in court or in his painful exchanges with the white woman Angela (" 'You have done a day's work' . . . There was no reply, nothing"; " 'You will come on Friday?' . . . But he made no answer").[25] Abel is thus lost between the "inability to speak" (P. Gunn Allen) and the ability not to speak. Silent on the one hand and "inarticulate" on the other, he must resort to physical violence as a means of expression; he kills the albino witch, just as other physically or socially speech-impaired characters, from Billy Budd to Bigger Thomas, strike against the ghosts of a power to which they cannot speak.

In typographic cultures, the anxiety of silence appears in the form of mute, looming presences: the "prodigious palpable hushes" that signal the "presence" in "The Turn of the Screw."[26] If the ghost of orality is a voice without a body, yet these alarming, dumb presences evoke writing as a body without a voice. Perhaps the reason why writing has no silence is that writing is *already* silence.

In Edith Wharton's story "Mr. Jones," a ghostly housekeeper named Jones rules for generations the life of a mansion and its inhabitants because he never answers their questions or complaints: "That's the terror of it . . . that's why she always had to do what he told her to. Because you couldn't answer him back." Mr. Jones's silence has the same power that W. J. Ong recognizes in writing: "There is no way directly to refute a text. After absolutely total and devastating refutation, it says exactly the same thing as before." The connection is underlined by the fact that Mr. Jones's power resides in writings, papers, and archives: "You hadn't ought to meddle with his papers, my lady . . . "[27]

The visible silence of writing is the way in which Edith Wharton's ghosts communicate with the living, to whom they send newspaper clippings, faded letters, folded, unreadable notes, and envelopes bearing faint names like graves with faded headstones, containing letters like corpses in a coffin:[28]

> The letter was always the same, a square grayish envelope with "Kenneth Ashby, Esquire" written on it in bold but faint characters. From the first it had struck Charlotte as peculiar that anyone who wrote such a firm hand should trace the letters so lightly: the address was always written as through there were not enough ink in the pen or the writer's wrist were too weak to bear upon it.[29]

Like Irving and Hawthorne, Edith Wharton is aware of the link between ghosts, sources, and foundations. "Sources, as a matter of fact, are not what one needs in judging a ghost story. The good ones bring with them the internal proof of their ghostliness; and no other evidence is needed." A ghost, in fact, only exists in language: "his only chance of survival is in the tales of those who have encountered him."[30] But, rather than the stories of oral tradition, Wharton has in mind the self-referential language of writing: her ghosts are not to be measured against the "real" world but against their own presence. The faded letters traced by an inexistent hand, like certain levitating letters that we find in Faulkner's novels, designate literature's effort to liberate writing from the weight of its written body, without disappearing altogether.

In another story, while the heroine's husband is busy composing a book on "The Economic Basis of Culture," she is surprised to discover "how little she knew of the material foundation on which her happiness was built."[31] A ghost will finally reveal to the heroine, by means of letters and clippings, that her husband's wealth was obtained by morally devious means; the property on which her pursuit of happiness is founded is a theft. The ghost of the dispossession of the Indians and that of future depressions are both evoked by a silent, self-referential ghostwriting, which needs no other source and foundation but itself and dissolves all others.

TURN-TAKING: HAWTHORNE, CRANE, HURSTON, MORRISON . . .

He ceases. At once the woman begins to speak, as though she has been waiting with rigid impatience for Byron to cease. She speaks in the same dead, level tone: the two voices in monotonous strophe and antistrophe . . .

—William Faulkner, *Light in August*

A group of women stand talking to each other in the crowd on the grass-plot of the Boston marketplace waiting for Hester Prynne to appear at the prison door. Each waits politely (and implausibly) for the others to cease before speaking in turn; nor does there seem to be any uncertainty as to who has the floor next. Yet Hawthorne is clearly uneasy with this fiction: " 'Ah, but,' interposed more softly a young wife, holding a child by the hand, 'let her cover the mark as she will the pang of it will always be in her heart.' "[32]

The verb he chooses to describe the young mother's speech reveals Hawthorne's awareness of the discrepancy between the choral scene he imagines and the monologic limitations of writing. "Interposed" evokes both "intercession" and "interruption": two ways of "interfering" with the others' "hard-featured" discourse, mitigating it with the soft urgency of feeling. Yet the linear form of writing allows the narrative no other choice but to represent the passionate interruption as a disciplined succession. Hawthorne is not alone in his unease at the gap between choral scenes and monologic writing. In one of Jack London's stories for instance, a storyteller is continually being interrupted by his audience; the frame narrator, however, announces that, in order not to overburden the story, he will not imitate the audience and will report the tale without interruptions. Again, the scene that London imagines is much more animated than the scene he can write.[33]

Orality allows more than one person to speak at the same time in the same place and is always accompanied by simultaneous, nonverbal communication. Writing, on the other hand, is purely verbal and can only express one thing at a time; furthermore, the space occupied by one text cannot be occupied by another. There is no way, therefore, that writing can reproduce the simultaneity and multivocality, the uncontrolled, competitive overlapping of voices in conversation.

The problem becomes even more pressing as the story moves from the parlor to the market square, to the army camp, to the forecastle of a whale ship, where the rules of etiquette that guaranteed harmony to the conversation no longer hold. In Stephen Crane's *The Red Badge of Courage*, the grammatical subject of *verba dicendi* is often a collective one ("the regiment," "the army"). Everyone speaks at once, interrupting and drowning each other, but this undisciplined dialogue can only be rendered as a linear succession studded with dashes:

> "[. . .] if anybody with any sense was a-runnin' this army it—"
>
> "Oh, shut up!" roared the tall private. "[. . .] you talk as if—"
>
> "Well, I wanta do some fighting anyway," interrupted the other.[34]

Collective simultaneous discourse can only be stylized, not reproduced. One way of dealing with this problem is to rely on the medium of writing's very limitations rather than forcing it to feats it cannot accomplish. The author may use the fact that writing can only carry one discourse at a time in order to restrict focalization, thus removing the question of simultaneity altogether. During a conversation with Daisy Miller and her mother, Winterbourne strays into "meditations" covering six typographic lines; later, Daisy scolds him: "You haven't spoken to me for half an hour." Even accounting for her colloquial exaggeration—let us say it had only been a minute—what were the two speakers doing meanwhile? The linearity of writing draws our attention toward one element at a time and allows us to forget Daisy and her mother. Yet, if James had been composing in a simultaneous medium—the theater, for example—he would have had to think of something for them to do and say as Winterbourne meditates.[35]

More complex strategies resort to the cross-cutting and montage of simultaneous discourses, or to the acceleration of rhythm and the elision of time between turns. In Zora Neale Hurston's *Their Eyes Were Watching God*, the collective subject ("the porch") is rendered by means of a quick succession of brief rhythmic clauses, by skipping the identification of speakers (as if the individuality of the speaker took second place to the collective discourse), by the omission of paragraphing and quotation marks at the end of each turn, and by the skillful use of collective free indirect speech. Together with the readers' habit of silent reading and with the visual syntheticism of print, these devices help create the impression that all are speaking at once, that all discourses mix and weave together in "words walking without masters; walking altogether like harmony in a song":

> "What she doin' coming back here in dem overalls? Can't she find no dress to put on?—Where's dat blue satin dress she left here in?—Where all dat money her husband took and died

and left her?—What dat ole forty year ole 'oman doin' wid her hair swingin' down her back lak some young gal?—[36]

Saul Bellow uses a similar approach in the narrator's dialogues with the "Spirit of Alternatives" in Dangling Man. These are long exchanges of brief lines with no indication of who is speaking, until the reader loses track of who is saying what—which is the point, since the dialogue is between two aspects of the same personality.[37] Toni Morrison's *Beloved* takes it one step further, representing the gradual fusion of three characters by starting with three separate chapters of stream of consciousness and then weaving them together into a dialogue with no demarcations, which turns into a multivocal and dialogic poetic utterance:

You are my face; I am you.
Why did you leave me who am you?
I will never leave you again
Don't ever leave me again
You will never leave me again
You went in the water
I drank your blood
I brought your milk
I will never leave you again.[38]

WITNESSES AND NARRATORS: BLACK ELK AND WASHINGTON IRVING, MALCOLM X AND HENRY JAMES

[A] Cree hunter . . . came to Montreal to testify in court concerning the fate of his hunting lands . . . But when administered the oath he hesitated: "I am not sure I can tell the truth . . . I can only tell what I know.

—James Clifford, *Writing Culture*

"Oral narrative invariably employs an authoritative and reliable narrator"; "Oral tradition . . . implies the existence of a narrator whose authority is never in doubt."[39] Such generally accepted statements apply, if anything, to the specialized repertoire of ritual and formalized discourse that attempts to create in the oral tradition the "literary" detachment and the impersonal stability of "texts." Actual oral narrators, however, are not a function of the text, but persons; even in the most ritualistic and formal performance, their right and competence to speak are always in question, as are the changes they make and the inextricable weaving of shared memory and personal experience in their rendering of the story.[40] Their words may carry the authority of tradition, but they are always entrusted to personal voices, fallible and precarious, always subject to the dialogic test of the response of an empiric audience.

Thus, though literary critics still claim that "there is no ironic distance between the author and the teller of a traditional story,"[41] yet oral narrators will often distance themselves from the tale and from other tellers. One Cree word for "storyteller" means "someone who lies without harming anyone." Zora Neale Hurston's storytellers call their tales "them big old lies we tell when we're jus' sittin' here on the porch doin' nothin' "—not exactly a term of authority or an authoritative context. An excellent example of modulated detachment between tale and teller is the beginning of Theodore Rosengarten's *All God's Dangers*. "But used to in them days, I think a heap of this old back yonder stuff was lies, a heap of it," says Ned Cobb, the oral narrator: "If I tell any kind of story that I think was just something told to entertain, I'll say 'That's what I heard So-and-So say', and so on. But my daddy told this for the truth."[42]

Black Elk also plays upon degrees of distance to shift the level of meaning. "This they tell," he says, concluding his story of the sacred pipe, "and whether it happened so or not I do not know; but if you think about it you can see that it is true." The truth of the story is the truth of art; it does not vouch for the facts but tells another kind of truth, and this is why it is told. Elsewhere, he articulates the same point: "Watanye said the story happened just as he told it, and maybe it did. If it did not, it could have, just as well as not. I will tell that story now."[43]

The distinction between "the truth" and "what I know" bases authority on the narrators' limitations rather than on their omniscience. Black Elk remembers the battle of Wounded Knee like the battle of Waterloo seen and not seen by Fabrizio Del Dongo in Stendahl's *La Chartreuse de Parme*. Earlier in the book, he describes another battle "like something fearful in a fog." Facts dissolve in the mist, but their experienced effect—condensed in the adjective *fearful*—remains. The limited point of view declares that the narrator may not know everything but he does know what he knows; hence "the quick urgency of personal testimony, the insinuating authority of the truly sincere" that Werner Berthoff describes as the "basic virtue" of all first-person narrative.[44]

Thus, Pretty Shield, a Crow woman, also founds the authenticity of the tale about a battle with the Lakota on her restricted point of view (and of listening):

> I saw what went on there . . . I did not cover my eyes. I was looking all the time, and listening to everything. I saw Strikes-two, a woman over sixty years old, riding around the camp on a gray horse . . . I saw her, I heard her, and my heart swelled, because she was a woman.[45]

The Autobiography of Malcolm X, another text founded on oral narration and dialogue, also establishes the authenticity of the tale by insisting upon the narrator's limited viewpoint, on his lack of understanding, and on his unmediated reactions, feelings, and memory:

> I remember being suddenly snatched awake into a frightening confusion of pistol shots and shouting and smoke and flames . . . I remember we were outside in the night in our underwear, crying and yelling our heads off.[46]

One reason these narrators insist on the limits of their authority is that, as opposed to writers, they are not alone but must be responsible to hearers who can in turn play the role of speakers and offer another version, another point of view. "It was customary," writes the editor of Yellow Wolf's biography, "to have witnesses to what was said. The listeners, should they detect error—intentional or otherwise—in statement, were privileged to make corrections." In this way, he adds, "oral histories are kept nearer the facts."[47] Thus, Black Elk opens his tale to other voices, suspending his narration to yield the floor to his friends gathered around him to listen to a story they already know.

In the introductory frame to *The Autobiography of Miss Jane Pittman*, Ernest J. Gaines recognizes and describes this process: "there were other people at the house every day that I interviewed her, and . . . Miss Jane was constantly turning to one of them for the answer." "When she was tired, or when she just did not feel like talking any more, or when she had forgotten certain things, someone else would always pick up the narration." Miss Jane, however, is always called upon to signal her approval or dissent from what is being said and no one would contradict her "because, after all, this was her story." In Goffman's terms, Miss Pittman remains the "author," while the supplementary narrators function as "animators." This dialogic, cooperative, plurivocal character of oral narration, however, seems to clash with the requirements of Gaines' fictional genre; in written autobiography, unity of voice is an intrinsic requirement for the construction of the self. Therefore, the frame narrator informs us that in what he presents as an edited transcript, "I have used only Miss Jane's voice."[48]

In oral narration, the multiplication of voices originates as a control procedure. Because oral cultures have no texts other than personal performances, the only way of going beyond the individual to achieve a sort of shared "text" is to let many individuals speak, converging toward a common ground of experience and words. This, however, is a self-defeating gesture, for it is impossible to build narrative authority by constantly curtailing the authority of each narrator. Furthermore, it is manifestly impossible to consult all the possible narrators and narratives of any event: thus, rather than creating a sense of approaching completeness, the heaping of tales only accentuates the sense of partiality. This is why the accumulation and fragmentation of narrators and narratees is adopted from the oral into the written literary tradition precisely as an index of crisis rather than control. Each narrative "voice" designates the emergence of partiality and individuality in the neutrality of writing.

The creation of a partial voice frequently takes the form of a dialogic apostrophe to the reader, as if imitating a face-to-face narrative situation: "Call me Ishmael." But the text's invitation to the reader is always an invitation to listen, never to speak; we can never actually "call" Ishmael. "And *only I* am escaped to tell thee," says Ishmael, clinching in the grammatical distinction of "I" and "thee" the immutable roles of the first-person narrator and the second-person narratee. Other shipwrecks have been more fortunate: "How the gallant squadron of Pavonia was snatched from the jaws of this modern Charybdis, has never been truly made known, for so many survived to tell the tale . . . "[49].What would the story of the white whale be, if Queequeg or Bulkington or Fedallah had also lived to tell us?

Irving uses the "plurality of historians" as a metaphor for the inconclusive fragmentation of voices in a free-speaking popular sovereignty. Like democracy, the plurality of voices confuses but allows choice—in fact, it confuses *because* it requires us to choose.[50] Readers must make their own way, like Hawthorne's young Robin Molineux. The story of the "Adventure of the German Student" reaches us through Irving's persona Geoffrey Crayon, who had it from a "nervous gentleman" who heard it from an "old gentleman with the haunted head," who claims he learned it from the student himself "in a mad-house in Paris."[51] In this chain of unreliable narrators, readers can (must) decide at which level they accept the story and how they feel about it: whether to be "mad" like the student, "haunted" like the old gentleman, "nervous" like the other gentleman, "inquisitive" like one of the listeners, "spectatorial" like Crayon, or pretend not to be there at all like Irving.

Yet, a radical difference remains. In oral performance, partiality underlines the speaker's responsibility, both for the contents of the speech and for the act of speaking. In writing, the interposition of limited, multiple, or unreliable narrators is one way of limiting the responsibility of the authorial figure and removing it from the scene. The partiality of oral narrators is an attempt to found meaning on their own limitations; the partiality of literary narrators stresses their fragmentation only to reconstitute completeness and order in the artistic form shaped by the authorial figure.[52]

In some ways, the absent authorial figure functions in literature as the voice of the interviewer functions in certain representations of oral history and narrative. The interviewer's voice is apparently suppressed in the monologization of *The Autobiography of Miss Jane Pittman*, as well as in such nonfictional works as *All God's Dangers* or *The Autobiography of Malcolm X*. However, beyond Miss Pittman's presence, the interviewer controls the story in silence (and in the invisibility guaranteed by writing), filtering, evoking, selecting, transcribing, and linking the voices of the actual narrators while keeping up the fiction that he is merely reporting, transcribing "the thing itself." Unlike Miss Pittman, however, whose control is made explicit by the fact that she is present and visible on the scene, the interviewer's control is disguised.[53] In the same fashion, literary authors grow invisible and omnipotent to the extent that they shift the burden of visible responsibility on to the partial narrators. Thus the artist deals with the increasing sense of the fragmentation and uncertainty of reality by founding "on his own partiality, in his own specialization, a new totality, a new unitary value of reality."[54]

Henry James writes: "It is scarce necessary to note that the highest test of any literary form conceived in the light of 'poetry' . . . hangs back unpardonably from its office when it fails to lend itself to *viva voce* treatment."[55] It would be a mistake to believe that James here is thinking of a mimesis of orality. On the contrary, the highly *written* quality of his phrasing requires a reading voice, not as a reproduction of the spoken word but as a strategy of control. James knows that reading is faster than speaking and is therefore aware of the dangers of the reader's global, simultaneous glance at the page. He asks for the controlled speed of the voice as a guarantee that the reader will devote to the text all the time and attention it requires. In fact, the "oral interpretation" of literature has long been a respected and widespread subject in American schools and colleges, where it was perceived at times as a critical exercise preparatory to textual "close reading" (the "pressure of the attention articulately *sounded*," as James put it).[56]

James often complains of the blurred, indistinct diction and the uneducated, "unsettled character" of "the colloquial *vox Americana*."[57] As a remedy, he suggests that speakers imitate the distinct diction of books, in which all letters are clearly and equally printed and the syllables are (at least in theory) "all sounded." The ideal reader *a viva voce* of his novels follows the same recipe. Each syllable in James's carefully wrought texts is important; each syllable must receive sounded attention. The voice James is looking for is one that has learned to model itself upon the example of writing.[58]

CHAPTER SIX

Symbols: The Oral Origins of the World

In the beginning was the Word . . . " Now what do you suppose old John *meant* by that?

—N. Scott Momaday, *House Made of Dawn*

At the beginning of *Moby-Dick*, a consumptive usher to a grammar school with a passion for etymologies informs us that in the word "whale" it is "the letter H, which almost alone maketh up the signification of the word"—and perhaps of the world, in whose deepest foundations and most secret ribs the whale rolls its "island bulk." The aspirate consonant is an image of the breath that brings clay to life, an implicit memory of the oral creation of the world and of the presence of the Word. But even in the biological processes of nature and the body, everything begins with the voice: Walt Whitman describes slang, the everyday speech of common people, as "the lawless germinal element, below all words and sentences."[1]

In this chapter I will explore the symbolic implications of voice and sound, and their relationship with the body, birth, and death. Pure spirit and fermenting matter, the voice dissolves the foundations of writing, of meaning and America, while raising a further, more essential foundation in the substance of prearticulated sound, in the myriad sounds of nature, in the word of creation, and in the cry of birth. The "house made of dawn" is the world: the voice announces the second foundation.

"But the beginning of things," says Kate Chopin, "of a world especially, is necessarily vague, tangled, chaotic, and exceedingly disturbing."[2] Because it attains the origin of everything, the voice evokes the chaos preceding and accompanying creation, the tangling of matter and spirit before life, and their dissolution and separation after death. Whitman's "germinal" ferment can signify both the stirrings of life and its corruption and decay. The ghost of the voice may freeze into the livid flesh of the corpse.

VOICE AND CREATION: EMERSON'S PRECANTATIONS

The Bible is an antique Volume -
Written by faded Men
At the suggestion of Holy Specters
—Emily Dickinson

"For poetry was all written before time was," says Emerson, "and whenever we are so finely organized that we can penetrate into that region where the air is music, we hear those primal warblings, and attempt to write them down." Our ear, however, is imperfect, and "we lose ever and anon a word, or a verse, and substitute something of our own, and thus miswrite the poem."[3] As Emily Dickinson knows, only a "warbling teller" can restore life to a creative word hollowed into dry Scripture.

Writing, Emerson explains, turns the "high chant" of bards and the song of prophets into dogma and institution, freezing poetic metaphor into literal truth. The prophetic voice must renew itself at every generation, as if uttered for the first time, lest it lose its correlation with an ever unfinished Creation that is performance rather than text. Only when we recognize Scripture, and scriptures, as inadequate transcriptions of an earlier orality or music can we recover the original authority and authenticity of divine and human word, and again connect the *vox populi* to the *vox Dei*. Hence Emerson's fascination for the "oralistic" hypotheses of the "higher criticism" of the Bible, according to which the origin of the Scriptures was to be found in the oral poetic and narrative tradition of the Near East.[4]

"Where now sounds the persuasion, that by its very melody imparadises my heart, and so affirms its origin in heaven?" Emerson's "Divinity School Address" is built around the contrast between sound, light, flux, and intoxication on the one hand, and immobility, petrification, and textualization on the other. The insubstantiality of voice is a figure of the transparent Oversoul, as are air and electricity, or the intoxicating influence of liquor and the enlivening power of water. "The Poet" explores the interplay in sound of cosmic and poetic creation; the world of ideas is a musical one, in which all things "pre-exist, or superexist in pre-cantations." Writing stands as a screen between us and this original sound; as Italo Calvino has written more recently, "the weight, the inertia, the opacity of the world [are] qualities that stick to writing unless one finds some way of evading them." The travesty of the word of Christ in Scripture is but the biblical type of the limits of poetry—this imperfect transcription of the music in the air.[5]

Emerson proposes to establish American culture on a new foundation, free from the hegemony of the book. In order to recover the blissful time when the world was "plastic and fluid in the hands of God," the reader must go beyond the text to rediscover the movement of time and the sound of the voice, "the seer's hour of vision" and the "the authentic utterances of the oracles." The new national literature will be based on nature, experience, and the tangible sound of popular orality: "the literature of the poor, the feelings of the child, the philosophy of the street, the meaning of the household life," "the ballad in the street; the news of the boat; the glance of the eye; the gait of the body." The "necessity of speech and song" proclaimed in "The Poet" may be fulfilled, as the "Divinity School Address" suggests, by such still viable forms as ritual, oratory, and preaching, in which the truth of the poets who "spoke oracles to all time" shall find a new voice.[6]

"Oracles to all time": even as Emerson sings the praise of fluidity, he affirms a need for permanence. The authenticity of the original sound becomes authority only when it somehow consolidates into text. Emerson offers to solve this contradiction by appealing to the institutions of the voice (oratory, preaching, and conversation) and by offering a theory of language and text, and a specific rhetorical form.

In the "Divinity School Address," Emerson uses images of petrification to represent the falsification of the truth and life of the voice. A few years later, however, in "The Poet," petrification is no longer described as an obstacle to the flow of language but rather as its natural concretion: "Language is fossil poetry. As the limestone of the continent consists of infinite masses of the shells of animalcules, so language is made up of images, or tropes, which now, in their secondary use, have long ceased to remind us of their poetic origin." Like organically composite stone, language is less an original expression of individual genius than a form of "wide social labor" and "popular tradition." By rooting themselves in this collective creative process, the poet's art and the reader's creativity restore the suspended life of fossilized tropes and figures. This insight anticipates Bakhtin's views on the social, dialogic nature of language and Jakobson's thesis on the creative processes of folklore. Whitman draws on the democratic implications of Emerson's insight by emphasizing how the implicit poetic and metaphoric power of slang and everyday language originates in its accumulated use by the common people rather than in a supposed original purity.[7]

After thus establishing the collective authority of language, Emerson secures that of the text by means of two orally-rooted rhetorical forms: proverb and aphorism. Proverbs are literally "fossil poetry": a collective linguistic and ideological concretion, a prescriptive truth "to all time," a minimal form of poetic folklore. Aphorisms, on the other hand, are poetry in the process of fossilization. They differ from proverbs because they are the work of an author rather than of folk tradition, but they share the proverb's rhetorical form; several of Emerson's (and Franklin's) aphorisms find their way into the oral tradition.[8]

Proverb and aphorism share the function of establishing an authority capable of compensating for the precariousness of the spoken or unauthorized word. Emily Dickinson, for instance, uses aphorisms as a corrective to improvisation, a "solution to the problem of authority" implicit in the transgression of a woman who wants to write.[9] Emerson's proverbs and aphorisms also oscillate between the oral and the written, the natural and the spiritual, and thus establish a precarious balance between authenticity and authority, between the oral foundation of the world and the written presence of the text.

THE TONGUE AND THE HEART: WHITMAN

O I perceive after all so many uttering tongues
And I perceive they do not come from the mouths of graves
for nothing.

—Walt Whitman, "Song of Myself"

The leaves of grass are also tongues, and the poem named after them refuses to be called a book, proclaiming itself to be "song," "chant," voice of a "singer" and "bard," or tongue of the reader: "I act as the tongue of you/ Tied in your mouth, in mine it begins to be loosen'd." In the "germinal" encounter of this tongue with the body lies "the origin of all poems":

I mind how once we lay such a transparent summer morning,
How you settled your head athwart my hips and gently turn'd
over upon me
And parted the shirt from my bosom-bone, and plunged your
tongue to my bare-stripped heart[10]

An erotic as well as a vocal organ, the tongue presides over the incarnation of insubstantial voice into the passional matter of the body. As in the encounter of the sea with the land ("the solid marrying the liquid"),[11] the mutual penetration of tongue and heart eroticizes the fusion of matter and spirit into concrete phonic substance:

loose the stop from your throat,
Not words, nor music or rhyme I want, not custom or
lecture,not even the best,
Only the lull I like, the hum of your valvèd voice.[12]

Seldom does Whitman succeed better in merging the poetic, syncretic and metaphoric power of slang than in that word, "valvèd." "Valve" is the stop that regulates the flow of air in musical instruments, of which the human throat is one. It is the shell that retains the voice of the sea; it is, as John Berryman points out, a "safety valve" for the soul to control and liberate the body. But in slang "valve" is also a sexual organ, both female (a concretion of "valve" and "vulva") and male ("a synonym of cock"). In this erotic mystic fusion, the metaphorical layers of popular speech merge with the syncretism of Latin and English, of high culture and low, of female and male.[13]

Tongue and heart meet in some mythical sphere before language, where the correspondence of sound and sense persists in the shared physical roots of the voice. "Only the lull I like": the inarticulate "hum" is described as pure flow, liquid "sea-drift" of sound, antecedent to the discrete articulation of linguistic meaning and musical scales, to the rise of discontinuity between the self and the world, between words and things. In the alliterative repetition of sounds, the hypnotic absorption of "I" in "like" becomes a metaphor of fusion, a paronomastic image of the lover enveloped in the object of love.[14]

I swear I begin to see little or nothing in audible words,
All merges toward the presentation of the unspoken meanings
of the earth,
Toward him who sings the songs of the body and of the truths
of the earth,
Toward him who makes the dictionaries of words that print
cannot touch.[15]

Meaning must be sought, then, in the expressive mimetic quality of figures of sound, alliteration, and onomatopoeia: the "blab" of the street, the "sluff" of boot soles, the "clank," "clinking," and "flap" of city traffic. Before this, there is music; to Whitman, the fact that the words of Italian opera were incomprehensible only enhanced its fascination.[16] Farther back, before music, we hear the sounds of nature: animal voices, the song of the thrush and the mocking-bird, the "barbaric yawp" from the roofs of the world. And at the origin of everything, "key" to all sounds of the natural world, we hear the "musical shuttle" of the sea.[17]

The liquid sound of the sea recurs in Whitman's images of the voice: the "liquid and free and tender" song of the bird in "liquid-flowing syllables," or the notes of the "liquid-full contralto." This quality is also underlined by the phonic symbolism of alliterating "liquid" consonants: "lean and loaf," the "lilacs" that "last bloomed," the "lull I like." The liquid flow of sound, the hypnotic untranslatability of lull and hum, associate the voice to the rhythmic coming and going of the tide, absence and presence, birth and death. In the ocean's undifferentiated mass, cosmic unity ("the float forever held in solution") coexists with democratic equality ("the rolling ocean, the crowd"). The liquid matter of the "password primeval" is "the sign of democracy."[18]

"You conceive too much of articulation," says Whitman, figuratively addressing language itself. Liquids are always continuous, never discrete or articulated. Whitman's prearticulated voice is the culmination of an American dream of a communal, egalitarian Eden free from divisions and articulation. An Appalachian folk song says that in Heaven "There'll be no distinction there"; similar images of prelapsarian Eden are to be found in the mixing of juices and flavors before Huckleberry Finn's "sivilization"; in the English countryside before enclosure in Irving's *Bracebridge Hall*; in the ancestral time when all shared the same name, before Christ began to save "only the individual soul" in Silko's *Ceremony*; and in the Appalachian paradise, without hierarchies and social distinctions, from which Faulkner's Sutpen descends to meet his fate.[19]

Democracy, however, ought to balance the egalitarian values of unity with the ability to articulate, rather than abolish, difference. Whitman's resistance to articulation and his attack on "linguists and contenders"[20]—against, that is, those whose task it is to articulate language and discriminate ideas—express his yearning for the deep organic unity that makes democracy meaningful; yet they also represent his inability to perceive democracy as a historically given form of organization of complex, diversified societies.

Rather than a pluralistic system, Whitman sings a democracy *en masse*, containing multitudes and unafraid to contradict itself because it takes equality for equivalence: "a vast cosmic democracy, without episode, separation or conflict" (Richard Chase), in which "the practical dialectics of the democratic relationship between the self and the masses vanishes into a universal identification of everything with the self" (Bruno Cartosio).[21]

Conflict, however, is implicit in the voice itself, in its relationship with writing, in the tension between the voice's tangible substance and its tendency toward dispersion and loss. Regardless of his stance as bard and singer, Walt Whitman is first of all a printer. "I was chilled with the cold types and cylinder and wet paper between us," he writes in the first version of *Leaves of Grass*, which he himself composed and printed.[22] His yearning for words that "print cannot touch" arises from the experience of the icy chill of typography.

> Were you thinking that those were the words, those upright lines? those curves, angles, dots?
> No, these are not the words, the substantial words are in the ground and sea,
> They are in the air, they are in you.[23]

"Camerado, this is no book,/ Who touches this touches a man," Whitman proclaims; "I touch your book," sadly responds Allen Ginsberg.[24] *Leaves of Grass* cannot help but be a book, and Whitman's dream of the voice is rooted upon typographical soil. Raised and educated in the written word, Whitman fears that he may be entrapped by it. "To avoid having his words lost to the winds," the critic Calvin Bedient has written, "Whitman required the technology of writing." Perhaps, the reverse is true: Whitman accepts the risk of losing his voice in the wind in order to keep his printed words from being imprisoned in ice.[25]

Rather than doing away with the authority of the text, then, Whitman's voice conveys the higher authority of a language that claims to be natural and universal because it incorporates the immediate evidence of senses and experience. As in Emerson, orality dissolves an authority in order to consolidate a stronger, more authentic, more arrogant one: "What I assume you shall assume"; "stop this day with me and you shall possess the origin of all poems." Bedient sees *Leaves of Grass* as "the triumph of oral imagination over writing, won at the mercy and through the triumph of writing itself." Perhaps we should again reverse the phrase: Whitman's poetry is the triumph of writing, won by means of the absorption in it of a triumphant orality.[26]

Through me many long dumb voices,
Voices of the interminable generations of prisoners and slaves
Voices of the diseas'd and despairing, and of thieves and dwarfs
Voices of cycles of preparation and accretion[27]

It would be silly to dismiss the importance of this revolutionary affirmation of the collective voice of the "deform'd, trivial, flat, foolish, despised." If ever literature affirmed the oral foundations of democracy, this is the moment. Yet an ambiguity remains. Whitman offers himself as a transparent medium, but he is not entirely so. In the plurality of roles staged by his performing voice, we recognize both the transparency of identification and the opacity of the mask, the difference/deferment of writing[28] and the delegated voice of representative democracy. "I *act* as the tongue of you" has both political and theatrical connotations. As the popular voice issues "refined" and "enlarged" from the filter of Madison's democratic institutions, so Whitman claims that the forbidden, indecent voices of "sexes and lusts" are "clarified and transfigured" as they go "through" his writing and voice.

"Through me . . . voices . . . of slaves"; one wonders what his contemporary Frederick Douglass would have thought, bent as he was on speaking through no one but himself, rejecting benevolent interpreters and paternalistic mediators. Perhaps the "dumb" voices of the oppressed find their sound through Walt Whitman. On the other hand, perhaps they will remain "dumb" as long as he speaks in their place. The masses may receive their voice from the poet, but they also confer and delegate their voice to him until they finally lose it in his.

Whitman's masses are no more articulated in social groups and classes than the sea is articulated in waves, or "primeval" sounds in words. Rather, they fluctuate in the uncertain region between the power they receive and the power they delegate, between popular democracy and the nationalization of the masses. "Only what nobody denies is so"; the unanimous popular voice that speaks through Whitman is a voiced mass, spontaneous and intoxicatingly liberated and real, but it is also the alarming, inarticulate, and formless voice of undiscriminating, "oceanic" consent.[29]

GOSSIP: GRACE PALEY, HENRY JAMES, AND THE DISSONANCE OF WOMEN'S VOICES

> You see," said Mr. Darwin, "to a Jew the word 'shut up' is a terrible expression, a dirty word, like a sin, because in the beginning, if I remember correctly, was the word.
>
> —Grace Paley, "Faith in the Afternoon"

Writing in the 1840s, the critic Henry Cary complained that he could hear nothing liquid or musical in the voices of American women. "Alas," he wrote, "for the husky impediments, the ear-piercing squeaks, the pistol-shot abruptness, the revolting harshnesses, the cracked-kettle intimations, the agonizing squeals, the slipshod drawls, the rumbling distances of sound." Sixty years later, Henry James perceived the excessive volume, the intrusive projection, the mumbled articulation of emancipated American women as an authentic danger to civilization.[30]

Yet, in James's sarcastic portraits—the vociferating Bostonian students who "ingeniously shrieked and bawled at each other" and "conversed at the top of their lungs," or the ladies who crowd squealing around one who tops them all with an "admirable yell"—we still hear the the "boldness and rotundity of speech" of their ancestors in the *Scarlet Letter*.[31] Or perhaps, an announcement of the resonant loudness with which Grace Paley's characters overcome the noise of the world: "There is a certain place where dumb waiters boom, doors slam, dishes crash, every window is a mother's mouth bidding the street shut up, go skate somewhere else, come home. My voice is the loudest."[32]

In the Victorian age, high volume, intrusive loudness, blurred diction seemed to define not only women's speech but all of American speech; they are a natural consequence of democracy and free speech. James's women, in fact, are very often, "simply, and ambiguously, America itself"; and America was, and is, a loud place. Grace Paley, again: "This is a great ballswinger of a city on the constant cement-mixing remake, battering and shattering, and a high note out of a wild clarinet could be the decibel to break a citizen's eardrum."[33] The dissonance of women's voices is part of the antiauthoritarian, often arrogant "barbaric yawp" that America shouts to the world: the sound of an intriguing primitive glamour, with definite undertones of threat.

In *The Bostonians*, as Tony Tanner points out, Henry James tells an emblematic story of the struggle "between the female voice and the male pen." Captured by Verena Tarrant's magical voice, Basil Ransom hastens to appropriate it, to bring it under the control of his own writing, and finally to silence it. But it is not an easy thing to do. "We don't here, you know," a lady told Henry James, "*acknowledge* authority." Grace Paley agrees: "We were, in fact, the soft-speaking tough souls of anarchy."[34]

In Paley's aptly titled story "The Loudest Voice," a storekeeper enjoins little Shirley Abramowitz to "Be quiet" as she reads out the brand names on the shelves: "the labels are coming off." In a tradition that associates writing to male control, these women's voices disrupt labels and definitions and inject an ambivalent resistance to control into their own writings. "The spontaneous, the instinctive, the natural, the informal, the anti-classical, and the artless: all these terms of art," writes Ellen Moers, "have been associated with the woman's voice from the beginning of time," so that "the raising of the woman's voice in letters" was identified with that "start of modern literature that we call Romanticism." Voice, then, is both a stigma assigned to women to brand them them as *incapable* of rationality and control and a weapon in the women's struggle *against* control.[35]

Women therefore often claim the oral origins of their writing as a challenge to the cultural order, vindicating despised, depreciated sources. "It is the responsibility of the poet to listen to gossip and pass it on the way story tellers decant the story of life," writes Grace Paley. "When people talk about the details of daily lives it is gossip; when they write about them, it is literature," notes linguist Deborah Tannen. "Mah tongue is in mah friend's mouf," says Janie Crawford in Zora Neale Hurston's *Their Eyes Were Watching God* (echoing Whitman's "I act as the tongue of you"), as if to indicate the cooperative, socializing quality of that exchange of secrets that men call gossip. Eudora Welty traces the sources of her narrative art to the sewing and gossiping sessions she listened to at home, in spite of her mother's protective attempts to keep her out. More broadly, Gertrude Stein insists: "I always listen. I always have listened. I always have listened to the way everybody has to tell what they have to say."[36] And Grace Paley, once more:

> In their gossipy communications, they ["certain Jews"] whispered the hidden or omitted fact (which some folks had

> already noticed): the Child WAS a girl, and since word of mouth is sound made in the echo of God (in the beginning there was the Word and it was without form but wide), ear to mouth and mouth to ear it soon became the people's knowledge, outwitting the computerized devices to which most sensible people had not said a private word for decades anyway.[37]

The myth of the oral creation of the world is woven here together with the history of a birth: a Creation and a Birth that is oral ("word of mouth"), ethnic ("certain Jews"), folkloric ("the people's knowledge"), and above all, female. The word is made flesh, and the flesh is a woman born of a woman. This word "without form but wide"—like the intangible voice expanding in the air, like the contourless ghost of origins—is irreverent and powerful, a Creator and a Trickster. Not only does it shake and undermine one form of writing, it prepares to found another. In the tradition of Hester Prynne, excluded from the church and the liturgies of public speech, these unauthorized voices control the secret of origins and the secret of birth.

BIRTHS OF THE VOICE: DICKINSON, ATWOOD, MORRISON, CHOPIN, WALKER

A word is dead
When it is said
Some say.
I say it just
Begins to live
That day.

—Emily Dickinson

This is a poem about birth: like a newborn child, the voice issues from the body to begin a new, independent life of its own. On the other hand, it is also a poem about death: in the metaphoric continuum of voice-breath-spirit-soul, the birth of the voice also stands for the immaterial soul's departure, to begin a new, eternal life as the body dies.

Like life itself, sound begins with expulsion from the body. As birth separates the new, living being from the mother, so the vibration of the voice disentangles tongue and air, speaker and utterance, in a process of origination, separation and identification in which the body is both the place of origin and the subject of loss.

"It's hot here, and too noisy": it is the childbirth scene in Margaret Atwood's *The Handmaid's Tale*. "The women's voices rise around me, a soft chant that is still too loud for me, after the days and days of silence. In the corner of the room there's a bloodstained sheet, bundled and tossed there, from where the waters broke." The women's voices are continuous as the hum of an incantation, rhythmical as a work song: " 'Breathe, breathe', we chant, as we have been taught. 'Hold, hold, hold. Expel, expel, expel.' "[38]

Continuity, rhythm, fluidity evoke what Julia Kristeva calls the "semiotic" sphere: the preverbal, preoedipal space before the original separation and articulation of language and self. Continuous sound, as opposed to articulated language, retains and expresses the memory of fusion and unity at the very moment of separation. Rhythm (what Kristeva calls "chora"), on the other hand, organizes the chaos of psychic impulses into an order implicit in the vocal and kinetic movement of the voice and the body "which precedes and underlies figuration and thus specularization, and is analogous only to the vocal and kinetic rhythm."[39] The breaking of the waters symbolizes both this primeval fluidity and the moment of separation, as in Atwood's childbirth scene or in Lee Smith's *Fair and Tender Ladies*, where it accompanies a preverbal cry emanating directly from the body:

> And then right before she came out I could *hear* it . . . I swear I could *hear* my bones parting and hear myself opening up with a huge horrible screeching noise, and all the splashing down my legs felt cold, not hot. Beulah says I screamed so much I embarrassed them all . . . So may be what I heard was my screaming, but I don't think so. I think it was my screeching bones.[40]

In Toni Morrison's *Beloved*, Sethe's dramatic delivery takes place while crossing the river and is prepared and soothed by the continuous, steady, healing hum of the girl Amy's good voice. Later, when the women of the neighborhood gather to exorcise the ghost of Sethe's murdered daughter, Beloved, out of the hummed words of their collective, antiphonal chant we can make out "only the earnest syllables of agreement that backed it: Yes, yes, oh yes. Hear me, hear me." Out of this *choral* litany, rises the scream of another birth: "And then, Ella hollered." Raped by her master, Ella "had delivered, but would not nurse, a hairy white thing . . . It lived five days never making a sound." Ella's inarticulate cry is the desperate recognition of that birth rejected into silence. The other women, however, also hear it as the memory of an earlier and more universal origin evoked by the voice: "They stopped praying and took a step back to the beginning. In the beginning there were no words. In the beginning was the sound and they all knew what it sounded like."[41]

This beginning before language separated from sound is the "time immemorial" recalled by the Pueblo storytellers in Leslie Silko's *Ceremony*, when "human beings could understand what the animals said" in the cosmic merging of all voices. In Morrison's *Song of Solomon*, Milkman Dead becomes absorbed in the night sounds of animals and hunters, and through them transcends his separate identity: "It was all language . . . No, it was not language; it was what was there before language. Before things were written down. Language in the time when men and animals did talk to one another." Later, Milkman discovers the roots of his family and racial history in the choral song and the endless circular dance of a children's ring game.[42]

The "semiotic" sounds of animals, water, and music open and close Kate Chopin's *The Awakening*. In the beginning, M. Pointellier is trying to read his newspaper but is distracted by the animal voices and musical sounds that surround him, all somehow related to women. Later, while he speaks in a printlike monotone, Edna goes outside to listen to other semiotic, liquid voices: "the hooting of an old owl . . . and the everlasting voice of the sea."[43]

Edna Pointellier "was not a mother-woman," and the most frightening episode in *The Awakening* is a scene of childbirth. Edna's story, however, is a rebirth in the name of sound, of voice, music, animals, the sea: "She was flushed and felt intoxicated with the sound of her own voice and unaccustomed taste of candor . . . It muddled her like wine, or like a first breath of freedom." The intoxication of wine and voice echoes Emerson, while the voice of the sea echoes Whitman: "The voice of the sea is seductive; never ceasing, whispering, clamoring, murmuring, inviting the soul to wander in abysses of solitude; to lose itself in mazes of inward contemplation."[44]

The everlasting voice of the sea returns in the first and the last scene, almost as an icon of the sea's enveloping caress and of the end's return upon the beginning, death's return upon birth. "She felt like some new-born creature"; hers, however, is a birth in reverse, a return to the womb, a prelude to death. The death scene at the end of the book is dominated by liquid imagery and prelinguistic sounds: the waves of the ocean, the vibrations of the air, the voices and smells of memory, the "hum" of animal rhythm. "She heard the barking of an old dog that was chained to the sycamore tree. The spurs of the cavalry officer clanged as he walked across the porch. There was the hum of bees, and the musty odor of pines filled the air."[45]

"I seed de beginnin, en now I sees de endin" says Dilsey in Faulkner's *The Sound and the Fury*.[46] The circular return of the end upon the beginning in *The Awakening* restates the mythical role of women as guardians of the boundaries of life, of the gateways of birth and death. Women's mythic power over the beginning is balanced by their power over the end, and the voice is one of the ritual instruments that preside over this function.

What is truly disturbing in Emily Dickinson's poem is that the life of the word, after it separates from the body, is both a life *and* a death, a life after death, a nonlife and a nondeath. The voice has a beginning but not necessarily an end; as Leslie Silko's medicine man says, what is said "cannot be called back" but goes straight forward indefinitely. "Word of mouth," Grace Paley says, is "without form but wide"; it has no body and no shape, no outlines and no boundaries, but expands in a circle of waves toward circumference. The end is the beginning, and the voice belongs to both: it announces the beginning and overcomes the end; it designates the body and also negates it.

Modern technology has given us a vehicle for this uneasy metaphor of deathlessness, of immaterial, disembodied life: the recorded voice. In many male authors of the 1970s and 1980s—De Lillo, Leavitt, McInerney, James Welch—the recorded voice is a metaphor of unreality: "We're all on tape. All on tape. All of us" (Don De Lillo).[47] Undue generalizations aside, in women writers the recorded voice as metaphor of unreality coexists more often with the recorded voice as the metaphor of a reality so unsuppressible and undaunted that it refuses to die. The recorded voice is both the negation of life and the negation of death.Both aspects can be found in Margaret Atwood. In *Cat's Eye*, the female voice of an answering machine speaks like "a disembodied voice" untouched by death: "an angel voice, wafting through the air. If I died this minute it would go on like that, placid and helpful, like an electronic afterlife."[48] The implication is that the recorded voice never dies because it never was alive; the secretarial voice on the machine is a metaphor for the alienation of women. On the other hand, in Atwood's distopia, *The Handmaid's Tale*, the heroine leaves behind a set of cassette tapes (a modern version of the classical theme of the rediscovered manuscript), representing a proud, unsuppressible historical memory. Beyond oppression, beyond women's exclusion from the written record, beyond death, this woman's voice lives on to tell the tale. She is still alive through her recorded voice because she never really died; her taped voice preserves the collective memory of women's resistance.

Ces voix qui nous viennent du passé, these voices that come to us from the past, is the French historian Philippe Joutard's description of oral history.[49] Once, literature knew only one type of undead, disembodied voices from the past: ghosts. Today, the voice of the dead is embodied and preserved on tapes, which guarantee the survival of memory and, in the process, turn our entire world into a haunted house. In Lee Smith's *Oral History*, the heroine, in search of her family history, leaves a tape recorder in the old family house in the Appalachian hills, and it picks up sounds that may be the wind or may be the ghosts of dead ancestors. The formlessness of the ghost stands before the uncharted territory after death as the semiotic formlessness of sound lies before the uncertain territory of birth. Thus Ann Rice, a popular writer of horror books, also uses tape recording as a metaphor of a problematic deathlessness: the vampire's frustrated desire to die. *Interview with the Vampire* opens with a typical fieldwork session, as a young student prepares to tape the vampire's life (or his death?) history: " 'But how much tape do you have with you?' asked the vampire . . . 'Enough for the story of a life?' "[50]

The association between tape and life makes sense. Scheherazade lived as long as she had a voice to tell her story; but if the story is recorded, the storyteller may live forever (on the other hand, if he had a tape recorder, the Sultan could have cut off her head and just listened to her tapes). In Alice Walker's *The Temple of My Familiar*, Miss Lissie, who is reborn after each death, is an incarnation of the eternal woman: through metempsychosis, she is able to connect the origins of the human species with the present as well as with an indefinite future. As she vanishes, she also leaves behind her voice on tape: out of a car's tape deck, the voice sounds "deeper and weaker, *older*," as if the very act of recording it had removed it from time. Like Dilsey, but on a much broader scale, Miss Lissie has seen the beginning and will see the end—or perhaps, will save us from it. "What does not end, Suwelo?" she asks: "Only life itself, in my experience."[51]

BABEL IN THE RUE MORGUE: POE

> No sooner had the reverberation of my blows sunk into silence, than I was answered by a voice from within the tomb!—by a cry, at first muffled and broken like the sobbing of a child, and then quickly swelling into one long, loud, and continuous scream, utterly anomalous and inhuman—a howl—a wailing shriek, half of horror and half of triumph, such as might have arisen only out of hell, conjointly from the throats of the damned in their agony and of the demons that exult in the damnation.
>
> —Edgar Allan Poe, "The Black Cat"

Around three o'clock one morning the inhabitants of the Quartier St. Roch in Paris were awakened by "a succession of terrific shrieks" from "two or more rough voices, in angry contention," which "seemed to proceed from the upper part" of a house in the rue Morgue.[52] The stairs of the rue Morgue do not descend to the roots of language but climb toward the Tower of Babel. The natural voices of animals do not express the original universal communication of all beings but the angry contention, the mutual incomprehensibility of all tongues.

Poe rehearses the whole symbolic paradigm of the voice as we have discussed it so far in this chapter, but reverses its connotations. For him, as for Whitman, the prelinguistic, inarticulate substance of the voice suggests a vision of democracy—as an indistinct chaos rather than universal unity. It signifies the materiality of life, not as birth but as magmatic matter recalcitrant to death. In the human heart Poe finds nothing "spontaneous" or "authentic," only horror, madness, and death. The voice of the heart ticks the mechanical rhythm of "The Telltale Heart"; animals shriek like the Black Cat, hiss like the black and white birds in *Gordon Pym*, announce inexorable doom in the raven's "Nevermore." Rather than securing the continuity of life, the survival of the voice blurs the distinction between reason and madness, life and nonlife, matter and spirit.

At the beginning of everything, once again, is the relationship of sound and matter. Agathos, one of the "angelic" spirits who speak after death in "The Power of Words," presents a problematic image of the oral creation of the world:

> And while I thus spoke, did there not cross your mind some thought of the *physical power of words*? Is not every word an impulse on the air? . . . This wild star—it is now three centuries since, with clasped hands, and with streaming eyes, at the feet of my beloved—I spoke it—with a few passionate sentences—into birth. Its brilliant flowers *are* the dearest of all unfulfilled dreams, and its raging volcanoes *are* the passions of the most turbulent and unhallowed of hearts.[53]

The unity of matter and spirit manifests itself in the phonic substance of words; the sound of speech, like Agathos's star, contains both the dearest flowers and the raging volcanoes of passion. The same polarity connects Poe's "angelic dialogues" to his horror stories; both groups are concerned with voices speaking after death, but while the "angelic" voices are disembodied and dispassionate, the others madly and obstinately refuse to leave the body. "I am dead" says M. Valdemar as his magmatic voice arises "from some deep cavern within the earth" and impresses the narrator "as gelatinous or glutinous matters impress the sense of touch."[54]

The phonic substance *comes alive* in the impulse of the vocal chords on the air, blurring the articulation between animate and inanimate matter, just as in the inexplicable mutual relationship between the stones of the House of Usher and the spirit of its inhabitants. A scream announces the rising from the grave of Madeline's undead body; "certain low and indefinite sounds which came . . . I knew not whence" announce her return, until the end comes with a "sound like the voice of a thousand waters."[55]

Ligeia's reincarnation also begins with vibrations and impulses on the air, "sounds, and . . . motions," a low and gentle sob and a deep sigh, resonant matter that clinches the female jurisdiction over the boundaries of life and death. In the "thrilling and enthralling eloquence of her musical language" and the "dear music of her low sweet voice," she combines song as the aesthetic ideal of transcending language and song as vocal flow of a magmatic, passional stream.[56]

If for Whitman music is poetry without words, for Poe poetry is music made words. Poetry appropriates music by means of alliteration, onomatopoeia, and phonic symbolism. Both in Poe's "The Raven" and in Whitman's "Out of the Cradle," a bird's voice represents the origins of poetry. In Poe, however, this voice is obstinate negation ("Nevermore") rather than free-flowing natural song. Before the words of the text stands the almost tactile "impression" of rhythm and sound: "the long *o* as the most sonorous vowel, in connection with *r* as the most producible consonant." While Whitman floats his song on the expanse of free verse, Poe subjects it to strict rules of strophe, meter, alliteration, paronomasia, and refrain ("the sense of identity—of repetition"). By means of this artificial discipline, poetry ("the rhythmical creation of beauty") controls the stream of sound, securing the rule of ideal form upon magmatic matter. Mastery of sound becomes power over sound, turning "The Raven" into a sort of ritual dance, a choreutic therapy in which each movement, as each of the speaker's questions, takes us inexorably back to the same place. Poe later repeats the process on a conceptual plane in "The Philosophy of Composition," superimposing a show of rationality over the phonic matter of poetry, replacing the dark sound of origins with the finalistic perspective of the *denouement.*[57]

Which brings us back to the theme of "William Wilson": the inscription of writing's control over the subversive passions of the voice. Metrics and poetics are a means to the same end: "to hold in check the working of passion," as Matthiessen writes, paraphrasing Coleridge. Both Poe's "almost neurotic devotion" to the rules of prosody and syntax and the dynamics of his detective stories express the same need: to restore "the intellect's power over the sensational," while giving the sensational a voice.[58] As the figures of sound force feelings into dance, so M. Dupin—a character conceivable only "in an age which had interiorized literacy," endowed with a logical mind akin to the straight lines of print and the linear plot, restores purloined letters to the rightful owners and silences the roaring voice of the murderous ape.[59]

THE GHOST AND THE CORPSE: FAULKNER

Let us take two passages, from William Faulkner's *As I Lay Dying* and *Absalom, Absalom!* respectively. This is Darl Bundren, describing the Bundren family house:

> I enter the hall, hearing the voices before I reach the door. Tilting a little down the hill, as our house does, a breeze draws through the hall all the time, upslanting. A feather dropped near the front door will rise and brush along the ceiling, slanting backward, until it reaches the down-turning current at the back door: so with voices. As you enter the hall, they sound as though they were speaking out of the air about your head.[60]

And here is Quentin Compson, in his "tomblike" room at Harvard, preparing to read his father's letter:

> Quentin . . . sat quite still, facing the table, his hands lying on either side of the open textbook on which the letter rested: the rectangle of paper folded across the middle and now open, three quarters open, whose bulk had raised half itself by the leverage of the old crease in weightless and paradoxical levitation.[61]

Italo Calvino would have recognized in these passages two ironic examples of what he called *leggerezza* (lightness, weightlessness).[62] In the first, the immaterial transparency of air, voice, and breeze is rendered through an object that, slight as it is, yet possesses a visible and tangible body—the feather. In the second, a solid object—a "bulk," resting on a table with all the materiality of writing—rises and levitates as if endowed with a spirit of its own. Intangible voice is embodied in the feather, the archetypical ancestor of the pen; tangible writing rises in weightless levitation, like a disembodied voice.

As we read further in *As I Lay Dying*, the relationship between the voice and the body grows more complex. This is Vernon Tull describing the singing and preaching at Addie Bundren's funeral:

> The women sing again. In the thick air it's like their voices come out of the air, flowing together and on in the sad, comforting tunes. When they cease it's like they hadn't gone away. It's like they had just disappeared into the air and when we moved we would loose them again out of the air around us, sad and comforting.[63]

The voices that "quaver away" in the air have more than one literary antecedent: Ligeia, who is impulse on the air before she becomes a sound and, finally, a body; or Irving's Ichabod Crane, whose "peculiar quavers" hang in the air of Sleepy Hollow long after he is gone. An almost direct quotation ("when they cease") and the tactile image of "thick" air (and, earlier, the "slanting" shape of the house) evoke another "imperial affliction sent us through the air" in slanted light and heavy vibrations of cathedral tunes. Transparent air thickens, flowing sound and wind freeze, weightlessness turns into "heft"; in turn, bodies shed their weight and float: "He heaves"—this is Jewel, lifting his mother's coffin—"For an instant it resists, as though volitional . . . Then it breaks free, rising suddenly as though the emaciation of her body had added buoyancy to the planks."[64]

On the threshold of *Absalom, Absalom!* we are greeted by the smell of wistaria, the sunlight slanting through the blinds, and a liquid voice inhabited by garrulous ghosts: "the voice not ceasing but vanishing into and then out of the long intervals like a stream, a trickle running from patch to patch of dried sand, and the ghost mused with shadowy docility as if it were the voice which he haunted where a more fortunate one would have a house." And the ghosts reverberate in the air with the sound of church bells, vibrating "in the same air in which the church bells had rung on that Sunday morning in 1833."[65]

Like the words of Poe's Agathos, the bells of Jefferson are "an impulse on the air." Their suspended sound is a metaphor of collective memory, while the impulse is the vibration of art, which sets the sound into motion and makes the air visible. Later, at Harvard, Quentin and Shreve condense the air and mold the shadows in "the visible murmur of their vaporising breath," generating visions and scriptures not unlike the "visible breath" of Black Elk's vision, walking with "visible tracks" on the road.[66]

Addie Bundren also seems to speak like a ghost. A woman on the edge of time, always dying, never gone, her voice seems to hover out of sequence, shaken back into sound by the tossing and lifting and heaving of the coffin. She speaks out of time like a ghost, but occupies the text as a corpse. Her body is buoyant and weightless, but its presence is inescapable. In fact, as her son Cash puts it, "hit was becoming right noticeable."[67] Along with the voice, the body sends other, disembodied messages through the air. Let us read in *Light in August*, holding our noses for the racial implications but smelling the metaphorical ones:

> Then he found himself . . . surrounded by the summer smell and the summer voices of invisible negroes . . . as if the black life, the black breathing had compounded the substance of breath so that not only voices but moving bodies and light itself must become fluid and accrete slowly from particle to particle.[68]

The linkage of voice, water, and smell is dear to Walt Whitman: "Loud in the pines and cedars dim/ Clear in the freshness moist and the swamp-perfume." But in *As I Lay Dying* there are no sprigs of lilac, no warbling thrushes, no athletic armpits whose scent is aroma finer than prayer. If anything, "Infection in the sentence breeds—we may inhale despair."[69] The room in which we listen to Rosa Coldfield's tale is filled with the "rank smell of female old flesh." And the smell of decaying female flesh *is* Addie Bundren's other voice, which Darl and Vardaman hear as they lay their ears on the coffin: "and then she talks in little trickling bursts of secret and murmurous bubbling"; "I put my ear close and I can hear her. Only I can't tell what she's saying."[70]

Whitman's pantheistic myth of decomposition and liquefaction ("I effuse my flesh in eddies") is returned in horror. Addie Bundren is a reincarnation of M. Valdemar, who lies dying and speaks from beyond death with a tactile, glutinous voice until he melts into "a nearly liquid mass of loathsome—of detestable putridity." Addie's revenge on her husband is to turn his name into a glutinous matter, "like cold molasses flowing out of the darkness into the vessel, until the jar stood full and motionless." When words coagulate into motionless shapes, they turn into writing, as in Mr. McEachern's voice in *Light in August*, "cold, implacable, like written or printed words."[71]

This takes us back to Quentin Compson's levitating letter and open book: a metaphor of the literary text endeavoring to disinscribe itself, to free the words from writing by borrowing devices and metaphors from orality. In *Absalom, Absalom!*, in fact, Faulkner is not so much trying to imitate or represent the dynamics of orality as to incorporate them as the text's organizing principle and its very grammar. *Absalom, Absalom!* is not *about* the oral tradition; it *works* like one. We enter the world of this novel as a stranger enters a culture, overhearing "the rag-tags and bob-ends of old tales and talking" from different sources at different times, and piecing them painstakingly together in an ever-elusive picture. In the first pages, for instance, Quentin sums up the story of Thomas Sutpen as he then knows it; two pages later the authorial voice repeats the story almost word by word but including an additional, essential detail ("the son who widowed the daughter who had not yet been a bride"). Gradually, through the repetition and variation of versions and fragments, we assemble a mosaic of hypotheses that takes the place of history.[72]

The discovery of oral devices in such an emphatically *written* text as *Absalom, Absalom!*, however, is not a critical solution but a critical problem. Do these devices mean the same thing in a work of literature as they do in oral discourse and tradition? Indeed, though they may look alike on the textual surface, *are* they the same thing?

In 1979, while carrying out an oral history project in Central Italy, I found myself sitting in the darkened parlour of old Miss Maggiorina Mattioli, listening to her tell the story of her life, like Quentin Compson in Miss Rosa's parlor. Like Miss Rosa, Miss Mattioli was a seamstress; like her, she took the initiative and control in telling the story. Miss Rosa summons Quentin because she wants her story told; I had sought out Miss Mattioli to ask her about her brother's involvement in the anti-Fascist underground, but she kept digressing because she was obsessed with the need to tell her own story—about a broken engagement and a burning insult she had suffered, like Miss Rosa, forty-three years before.

More striking than the analogies between the stories, however, was the analogy between the ways of telling. Both narrators weave tantalizingly in and out of chronological sequence, shift points of view, make extensive and competent use of incremental repetition. Miss Mattioli introduces the story of her broken engagement in the form of a digression ("Well, at the age of nineteen I became engaged. To a man who gave me so much pain, God only knows. He kept me in agony for seventeen years. Think of that—seventeen years. A whole life. I was a child before, and then I was an old woman") and then repeats it, verbatim but with an additional, essential detail: "Look: me, the daughter of an anti-Fascist, I couldn't stand those people, and yet I fell in love with a Fascist. I loved him so much. Seventeen years. Seventeen years. A whole life. I was a child before, and then I was old").[73]

If we lay Faulkner's incremental repetitions side by side with Miss Mattioli's, they look very much alike. Yet one is literature, and the other is a different art. The difference lies in the *process* of enunciation rather than its *product*, in the performance rather than the text. Mattioli, an accomplished storyteller, knows that her story is always on the verge of vanishing like a ghost; therefore, she uses repetition as a weapon in her struggle to hold still the unceasing flight of the voice, to test the reception, expand the performance, secure recollection, fill gaps, repair errors. Faulkner, on the other hand, uses a technology of the word so obsessed with repetition and reproduction (thousands of identical printed copies, infinite possible rereadings of an unchanging, established text) that he is in constant fear that his text may freeze into a motionless corpse. His effort, therefore, is to turn repetition into motion, reproducing in reverse the ephemeral voice's struggle to turn motion into stability.

Early in *Absalom, Absalom!*, the authorial voice informs us that Sutpen's story was "a part of the town's—Jefferson's—eighty years' heritage." In an interview, a black preacher says, "I had not reached my thirteenth birthday—fourteenth birthday, rather, you know."[74] Both narrators use the "oral" device of "repair," or paratactic correction, but bend it to opposite strategies. The oral narrator wants to recover the past as precisely and authentically as possible, and when he catches himself in error he adds the correct information. Faulkner, on the other hand, wants to convey a sense of the blurring of control; he could have replaced the generic "town" with the more specific "Jefferson" in manuscript or in proof, but he chooses to pretend that, like Silko's witches, he has no power over words once they are uttered. The oral narrator was struggling *against* time, to recover the actuality of the past; Faulkner is struggling *for* time, to inject into his text the time-bound marks of orality. Orality and writing exchange weapons to defend themselves against the opposite threats of vanishing or freezing: voices freeze, letters levitate.

The fact that to create the illusion of time Faulkner uses the same device that orality uses to create a sense of timelessness, however, is not without consequences. In the same gesture, in fact, he injects time and subtracts time; he introduces time and motion *in order* to stop them, like a still picture frame, or like Clytie and Rosa's suspended struggle on the stairs. In Mr. Compson's levitating letter, he creates a metaphor of the open, moving literary text, only to turn it into a closed static formula—"the open letter on the open book"—repeated over and over again.

The coagulated voices and the corpse in *As I Lay Dying* and the levitating letter and the ghosts in *Absalom, Absalom!* are a summation of the double bind that ties writing and voice to body and death. The voice is metonymically associated with the body because it originates in it; but it is metaphorically opposed to the body because the voice's substance is immaterial and intangible. On the other hand, writing is is metaphorically associated with the body because it is tangible and material (the "corpus" of an author's works) but is metonymically opposed to it because texts can be detached from the writer's physical presence. In their mutual search, voice and writing generate converging symbols: the ghost, a missing body materializing; the corpse, a present body dissolving. The hinge between them is the place where Addie Bundren and M. Valdemar precariously lie: death, which the voice negates with its motion and reproduces with its vanishing; which writing denies with its permanence and reproduces with its rigidity.

Miss Rosa Coldfield, according to Mr. Compson's letter, may hope to stop being a ghost—but only when she becomes a corpse. The final run-on sentence of his levitating letter describes her funeral: "The weather was beautiful though cold and they had to use picks to break the earth for the grave yet in one of the deeper clods I saw a redworm doubtless alive when the clod was thrown up though by afternoon it was frozen again." Like the literary text infected by orality, the "cold field" in which Miss Rosa is buried breaks open only to close again, discloses life only too enclose death, unfreezes only to freeze once more. Nothing remains but a voice: the idiot Jim Bond, haunting the ashes of Sutpen's house like the ghost of Ichabod Crane, howling and stopping and howling again. "You still hear him at night sometimes," says Shreve: "Don't you?"[75]

Part Three

Second Foundation: The Text upon the Voice

CHAPTER SEVEN

LANGUAGES OF REALITY

> —that this nation, under God, shall have a new birth of freedom—and that government of the people, by the people, for the people, shall not perish from the earth.
>
> —Abraham Lincoln, "Address at Gettysburg, Pennsylvania," November 19, 1863

The Founders' America ends with the Civil War, overwhelmed by its own silences. The written Constitution could not *contain* slavery; it could neither name it, nor live with it. At Gettysburg, in the depth of the Civil War, Lincoln's voice revives a new America, recalling the sources behind and before the Constitution—the Declaration of Independence and "the people."

Writing had sanctioned the birth of America; an oral performance, aptly, announces a "new birth" at Gettysburg. No voice was better suited to announce this second American foundation than that of Abraham Lincoln: a farmer's son, a self-made man, a lawyer and humorist, who was able to invest humble, ordinary speech with the eloquent yet familiar dignity of the Anglo-Saxon lexicon, of Shakespeare, and of the Bible.[1] Through the spoken word and a direct appeal to the people, Lincoln attempts what the Constitution's deferment of writing and representation could no longer accomplish: the restoration of a sense of legitimacy and community to a nation torn by war and self-doubt. After the Civil War, the Constitution continues to function to a large extent as a symbol or icon—a hallowed, often hollowed, textual monument to the identity of a deeply changed nation with a deeply changed relationship between government and the ambiguous entity called "the people." While the generation of Franklin and Madison had puzzled over the meaning of popular sovereignty, Lincoln skips the question altogether, as if repeating the words *the people* and juxtaposing them to the word *government* were enough to dispel the problem of just how "the people" are to govern.

After the next great crisis of American history, the crash of 1929, Franklin D. Roosevelt also resorted to oral communication—public speeches and broadcast "fireside chats"—in order to appeal directly to the people and the "forgotten man" and involve them in reconstructing the stricken nation. Both Lincoln and Roosevelt stand for deeply democratic impulses: national unity, the abolition of slavery, the expansion of citizenship to include a guarantee of material subsistence and workers' rights. In both cases, however, the appeal to the people as the source of legitimacy and identity coincides more with a tightening and centralization of government than with a broadening of actual popular participation and power.

The period of the Civil War and the Reconstruction ends in renewed offensives against "the people": the restoration of the planters' power over the former slaves in the South, General Sheridan's campaigns against the Native Americans in the West, the repression of the great railroad strike of 1877.[2] "The people" remain as an ideal and ideological point of reference, democratic and demagogic, but the active exercise of power (as opposed to mere consent) grows increasingly remote. The more the people are included ideologically and rhetorically, the more they are excluded from the sphere of actual power and concrete politics. Representation as performance outweighs representation as expression of sovereignty.

Both Lincoln and Roosevelt inaugurate eras in which "representation" and "the people" are literary as well as political passwords. "Capturing the special immediate air of American reality in the familiar American dialect"[3] is the agenda of realism, proletarian literature, much ethnic writing, as well as of regionalism, local color, humor, and of the literary use of folklore. The "new birth" of America is accompanied by an attempt to create a specifically "American" literature by basing the literary text on the American voice. Orality no longer signifies the immateriality of sound, but the immediacy of the body; the age of realism is fascinated by the idea of "reproduction," both biological and technological.[4] But, as George Washington Cable had already realized, "reproducing" the voice and the body and "representing" the people may be as frustrating as pursuing Achilles' mythical turtle. Closer and closer and ever inaccessible, orality remains an elusive object of desire, which arouses and frustrates the realistic impulse. Evanescent as breath, it cannot be grasped by material technology; concrete as the body, it eludes the abstract codes of linguistic and literary representation. The text based on the voice rests on shifting, immaterial foundations.

"TOUGHER THAN THE REST": THE ROUGH SINCERITY OF THE AMERICAN LANGUAGE

As we already noted, "all of modern American literature comes from a novel by Mark Twain called *Huckleberry Finn*." At least, this is what Ernest Hemingway claimed, thus identifying the national literature with the tradition that goes from Mark Twain, through Stephen Crane, Sherwood Anderson, and Gertrude Stein, to himself and his descendants. What makes this tradition "American" are its roots in common, everyday speech: "common language, the language of normal discourse, the language we speak to each other in" (Raymond Carver). "The genius of the United States," Whitman proclaims, "is . . . always in the common people. Their manners, speech, dress, friendship" and "the fluency of their speech—their delight in music." "But mostly," Dos Passos concludes, "U.S.A. is the speech of the people."[5]

America, Whitman claims, is "the accretion and growth of every dialect, race, and range of time," and its language is the syncretic incorporation of the contribution of many peoples and languages. As in the ideal democracy, also in language "final decisions are made by the masses, people nearest the concrete, having most to do with actual land and sea." Slang, the source of "perennial rankness and protestantism in speech," sets the tone for the irreverent vulgarity of a literature that cultivates all the excesses and passions of popular discourse.[6]

"I hear America singing": Whitman's America sings with the rough, gravelly voices of Louis Armstrong and Bob Dylan, Almeda Riddle and Ma Rainey, Little Richard and Tom Waits. "None of the folks I know," Woody Guthrie wrote, "have got smooth voices like dew dripping off the petals of the morning violet, and still they can and do sing louder, longer, and with more guts than any smooth voice that I ever heard." Woody Guthrie's soundscapes have the texture of the American landscapes of the "ashcan school" of painting: "I had rather sound like the ash cans of the early morning, like the cab drivers cursing one another, like the longshoremen yelling, like the cowhand whooping, and like the lone wolf barking." "You got to have smelt a lot of mule manure before you can sing like a hillbilly," Hank Williams used to say, voicing in his own way the need for a direct relationship between art and reality. Emerson had announced that "Life is our dictionary," and Hank Williams agreed: "[a] hillbilly . . . sings more sincere than most entertainers because the hillbilly was raised rougher."[7]

Rough sincerity, says Constance Rourke, has always been a principal American virtue. According to Hugh Henry Brackenridge, American English is better than England's because the latter does not possess "*vrai naturelle* or simplicity of nature." To Cooper, Hawthorne, and James, who listed what America lacks before it can have a literature, romantic, realist, and proletarian writers responded with America's rough, tangible truths. Emerson: "Our logrolling, our stumps and their politics, our fisheries, our Negroes and Indians, our boasts and our repudiations, the wrath of rogues and the pusillanimity of honest men, the northern trade, the southern planting, the western clearing, Oregon and Texas, are yet unsung." Lafcadio Hearn, in 1881: "What is wanted now is something distinct and unique and truthful which cannot be found in the factitious life of drawing-rooms, but in the workshops and factories, among the toilers on river and rail." And Joseph Freeman, in the radical manifesto of *New Masses*: "The stockyards of Chicago, the steel mills of Pittsburgh, the mines of West Virginia, the lumber camps of Washington and California, the lynching of Negroes in the South, the clothing industries in the East, the Klan, tabloid newspapers, automobiles . . . these have still to find expression in imaginative, essential and permanent forms."[8]

This essential voice, shaped by the puritan plain style and the Anglo-Saxon lexicon, steeped in the cowboy's reticent code and the Native American's laconic oratory, and influenced by the transparence of scientific discourse, finally affirms one idea: that America is more simple, more authentic, more *real* than the rest of the world.

Which poses a paradox. An English traveler in the early 1800s wrote that Davy Crockett's voice was "was so rough it could not be described—it was obliged to be drawn as a picture." This American voice is so tangible and concrete that it ultimately coalesces into graphics. Davy Crockett's verbal expansiveness and patriotic bragging coagulate in the reticence and silence of the hard-boiled hero. Hemingway's "American" literature "achieves eloquence by saying as little as possible." The hard-boiled hero speaks reluctantly out of the corner of his mouth, hardly moving his lips, drying vernacular and colloquial speech to the verge of silence.[9] The mobile authenticity of feeling and the imperturbable authenticity of silence feed a dialectics between the hard and the soft: the hard-boiled shell protects a tender yolk, the tough stance hides a feeling heart. Grace Paley's "anarchic" voices are both "tough" and "soft-speaking"; Louis Armstrong "performs the magical feat of making romantic melody issue from a throat of gravel." Damon Runyon's gold-hearted vernacular gangsters, Humphrey Bogart's laconic heroes, or the Bruce Springsteen ilk of rockers can be "tougher than the rest" precisely because they are "rough and ready for love."[10]

Rather than denying sentiment, then, this voice inscribes it on the body, guarantees its durability and substance in the hard-drawn lines of the countenance. The tight-drawn lips of laconic hard-boiled heroes are as sentimental as, but more reliable than, Arthur Dimmesdale's fervid trembling mouth. As if turning the scarlet A upside down, Dashiell Hammett begins: "Samuel Spade's jaw was long and bony, his chin a jutting V under the more flexible V of his mouth. His nostrils curved back to make another, smaller, V. His yellow-grey eyes were horizontal. The V motif was picked up again by thickish brows."[11]

CAPTURING THE AMERICAN DIALECTS: FROM COOPER TO ETHNIC MODERNISM

> In this book a number of dialects are used, to wit: the Missouri Negro dialect; the extremest form of the backwoods South-Western dialect; the ordinary "Pike-County" dialect; and four modified varieties of this last.
>
> —Mark Twain, *Huckleberry Finn*

> Dialect, general or special—dialect with the literary rein loose on its agitated back . . . to feel the thick breath, to catch the ugly snarl . . . was to be reminded afresh of the only conditions that guard the grace, the only origins that

> save the honour, or even the life of dialect; those precedent to the invasion, to the sophistication, of schools, and unconscious of the smartness of echoes and the taint of slang.
>
> —Henry James, "Preface" to *Daisy Miller*

Two vernacular characters stand on the banks of Lake Glimmerglass in the early pages of Cooper's *The Deerslayer*: the huge, uncouth Harry Hurry and his young companion, Natty Bumppo. They represent two contrasting visions of the "natural man," signaled by the narrator's attitude toward their speech. Harry Hurry's "uncouth dialect," studded with errors and "malapropisms" caused by "ignorance of English," is a symptom of "his dogmatical manner of disposing of all moral propositions." Natty Bumppo's "peculiar vernacular," on the other hand, is endowed with a captivating "quaintness," which expresses "his untaught, natural courtesy." "The freshness of his integrity, the poetry and truth of his feelings, and even the quaintness of his forms of speech" are all part of one moral and linguistic paradigm.[12]

Cooper's dialects are of questionable authenticity, but they are important markers of sociological and textual otherness and voice the variegated pluralism and cultural conflict of early American society. They are sounds of difference, if not of discord, like the screams of terror, war shouts, and gunshot roar that, in *The Last of the Mohicans*, constantly interfere with the musical voices of Indians and the singing of Psalms. In this way, Cooper implicitly undermines the Founders' project of a linguistically as well as politically homogeneous America.[13]

"New circumstances," Thomas Jefferson noted, "call for new words." Noah Webster, in his search for an American English, claimed that "we have the fairest opportunity of establishing a national language . . . that ever presented itself to mankind." "The concept of a unified language," writes Bakhtin, "is the theoretical expression of the historical processes of linguistic unification and centralization, the expression of the centripetal forces" of society and of the state. In the United States, however, a relatively unified language preceded the birth of the national state—which, on the other hand, was an act of separation and expansion rather than a centripetal process of unification. The problem, for Jefferson as well as for Webster, was not only that of unifying America's language but also of differentiating it from that of Great Britain's. American English was to be homogeneous internally because it would be planned on rational and universal criteria. It would differ from British English because it would be based on common, spoken usage filtered through republican institutions and through the practice of the educated classes, rather than relying on aristocratic and artificial written models.[14]

But the social and linguistic processes that differentiate the American language from Great Britain's do not stop at America's boundaries. Not only are significant traces of British regional differences retained, if transformed, in American regional cultures; but the temporary koine shaped by the mixing of people and languages on the frontier and by urban social mobility soon erupts again into a plurality of dialects, slang, and sociolects. Even the variety of the land differentiates the language: geographical expansion is also a linguistic expansion, which adds and imports new words into the language to designate new-found places, plants, animals, and peoples.[15]

Dialect, then, implies a challenge to the rationalistic order of language, an element of irreverence. It introduces alien sounds, ignores the rules of spelling, and seems at times to break altogether free of the written word. This is why the metaphor of "unshackled dialect; fettered by no rule of delicacy, or feeling of humanity," like an escaped convict, is shared both by Hugh Henry Brackenridge and Henry James.[16] "Yoo kin spell an' punctooate thet as you please," says Hosea Biglow, James Russell Lowell's dialect-speaking Yankee character, reiterating the prison metaphor: "I allus do, it kind of puts a noo soot of close onto a word, thisere funattick spellin' doos an' takes 'em out of the prison dress they wair in the Dixonary." Vernacular humorists, Neil Schmitz says, "rong riting, impose *vox* upon *littera*," moving freely in the no-man's-land between phonetic matter and scriptural code. Thus the imaginative, baroque spelling of literary comedians like Artemus Ward, or the boundless linguistic invention of George Washington Harris's Sut Lovingood involve readers in the reconstruction not only of the text's languages but also of their own.[17]

And yet: what Lowell refers to is not an *invention* but a *transcription*. Phonetic spelling is both a recognition of dialect's evasion from the prison house of writing and the erection of another house capable of containing it. It breaks with fidelity to orthography only to seek another allegiance in fidelity to sound. Humorists, from Lowell to Will Rogers, deride the arbitrariness of the orthographic norm, yet vernacular realism makes a fetish out of the phonological authenticity of reproduction. Rather than the independence of writing and voice, the goal is a writing revived by the voice and therefore capable of holding it.

Voice, however, will not keep still. The painstaking reproduction of sound "pulverizes" the phonetic matter of language, resulting in frustrating texts that are "difficult to read and difficult to print." The reader's attention is directed toward the discrete detail of transcription rather than toward the flow of voice and meaning. Ironically, these accurate renderings of oral discourse are perhaps the only texts that cannot be read aloud.[18]

Difficulties of deciphering aside, not even the most accurate transcription can indicate to the readers how to reproduce the actual sounds of dialects with which they are not already familiar. Karla Holloway observes that the appreciation and understanding of the sermon in Zora Neale Hurston's *Jonah's Gourd Vine* "lies in being able to hear the delivery." This, however, is possible only to "those who are familiar with both the dialect and the structure of the black sermon form"—to those, in other words, who do not need phonetic script at all. Cleanth Brooks has said that, when a Eudora Welty character says "thing," a reader familiar with southern speech needs no phonetic aid to imagine something like "thaing." On the other hand, however, no acrobatic spelling could enable a nonsouthern reader to pronounce "thaing" correctly. William Faulkner also insists that "if the writer puts too much attention to transcribing literally the dialogue he hears, it's confusing to people who have never heard that speech," while a native "would know how it sounded" no matter how it was written.[19]

Another problem lies in the widespread convention that equates the credibility of literary dialects with consistency. While actual persons shift between registers and varieties of the language according to situations and contexts, literary vernacular characters are supposed always to stick to the same variety and often to the same register. All the members of a literary linguistic community are expected to speak alike, which is why Mark Twain must warn his readers that the differences in *Huckleberry Finn* are intentional. Literary dialect, in other words, functions as a sign of difference on the national plane only at the cost of having no internal differences of its own; the "Nation of nations" is composed of a plurality of nations with no internal pluralism.

This effect is reinforced by the fact that transcription signals the contrast between national standard language and popular regional dialects but ignores the regional variants that also occur in the speech of the educated classes. Standard American English as spoken in New York, in fact, does not sound the same as standard American English pronounced in New Orleans. These differences (which make up the regional "accents") lie mostly in subphonemic and suprasegmental traits, which are very noticeable to the ear but escape transcription. Thus, the Canadian Shreve must have heard a southern accent in Quentin Compson's very correct English; as the local children say, "he talks like they do in minstrel shows." The traces of Quentin's accent, however, are hard to detect in the written dialogues of *The Sound and the Fury* or *Absalom, Absalom!*. "Few authors record regional traits unless they also signal class differences"; the conventions that require phonetic transcription for the black servant Dilsey exclude it for the young master Quentin, even though they must have often sounded somewhat alike.[20]

Indeed, Quentin's suppressed "minstrel show" sound is a good metaphor for the suppression of the black sound beneath the American text; one of the best-kept secrets, like the recently discovered black sources for *Huckleberry Finn*, of all of American literary history. An early, subversive use of the untranscribable continuity between southern and black English, as an indication of the invisible black presence and a subversive critique of the myth of racial purity, is in Charles Chesnutt's *The House Behind the Cedars*. The light-skinned hero passes for white in part thanks to his good education; yet he retains in his speech "a faint suggestion" of black accent, which no one notices because "the current Southern speech . . . was rarely without a trace of it."[21]

The laws of writing and the rhetoric of class, however, again segregate what Chesnutt has subversively mixed. Mr. Ryder, the light-skinned, wealthy, and educated protagonist of Chesnutt's "The Wife of His Youth," likes to declaim Tennyson's poems, though "his pronunciation was somewhat faulty." Again, no trace of these imperfections can be detected in the text's presentation of his speech; indeed, the opposition between Mr. Ryder's educated speech and his old wife's dialect is used to underline the social distance that time has created between them. Later, he repeats her story to his dinner guests "in the same soft dialect, which came readily to his lips"; but this performance is rendered in indirect speech, as if the text could not contain a dialect performance by an educated character any more than it could have contaminated with vernacular accents the recitation of Tennyson's poems. Apparently, dialect and literary language can exist in the same text only when they are relegated to separate characters or discourses.[22]

Rather than phonetic authenticity, then, the criteria for the literary use of dialects are to be located in their integration with the text as a whole and in the attitude of the narrator. The same dialect may appear in equally authentic but very different forms in different texts, according to its functional and symbolic role. Equally accurate renditions of the same dialect may look very different on the page because they stress different traits, according to varying functions. In Harriet Arnouw's *The Dollmaker,* the accurate presentation of Appalachian English (including the phonetic level) underlines its contrast with urban varieties of working-class English. By tracing the changes in the dialect spoken by her characters, the author outlines a history of uprooting, conflict, and contradictory and painful adaptation. In James Still's *River of Earth,* a rarefied, selective stylization evokes the rhythms, sounds, and phrasings of the speech of an Appalachian community, avoiding phonetic representation but insisting on the richness of figuration and ornament. In Gurney Norman's more recent *Divine Right's Trip*—which has been labeled both as "a folk tale" and "a postmodern novel"— a young hero, divided between regional Appalachian origins and metropolitan counterculture, expresses a composite identity in a vividly hybrid language that contains incessant shifts of code and register.[23]

Stylization and hybridism take dialect out of conventional clichés and into modernism. The representation of African-American speech, for instance, takes a new direction from a text that is also a manifesto of literary modernism, Gertrude Stein's "Melanctha." Stein ignores mimesis in favor of a selective stylization of grammatical, rhythmic, and rhetorical traits, and integrates dialect in the text in a completely new way. By abolishing all distance between the narrator's language and that of the characters in a unified flow of discourse, Stein lifts the veil of inferiority that local color and the plantation tradition had imposed on black literary vernacular. Rather than Paul Laurence Dunbar's "jingle in a broken tongue" or James Weldon Johnson's instrument with only two stops (the comic and the pathetic), dialect becomes a fully validating language that adequately voices the complex feelings and experiences of fully developed characters. Later, in *Their Eyes Were Watching God*, Zora Neale Hurston again stresses phonetic difference; but the central aspect remains the figurative quality, the "will to adorn" that characterizes black English and results in a "speakerly" text in which "the resonant dialect of the character's discourse has come to 'color' the narrator's idiom."[24]

When difference is no longer taken to mean inferiority, dialect becomes a literary expression of the specific modernity of an America in which every speaker is exposed to a plurality of linguistic norms and is often the bearer of a plurality of languages. American English is learned "from the mouths of Polish mothers," William Carlos Williams said.[25] Modern American literature is born of the mixing of tongues between the "foreign" immigrants and the "native" American varieties of English. This is even truer in the polyglot tradition of Jewish orality and writing. The sounds of Henry Roth's ethnic ghetto mingle "the Yiddish spoken at home . . . the Hebrew which David learns at *chedder*; the street jargon he speaks with other children . . . [his mother's and aunt's] Polish, and the varied symphony of ethnically connotated languages which rises in the final chapters."[26] Certain passages are tours de force of code-switching and code-mingling:

> Shebchol haleylos onu ochlim—. De rain wedded my cockamamy! Oh! Leggo! You can't cover books wit' newspaper. My teacher don't let. An aftuh she took mine bean-shooduh, she pinched me by duh teeth! Lousey bestia! Bein yoshvim uvein

mesubim. So wad's de nex' woid? Mine hen'ball wend down
duh sewuh! Now, I god six poinduhs![27]

To Henry Adams this was the speech of "a furtive Yacoob or Ysaac . . . snarling a weird Yiddish to the officers of customs"—the sound not of the birth, but the death of a world. To Henry James, the ethnic ghettoes of New York appeared as "torture rooms of the living idiom."[28] Ethnic heteroglossia, however, does not recover "authentic" old dialects but generates miracles of forward-looking contamination. For instance, Abraham Cahan's characters speak "a Yiddish studded with distorted American words and phrases, occasionally signalling varieties of Americanized Yiddish and Polish and Lithuanian inflections"[29] even the narrative voice embeds adapted fragments of English into Yiddish phrases incorporated in turn into English contexts. In a different time and cultural area, "spanglish" and "code-switching" become metaphors of identity in Latino texts that include their own translation and comment. "Ethnic modernism" becomes a constituent part of American modernism *tout court*.[30]

One final remark. Dialect speakers, in the modern age, are also capable of writing. Therefore another modality of the representation of nonstandard varieties of English must be sought in folk writing, and in its literary representations. Rather than attempting a phonetic reproduction of speech, folk writing usually attempts to approximate the standard norm of writing, which, however, it masters imperfectly and does not always fully accept. This can be recognized both in an ethnic text (the historical tale of "The Stone and Kelsey 'Massacre' [1932], by William Raiganal Benson, a Pomo Indian from California), and in a literary mimesis of vernacular writing (Celie's letters in Alice Walker's *The Color Purple*):

> Stone came out with pot full of fire which was taken from the fireplace. and said to the indians. whats the matter boys you came Early this morning. some thing rong; the indians said. O nothing me hungry thats all.[31]

> Last spring after little Lucious come I heard them fussing. He was pulling on her arm. She say It too soon, Fonso, I ain't well. Finally he leave her alone. A week go by, he pulling on her arm again. She say Naw, I ain't gonna. Can't you see I'm already half-dead, an all of these children.[32]

Both texts avoid phonetic reproduction, retain traces of oral syntax, and use a register halfway between standard and dialect (Celie reproduces sound when she writes *an* for and, but writes *Lucious*, hypercorrectly). They differ, however, in the use of more strictly scriptural marks, such as punctuation and capitalization. Alice Walker's Celie uses a simplified but regular punctuation, with periods, commas, capitals, and apostrophes in the right places, while Benson's is less regular and more complicated. He uses more punctuation marks, but more erratically; his capitalization is also irregular (but he always capitalizes proper names) and his punctuation follows the movement of the voice, attempting to separate narration and dialogue. There are no apostrophes (compare Benson's "whats" with Celie's "ain't"). Ultimately, Celie's writing lies within the framework of specific literary precedents: Hurston's free indirect speech, Stein's syntactic and lexical minimalism. Benson, on the other hand, seems to have reluctantly come out the realm of orality, to inhabit the space of a "mis-writing" between graphics and sound (as well as between his own handwriting and his editors' reading and printing), in which no convention is possible.

MARK TWAIN'S TOWER OF BABEL

Monsieur le Landlord—Sir: *Pourquoi* don't you mettez some savon in your bedchambers?

—Mark Twain, *Innocents Abroad*

To *know* something is to kill it . . . One should be sufficiently intelligent and interested to know a good deal *about* any person one comes into close contact with.

—D. H. Lawrence, "Edgar Allan Poe"

Let us return to the beginning of *Huckleberry Finn*: "You don't know about me." This deceptively simple opening clause lies across a double edge: between dialect and colloquial speech, and between ordinary language and poetry. This is true both at the level of sound and at the level of meaning. Rhythmically, the clause is composed of two anapests; the rhythm of everyday speech is also the metrics of poetry. Semantically, the modifier "about" suggests that what we know of Huck cannot be contained in the binary logic of positive knowledge and ignorance. However we know Huck, we do not know him in the deadly sense described by Lawrence. We have always already begun to know about him, but we will never finish knowing him; knowledge is an elusive, indefinite process rather than a finished product. It is significant that this clause challenges translation. Italian translators, for instance, have been forced to choose between suppressing it ("*Non mi conoscete*," "you don't know me") or exaggerating it ("*Voi non potete sapere niente di me*," "you can know nothing about me")—as if we could only know either all or nothing. On one level of meaning, then, this beginning combines the semantic fuzziness of orality with the open ambiguity of poetry.[33]

All lines and definitions are fuzzy and blurred in *Huckleberry Finn*. The island is "*sort* of lonesome," the river is "*kind* of solemn," the

judge is "*kind* of sore." Everything is "maybe" or "mainly"; every rule has an exception ("I never seen anybody but lied, without it was Aunt Polly"). The syntax of orality, through paratactic correction and repair, reinforces Huck's moral vision,
which rejects final judgments or neat distinctions between felons and victims. The King and the Duke, for instance, are "villains," but when they are tarred and feathered they become "poor pitiful rascals" and ultimately, in a grand narrative repair, "human beings."

Let us take a step forward: "You don't know about me *without you have read*" Another paratactic correction and another fuzzy border. Between "without" and "you have read," we step across the border between colloquial speech and dialect. After "without," standard diction expects an indirect construction ("without having read," or even—with one of those nominalizations so dear to the syntax of writing—"without your having read"). The main effect of "without you have read" on the standard-language reader is, thus, a sense of missing connection. We understand what it means, associating the connotation of deprivation in "without" with the act of reading to which it refers. But in doing so we skip, consciously or not, over a fracture in the flow of the language. Huck's narrative constantly requests us to perform this kind of operation, bridging gaps opened by prepositions turned into adverbs or by missing auxiliary verbs and relative pronouns: "I never/seen anybody but/lied without/it was Aunt Polly"; "I couldn't/stood it much longer," "she/done it herself." The bars stand for microfractures in the grammatical chain of language; in order to understand, we need to slide from an analytic to an associative frame of mind—that is, from the discreteness of grammar and syntax to the continuum of poetry.

This process also reverberates on Huck's moral vision. A vanishing suffix can turn the explicit judgment of an adverb into the neutral observation of an adjective. The Widow Douglas, for instance, is not "dismal*ly* regular and decent," but "dismal regular and decent"; with the help of alliteration, "dismal" and "decent" deploy at the sides of "regular," as if striving to draw it toward its two opposite potential meanings. There are two ways of being "regular"—one "dismal" and one "decent"—just as there are two Providences, Miss Watson's and the Widow Douglas's.

The associative frame of mind, in fact, supports not only an ethics and a poetics but a cosmogony as well. In the description of dawn on the river, darkness and light, water, earth, skies, emerge progressively, without breaks, in the osmotic evolution of run-on sentences and the progression of gerunds. This is a gradual revelation of a new world, a far cry from the abrupt *fiat lux* and the sharp separations of Genesis: "The first thing to see, looking away over the water, was a kind of dull line—that was the woods on t'other side—you couldn't make nothing else out; then a pale place in the sky; then more paleness, spreading around; then the river softened up, away off."[34]

One more step: "without you have read *a book*"; Huck's addressee is a reader of books, a citizen of the republic of letters and standard English. Only such readers will be jolted by his "without" and find his dialect refreshing and transgressive; members of Huck's own linguistic community would find it only "regular." Only a standard reader may perceive dialect as poetry; on the linguistic as well as on the moral plane, Huck is not trying to break rules but only to follow different ones. The "poetry" of his language is not intrinsic to dialect per se but springs from the intentional overlapping of two different linguistic norms. To thc multiple voices and dialects in Huck's speech, we must add, therefore, the plurivocality generated by the encounter of these voices with the standard language of the absent author and the implied reader.

"The novel," Bakhtin writes, "can be defined as diversity of social speech types (sometimes even diversity of languages) artistically organized." Though Bakhtin never mentions Mark Twain, the latter's work displays many of the features discussed by Bakhtin: the "internal stratification" of languages, the interaction of lowbrow and highbrow cultures, the interplay between folk laughter and literate culture, and the "heteroglossia of the clown," which proclaims that there is "no language center at all" and that all established languages are "masks." Yet something in Mark Twain escapes Bakhtin's definitions.[35]

"Out of this stratification of language," says Bakhtin, the artist "constructs his style, while at the same time he maintains the unity of his own creative personality and the unity . . . of his own style." But in the writer who chose to call himself Mark *Twain*, linguistic interplay generates fragmentation, dissonance, and duplicity rather than dialogue and polyphonic orchestration. As David R. Sewell points out, "heteroglossia and cacophony minimize underlying unity."[36] Too archaic and too modern, Mark Twain's clownish heteroglossia remains too close both to the immediate sources of folk laughter and to the modernistic dissonance of alienation. Rather than "compelling language ultimately to serve all his own intentions," Mark Twain allows the multiplicity of languages inside him to fragment his authorial persona and to disrupt the cohesion of his texts.

"What a jumbling together of extravagant incongruities; what a fantastic conjunction of opposites and irreconcilables," says the narrator of *A Connecticut Yankee at King Arthur's Court*. He is talking about himself, but he could be describing the text that contains him, hanging between parody and tragedy, between derision of the feudal past and a desolate vision of the bourgeois present and future. In "this plodding, sad pilgrimage, this pathetic drift between the eternities," all he can hope for is to "save that one microscopic atom in me that is truly *me*." Yet the ambiguity and elusiveness of this authentic "me" is the basis of the play of parody, hybridization, and anachronism both in this novel and in the identity of its author and his relationship with America.[37]

Mark Twain always resides in split universes: orality and writing, standard language and dialect, East and West, Europe and America, past and present, the humorist's platform and the parlors of the Hartford elite. Rather than seeking harmony and balance, however, he makes literary capital out of his dislocation and laceration, using it as the matrix of his perception of an increasingly fragmented and multiple America. The America of the industrial revolution seems to lack a center, and its heteroglossia consists less in varieties of English than in the dissonance of the foreign tongues flooding in through Ellis Island. Identities are varied and shifting, but none is satisfying and convincing. As in the accelerated mobility of the Gilded Age, discoursive and literary genres move up and down the social ladder, mix, overlap, and blur into one another. Only in these conditions could a platform humorist and a provincial journalist write, in dialect, the novel from which "all American literature begins."

BEWARE OF SIGNS: THE POETRY OF PEDRO PIETRI AND THE SWITCHING CODES OF THE HISPANIC VOICE

Ay! To make love in Spanish, in a manner as intricate and devout as la Alhambra. To have a lover sigh *mi vida, mi preciosa, mi chiquita,* and whisper things in that language crooned to babies, that language murmured by grandmothers, those words that smelled like your house—

—Sandra Cisneros, *Woman Hollering Creek*

Recuerdo que una vez le dijo a la raza que leyeran los poemas en voz alta porqué la voz era la semilla del amor en la oscuridad.

Tomás Rivera, *. . . y no se lo tragó la tierra*

Over a background of talking, laughing voices, applause, cheering, and an occasional crying child, the Nuyorican poet Pedro Pietri chants, shouts, laughs, sings, whispers and groans his "Puerto Rican Obituary" and other poems, crossing and recrossing the blurred border of English and Spanish as shaped by the New York experience. "Beware of signs that say/ 'Aquí se habla Español',"[38] he chants. The record conveys the thick mock-Anglo accent in which Pietri delivers the Spanish words: the stress on the wrong syllable (*Aqui*), the retracted English *l*, the inability to pronounce the Spanish *ñ* (*Espaniol*). A whole layer of meaning is couched in the play on accents; rather than the oral rendition of a written text, this is a performance inspired by and conceived for the living voice.

The Hispanic tradition in America has relied largely on the vivid sounds of the spoken language, weaving the interplay of voice and writing into the intricacies of linguistic code-switching between varieties of English, varieties of Spanish, and (especially in the case of Chicano authors) pre-Hispanic substrata.[39] Just as in the case of Mark Twain the life of the text is in the space and motion between the text's dialects and the reader's standard English, in the Hispanic literature of the United States the dramatic and ironic space and motion between languages (and between their registers, variants, and emotional associations) is the life of a new poetic tradition. As the Nuyorican poet Tato Laviera puts it:

LA VIDA es un inglés frío
        un español no preciso
        un spanglish disparatero.[40]

Heteroglossia is embedded in the very titles of Hispanic texts, as translation (Tomás Rivera's *y no se lo tragó la tierra . . . And the Earth Did Not Devour Him*), bilingualism (Carmen de Monteflores

Cantando bajito/Singing Softly), code switching and hybridation (Tato Laviera's *La Carreta Made a U-Turn*).[41] The play of hybridation and interlingualism combines with the interaction of orality and writing: "poets who were born and raised in New York, like Miguel Algarín, Tato Laviera, Pedro Pietri and Sandra María Esteves, write in English or in Spanglish, and strive to create an oral, bilingual context which reflects the popular culture and the social conditions of the *puertorriqueños* in El Barrio."[42] The streets of El Barrio or the cafés of the Lower East Side are the stage for the performances of highly sophisticated oral poets such as Miguel Algarín, an academic fully at home in the oral tradition, or the mythic Jorge Brandon, who (like an oral Emily Dickinson) "does not allow anyone to see his work written or to publish any of his poems," but transcribes them in "mnemonic patterns" with personal codes and rehearses his performances accurately on the tape recorder.[43]

Pedro Pietri is fully immersed in this cultural environment (he is known to have distributed his poems in front of the New York Public Library, printed on envelopes containing condoms; in the age of Aids, he explained, it is another way for a poem to save a life). What he brings to it, however, is a highly self-reflexive attention not only to the role and metaphoric implications of orality and performance but also of writing and, especially, of the electronic reproduction of the voice. All the technologies of the word are consciously involved in the creation and meaning of a type of poetry conceived through the voice, composed in writing, performed orally, and reproduced electronically.

It is the recording that allows us to perceive his ironic use of the Anglo accent in *Aquí Se Habla Español.* The Anglo distortion of the sounds of Spanish stands for the distorted communication generated by unequal social relationships, but it also takes on broader meanings. "Beware of signs," Pietri warns us; and indeed, how can a *sign* have an *accent*? Indeed, how can a sign *say* anything? As Inca Atahualpa told Francisco Pizarro, books make no sound and "don't say a word." Through the polysemy of "sign" and the discrepancy between Spanish speech, Spanish writing, and Anglo reading, Pietri evokes the historic metaphor of the "talking book": a figure of the encounter between colonialism and the Third World (as in the African-American autobiographies of James Albert Ukawsaw Gronniosaw and John Marrant); of the relationship between literature and the market place (as used by Jonathan Swift and Washington Irving); and, ultimately, of the essential unreliability of all signs.[44] After all, the talking book is essentially a forerunner of the record.

Pietri's sources and environment are rooted in the orality of Puerto Rico and Spanish Harlem: long ballads sung by relatives and friends, early poems made up and recited in bars and at parties. Records, however, are an early influence, a vehicle of the music in the air of the ghetto environment: "Why Do Fools Fall in Love," a hit by a neighborhood rock and roll group, Frankie Lymon and the Teenagers, "gave us a motive to survive—it doesn't have to be that bad if we get a rock and roll group, we sing good, we can survive in society."[45]

Pedro Pietri incorporates in his poetic performance all the personae of oral bards, recording artists, and verbal heroes of this culture. His delivery ranges from the mimicry of the monotone of print to the impersonality of the ballad singer; from the straight-face of the standup comedian to the incantatory patterns of preaching, praying, and nursery rhyming; from the street poetry of the dirty dozens to soap box oratory—and the parodies of each. His plays stylize choral, antiphonal patterns of formalized collective speech and amplify the voice of the community shouting slogans, mumbling litanies, and calling out Bingo numbers. The interaction of English and Spanish sounds enhances the ironic contrast between the formulas of official discourse and the flow of street talk, a contrast underlined by puns and oxymorons ("the make-believe steaks/ and the bullet-proof rice and beans") building breathlessly upon one another in rapid self-contained units, like the one-liners of a standup comedian.

Therefore, Pietri's orality, as is the case with all contemporary Nuyorican poetry, is not an archaic residue, but a result of the urban experience. "Suicide Note of a Cockroach in a Low-Income Housing Project"[46] tells the same story as the African-American folk ballad of "The Boll-Weevil"; the black sharecropper and the ghetto dweller each identify ironically with the pests that destroy their crops and infest their homes because both recognize in these indestructible insects their own undaunted will to survive. Pietri's irony, however, is darker and cooler; his cockroach does die eventually, and its long suicide note is less reminiscent of folklore than of Amiri Baraka's *Preface to a Twenty-Volume Suicide Note.*

In this context traditional oral devices acquire new meanings and functions. Repetition underlines the radical displacement of meaning in a world in which things are no longer themselves; the paratactic accumulation of fragments of nightmares suggests another oral poet of the electronic age, Bob Dylan. The oral criticism of "signs" discloses an absurd metropolitan landscape of distorted experience and perception.

I once met a Bus Driver
With fifty fifty vision
Who had a sign on his neon mind
Informing the passengers
The exact fare to go somewhere
On this bus will be announced
A few weeks after the trip ends
DO NOT OBSERVE THE NO SMOKING SIGN
Anyone caught using seatbelts on the bus
Will not be allowed to ride with us.[47]

On one level, this is a poem about the immigration experience. As Pietri explains in another poem, only when they land at the airport, lost in a maze of innumerable threatening signs, do the immigrants understand how much the fare really cost them:

We follow the sign
that says welcome to america
but keep your hands off the property
violators will be electrocuted
follow the garbage truck
to the welfare department
if you cannot speak english.[48]

On another level immigration is metaphorically and literally woven with the everyday experience of death, the passing of another border: "So the whole preoccupation with that was that all we did when we came here was to attend one funeral after the other: my grandfather committed suicide in '48, he came here in '47. My father died of double pneumonia in '49." The immigrants are not ready for the atmospheric and social climate, and the streets around them are lined with "funeral parlors with neon signs that said/ Customers wanted no experience necessary."

The ordinary experience of death is also a metaphor for assimilation and frustration "in the nervous breakdown streets/ where the mice live like millionaires/ and the people do not live at all." In this "world of walking canes and pace makers," inanimate objects walk, humans move to the step of machines like zombies or ghosts, and the recorded voices of bus drivers, answering machines, and poets are a metaphor for living death.[49]

The bus driver is like Edith Wharton's ghost butler: there is no way humans can contradict him, because his voice is a tape and his brain is a neon "sign" and there is no way of talking back to him. More frustratingly, his command is a double bind; smoking on the bus is both forbidden and obligatory. All signs repeat the same message; whatever we do, we are always following a sign.

The act of writing, too, becomes enmeshed in double bind. Pietri describes writing as a solitary confrontation with the "flawless," "magnificent blank page." The page is both an inanimate object that resists the writer's expression and an innocent target of his aggression, which destroys the page's "privilege to be blank." The struggle between the pen and the page, then, mimes in sexual metaphor the dilemma of an innocence that cannot be possessed without violating it. If he writes, the poet turns into a talking sign; if he does not, he is locked in silence: "I know it will be very unwise of me/ To lose sleep over writing this poem/ When the correct thing for me to do/ Is to lose sleep over keeping the page blank."[50]

This struggle is doubled by the tension between spelling and sound: "To the United States we came"/ To learn how to mispell our names." Newspapers, official records, all sorts of documents miswrite the names of the immigrants, who respond by subverting and distorting the order of writing. "The end has come to the correct spelling of words," Pietri announces: "There is no alphabetical order/ To restrain the element of surprise." But after they arrive "All the way to the last/ Letter of the alphabet," the weary warriors of signs return to the dark of their rooms, with a "blank expression" similar to a page, on which we can imagine the writing of the neon signs flashing outside their windows.[51]

Things talk to us, write upon us, and we can neither talk back nor talk to each other. Writing and recording vampirize the human voice; communicating with the dead is Pietri's metaphor for the anxiety to communicate with the living who have become indistinguishable from the dead. But we cannot talk to the dead if they do not talk to us; if our messages remain unanswered, we too, turn into walking and talking signs. "Adults . . . are buried, when the conversation is dropt."[52]

A conversation is a bilateral exchange; but when signs communicate in one direction only, they die and kill. To the unilateral, frozen messages of the dominant culture, Pietri opposes the multilateral flexibility of the antiphonal, conversational living voice; the audible presence of the audience in his recordings becomes a way of preserving this exchange and turning recording into a metaphor of survival. Perhaps, on the lower frequencies, Pedro Pietri speaks for us. Like the migrants in the last lines of his "Puerto Rican Obituary," we are dead, and we shall not return from the dead until we stop "neglecting the art of our dialogue for broken-English lessons."

CHAPTER EIGHT

FRAMES

Because I see—New Englandly—
The Queen, discerns like me—Provincially
—Emily Dickinson

Unlike most European nation states, the United States did not originate in the unification of preexisting political entities, but in separation from one. Difference, therefore, is inherent in American identity, both as pluralism and cultural wealth and as a constant threat of fragmentation. We have already seen how linguistic difference is controlled and appropriated in the literary use of dialect and heteroglossia. We will now look at the ways in which other dangerously attractive cultural differences, grounded in folklore and localism, are represented and distanced in the literary text.

In literature, as in society, the problem is how to include these differences and their bearers and yet keep them under control. In the case of folklore this results in its presentation as an ideological projection of organic otherness, attractive in itself but safely inaccessible to the reader. Vernacular humor is admitted in the text, but enclosed in the *cordon sanitaire* of the frame narrative so that control remains in the hands of the spectatorial, gentlemanly frame narrator, with his reassuringly standard diction. Localism and regionalism oscillate between protest and consolation, between vindication of partiality and acceptance of subordination.

Control, however, is hardly ever truly achieved. The devices invented to protect language and culture from the intrusion of folk, vernacular, and regional voices turn regularly into their own opposites; each effort to reinforce hierarchy is an admission of its erosion, each statement of distance and difference from external otherness becomes a recognition of the otherness inside.

THE PORCH AND THE FORECASTLE: IMAGING FOLKLORE

"As I mounted to the deck at the call of the forenoon watch," Melville's Ishmael recalls, "so soon as I leveled my glance toward the taffrail, foreboding shivers ran over me. Reality outran apprehension; Captain Ahab stood upon his quarter-deck."[1] Thus enters the most memorable character in American literature. Ishmael prepares Ahab's entrance with all the folk fascination for signs and omens, and announces him with a formula lifted straight from the folk songs of the sea: the captain "stood upon his quarter-deck." At midnight, on the forecastle, a Nantucket sailor repeats it in song:

Our captain stood upon the deck,
A spy-glass in his hand,
A viewing of those gallant whales
That blew on every strand.[2]

Countless songs of sailors and whalermen focus on the solemn image of the captain standing on the quarter-deck holding the spy-glass. Another song says that "The captain stood on the quarter-deck,/ And ice was in his eye." And *Moby-Dick:* "Captain Ahab stood erect, looking straight out beyond the ship's ever-pitching prow."[3] Ishmael and the crew, then, see in Ahab an incarnation of this folk image of authority, standing straight and still, ambiguously powerful and hostile. In another song that includes the same formulaic image, "The Greenland Whale Fisheries," the ambiguity is revealed in full. When a whale destroys a boat and kills four sailors, in some versions the captain weeps for his men, but in others he is, like Ahab, more concerned about the ungraspable whale:

"Bad news, bad news," our captain he cried
For it grieved his heart in full store,
But the losing of that hundred barrel whale,
It grieved him ten times more, brave boys.[4]

"D'ye see him?" Ahab asks anxiously in the last days of the chase; eventually, he will be the first to sight the whale. In folk songs the captain's spy-glass designates the vision that legitimates authority. But folklore also teaches that power and vision do not always confer salvation. Sometimes, as in one of the songs created by the wild sailors of the Erie canal (whom Ishmael describes in the Town-ho story), even the captain's enhanced vision is powerless:

The captain came on deck
With spy glass in his hand,
But the fog it was 'tarnel thick,
He couldn't spy the land.[5]

Ahab, then, is shaped at least as much from folklore as from Shakespeare and the Bible. In this, Melville is no exception; from Irving to Hawthorne, from Mark Twain to Faulkner, structural and thematic concern with folklore, myth, and ritual has been a crucial aspect of the mainstream of American literature. The democratic roots of the popular imagination in America are also to be found in the tangle of folk expression and mass culture, oral tradition and the popular press that makes up the culture of the people.[6] Yet the relationship between folklore and literature has been far from simple or univocal.

"My home was in a quiet village on the banks of the Arkansas, to which, hitherto, newspapers, and printers, and persecution had never come . . . We knew nothing of books. At evening, when the labours of the farm and garden would be over, I told stories and sung the prettiest songs to them, and all of them loved me." William Gilmore Simms's story "The Sins of Typography" (1824) is an early example of concern with the ambiguities of literary folklore: a curious tangle of parody and parroting of romantic clichés about the organic folk community and its dissolution through the printed word (a very resistant cliché, if three generations later Henry James was still complaining of "communities disinherited of the felt difference between the speech of the soil and the speech of the newspaper.") "We had no strife—we knew no discontent," recalls Simms's narrator: "There were no artificial standards of taste or of opinion, to make one discontented with his own, and jealous of the person or the pretensions of his neighbor." Daniel Hoffman describes this image as "the Rural Village as the locus of paradisal symbolism," and Mark Twain attacks it fiercely in his representations of rural villages on the banks of the Arkansas as a concentrate of violence and squalor rather than an idyll.[7]

The principal attraction of this folk paradise is the absence of "strife" and "discontent," its homogeneity and lack of internal articulation. These imaginary traits offer a pleasant contrast to the urban, typographic experience, represented by the discrete articulation of the alphabet and the press and the strife and discontent of pluralistic politics. The supposed separate homogeneity of the self-enclosed folk community allows the observer to contemplate it from a safe distance, regretting the warmth of organic unity but retaining the privilege of moving freely as an individual outside of it.

In fact, when homogeneity is imposed upon the observer's own world, rather than pastoral idylls we discover totalitarian dystopias. In Ray Bradbury's Fahrenheit 451, the "secondary orality" and the visual environment of the electronic age do not generate the fusional warmth of the organic community but flat mass subordination and amalgamation. Yet Simms's and Bradbury's characters describe the effects of print and books in essentially the same terms; for both, books create and disseminate doubt, introduce difference, and separate individuals from one another. Simms: "The accursed books . . . taught us selfishness," "There was no longer communion"; and Bradbury: "[books] make everyone unhappy with conflicting theory and thought."[8] At the beginning of the age of the popular press, Simms displayed an ironic nostalgia for the lost orality of folkloric subjects other than himself. At the dawn of the electronic revolution, Bradbury turns the press into an object of nostalgia and regret in the light of a dystopian future that is also his.

This is why Bradbury finally creates another version of Simms's primitive riverside community. The runaways gathered by the river and around the fire are both an oral and an interpretive community; they are homogeneous because they don't interpret at all but memorize texts and repeat them orally, with no function but to preserve them. At this point, books no longer generate doubts but are identified with a stable, unquestioned heritage. Beyond the identification between typography and critical thought, Bradbury rediscovers the substratum of consensus that supports the authority of books and print. Like Pedro Pietri's dangerous signs, books teach us to doubt everything, except themselves.

The typographic imagination legitimates itself by identifying with an individualistic, rational modernity, wedged between the "primary" orality of folklore and the "secondary" orality of electronics. Print is thus symmetric to an image of enlightened democracy wedged between the twin darknesses of feudalism and totalitarianism. Between a dubious golden age and a looming dystopia, the existing reality is the best of all possible worlds. On the other hand, by dealing with the double homogeneity of the folk community and the electronic mass audience, the culture of print explores its own regrets and fears about the realities it perceives beyond its boundaries: in time (origins, night, apocalypse), in space (the country, the frontier, the cosmos), and in the psyche (the body, instincts, the unconscious, thought control).

While a future electronic mass society is usually represented in dystopic terms, the homogeneous folk community appears in literature mostly as a positive myth of origins, salvation, foundation. This myth has both "populist" and "elitist" versions. The most established "populist" version was offered in the 1930s by Constance Rourke. American literature and the national character, Rourke claimed, are rooted in the "common soil," oral and written, of "an anterior popular lore that must for lack of a better word be called a folk-lore." The comic and epic masks of the Yankee, the black minstrel, the backwoodsman, the Irish "b'hoy" replace—with a brand new expansive vigor, exuberance, irreverence—the rural folk characters of European Romanticism. This folklore is a rich vein of new life for the new nation and its literature.[9]

The "elitist" version, in turn, can be identified most of all in the myth and ritual school of criticism inspired by T. S. Eliot. This approach sees folklore and myth as part of the atavistic heritage of all mankind rather than as an expression of a folk community (and least of all of the emerging new popular subjects). Its unifying power is retrieved by attempting to gather all stories under great comprehensive and interrelated myths—the death and rebirth of a God, the initiation of a hero. The painful diversity of human experience and its conflict with the world become reconciled in a universal, archetypical, and ritual background and in the vision of an organic (and originally monarchic and feudal) state.[10]

In both modes the presuppositions of homogeneity and self-enclosed separation of folk cultures reverberate in textual and formal problems. In the "populist" mode separation turns folklore into a discrete body of quotable information, a documentary or coloristic "reality effect." This satisfies those folklorists who search the literary text for discrete "items," such as proverbs or traditional customs, which can be catalogued and classified; yet this approach may end up paying more attention to Rowland Robinson and Harden E. Taliaferro than to Melville or Hawthorne.[11] Homogeneity, in turn, makes "populist" folklore incompatible with the novel as a genre. Whereas the novel develops psychological realism and accurate study of individual characters, folklore is invoked precisely to exorcise individuality. This applies not only to the conflated and magnified stereotypes of such "folk novels" as Roark Bradford's *John Henry* (1931) but even to the characters of the "proletarian" novels of the 1930s. Whether they belong to the rural South or to the working-class North, in fact, they tend to speak in formulaic, suspended allusions, in which "all utterance is but a courteous acknowledgment of the wisdom of the tribe."[12]

In the archetypical approach, instead, myths, rituals, and heroes tend to exist in a rarefied, monologic, antecedent universe. Raised in a myth- and ritual-centered Native American culture, a critic such as Paula Gunn Allen is well aware of these discrepancies: "Myth criticism to the contrary," she argues, "Western novels are not ritual-based"; when they "incorporate" elements of myth or ritual, "these borrowings are intellectual, aesthetic, or allusive." [13] Myths and rituals are never embodied in specific texts, environments, or performances, or in flesh-and-blood narrators or performers. No one ever celebrates the initiation ritual, no one ever tells the story of the Fisher King—as if myths and rituals could really have any life or meaning outside of these concrete occasions, in an abstract, disembodied universality. Ralph Ellison writes:

> But the places where a rich oral literature was truly functional were the churches, the schoolyards, the barbershops, the cotton-picking camps; places where folklore and gossip thrived. The drug-store where I worked was such a place, where on days of bad weather the older men would sit with their pipes and tell tall tales, hunting yarns and homely versions of the classics. It was here that I heard stories of searching for buried treasure and of headless horsemen, which I was told were my father's versions told long before.[14]

The most important thing, then, is space. In specific places, identifiable contexts, such as Ellison's drug store, the stylized folk community of Melville's forecastle, or the dialogic anthropology of Zora Neale Hurston's porch and turpentine plantation, recognizable people enact plurivocal and heteroglossic performances. Folklore never occurs separately, in isolation, but is animated by a plurality of voices, languages, and genres of discourse, woven together with ordinary conversation and with literature itself. In Ellison's recollection, the headless ghost rises once more from the papers of Diedrich Knickerbocker to mingle among the oral folklore from which Irving had lifted him in the first place. In *Mules and Men*, Hurston mixes songs and folk tales in the agonistic stream of conversation and performance, so that the documentary prepares the narrative strategy of her novel, *Their Eyes Were Watching God*.

Also, although folklore is shared cultural property, it comes to life only in the interaction of individuals in social contexts. Thus the best representations of folklore in literature are not those that stress homogeneity but those in which voices and identities remain distinct, and conflicts are neither abolished nor silenced.

Hurston's turpentine camp workers flash knives and draw guns with alarming frequency and enthusiasm. The thirty "isolatoes" of the Pequod crew slide from song and dance all the way to the edge of a race riot; only under the cohesive spell of Ahab's powerful voice do the members of the crowd become "welded" into a homogeneous—and subordinated—whole. Melville's respect for the common man includes a recognition of his weakness and his dark side; the folk community of the forecastle is not exempt from the complexity of human nature. By acknowledging the internal differences and conflicts in the folk community, and integrating folklore into the symbolic continuity of the text, Melville and Hurston rescue the folk community from its reassuring separateness while depicting it in different but equally accurate and credible representations.

This is part of what Melville's quarter-deck and forecastle are about. Taken together, these spaces constitute the ship as metaphor of the state and society: the folk community is included in the hierarchies of a political "community." We are all on the same boat, but we are not equal in it. Together with his comrades, Steelkilt—the sailor of the Town-ho in *Moby-Dick*, who might have heard the Erie Canal songs about the blind captains in the fog—prefers to sink the whole thing rather than keep pumping water for the officers and owners. Like him, Shine, the eponymous black stoker who is the hero of countless "toasts" and "dozens" in black urban folklore, emerges from the hold of the Titanic just in time to jump into the water and leave the white captain and his daughter to their fate: "Get your ass in the water and swim like me."[15]

Perhaps, then, the literary use of folklore is an attempt to keep Shine and Steelkilt on board and in the text, pumping water, fire, and meaning for us but staying in their place below, without invading the textual space of command or jumping into the water to swim home.

INTRUSIONS: ADVANTAGES AND DANGERS OF VERNACULAR HUMOR

Quit yer kerd playin' an' writin' an' listen tu me.

—George Washington Harris, "Sut at a Negro Night-Meeting"

"If my memory fail me not, the 10th of June, 1809 found me at about 11 o'clock in the forenoon, ascending a low and gentle slope in what was called the 'Dark Corner' of Lincoln [County]. I believe it took its name from the moral darkness which reigned over that portion of the county at the time of which I am speaking." Thus begins a foundational text of frontier humor, Augustus B. Longstreet's *Georgia Scenes*: a rural ride among natural scenery and singing birds, until "moral darkness" intrudes in "loud, profane and boisterous voices."[16]

Vernacular voices always seem to invade the silent space of reading and writing. "While I was thus busily employed in reading . . . we were startled most unexpectedly by a loud Indian war hoop": this is how the "Big Bear of Arkansas" breaks into Thomas Bang Thorpe's classic story. Sut Lovingood interrupts the narrator's reading and card playing; Uncle Julius, the black vernacular storyteller in Charles Chesnutt's *The Conjure Woman*, keeps interfering with his master's book reading. Scotty Briggs, the flamboyant frontier fireman of Mark Twain's *Roughing It*, walks into the minister's study and lays his helmet on an "unfinished manuscript sermon" (echoes of Dimmesdale!); vocal intrusion is also physical invasion, a compound violation of the code of manners, the supreme law of literary conversation.[17]

Not long after Longstreet's rural ride, on July 27, 1844, Nathaniel Hawthorne was meditating in the woods near Concord, Massachusetts, when "Hark! there is the whistle of the locomotive—the long shriek, harsh, above all other harshness." Leo Marx reads this episode as an example of what he calls the trope of the interrupted idyll: the irruption of an alien, aggressive sound into nature's pastoral garden. In Hawthorne the sound belongs to the machine and designates the conflict between the pastoral ideal and modern technology. In Longstreet, instead, it comes from the vernacular voices and announces the conflict between the pastoral ideal and the reality of the popular world. Both the machine and the people, however, are aspects of the same process: America's territorial, technological, industrial, democratic expansion between the age of Jackson and the Civil War.[18]

In fact, long before he heard the machine in the garden and a few years before Longstreet and his successors, Hawthorne had represented the stormy eruption—"in senseless uproar, in frenzied merriment"—of folk laughter in the reckless, desecrating carnival of "My Kinsman, Major Molineux": "The contagion was spreading among the multitude, when all at once, it seized upon Robin, and he sent forth a shout of laughter that echoed through the street." These are the years when the impact of the frontier and the nascent urban popular culture give birth to what has been described as the "carnivalization of American language." H. L. Mencken's "hordes of the ignorant and illiterate" and Constance Rourke's "mass of the people . . . the insurgent, the revolutionary class" lay their hands on the language and thus create mass culture and American humor. Hawthorne's carnival parade and collective laughter, like the mad subversive laughter of Poe's "The Haunted Palace," describe the frightening association between the rise of humor and the unruly rise of the Jacksonian common man.[19]

Hawthorne's "contagion" metaphor is significant; as Poe will later describe in "William Wilson," the structures of control are contaminated by what they are supposed to control. Even literacy functions less as a means of rational control than as a vehicle for the irreverent popular press, a writing tainted by the intrusion of the popular voice. Significantly, the litigious voices that interrupt

Longstreet's rural ride in *Georgia Scenes* turn out to belong to one person, quarreling with himself—just as, symmetrically, both the vernacular dialogue and the elegant narrative frame issue from the same authorial subject. The self-controlled gentleman who handles the narrative chores in this and other similar texts is, in his way, also divided; the zeal with which he rushes to the scene of the supposed fight, and his transparent disappointment when he realizes that there is no fight at all, reveal how much he needed a fight, both to confirm his gentlemanly superiority[20] and to externalize a negated part of himself.

This internal dualism, and the social tension underlying it, must not, however, be allowed to break out into open conflict. For Longstreet, too, realism is all right only in its place. The problem, then, is to create devices to ward off contagion, to distance the vernacular intrusion, by representing it as mere verbal theatrics and by assigning it to a foregone past rather than an emerging present. This is the function of the narrative frame: a *cordon sanitaire*, a "literary picket fence" that separates the threat and fascination of vernacular orality from the observer's stance of detached writing.[21]

By stressing terms such as *scenes* or *theatrics*, Longstreet erects the diaphragm of a conventional fourth wall between the acting characters and the spectatorial writer. The frame narrator is thus allowed to pretend that the words of the vernacular characters are not his own but only the transcription of someone else's voice: a discourse reported but not repeated, and often not even interpreted, ostensibly not understood. To the readers, the frame becomes a metanarrative that guides them in discriminating between the different layers of the text. This concentric structure draws attention to the core of vernacular orality but away from the contradictions of the literary writing around it.[22]

The only sentence that the narrator addresses to the vernacular character in *Georgia Scenes* begins with "Come back, you brute!" In most humorous stories the core vernacular characters and the gentleman in the frame are allowed to speak only in separate portions of the text, hardly talking to each other beyond the few words necessary for contact. In this, American humor resembles the bulk of anthropological writing in which, as Dennis Tedlock has repeatedly shown, the discourse of the observer and the discourse of the observed are carefully kept apart. And in fact, as an account of encounters between cultural differences, most American humor does possess an anthropological dimension.[23]

The representations of contact with cultural otherness, however, are also, by contrast, allegories of the observer's identity.[24] In fact the fiction of reported speech is a transparent one; rather than the discourses of two separate subjects, American humor is the double-voiced discourse of a "twain" authorial figure. The split identity is also suggested by the most recurrent rhetorical figures and humoristic devices, based on incongruity, duplicity, contrast, and fragmentation, and enhanced by the dissonance between the sedate prose of the frame and the excited, violent, gothic, fantastic voices of the internal story. The frame, then, not only protects the authorial subject from the intrusions of the external other but also attempts to control, while recognizing them, the irrepressible voices that rise from within and from below.

APPROPRIATING FOLK LAUGHTER: FROM ROBIN MOLINEUX TO SUT LOVINGOOD

Distancing is not the only available strategy of control. A subtler, more effective approach consists in pretending that there is no distance and no difference at all: assimilating folk laughter into the discourse of authority. The collective laughter in "My Kinsman, Major Molineux," after all, does not start in the street below but proceeds from a balcony "over the heads of the multitude"; it does not come from the crowd but from the authoritative "old citizen."[25]

The "convulsive merriment" on his face looks "like a funny inscription on a tombstone": a sarcastic reference to Franklin's autobiographical epitaphs, perhaps, but also a parodic forerunner of the scarlet letter. In fact this "inscription" also concerns the relationship between subversion and control. The dignitary's stockings are hanging around his legs, his wig is askew like a mock Phrygian cap, his only attire is a nightgown, yet he still wields the "polished cane" of authority. Order rules by disguising itself as disorder. The nocturnal revolutionary carnival is anticipated and directed by the new wielders of power.

Rather than abolished, then, distance is manipulated. Rather than preventing the crowd's access to power, the strategy consists in organizing the authorities' access to the crowd by pretending to be part of it. Power laughs with the mob, and the mob takes up and amplifies power's laugh. This ambivalent laughter frightens the more timid bourgeois and accentuates their law-and-order syndrome; but it offers to the crowd a normative mirror, a plausible other-directed image of themselves.

Hugh Henry Brackenridge anticipates this strategic use of humor during the Whisky Rebellion of 1794. Caught between the authorities and the rebels, he pretends to approve the actions of the multitude, speaks to them "with some humor and making them laugh," raising "a good deal of pleasantry at the expense of the Executive" but always intending to "put them in good humor and at the same time lead to the point I had in view"—that is, ending the rebellion and restoring order. His success is ambiguous; in the end the multitude no longer trust him, and the authorities suspect him of conniving with the mob. His is the fate of all humorists who touch folk laughter and orality in order to domesticate them and thus become suspect of infecting writing. Like many future humorists, Brackenridge spends the rest of his life in an effort to recover his respectability.[26]

"In popular governments," Edmund S. Morgan writes, "the fictions that enable the few to govern the many exalt, not the governors, but the people governed . . . the exaltation of the people can be a means of controlling them." Beginning with the spectacular national-populist rhetoric of the 1840 presidential campaign, the elite learns to accompany the rise of the common people in order to govern them, to appropriate popular identities and forms of expression in order to—as Brackenridge put it—"take the business out of the hands of the multitude."[27]

The adoption of this strategy, however, is not entirely a matter of choice. It is also a necessity imposed by the fact that sheer repression and negation no longer work. No matter how distorted and manipulated, the presence of the multitude is ineludible. Humor, then, is the ground where a discourse rising from below encounters its manipulative echo from above; an antiseptic device, which may at any time turn into a vehicle of contagion. Across the frame's *cordon sanitaire*, in an endless play of mirrors, the elite imitates the masses while the masses imitate this imitation of themselves.

The minstrel show is a typical case of this double ambiguity. Whites wear the face of black people represented as stereotyped, exuberant, and irresponsible creatures of appetites, desiring bodies—attractive and frightening images of what the whites themselves could become if controls were removed. On the other hand, blacks take advantage of this image that, while distorting them, still makes them visible. Thus the cliché of the primitive, hedonistic African-American "inadvertently permitted the black man to salvage large parts of a preindustrial, anti-Victorian, and anti-Puritan working-class culture which went into the making of twentieth century American popular culture."[28]

In written humor also the distance between the gentlemanly frame narrator and the vernacular characters is eroded and reversed. The gradual emancipation of the lower classes requires increasingly subtle techniques of control. When the narrator of George Washington Harris's *Sut Lovingood's Yarns* pleads "You must have a preface, Sut. . . . What shall I write?" it looks as if he were imploring his increasingly independent and intrusive character to leave him a little space and a simulacrum of a frame; but on another level he is also hiding behind that character, speaking unseen through what is supposed to be Sut's voice.[29]

Edmund Wilson has called *Sut Lovingood* "by far the most repellent book of any real merit in American literature." This is the best possible homage; it recognizes Sut's merits without having to make him respectable as a standard of liberation. We can recognize in Sut Lovingood, without having to read him as the vehicle of an alternative ideology, the antirepressive energy of a fragmented, desiring body; an alogical, obscene voice that tears language apart at the seams; and a constant derision and evasion of sentimental clichés.[30] In the reciprocal mimetism of frontier humor, Sut offends respectable people by embodying what they negate and repress in themselves; but he also indicates to the folk what they must become: that is, mere bodies, inhabiting the restricted space in which all transgressions are possible because they make no difference anyway.

Sut is doubtlessly one of Huckleberry Finn's ancestors (though it would be hard to conceive of his writing the letter to Miss Watson and tearing it up), as well as of Faulkner's Snopeses. But Sut, a native of the Tennessee mountains, also represents the first literary appearance of another imaginary creature of primitive appetites: the stereotyped Appalachian hillbilly, the eternal child of a belated wild frontier. If Sut is free from the repressions of civilization, it is in part because he anticipates the happy stupidity of Li'l Abner and the savagery of James Dickey's hillbillies in *Deliverance*[31]—barbarians, idiots, rapists, persuaded that they are, and cannot be, anything else.

THE MASK AND THE ROOTS: CHARLES W. CHESNUTT'S *THE CONJURE WOMAN*

It is a peculiar sensation, this double-consciousness, this sense of always looking at one's self through the eyes of others, of measuring one's soul by the tape of a world that looks on in amused contempt and pity. One ever feels his two-ness—an American, a Negro; two souls, two thoughts, two unreconciled strivings; two warring ideals in one dark body, whose dogged strength alone keeps it from being torn asunder.

—W. E. B. DuBois, "Of Our Spiritual Strivings"

The humorous, framed vernacular story, image of a divided individual and collective self, culminates and ends with the plantation tales of Charles Chesnutt's *The Conjure Woman.* The frame narrator, John, is a Northern white man who moves to the post-Civil War South with his wife Annie, buys a vineyard, and tries to run it with modern business methods. The internal vernacular narrator is the former slave Uncle Julius, who tells his employers prodigious stories of magic transformations set in the times of slavery.

Uncle Julius's tales build a double strategy of defense and countermanipulation. On the one hand they are stories of how the slaves' magic power over nature checks the masters' power over society and the economy. On the other they are always told in view of some practical goal, manipulating his employers' sentiments and feelings of guilt. For instance, the story of Po' Sandy, who has the conjure woman turn him into a tree to avoid separation from his woman, and is then cut down, sawed and planed under her eyes, is an impressive metaphor of the masters' total power over the slave's body. Uncle Julius, however, tells it primarily to persuade Annie that a certain cabin she wants to turn into a kitchen was built with the boards made from Sandy's body and is haunted by his ghost (actually, Uncle Julius's church has been using that cabin for its meetings, and he wants to retain its use). He succeeds because Annie changes her mind after hearing his story. Roles are reversed; the vernacular core character breaks through the cordon sanitaire of the frame and manipulates the master of the frame narrative, like a trickster figure who manipulates the powerful with cunning and dissimulation.

Thus Uncle Julius is the cultural winner. His vivid dialect prevails over John's conventional diction; black oral tradition and magic knowledge prove infinitely more fecund than white bookish positivism. But cultural victory is not accompanied by economic victory. Uncle Julius obtains small sentimental and domestic successes, thanks to Annie's feminine mediation, but he is always thwarted when it comes to matters of property and ownership. For instance, he tries to scare John out of buying the vineyard (so that he can go on enjoying its fuits) by telling him that it is "gophered"; John, however, enjoys the tale but goes on to close the deal anyway. Uncle Julius embodies folk imagination, but John retains economic control precisely because he is wholly impervious to the meanings of imagination.

The dualism between Uncle Julius's artistic and John's economic victory suggests that there is a shared, common ground underneath their contrasting discourse. A book such as this, based on fluid identities and transformations, cannot be read in rigid terms of black and white, and Chesnutt in fact constantly hints at forms of communication and mediation across the narrative frame as well as across the color line. After all, whites, too, believe in "conjure" and often resort to it with the help of blacks, who act as mediators between them and nature. For instance, Uncle Julius's magic rabbit foot heals Annie's depression. Though it never occurs to her that Uncle Julius is a citizen with equal rights, Annie glimpses the metaphoric truth in his tales and mediates between her husband's economic positivism and the folk imagination of the black former slave.

Most important, the "two-ness" is also inside Uncle Julius himself. At his first appearance, John notes that "he was not entirely black," and a "slight strain of other than Negro blood" may explain "[the] shrewdness in his eyes, too, which was not altogether African."[32] This may be a projection of John's racial imagination, but it may also be Chesnutt's way of blurring the color line, attenuating the dualism between blacks and whites, frame and character, while at the same time doubling it in the "two-ness" within the black identity itself. Free-born, educated, light-skinned, moderately wealthy, and living in the North, Chesnutt looked, spoke, and behaved as much like John as like Julius. His public speeches and statements prove that he is as much at home with John's formal diction as he is with Julius's dialect.[33] As is always the case in vernacular frame narratives, the two languages in the text are both his, and both Julius and John represent two aspects of the same divided authorial identity.

The Conjure Woman becomes, then, a metaphor for the artificial, violent split between black and white America and for the consequent split within black identity. It is, however, also an attempt to create a ground where identities can coexist. Chesnutt never ceased wondering whether he had to give up his identity as "Negro" in order to rise as "American," or (as it would ultimately be the case with DuBois) if he had to give up his "American" citizenship in order to affirm himself as "Negro." This book is an attempt to bridge the gap, to overcome the two-ness, or, indeed, turn it to advantage.

Uncle Julius's voice and John's writing, in fact, entertain a reciprocal relationship of vivification and control, not unlike that which exists between the voice of the heart and the scarlet letter. In "The Gophered Grapevine," a Northern expert nearly kills the vineyard's roots to increase production. By creating Uncle Julius, Chesnutt revives the roots he had almost desiccated in the process of becoming John—but he makes sure that the ownership of the vineyard remains safely in John's hands.

REAR WINDOW: REGIONALISM FROM HARTE TO HITCHCOCK

> —to sound urban when you're rural, English when you're American, white when you're black, male when you're female, bluegrass when you're Appalachian [is] the literary equivalent of Walter Cronkite's accent . . . we might as well seek truth from the telephone computer which tells us "the number is . . . " or expect welcome from the Atlanta airport simulated guide, "You are entering the People mover. There will be no food or drink beyond this point.
>
> George Ella Lyon, "Literature in Its Place"

Let us take a short story by Bret Harte, "Melons," a paradigm and parody of the motifs and ingredients of regionalism and local color:

> McGinnis' Court was a democratic expression of some obstinate and radical property-holder. Occupying a limited space between two fashionable thoroughfares, it refused to conform to its circumstances, but sturdily paraded its unkempt glories, and frequently asserted itself in ungrammatical language.[34]

"Democratic expression," regionalism speaks for a minor America, outside the streams of geographic and economic expansion. The obstinate smallholder who resists the passing of the "thoroughfares" is a minor hero of democratic individualism that we will find again in the populist struggles against the railroads and Eastern finance capital, and in countless Western movies. This is the antagonistic dimension of localism: the small versus the great, the individual versus the corporation, community versus centralized impersonality, spoken dialect versus official documents. On these bases, realist regionalists such as Joseph Kirkland, Harold Frederick, and Hamlin Garland lay the groundwork for what Alfreed Kazin called "a modern literature of protest."[35]

McGinnis' Court, however, is also "a limited space," not unlike the still waters of Sleepy Hollow, forgotten beside the main streams and thoroughfares of progress and history. Local color writing is also a limited space, a neglected interstice that cultivates its own minority in minute depictions of picturesque, irrelevant partialities, "a politically impotent Maine fishing village or New Orleans creoles or a Tennessee mountain community," as "the less arduous literary course."[36] The vernacular aggression of *Georgia Scenes* is reduced to the "unkempt" manners and innocuously ungrammatical language that the narrator can afford to view with paternalistic irony and tender nostalgia.

Hamlin Garland reacts to this image in *Main Travelled Roads*. In the story "Up the Coolly," the narrator compares the conventional landscape of two pictures hanging on a wall with the realistic view of the "sombre landscape" framed by the window: "a melancholy subject, treated with pitiless fidelity. A farm in the valley!" This allegory of the contrast between local color and regional realism shows that the closed space of the coolly is not a residual enclosure of a romantic past but the blind alley into which farmers are pushed by modern social forces. The truth of "these lives which the world loves to call peaceful and pastoral" is "infinite tragedy."[37]

The window frames a reversed pastoral scene. The "sullen and weary horses" in the rain and the weeping boy guarding the cattle would be another conventional picture if it were not for the inextricable materiality of the soil, "black and sticky and with a dull sheen upon it," which seems to suck the people and animals in, never to let them go. In regional writing, Edward Eggleston wrote, people appear as "the logical result of the environment": natural fruits of the land, or, as in this case, imprisoned in it. This is why regionalism stresses place and landscape much more than dialect; if (as Kazin claims) Garland is the first writer who makes American farmers talk like real farmers, it is perhaps because they don't speak very much at all.[38]

Regionalism and local color, according to Garland, mean that artists spontaneously reflect the life surrounding them. Since life is different in each part of the country, each place will leave its distinct mark and "utter its own voice." Regionalism, however, insists on claiming the national function of rooting general identity in the heart of partiality, making decentralization a constant impulse throughout the history of American literature. "The 'great American novel' . . . is appearing in sections," Eggleston suggested, as a mosaic of stories and local differences: an idea that Dos Passos takes literally, in the great work of montage he calls *U.S.A.*[39]

Localism, then, becomes an ironic extension of the nationalist vector of independence as separation; arguments in favor of local literature repeat those in favor of national literature against British models. "New York, like Boston, is too near London," Garland complained. For the Kentucky poet George Ella Lyon, the difference between "Appalachian" and "bluegrass" within her own state lies on the same continuum as that between "American" and "English."[40]

Regionalism, therefore, becomes central and problematic in the context of national identity crises such as the Civil War or the Depression, when efforts to contain all of America within the covers of one book, as Whitman had done, seem to fly apart (just as ethnicity will be central and problematic in the crisis of the 1960s, after Berkeley, Watts, and Vietnam). But this centrifugal impulse also contains its opposite: a search within each fragment for America's essential unity. The universal and national values, lost or degraded in the cities, are preserved intact in the industrious frugality, the democratic individualism, the wholesome irreverence of the provincial experience.

"I have travelled widely in Concord," Thoreau said; the transcendental unity of human nature recreates the cosmos within each microcosm. An old hillbilly woman in Lee Smith's "regional" novel, *Oral History*, reiterates: "I have traveled a lot in these parts," making up in depth of time and involvement what she apparently lacks in width of space. And yet, Garland insisted, "it is the difference which interests us"; if differences cannot be reduced to unity, difference itself becomes the only universal experience.[41] We are all "provincial," like Emily Dickinson's Queen—and Queen Victoria certainly *was* provincial, walled inside Buckingham Palace and the limited mentality that is named after her.

And yet, though limited, the Queen had the power to impose her perception on the whole world, and so did Emily Dickinson's "imperial self" inside her room at Amherst. This power, however, is out of the reach of Garland's farmers and the residents of McGinnis' Court. Though their universe is limited to a few blocks in Manhattan, "no one calls the New York writers regional," writes George Ella Lyon. Perhaps, it is because that limited space, and no other, irradiates voices that are heard around the world. Universalizing partiality, then, can be both a consolation for local powerlessness and a political response to the globalization of power, to the "extraterritorial" claims of parts that, like Queen Victoria, claim that they are all: the metropolis, the bourgeoisie, whites, males.

The tension between localism and partiality implies the question of point of view. The space of McGinnis' Court is as circumscribed as the point of view of Henry James's characters (and aren't they "regional," too, Americans in a Europe that thinks it is the world?). As Henry James teaches us, the house of fiction has "not one window, but a million"; from some of these windows, Hamlin Garland's and Bret Harte's narrators look upon the world.

> My window—a rear room on the ground floor—in this way derived blended light and shadow from the court. So low was the window sill, that had I been the least predisposed to somnambulism it would have broken out under such favorable auspices and I should have haunted McGinnis' Court. My speculations as to the origin of the court were not altogether gratuitous, for by means of this window I once saw the Past, as through a glass darkly. It was a Celtic shadow.[42]

Bret Harte's window, like James Stewart's zoom lens in Alfred Hitchcock's *Rear Window*, is a way of framing the world. Hitchcock's film, in fact, makes a subtle ironic use of the narrative conventions of local color: small pathetic stories held together by the unity of place, framed from above through a glass and a window. Unlike Stewart's revealing lens (or Garland's transparent window), however, Harte's glass is darkened. Rather than the realistic novel's or detective movie's illumination of reality, the rear window on McGinnis' Court offers us the filtered light of sentiment and nostalgia. Like all the frames of humor and local color, Bret Harte's window is an ambiguous distancing device. The low sill seems intended to allow the artist to reach outside toward "the people" but it also allows the people to intrude into the artist's space. And the glass, a rigid barrier between inside and outside, performs the same function as the cast on James Stewart's broken leg: it allows the observer and the observed to see each other, but not to touch.

Because contact, the intrusion of the courtyard into the room, of the observed into the space of the observer, is still dangerous. In *Rear Window*, James Stewart is forced to use his camera as a weapon, not to see but to blind, shooting the light bulb in the face of the killer. More modestly, Bret Harte's little Melons is expelled from the courtyard for stealing the narrator's bananas. But the observer's descent out to the observed space of the courtyard is even more dangerous. James Stewart breaks another leg (and his girlfriend is nearly killed), while Bret Harte's narrator becomes a ghost in the nocturnal, Celtic shadows and phantoms of the past. Ultimately, reaching out to the people does not yield local color's reassuring nostalgia or realism's contact with experience, but the disturbing discovery of an impalpable fantastic universe.

CHAPTER NINE

The Red and the Black

"The native voice in American literature is indispensable. There is no true literary history of the United States without it, and yet it has not been clearly delineated in our scholarship": thus N. Scott Momaday, in the opening essay of the 1988 *Columbia Literary History of the United States*. At the beginning of the twentieth century, W. E. B. DuBois made similar claims for African-American orality, when he described black music as "the singular spiritual heritage of the nation, and the greatest gift of the Negro people."[1]

Both statements are compelling claims of the rights of citizenship for minorities that have been historically excluded. However, a residue of ambiguity still remains in the belated recognition of the native or the African-American voice. Placing native voices at the source of national writings, Momaday concludes that "the continuity is unbroken. It extends from prehistoric times to the present, and is the very integrity of American literature." Rather than questioning the identity and possibility of a national literature, then, Native American orality is used as its new foundation, helping America assimilate the difference of those antagonistic or alternative voices it could not silence. Native Americans and African Americans replace, in this process, the ancestral, "feudal," "oral" "folk" origins America was supposed to lack. Ironically, in this light, the reclaiming of the native voice makes American literature look much more like the European national literatures from which it seeks to differentiate it.

Fortunately, things are more complicated. American literature is not an integral, unified, and continuous line but a much more fascinating weave, dialogue, and conflict among several distinct, interacting lines: the white mainstream, the Native American tradition, African-American expression, and other important strands—particularly the Jewish and Hispanic. Each of these traditions is distinguished by a different type of interaction between orality and writing. As we have already seen, in the hegemonic mainstream legitimacy, authority, and identity are founded on writing while orality intervenes either as a threat or as an alternative foundation. Native American and African-American cultures, instead, both found identity and authority on orality and the voice, but they relate to writing in significantly different ways.

Native American authors endeavor to overcome the opposition of writing and voice, and to include writing as an extension and continuation of a unitary history of language. African-American literature, instead, goes through a phase of problematic appropriation of writing and critique of the limitations of orality; and then, from the vantage point of a full possession of writing, goes back to claim its oral origins and foundations. This chapter is dedicated to an exploration of these dialectics.

INDIANS AS FOUNDERS: NOTES ON JEFFERSON'S *NOTES*

The red aborigines,
Leaving natural breaths, sounds of rain and winds, calls as of
birds and animals in the woods, syllabled to us for names,
Okonee, Koosa, Ottawa, Monongahela, Sauk, Natchez,
Chattahoochee, Kaqueta, Oronoco,
Wabash, Miami, Saginaw, Chippewa, Oshkosh, Walla-Walla,
Leaving such to the States they melt, they depart, charging
the water and the land with names.

Walt Whitman, "Starting from Paumanok"

The sound of a native voice is evoked in a text that may well be counted as one of America's birth certificates: Thomas Jefferson's *Notes on Virginia.* Written during the Revolutionary War by one of America's recognized Founders, *Notes on the State of Virginia* is intended to prove to European critics that the new continent is fully adequate for the physical, intellectual, and moral development of human beings. To prove his point, Jefferson resorts to what he presents as an Indian oral text, a speech attributed to the Mingo chief Logan, "a specimen of the talents of the aboriginals of this country, and in particular of their eloquence." Through the voice of its native inhabitants and the myth of the "eloquent savage," Jefferson appropriates to the new nation the virtues and possibilities of the new land.[2]

"I appeal to any white man," Logan's speech begins, "to say, if ever he entered Logan's cabin hungry, and he gave him not meat; if ever he came cold and naked, and he clothed him not." Like the colonization myth of Pocahontas, the independence myth of Logan identifies the Indians with nurture. They are part of the benevolent American nature that feeds and clothes the newcomers, becomes part of them, and then vanishes. Logan, whose family was murdered by whites, ends with a peroration that generations of American schoolchildren would later learn by heart, a prototype of the stoic, doomed Indian: "There runs not a drop of my blood in the veins of any living creature . . . Who is there to mourn for Logan?—Not one."[3]

"They melt, they depart," Whitman wrote, and no one lives to mourn for Logan. Likewise, James Fenimore Cooper's Indians are, by definition, *the last* of the Mohicans. In the popular Indian plays of the early nineteenth century, Indian voices are heard most frequently in death song and funeral speech. On the one hand, Indians are reduced to "children of the Great White Father" and "wards" of the government; on the other, they are molded into ancestral images. Pocahontas is "the mother of us all" and Logan appears in the Indian plays as an "improbable ghostly ancestor," who deeds his identity and his land to his adopted white children and heirs.[4]

Constance Rourke reads the reports of early Indian treaties, with their characteristic dialogue of pioneer wit and native gravity, as one of the sources of American theater. For the Indians, however, those treaties were not theater, they were political agreements to be taken seriously.[5] Likewise, if Logan ever spoke at all, it was not to found Jefferson's tradition but to protect his own. The native voice was not speaking in order to join the United States but to remain distinct and independent from them. Perhaps the risk that his voice may be used as the foundation of someone else's authority is the reason why Chief Bromden, in Ken Kesey's *One Flew Over the Cuckoo's Nest*,[6] chooses to pass for deaf and dumb.

THE MAN MADE OF WORDS: MOMADAY, SILKO, WELCH

While composing the last pages of *The Way to Rainy Mountain*, N. Scott Momaday included a recollection of the old woman Ko-sahn, who had sung and told for him the memory and history of the Kiowa people. "For some time," he writes, "I sat down looking at these words on the page, trying to deal with the emptiness that had come about inside of me. The words did not seem real." But then the writer's eye fell on the name. And suddenly, as if that name embodied "the whole complexity of language . . . I had the sense of the magic of words and of names. Ko-sahn, I said, and I said again KO-SAHN." And Ko-sahn "stepped out of the language and stood before me on the page."[7]

It would be a mistake to read this story in terms of a simple opposition between the "emptiness" of writing and the vivid presence evoked by the voice. Before Momaday calls out her name, in fact, Ko-sahn is already alive and present there, "on the page." She can be evoked precisely because Momaday has objectified his own discourse by writing it; the words stand motionless on the page, so that they can be scrutinized, reread, reversed ("I went back over the final paragraphs, backwards and forwards, hurriedly"), spoken to. The voice's magic of identification between word and subject is reinforced, then, by writing's magic of separation between word and subject: Ko-sahn is doubly *there*, as she speaks from the air and yet stays written on the page.

Two forces catalyze this process: the power of names and the memory of traditional Native American writing. "And all at once everything seemed suddenly to refer to that name"; but the name only refers to itself. "Naming is coincidental with creation," writes Momaday. Names are the heart of ritual because they are a distinct sphere of nonreferential language, akin to the sphere of myth. Naming Ko-sahn is, literally, to recreate her, to repeat visibly the entire creative process of which her narrative, ritual words are vehicle and symbol.[8]

Ko-sahn also implies the other catalyst, Native American writing. The type of collective memory she embodies is the same that is inscribed in the winter counts in which the pictographic annals of tribal memory are preserved. Inasmuch as they are a graphic trace, winter counts are "writing"; they, however, do not write words. Like Leslie Silko's sand paintings, geometrical forms that "are said to designate mountains, planets, rainbows" and that she learns to reproduce in the form of words; or like Momaday's own painting and graphics, winter counts are narrative matrixes rather than transcripts. The stories they tell cannot be read but must be recalled every time by the "reader's" memory and imagination. "It was the pictures I remembered and the words that went with them," says Black Elk, recalling his vision.[9]

Following a dream, the eponymous hero of James Welch's *Fools Crow* comes to the place where Feather Woman, a character in the Blackfeet creation myth, is painting figures on a skin. To him, however, the skin looks as empty as Momaday's page. He picks it up, turns it over (as Momaday does with his text), but finds nothing—nor can he remember the images he had seen issuing from the woman's hands. Only after Feather Woman tells him her story (which he already knows, because it is part of the holy stories of his people), do the images come back. At first, they seem like "a poorly done winter count," but gradually they become animated, like Ko-sahn on the page, and reveal the future of Fools Crow's people. Feather Woman's "writing," then, does not represent history but evokes it in the beholder, who perhaps knows it already without knowing, because it is historically inevitable.[10]

Writing and voice, seeing and listening, then, are not representations of each other but autonomous, interrelated manifestations of language, imagination, and memory. Reading a winter count is like reading a landscape; there are no words in it, but one can see and hear everything and then seek the words in one's own self. When Ko-sahn shows him the tree by which his grandmother was born, Momaday notes that it looks like all the others. But "in her memory Ko-sahn could see the child. I think she must have remembered my grandmother's voice, for she seemed for a long moment to listen and to hear."[11]

By rooting language in the land (or, more ambiguously, in "racial memory"), Momaday runs the risk of naturalizing the native voice out of history. From the Native American point of view, in fact, the identification with nature means inclusion in the cosmos, but from the point of view of Western culture, it means exclusion from history. Momaday, straddling the two worlds, reflects this ambiguity in the form of a discrepancy, within the same text, between his critical discourse and his artistic practice.

As a critic, Momaday defines writing as "recorded speech." He speaks of orality as "pre-literate storytelling" and of literature as the "end product of an evolutionary process" in which "the so-called 'oral tradition' is primarily a stage," necessary and, of course, "originary," but implicitly primitive. Thus, he seems to subscribe to a conventional concept of linear, typographic, progressive time. As an artist, however, he paints—through the character of Ko-sahn—a relationship between orality and writing based less on linear succession than on expansion, simultaneous interaction, and mutual change.[12]

Change is the nature of orality, and writing helps orality change. It is wrong to imagine that rituals must always be performed in the same way, says the medicine man Betonie in *Ceremony*: "if only in the aging of the yellow gourd rattle or the shrinking of the skin around the eagle's claw, if only in the different voices from generation to generation singing the chants . . . they have always been changing." Rather than freezing in immutable repetitions, the mutable adaptability of orality absorbs the new: "After the white people came, elements in this world began to shift, and it became necessary to create new ceremonies." And because the white people brought writing with them, writing must also be integrated and controlled in the osmotic continuity of the voice.[13]

Newspapers, old telephone books, ancient picture calendars, are all "part of the pattern" in Betonie's ceremony. The "bundles" of newspapers are reminiscent of medicine bundles (Silko herself speaks of this novel as a "bundle of stories"). The telephone books contain the names ("I brought back the books with all the names in them"), the calendars contain time. Rather than melting and leaving their names to the land, these Indians appropriate the invaders' names and change their sense of time. Betonie keeps them all jumbled, "the sequences of years confused and lost," as in the associative simultaneity of memory; and, rather than consulting the dates, Tayo associates the "Indian scenes" on their covers (reminiscent of winter counts) with personal recollections.[14]

Ko-sahn and Betonie, then, are figures of an integration of orality and writing, in which orality does not give up any of its authority and power. Whether it founds the literature of the United States or not, Indian orality does not melt into it. "It is carried on in all languages," Betonie's ancestor told him, "so you have English too." English *too*, writing *too*: they are not to be avoided or feared, because they cannot threaten the originary and antecedent, contemporary and active power of language and voice. Under these conditions, as the poet Simon Ortíz says, writing is not "a bridge crossed, but actually part of that path or road or journey that you are walking"—an extension of the intrinsic plurality of tongues in the native cultures.[15]

This vision, however, must measure itself against a history in which writing has arrived mostly in the guise of a violent imposition. In *Storyteller*, Silko describes how her Aunt Susie was equally at ease in telling traditional tales and in reading history books. But she also tells the story of Ayah, so proud of being able to write her name that she unknowingly signs the papers authorizing the whites to take her children away to a boarding school where they will learn writing and English and forget who they are.[16]

Power also impinges on the written representations of Native American cultures, beginning with the transcription and translation of traditional oral texts. Native American discourse has been often ossified and reified in the conventions of writing and in the perceptual frames of external observers, even when it retained traces of the dialogic relationship between Native tellers and white *scripteurs*. Even in the work of Native American writers, the extension of orality into writing is not a totally transparent passage; the prerequisites and devices of writing, print, and literature inevitably leave their mark on the native voice.[17]

Leslie Silko's *Ceremony*, for instance, is not only a description or account of a traditional ceremony, it *becomes* that ceremony itself. In typographic cultures, however, novels are *already* ceremonies: ceremonies of estrangement and alienation that interfere with the ceremony of healing celebrated by Betonie and Silko.

Urban readers may be more responsive to Tayo's modernistic alienation and fragmentation than to his ritual recomposition. They will tend to read the "witchery" as metaphor, and to notice that its defeat is only temporary, only "for now." It may be that Silko's novel is the dialogic hinge between these two different ceremonies: a way of recognizing the existence of alienation and witchery without being overwhelmed by them, and of making the best of the intervals of sanity and peace between the witches' cyclic returns.[18]

CROSSINGS: THE ORAL FOUNDATIONS OF AFRICAN-AMERICAN WRITING

While an intrinsic ardor prompts to write,
The muses promise to assist my pen;
'Twas not long since I left my native shore
The land of errors, and Egyptian gloom.

—Phillis Wheatley, "To the University of Cambridge, in New England"

In the same book in which he praised Chief Logan's Indian orality, Thomas Jefferson dismissed the African-American, female writing of the slave Phillis Wheatley as "below the dignity of criticism." Orality, which he considered a sign of Native American eloquence and wisdom, is now described as a mark of African childishness and illiteracy. From Wheatley onwards, then, African-American writing "arose as a response to the allegation of its absence" and functioned less as an extension of the oral roots of identity than as an emancipatory alternative.[19]

In the African diaspora, Ishmael Reed writes, "Dance and drums preceded the word." Especially after the 1960s, the history and theory of African-American literature claim oral and folk foundations. As Houston A. Baker, Jr., has written, "at the foundation of the black American literary tradition stands folklore," so that "even the most recent black American writer is closer to the earliest folk expressions of his culture than are the recent writers of most other groups." Orality, music, street language, the blues, and signifyin' are reclaimed as the basis of a black aesthetics independent from Euro-American models.[20] "We can learn more about what poetry is by listening to the cadences of Malcolm's speeches than from most of Western poetics," writes Larry Neal: "Listen to James Brown scream. Ask yourself, then: Have you ever heard a Negro poet sing like that?" And Rap Brown, the revolutionary orator of the 1960s, recalls: "I learned how to talk in the street, not from reading about Dick and Jane going to the zoo and all that simple shit . . . Hell, we exercised our minds by playing the Dozens."[21]

However, it was not always this way. The separation from the African "native shore," which Phillis Wheatley identifies as the origin of her writing, is symbolic of a phase of radical separation from the oral foundations of culture in the history of African-American literature. To take up Simon Ortíz's metaphor, for African-Americans writing has been neither the crossing of a bridge nor just a continuation of the path; rather, the space between orality and writing parallels in language the space of the Atlantic passage. Writing had to be conquered, as a form of emancipation (hence, the "greed for letters" of the first freedmen, the yearning of DuBois' disciples for "book-learning," the citizenship schools of the civil rights movement), before the places and meanings of the voice could be reclaimed in the process of liberation.[22]

The "two-ness" of African-American artists also derived, then, from this internal gap. There is always a self-reflexive distance, a doubling—if only that between subject and mirror—in the "*re*cognition" or "*re*discovery" of folklore by African-American writers. Zora Neale Hurston offers a poignant image of this necessary distancing: folklore "was fitting me like a tight chemise. I couldn't see it for wearing it . . . Then I had to have the spy-glass of Anthropology to look through at that." "For me," Ralph Ellison writes, "the stability of the Negro American folk tradition became precious as a result of an act of *literary discovery*"; in the American context, the metaphor of discovery inevitably evokes another crossing of the Atlantic, perhaps a return to the other side, to re-discover African roots.[23]

Robert B. Stepto has identified in African-American literature the two basic plots of "emersion" and "immersion," departure and return: the escape from the South toward the emancipated, literate North, and the return to the rural, familiar, oral roots of a "symbolic South." Significantly, this pattern does not exist in Native American literature, which has no "North" to emerge to; leaving home (for the Army, for jail, for boarding school) is never an act of emancipation but always a trauma, the formal equivalent of the Atlantic passage. Indian novels focus rather on "homing," on the return to a community that is still that of the ancestors, in which the originals language and institutions are still preserved.[24]

African-Americans, instead, only return to Africa metaphorically or mythically, like Toni Morrison's flying Africans in *Song of Solomon*; or they do so in a critical, distancing key, like Alice Walker's Nettie in *The Color Purple*, or Richard Wright in *Black Power*. The rural and oral South, on the other hand, has *become* home only after they have left it; only separation and distance remove the connotations of oppression to enhance those of identity. Only after emerging from a South in which they were not allowed to read and write did the younger African-American writers return home to create a new, distinct literature founded on the rediscovered memory of the voice.

PURLOINED LETTERS: FREDERICK DOUGLASS'S PURSUIT OF LITERACY

For they that carried us away captive required of us a song;
and they that wasted us required of us mirth, saying, Sing us
one of the songs of Zion.
How can we sing the Lord's song in a strange land?

Psalm 137

At the beginning of his *Narrative*, Frederick Douglasss writes: "I have no accurate knowledge of my age, never having seen any authentic record containing it." Like Hawthorne in "The Custom House," Douglass identifies a link between birth/origin and the written record. However, while Hawthorne plays ironically on documentary "authenticity" and "authority," Douglass needs "authentic" documents to certify an uncertain oral genealogy ("My father was a white man. He was admitted to be such by all I ever *heard speak* of my parentage" [italics mine]). Hawthorne's tradition is founded on writing, and he uses orality as an ironic dissolution of certified history and authority. Douglass and Wheatley, born in an oral environment and living in literate surroundings, establish African-American literature upon the voice's yearning for the material foundation and the guarantees of writing.[25]

The "primal scene" in the *Narrative* concerns the acquisition of literacy. Frederick's mistress, Mrs. Auld, begins to teach him his letters, until her husband forbids her, saying that "Learning would *spoil* the best nigger in the world," making him "unmanageable" and "unhappy." At this point, writes Douglass, "I understood the pathway from slavery to freedom." From the start, he conceives of the acquisition of writing as an antagonistic enterprise. "In learning to read," he comments, "I owe almost as much to the bitter opposition of my master, as to the kindly aid of my mistress. I acknowledge the benefit of both."[26]

The slave's writing, then, is neither a heritage nor a gift: it is a theft. Douglass reads his young master's books in secret, deduces the letters from the signs in the shipyard where he works, cheats the white children into teaching him more letters. "During this time, my copy-book was the board fence, brick wall, and pavement; my pen was a lump of chalk."[27] Later, Richard Wright and Malcolm X tell similar stories of stolen literacy: Richard's discovery of literature in books he pretended to borrow from the white library for someone else (*Black Boy*); Malcolm X's discovery of history in the process of copying out the dictionary in jail (*The Autobiography of Malcolm X*).

By keeping their slaves away from writing and confining them to compulsory orality, the masters attempted to turn the voice into a reassuring mark of subordination. A typical story is that told by the slave narrator Patsy Alexander, about an old man who, to avoid being caught reading, would hide his book in his pocket "and start singing like nothing was the matter."[28] Nothing *is* the matter in a singing slave; this is why, in the *Narrative*, Douglass compounds his theft of literacy with a refusal to lend his voice to his master by singing hymns for the slave breaker, Mr. Covey: "As he was a very poor singer himself, the duty of raising the hymn generally came upon me. He would read his hymn, and nod at me to commence. I would at times do so; at others, I would not. My non-compliance would almost always produce much confusion."[29]

The symmetry between stolen letters and withheld voice is a crucial African-American tradition. Stories about denial of the voice appear also in *Native Son* or *Invisible Man*: Bigger Thomas refuses to sing spirituals for his employer's daughter, and the invisible man is embarrassed when his white comrades expect him to sing.[30]

More than one critic has felt, instead, that this double movement—the appropriation of writing, the refusal of voice—removes Frederick Douglass from the oral bases of African-

American culture, leaving him "imprisoned by the notion of literacy that he hopes will liberate him" and by an "uncritical acceptance" of writing. Houston A. Baker, for instance, has written:

> Once literacy has been achieved, the black self, even as represented in the *Narrative*, begins to distance itself from the domain of experience constituted by the oral-aural community of the slave quarters . . . The voice of the unwritten self, once it is subjected to the linguistic codes, literary conventions, and audience expectations of a literate population, is perhaps never again the authentic voice of black American slavery.[31]

One, however, can hardly deny "authenticity" to the slave's wish to "distance" himself from the slave quarters. Douglass, in fact, uses his stolen literacy precisely to that end: he forges passes in order to escape, that is, to "steal" himself and his fellow slaves. Rather than as a means of access to hegemonic discourse, Douglass uses literacy to escape it. He does not hate slavery because he has learned to read—rather, he understands the importance of learning to read because he already hates slavery. Mr. Auld, he recalls, "wanted me to be a slave; I had already voted against that." Later, he attributes his "love for letters" not "to my presumed Anglo-Saxon paternity, but to the native genius of my sable, unprotected, and uncultivated mother."[32]

In the hands of Douglass, and slaves like him, writing changes meaning and direction. Harriet Jacobs, for instance, makes a sophisticated use of the ambiguities of writing to advance her own liberation. When her master realizes that she can read, he thinks this will help him seduce her, and sends her notes and letters. Jacobs denies that she is able to read them, withholding her literacy from her master just as Douglass had denied his voice to

Mr. Covey. Later, she escapes and spends seven years hidden in a garret across the street from her master's residence. From this refuge she reverses the flow of communication and literally turns the master's literacy against him, by writing him letters that her friends mail from New York, causing him to believe she is hiding there. The master had attempted to use writing in order to access her body; Jacobs, in turn, uses the separation of writing and body to distance herself from him.[33]

Stories of antagonistic and secret literacy are frequent in African-American literature. In Margaret Walker's 1966 novel, *Jubilee*, the slave preacher Brother Zeke hides his literacy in order to use it against his masters. At the beginning of the century, in *The Colonel's Dream*, Charles Chesnutt had told the story of a double denial, of both literacy and voice. Used sexually and then discarded by her master, the slave Vinnie pretends that she is both deaf and dumb, and too silly to learn to write; she is thus unable to communicate to him the whereabouts of a supposed treasure. Only after her mask of silence drives her master to madness and death does Vinnie speak again.

Douglass also manipulates voice and writing to overturn control. Even after his escape, under the pressures of his abolitionist friends, he defends his right to write and to have his own newspaper. "Give us the facts," they tell him, "we will take care of the philosophy." But Douglass will not lend himself as raw material to his protectors' elaborations. Rather, he is the one who interprets and authorizes them, just as he had turned observer and judge of his own masters. When he describes how slavery dehumanizes the kind mistress Sophia Auld and turns Captain Anthony into "a wretched man, at war with his own soul," this black writer appropriates the roles of authority and visibility associated with writing and denied to him by slavery. In the process, he substracts writing from the masters' exclusive domain, and thus transforms its very nature and meaning.[34]

The achievement of literacy, furthermore, does not mean the obliteration of all orality. Its traces can be recognized in the autobiographical syncretism that reveals elements of performance in the text, in the short-circuiting of story and discourse, in the frequent digressions, and in the irruptions of Douglass's (occasionally rhetorical) oratorical and preaching voice, studded with exhortations, parables, alliterations, repetitions, balance and parallelism. To all this, *My Bondage and My Freedom* later adds a less guarded use of dialogue and black speech.[35]

In fact, Douglass's denial of his voice to Mr. Covey also implies a recognition of the voice's power. Douglass withdraws his voice because he knows the master needs it; silence is a form of boycott. The contrast between Covey, who reads the hymn, and the slave, who is supposed to sing it, is a metaphor for writing's need of the voice and the master's need of the slave. The same applies to the parallel episodes in *Native Son* and *Invisible Man.* Bigger inwardly laughs at the whites who try ineptly to sing a spiritual but is bothered when his mother's sings them; the invisible man, surprised by the request that he sing a spiritual, is stopped by his political guardian before he has time to decide whether to accede or not. Between Bigger's reiterated "I can't sing" and the the invisible man's bewilderment at Brother Jack's "The Brother *does not sing*" lies the space between the African Americans' refusal to lend their voice to the whites and their intention to control its uses themselves.

In a memorable passage, Douglass describes the double function of the slave songs as both a form of expression from below and a means of control from above. "Slaves were expected to sing as well as to work. A silent slave was not liked, either by masters or overseers. 'Make a noise there! Make a noise there!' and 'bear a hand,' were words usually addressed to slaves when they were silent." Singing, then, was both "a means of telling the overseer, in the distance, where they were and what they were about," and an expression of "the natural disposition of the Negro to make a noise in the world," by making "the grand old woods for miles around reverberate with their wild and plaintive notes."[36]

The voice, then, is both the master's way of locating the slaves, and the slaves' way of locating themselves. Control is resented, but presence is irrenounceable. Therefore, as in Douglass's and Bigger Thomas's silent irony toward the unmusical whites, the voice protects itself by closing up, turning double, cryptic, secret. In their night meetings, slaves kept a pot turned upside down, in order magically to keep their voices close to the ground and away from the ears of masters and overseers; in the daytime, when the masters could hear, "they would sing, as a chorus, to words which to many would seem unmeaning jargon, but which, nevertheless, were full of meaning to themselves."[37]

"I did not, when a slave, understand the deep meaning of those rude and apparently incoherent songs," Douglass continues: "I was myself within the circle; so that I neither saw nor heard as those without might see and hear." In *My Bondage and My Freedom*, the circle designates both the most intense communal experiences and the cryptic, inward quality of a voice that, in order to protect itself from outside interference, becomes indecipherable to its own creators and bearers. This voice can only be deciphered by standing outside the range of its circumference. He who would understand the meaning of slavery, Douglass writes, "must place himself in the deep piney woods," and thence, unseen and outside the circle, "in silence, analyze the sounds that shall pass through the chambers of the soul." Only a distant and silent point of view, like that of writing, seems adequate to articulate and represent the unexpressed sounds of the soul.[38]

There is, however, such a thing as being too far out of the circle. In *Life and Times*, Douglass describes the Scala Santa ritual he saw in Rome, in which enthusiastic devotees climb a long flight of steps on their knees, and comments: "This is nothing to me, but it surely must be something to them." Only from outside the circle can one understand the meaning of folk culture and develop a metalanguage to describe it; but only from the inside it is possible to *know* it. The compelling power of Douglass's images of slave folk expression derives from his combined perspective of detached observation and inside involvement.[39]

Douglass uses a revealing metaphor to explain the power of his stolen literacy. "Books," he writes, "gave tongue" to thoughts that would otherwise have been lost "for want of utterance." His contemporaries, such as Whitman or Poe, move back from writing in search of an utterance below and before articulation. Douglass, instead, assumes the articulation of writing as the starting point for the reconstruction of his voice. The *Narrative* culminates precisely with the recovery of the voice: "While attending an antislavery convention at Nantucket, on the 11th of August, 1841, I felt strongly moved to speak."

This is both a second birth and a completion of his process of liberation. In the story of his rebellion to Covey, Douglass had written: "You have seen how a man was made a slave, now I will show you how a slave was made a man." As he takes the floor at Nantucket, he undergoes the same transformation. Before speaking, "I felt myself a slave"; but after he has started, "I felt a considerable freedom."[40]

Books "gave tongue" to Douglass and enabled him to speak. In turn, his reconstructed voice and public speaking enable him to write the autobiography. Before it was written in the *Narrative*, the story of how Douglass stole literacy from Mr. Auld had been told orally at abolition rallies. *The Liberator* reports it in the account of one of Douglass's lectures, and concludes: "He was not up as a speaker, performing. He was an insurgent slave, taking hold on the right of speech."[41]

REBELLION AS HOLIDAY: RALPH ELLISON AND THE LIMITS OF FOLK CULTURE

When the narrator of Ralph Ellison's *Invisible Man* first arrives in Harlem, he is struck by the attitude of the people there. "I wasn't sure whether they were about to celebrate a holiday or join a street fight," he muses. The ambivalence between holiday and riot, ceremony and rebellion is one of the organizing symbols of the Harlem episodes of the novel, and of Ellison's attitude toward African-American folklore and oral tradition. Later the hero describes the ghetto rebellion as "a holy holiday for Clifton," the young leader murdered by the police.[42]

Like *Ceremony*, *Invisible Man* is a circular ritual of temporary healing. Ellison, however, is less optimistic than Silko about ceremonies, in which he recognizes both identification and alienation, affirmation and defeat. In folklore, indeed, holidays are a time out of time, an extraordinary intensification of collective life and cultural expression, in which play, ritual, and wasteful consumption are mixed with penitence and sacrifice. Festive time is both antagonistic and complementary to ordinary time. Holidays suspend norms and heal identities, but in this way they make it possible for things to resume and go on as usual after the ritual time is over (as in Frederick Douglass's description of the slaves' Christmas holidays).[43] Ellison sees the same ambivalence in the ghetto rebellion; in it, the human potential and the shared culture of the black community achieve their fullest expression, only to be annihilated and destroyed.

The different quality of time is announced in the very beginning of the chapter on the rebellion. "Time burst": the sound of air escaping from a tire hit by a bullet announces both the explosion of the ghetto's compressed anger and the "sudden and brilliant suspension of time" in which the rebellion takes place. This exploded time is both a "suspension" and a continuation of ordinary time. "Tonight is some night," says a voice in the street, and another replies that "it's 'bout like the rest . . . full of fucking and fighting and drinking and lying." The holiday/rebellion reveals what is invisible and repressed by making it temporarily public and permissible.[44]

The first norm to give way is the centrality of economy and property. The rioters loot stores and carry away a stolen safe; flour sacks burst, chickens lie rotting on the pavement. Dupre, the spontaneous leader of the revolt, kicks a pound of butter that at any other time he would probably economize carefully. On top of a milk wagon drawn by laughing, drinking, singing men, a huge woman belts out a blues song, drinks beer from a barrel, and greets the crowd "like a tipsy fat lady in a circus parade." Fat, sensual, loud, the woman throws down milk bottles that burst on the pavement and mix with the beer with which, in mock benediction and ceremonial waste, she has sprinkled the crowd.[45]

The insistence on waste and destruction indicates that what the rebels seek is an emotional rather than an economic compensation: a ritual devaluation of the objects and commodities that rule their lives, a declaration of an at least temporary independence from them. But somehow the ordinary hierarchies are preserved; the devaluation of commodities respects the hierarchy of their valorization in advertising. The hats are Dobbs, the beer is Budweiser; the nocturnal rebels no longer accept second-class goods but derive the definition of first-class from those very powers that deny them by day.

The ambiguity of the rebellion-as-holiday culminates when Dupre and Scofield direct the burning of the decaying, infested building in which they live. In this episode, the peak of self-expression and identification coincides with the peak of self-destruction. "They organized it and carried it through alone; the decision their own and their own action. Capable of their own action," says the narrator. "My kid died from the t-bees in that death-trap," Dupre explains, "but I bet a man ain't no more go'n be *born* in there." In rebellions and holidays, the oppressed prove that they are capable of running their own lives. Yet the house they burn is the one they live in, and they, not the landlords, will be homeless when daylight returns.[46]

A deeper layer of symbolic ambiguity is revealed by the narrator's reactions to the sight of the milk dumped by the fat lady and mixing with beer and kerosene on the pavement: "Milk and beer—I felt sad." The narrator has just come from an encounter with a white woman, and the mixing of liquids upsets him because it evokes another taboo. "The spilling kerosene splashed into the pale spilt milk"; the redundancy of "pale" reinforces the color imagery, while the alliterations of "sp" suggest another pale liquid, poured and wasted on the ground, as in the biblical episode of Onan. This, then, is the meaning of this festive rebellion, and of the culture it expresses: a huge act of wasted creativity and fertility. Spilt milk, indeed.

"If it hadn't been for the referee," the fat lady on the wagon sings, "Joe Louis woulda killed Jim Jefferie." The song evokes Joe Louis as a mighty symbol of identification, but it also suggests that there is a crooked match going on.[47] The rebels can't win. Earlier, a group of boys in blonde wigs, pursuing others with dummy guns, have staged a ritual revenge for Clifton's death; but later real policemen come after them with real guns. "It was suicide, without guns it was suicide," the hero comments. Later, however, he realizes that the rebellion has been manipulated by the Brotherhood, to waste in repression the ghetto's militancy they no longer need. Like spilt milk, the explosion will bring the ghetto back to its usual passivity. "It was not suicide,"he realizes, "but murder." Finally, recovering the ceremonial holiness and hopelessness of the act, he calls it "sacrifice."[48]

Noble but self-deafeating, the rebellion reveals the brutality of history but is powerless to change it. Indeed, it ultimately reinforces its drift. Like Douglass's circle, the rebellion is a self-enclosed space and time: the expression and the metaphor of a folk culture conceived as an indispensable resource of collective humanity, but also as a limit and a boundary that prevents its members from achieving universality and realizing their full humanity.

All the genres and forms of folklore perform a validating function in *Invisible Man*, both in rich, mutual interplay and in admirable synthesis with literary modernism.[49] Ellison, however, insists that, like the ceremonial peaks that are its highest expressions, folklore and the oral tradition are limited and inadequate. "The blues are very important to me," he says, "but they are also limited." To achieve universality, the artist must "transcend the blues." Ellison feels that he must justify his use of folklore with the appeal to canonic literary authorities: "I use folklore in my work not because I am Negro, but because writers like Eliot and Joyce made me conscious of the literary value of my folk inheritance."[50] In this way Ellison's critical discourse reacts to the crippling stereotype that expects the "Negro writer" to be stuck with an exclusive use of folklore. But he pays the price—though more in critical discourse than in creative practice—of evaluating African-American orality less on its own terms than on a "universal" standard ultimately identified with the Western literary tradition.[51]

Commenting on images of the Civil Rights movement, Ellison notes that "the skins of those thin-legged little girls who faced the mob in Little Rock *marked them as Negro*," but the spirit that moved them was "the old *universal* urge toward freedom. For better or worse," he concludes, "whatever there is of value in Negro life is an *American* heritage and *as such* it must be preserved" (my italics).[52] In this passage, "universal" is opposed to "Negro" and is virtually synonymous with "American"—as if "American" were not also a partial identity, a limited and limiting label, another way of seeing "provincially." But there are partialities that recognize themselves as such, and there are hegemonic partialities that manage to pass for universals.

"OUR MOTHERS' GARDENS": ZORA NEALE HURSTON IN THE INNER CIRCLE

"I was glad when someone told me 'You may go and collect Negro folk-lore.' " Zora Neale Hurston's *Mules and Men*, the story of her field work collecting folk tales and songs in her native Eatonville, is a prototypical tale of immersion and return, an anthropological documentary on the retrieval of familiar folklore, and a preparation for the writing of her finest novel. Hurston retraces Frederick Douglass's steps backwards: while he moves from South to North and from orality to writing, she travels South toward the oral tradition. While Douglass must break out of the cultural barriers of illiteracy in order to emerge from the slave quarters, Hurston must break into cultural and class boundaries in order to reenter the quarters' oral culture: "I mentally cursed the $12.74 dress from Macy's that I had on among all the $1.98 mail-order dresses." Only after stepping outside the circle can Douglass describe the spirituals; but only after she proves she can sing the folk songs can Hurston say that "I was in the inner circle."[53]

In this way, Zora Neale Hurston founds an African-American tradition of women's writing, "a generation of female/feminist writing defining itself in relation to a maternal, largely oral past."[54] Her most direct descendant, Alice Walker, goes *In Search of Our Mothers' Gardens*, and each word of this title—the search, the garden, the mothers—is significant. Rather than "transcending" the boundaries of their culture toward an elusive universality, these artists dig toward an exclusive, deep center of identity located in the earth, the South, maternal warmth, communal solidarity, and the women's arts of oral storytelling and quilting. By setting *Their Eyes Were Watching God* in an exclusively black town in Florida, Hurston manages to convey "a sense of black people as complete, *undiminished* human beings." They do not need to leave the circle in order to be universal, because—in Alice Walker's words—in their "self love . . . love of community, culture, traditions" lies the power "to restore a world. Or create a new one."[55]

Hurston relies on no outside authorities to justify her literary use of folklore, nor does she need to "transcend" the blues or the folk tales. On the contrary, from the vantage point of African-American orality, she "signifies" ironically upon the literary canon. For instance, the invitation to the soul at the close of *Their Eyes Were Watching God* looks like pure Whitman; but Hurston reverses Whitman's triumphant expansion into an intimate, inward gathering gesture: "She pulled in her horizon like a great fish-net. Pulled it from the waist of the world and draped it over her shoulder. So much of life in its meshes! She called in her soul to come and see."[56]

Again, Hurston shares Emerson's myth of the originary unity of humanity before "the gods, in the beginning, divided Man into men." But her voice sounds less like Emerson's than like one of the bards and storytellers who are Emerson's imagined sources. In Hurston's telling, Emerson's abstract conceit melts into light and music, in biblical sonorities, in the wise, anthropomorphic naiveté of the folk tale and sermon: "When God had made The Man, he made him out of stuff that sung all the time and glittered all over. Then after that some angels got jealous and chopped him into millions of pieces, but still he glittered and hummed."[57]

Earlier, when Janie is beaten by her husband and her image of him "fell off the shelf inside her," Hurston signifies on one of Emily Dickinson's domestic metaphors:

It dropped so low—in my Regard—
I heard it hit the Ground—
And go to pieces on the Stones
At bottom of my mind—[58]

"I denounced Myself," Dickinson continues, "For entertaining Plated Wares/ Upon my Silver Shelf—." But there is no silver shelf in Janie's kitchen. The closest, ironic approximation, the equivalent of Dickinson's plated wares as a figure of glittering, superficial worth, is Jody's golded-up spitting pot.

The irony toward canonical literary authorities is accompanied by deep tensions toward the central themes of the novel: the discovery of the voice, nature, sexuality. In order to find her voice, Janie must rebel against the authoritarian orality of power embodied by her husband's "big voice." Jody's voice is as immutable and violent as an imitation of hegemonic writing; he "talks tuh unlettered folks wid books in his jaws," his voice has the sound of the whip in it, and he listens to and is influenced by no one. On the other hand, though Janie yearns to join the sessions of joking and storytelling on the store porch, she retains a degree of spectatorial detachment from the communal orality of folk sitters and talkers as well. When she finds her voice, it will be separate from theirs. Even her own narrative is filtered through a third-person narrator and free indirect speech, the figure of a divided self, only conceivable in writing.[59]

An unpacified ambiguity also runs through the novel's themes of sexuality and nature. Janie's first discovery of sexuality, after the pastoral vision of the bees and the pear tree, ends in an image of violence when Nanny "peered out of the window and saw Johnny Taylor lacerating her Janie with a kiss." Later, Janie's immersion into the community, the black workers, and the natural environment of the Florida "muck" is also steeped in ambiguity. The muck has been described as a "trope of erotic love, the antithesis of the bourgeois life and order," the equivalent of the " 'green world' in Shakespearean romance," a fit setting for "two lovers who dared to be happy in a society where happiness is sinful."[60] However, the muck also contains the elements of chaos: the mud, the hurricane, the flood, the night, the mysterious stirring of the deep, magmatic layers of identity. Twice, Hurston links the lake's overflowing to the dark side of sexuality: "the monster began to roll in his bed," "the senseless monster in his bed." The bite of a mad dog turns Tea Cake, too, into a monster in his bed; the first thing the doctor orders Janie to do is to separate her bed from his. At last, delirious Tea Cake attempts to bite her, and Janie kills him in self-defense. Her love life, begun with a kiss as "lacerating" as a bite, ends with Tea Cake's biting teeth sunk in her arm.

"And she was beginning to feel fear of this strange thing in Tea Cake's body." By killing the maddened Tea Cake, Janie kills sex as bestiality, physical aggression, laceration, and bite, and builds an altar to love as kiss, memory, and disembodied dream. The image of Tea Cake's "bloody body" melts into the music, sobbing, and sighing that fill her room with the familiar constellation of memory, sound, and ghost. Tea Cake's return is announced by breaths and sighs, like Ligeia's, but he comes back as dream rather than nightmare, not with a bite but with a disincarnated kiss: "Tea Cake, with the sun for a shawl. Of course he wasn't dead . . . The kiss of his memory made pictures of love and light against the wall."[61]

"Ah done been tuh de horizon and back," says Janie. Like Rip Van Winkle, she must now only remember and tell. As memory turns the body into thought and dream, so the voice turns experience into sound and words. Janie's final speech is a distancing from communal orality, a declaration of the limitations of language compared to experience. Yet, the words in which it is couched are a triumph of rhythm and sound and of the "will to adorn" of black orality: "It's uh known fact, Pheoby, you got tuh *go* there tuh *know* there. Yo' papa and yo' mama and nobody else can't tell yuh and show yuh." As she gathers the net of the horizon around herself like a shawl, Janie also gathers in herself the communal voice, excluding the others. Her new-found voice speaks inward, to itself alone.

BLOOD, MILK, AND INK: TONI MORRISON'S *BELOVED*

We have a ghost in here," she said . . . Paul D. scratched the hair under his jaw. "Reminds me of that headless bride back behind Sweet Home.
Remember that, Sethe? Used to roam the woods regular.

—Toni Morrison, *Beloved*

Toni Morrison's *Beloved* begins with a talking house, a headless ghost, a name written on a "dawn-colored stone." Sethe, a fugitive slave, has killed her still-nameless baby daughter to save her from the slave catchers. After she leaves jail, she pays with her body ("ten minutes for seven letters") for the writing of the first word on the baby's headstone: *Beloved*. This word will be her daughter's name when, unwilling to stay dead, she returns to haunt the house, first as a baby ghost and then with a new-found girl's body.[62]

Sethe knows well the ties between writing, sex, body, and death. On the farm from which she escaped, her work was to make ink, and she still carries a "blooming tree" of scars on her back, written by the blows of the whip. But now her house is filled and surrounded by voices, "the mumbling of the black and angry dead," crowded in slave ships and premature graves. Like the House of Usher, 124 Bluestone Road is alive, pulsating, "as a person rather than a structure."[63]

Sethe had to take upon herself the responsibility of life and death, and the voices and impulses on the air respond by abolishing the distinction between the living and the dead, between shifting voices and inert matter. Sethe could not distinguish between herself and the others and killed her daughter as if amputating a piece of herself, and now the child steps across the border of life and death, returning as a delightful and monstrous

Ligeia, with the same deep musical voice, sucking from Sethe the life Sethe tore from her.

Beloved is about separation and fusion. It is about the difficulty of being an individual, of distinguishing one's self from the others, the living from the dead, individuals from the collectivity, the present from the past, people from things. "This here now Sethe didn't know where the world stopped and she began," thinks her man, Paul D. "I am not separate from her" Beloved reiterates, "there is no place where I stop."[64]

The attraction and danger of fusion are represented by the text's pervasive liquid imagery: ink, milk, water, amniotic fluid, urine. Beloved reappears out of the waters, and Sethe greets her with a flood of urine that is a new breaking of the waters of birth. Sethe's first daughter, Denver, was born while crossing the Ohio river, the liquid border between slavery and freedom. To keep her from the slave catchers, Sethe tries to kill her together with Beloved, and Denver drinks on Sethe's breast her sister's blood mixed with her mother's milk. When Beloved returns, Denver is also absorbed into her presence and cannot part from her.

The necessity and trauma of separation, on the other hand, is evoked by the images of beheading and strangulation: Beloved's beheading, her hands around Sethe's throat, the hanging of Sethe's mother, the collars around the slaves' necks, the story of the slave Stamp Paid who breaks the neck of his wife violated by the master. The neck is the breaking point, the delicate junction of body and head, the weak link in the chain—but still a link and therefore also a metaphor of unity. This is expressed in the recurrent images of eroticism associated with the neck: the lovemaking of the turtles, Beloved's kiss on Sethe's neck. Finally, the neck, the throat, is also a channel of communication with others, because the voice goes through it on its way out. Choking is also a metaphor of isolation, as in the case of the kindly Mrs. Garner, deprived of her voice by a swelling of the neck. If beheading is a figure of the separation of the self, choking is a figure of the separation of the self from others in silence.

The dialectics of separation and fusion shape and lacerate the two realities that stand at the center of everything: the archetypical experience of motherhood and the historical fact of slavery. "Beloved she my daughter. She mine"; "I am Beloved and she is mine": thus begins the series of monologues that eventually fuse into one, lyrical voice.[65] In *The Bluest Eye* (1970) and *Sula* (1973), Morrison had already represented motherhood as an irreconcilable dilemma between separation and fusion, love and possession. In *Beloved*, Sethe's motherly attachment becomes the paradigm of her relationship with the world. The mixing of blood and milk underlines the biological flow between mother and child. When the overseer's nephews "steal" Sethe's milk on the plantation, it is as if life itself stops flowing within and from her.[66]

Slavery, like motherhood, is also based on the dialectics of separation and fusion. Slaves are not recognized as separate individuals (at Sweet Home, five of them are named Paul, and one bears a number for a name: Sixo), but they can be ruthlessly separated either by sale or by death. The slaves' effort, then, is both to claim their separate identity and to build a community. In this they are frustrated by the master's "paternal" power. All the slaves are the master's "children" (it does not occur to the paternalistic master of Sweet Home that his adult slaves may want women); and all the slave children are the property not of their mothers, but of the master (Sethe's stolen milk is also a metaphor for this stolen motherhood). Sethe's possessive attachement to her daughter is both a datum of universal motherhood and a historical consequence of her precarious hold on Beloved under the master's power. The combination results in paroxysmal excess, and loving fusion ends in bloody separation: beheading Beloved to deny her to the master, Sethe also denies Beloved not only her life, but her face—her identity, her voice.

A formal definition of the slave is "an extension of the master's will." The power to absorb another human being within themselves generates in the masters a delusion of unlimited expansion: white people, too, "don't know where to stop." Beloved sees white people as "men without skin," because the thin partition between these individuals and the world around them is so transparent that it is almost nonexistent. Sethe denies Beloved's form, but the form the whites deny is their own, because they do not know where other forms begin. Thus, while Sethe's inability to separate herself from the world generates the figure of beheading, the whites' unlimited expansion turns them into ghosts—a recurrent image of whites in African-American literature, from Olaudah Equiano to Alice Walker, inspired by the whites' diaphanous skin and lack of limits.[67]

Yet these two ways of negating the limit have something in common. Because of slavery's hegemonic power, slaves, too, view the world partly as the slaveholders make it. Treated and defined in terms of *ownership*, they too are liable to conceive of property as a paradigm of relationships between human beings. When Stamp Paid walks toward Sethe's house, out of the urgent, angry voices that surround it, he can make out one word only: "*mine*." The monologues of Sethe, Beloved, and Denver all reiterate an obsessive anaphora: "She is mine." Against the master's ownership, Sethe claims her own: "Beloved, she my daughter. She mine." In this book, then, slavery is present both as historical memory and as the metaphoric paradigm of the process that turns love into possession, the *beloved* object into beloved *object*.[68]

The mark of the whip on the slave's body, then, is also a metaphor for the marks left by hegemony on the slave's deepest feelings: a literal and symbolic writing of the masters *on* their subjects, a metaphor of the hegemonic power of all writing on its subjects.

In their final years at Sweet Home, Sethe and her fellow slaves are subjected to a new overseer—a schoolmaster with anthropological ambitions—and they are also the subject of the book he is writing about them, with the ink they themselves have made. The schoolmaster measures the slaves' limbs and turns them into a chart, like Jefferson's Indians reduced in the form of a catalogue: "put her human characteristics on the left, her animal ones on the right. And don't forget to line them up."[69] Ink, squeezed from plants and from human work, transforms these organic realities into inert signs on a notebook's pages.

Anthropological writing, then, is a paradigm of all hegemonic writing: the expression of the observing culture's power to reify the observed *subject*. Later, Beloved's death and Sethe's life are likewise molded into writing by the newspaper. "That ain't her mouth," insists Paul D., looking at her printed picture, as if to say that the story written there is not the same as the story that she tells.[70]

On a lower, self-reflexive frequency, Morrison suggests that this ambiguous power is also inherent in her own writing, which guiltily comes alive by impregnating itself with the history and life of her subjects. "He couldn't have done it if I hadn't made the ink," says Sethe of the schoolteacher. But this novel, like the whip's marks, is also a writing *on* Sethe, and it could not have been written if women like her had not made the ink, shed the blood, poured the milk. The sense that literature, too, is the blood and milk of human lives dried in ink on the page may be why Morrison insists that "it was not a story to pass on," not a story to hand over, and not a story to ignore. Because it would be sinful, and impossible, both to remember this story and to forget it.[71]

The ambiguity of writing is also restated at the level of the plot. When Mr. Garner offers the slaves of Sweet Home the possibility of learning to write, he meets with both acceptance and resistance. On the one hand, the slaves believe that "nothing important to them could be put down on paper." Sixo, the most independent and "African," repeats Plato's argument: writing, he says, "would change his mind—make him forget things he shouldn't and memorize things he shouldn't and he didn't want his mind messed up." On the other hand, however, Halle, Sethe's future husband, realizes that he will need literacy. He has been allowed to hire himself out to raise money to buy his mother's freedom and knows that "if you can't count they cheat you. If you can't read they beat you."[72]

Writing allows Halle to project an individual future, distinct from his peers and antagonistic to the master. By objectifying the world and identifying the writer, writing becomes an instrument of self-creation, of independence from possessive, fusional relationships. Beside identification, however, writing also serves communication, enables the relation to others; thus Halle learns to write to liberate not himself but his mother. In the brief "days of company" after Sethe's arrival at Bluestone Road, writing is woven into her process of socialization with the neighborhood women, together with conversation and sewing: "One taught her the alphabet; another a stitch."[73]

Writing thus mediates between the polarities of fusion and separation, of voice and silence, by introducing the intermediate terms of identification and communication. This process shapes the story of Denver, perhaps the most stoically heroic character in the book. Twice, writing accompanies Denver's effort to become independent of the fusional world of 124 Bluestone Road and to establish autonomous relationships with the community and the neighborhood. The first time she crosses the threshold of nothingness beyond her porch, Denver meets a lady who teaches the neighborhood children to read, and is entranced by the socialization of school and by the discrete, physical beauty and identifying power of the alphabet ("the capital *w*, the little *i*, the beauty of the letters in her name"). She loses all this, and sinks into silence, when a child asks her about her murdered sister.

Later, however, after Sethe and Beloved exclude her from their fusional relationship, Denver again ventures away from home, weaving self-construction with communication. By accepting her neighbors' material help, she makes amends for Sethe's isolating sin of pride. By planning (with the help of white abolitionists) to go back to school, she transforms her solitude into the project of a personal future.

Throughout her search for writing, Denver is entranced and haunted by her mother's stories about her birth. Oral, maternal storytelling is frequently described by metaphors of nourishment.[74] As she listens to these stories and repeats them to Beloved, Denver reenacts the scene of her birth, reminding herself and her mother of the time when they were one thing and milk flowed out of Sethe's breast as words now flow from her mouth. But Denver's birth is only complete when she steps from matrilinear orality into the personal autonomy of writing, separating from the mother's body to give birth to herself.

And yet, from her mother's story Denver has also learned that writing is a dangerous thing, the tool with which hegemony writes the life of its subjects. Denver thus recognizes in her benefactors' offer of sending her to college also an attempt to rewrite her according to their *design*, in an ambiguous convergence of Mr. Garner's paternalism and the schoolteacher's anthropology. "She says I might go to Oberlin . . . She's experimenting on me." And Paul D., who has not forgotten the experiments on Sethe's body, sums it up: "Nothing in the world more dangerous than a white schoolteacher."[75]

CHAPTER TEN

THE SOUNDS OF SILENCE

At rows of blank-looking counters sat rows of blank-looking girls, with blank white folders in the blank hands, all blankly folding blank paper . . . Not a syllable was breathed. Nothing was heard but the low, steady, over-ruling hum of the iron animals. The human voice was banished from the spot . . . The girls did not so much seem accessory wheels to the general machinery as mere cogs to the wheels.

—Herman Melville, "The Paradise of Bachelors and the Tartarus of Maids"

"Blank," like the page awaiting to be written, is Melville's obsessive word for the voiceless epiphany of the working class: a new variable in the relationship between language and democracy, the tangible and invisible, pervasive and ungraspable collective protagonist of the age from the Industrial Revolution to the Great Depression, and after.

America does not acknowledge the existence of classes. The working class, therefore, is denied twice: first, because it is a class; second, because, among classes, it is the newest and the most dangerous. In the literary imagination of the industrial age, the shape of the working class is unknown, its place is darkness, its language silence—thus making the working class a sort of general signifier for all that is repressed, marginal, and unspoken in society. Identified with the passive inertia of tired bodies and minds, the working class can only be represented by negation, only be named where the text breaks down.

The Great Depression changes this scheme radically. In the apocalyptic scenario of the crisis, the "natural" materiality of the proletarian world becomes a last resource of certainty, something to hold onto in the breakdown of the "artificial" socio-economic system. The inert gaze lights up in wisdom and vision, the body radiates vigor and fertility. And the collective proletarian voice—spontaneous, earthy, laconic, expressive—seems to restore meaning and validity to an exhausted and inflated national language.

But when one reaches out to touch this earthy body, to reproduce this authentic voice, they also vanish, or are revealed to be shifting, elusive signifiers of desire rather than of reality. Rather than experienced reality, documentary fidelity uncovers the inevitable limits of representation.

THE OUTLINES OF THE NIGHT: *LIFE IN THE IRON MILLS*

"A cloudy day: do you know what it is in a town of iron works?" Rebecca Harding Davis's *Life in the Iron Mills* (1861) is the first full-fledged American literary portrait of the "dark satanic mills" of the industrial revolution, a "city of fires" burning in the night among "revengeful ghosts in the red light." In this light, Davis's dialogic opening asks the "terrible dumb question": what is this brave new world? Or, as the Dickensian flatness of the title suggests: is it really "life" that burns "in the iron mills"?[1]

Prophetically, she begins with the air: "The sky sank down before dawn, muddy, flat, immovable. The air is thick, clammy with the breath of crowded human beings. It stifles me." This viscid air is too heavy to vibrate in sound waves and chokes the breath and the voice back into the throat. On the first industrial landscape of American literature, silence weighs like smoke, dust, fog. "I can paint nothing of this, only give you the outlines of a night"; we cannot penetrate the formless darkness of working-class existence but only trace the external outline of this black hole. The proletariat makes its literary entrance under the sign of blankness, inertia, silence: a "dumb secret" buried in "apathy and vacancy."[2]

The central symbol of the story is the statue that the factory worker Hugh Wolfe carves out of *korl*, the slag from the kilns: "a nude woman's form, muscular, grown coarse with labor, the powerful limbs instinct with some one poignant longing. One idea: there it was in the tense, rigid muscles, the clutching hands, the wild, eager face, like that of a starving wolf's."[3]

In this incipient self-representation, the working class stands for the body, for slaves, for women, for artists, as a general signifier of negation. The "slavish" and "negro-like" Ohio river reminds us with it "weary, dumb appeal" that Wheeling, (West) Virginia, is still part of the slave South.[4] But the statue itself is a woman's figure, in which the narrator recognizes her own negated voice as a woman and as an artist. She lives and writes in the same house previously occupied by Wolfe, and keeps the statue in her library, between a broken-winged, sooty angel on the mantel and a caged, desolate singing bird. As she writes, she looks up from her page to the statue, as if to contaminate her own writing with its silenced scream.

As Tillie Olsen has shown, the working-class artist Wolfe and his statue are the image of the author's own struggle to express herself, first against the constraints of domestic fate, and then against the silence that falls upon her literary work. Wolfe himself has a "meek, woman's face" and shares the intense sensitivity and weak nerves that are the conventional attributes of artists and women, certainly not of mill hands. Perhaps the darkness and silence of working-class life can be perceived only through a character who at least gropes and tries to scream, revealing the background against his own incipient difference. As the slave's condition was made visible mainly in the stories of those who had escaped from it, so the unimagined working-class life can only be represented through Wolfe's "frantic anguish to escape—only to escape," as the woman in his statue tries to emerge from the matter that imprisons her.[5]

Wolfe's desolate "It's all wrong . . . all wrong" is the working-class version of Melville's Bartleby's "I would prefer not to." But Bartleby's silence is a challenge to the unlistening world, while the silence of Wolfe and his statue is the voicelessness of those who, deprived of as yet unimagined speech, endeavor to reconstruct it by piecing together left-over, discarded fragments, second-hand materials. Wolfe's thirst for beauty, like the statue's hungry look, is a physical expression of formless spiritual desire. "Whiskey ull do it, in a way," says Wolfe, reminding the reader of Emerson's idea of inhebriation as a surrogate of inspiration and the spirit.[6]

"Let them have a clear idea of the rights of the soul," says a visitor, a friend of the owner's son, "and I'll venture next week they'll strike for higher wages." The visitors realize Wolfe's genius and recite the litanies of democracy: "Make yourself what you will, it is your right." But when he asks for help, they answer curtly: "I have not the money, boy."[7]

"Money? . . . That is it? Money?" Capitalism's hidden nexus between money and the rights of the soul has perhaps never been stated more sharply. Only when he has money will Wolfe have a voice. A strike for higher wages would indeed be a battle for the rights of the soul, as well as a metaphor for the artist's struggle for the right of expression.

Deb, Wolfe's crippled companion, is the first to understand all this. While the visitor deals his pretty words, she stretches out her hands, steals his money, and gives it to Wolfe, who is hesitant to keep it. As he wanders in the streets, trying to make up his mind, he sees the setting sun penetrating the fog to reveal a world of shifting colors, "drifting, rolling seas of crimson mist," with silver hues and scarlet depths. "Wolfe's artist-eye grew drunk with color," and, with a new "consciousness of power," he closes his hand on the money.[8] The worker's hand (workers, says the owner's son, "should be machines,—nothing more,—hands") becomes the hand of the artist. Just like Frederick Douglass's literacy, working-class expression begins with a theft.

Of course, Wolfe is discovered and pushed back into the empty darkness of a "Silence deeper than the Night!" He calls out from the window of his cell, but no one hears. Like Bartleby, Billy Budd, Bigger Thomas—all guilty, like him, of using their hands in place of a hindered tongue—Hugh Wolfe, artist and criminal, dies in prison.[9]

"His dumb soul was alone with God in judgment. A Voice may have spoken for it from far-off Calvary." On that fatal night in the factory, a visitor had said that perhaps the working class would generate its own Messiah. But even in the sight of God, Wolfe's soul remains "dumb," voiceless. Instead of helping him to speak, the Messiah's big voice will speak *for him*—that is, in his place.

JACK LONDON'S MISSING REVOLUTION: *THE IRON HEEL*

—and I had the sense that the deeper meaning of the story was in the gaps.

—Edith Wharton, *Ethan Frome*

Toward the end of Jack London's *The Iron Heel* (1905), Avis, the narrator, recalls: "Many events are focused sharply on my brain, but between these indelible pictures I retain are intervals of unconsciousness. What occurred in those intervals I know not, and never shall know."[10] *The Iron Heel* is a prophecy of future class struggle, of the rise of a fascist dictatorship, and of the final advent of a utopia of socialist brotherhood. It is the story of the revolutionary Ernest Everhard, told by his wife Avis in an incomplete manuscript discovered and published with commentary by the future historian Anthony Meredith. In this stratification of voices and writings, there remain significant "gaps," "intervals," and "blanks," of which, as in Rebecca Harding Davis's night, all we can know are the outlines.

Avis's narrative is framed by Meredith's critical apparatus, and in turn envelops Ernest's reported direct discourse. These three "voices" correspond to three types of knowledge and three modes of discourse: Ernest possesses theoretical and philosophical knowledge, explained mainly in oral, philosophical dialogue and political debate; Avis bears direct experience, reported in written narrative; Meredith is the depositary of historical knowledge, presented as critical paratext. Avis's narrative clothes Ernest's ideas with experience; Meredith's commentary confers to Avis's tale the credibility of documentary, and functions as a distancing frame to protect the reader from too close contact with the story.

Between the three discourses, however, there are also radical discontinuites. Avis's manuscript is incomplete, and a gap of fifteen years occurs between its writing and the events it describes; Meredith's comment, in turn, is composed centuries later, after the advent (which the book does not describe) of a socialist brotherhood. All the crucial events—the hero's death, the vanishing of the principal narrator, the rise of socialism—take place in these gaps between stories and between discourse and history. An iconic moment occurs when, at the peak of the rebellion of the "people of the abyss" and its violent repression, Avis faints, and the dramatic events that follow vanish in a "kindly blank."

The most important gap, located between Avis's text and Meredith's notes, concerns the event around which everything revolves but which no one manages to represent—the Revolution. The impossibility of representing the revolutionary transition from socialism to capitalism was already manifest in Edward Bellamy's earlier socialist classic, *Looking Backward* (1888). During a metaphorical earthquake, Bellamy's hero falls into a deep mesmeric sleep, from which he awakens only when the change has already taken place. Even the American Revolution had appeared, in Rip Van Winkle's long sleep as well as in the gap between tales and frames in Hawthorne's "Legends of the Province House," as a sort of black hole, a trauma designated only by silence. Jack London's proletarian revolution in *The Iron Heel* completes an American paradigm of missing revolutions.

Like the revolution, its supposed social agent—the industrial working class—also eludes representation. The text seems to hover at the margins of the working class, never actually touching it. Early in the novel, for instance, Everhard meets and debates representatives of various social groups—priests, capitalists, small entrepreneurs—but no industrial workers. Later, Avis and her friend Bishop Morehouse start on a journey in the underworld, a quest for the working class, but they only encounter former workers, marginal proletarians, invalids, the unemployed. In both cases, the working class is defined only by what it is not, or no longer is.

The central metaphor for this representation through negation is the missing arm of the former worker Jackson, torn by a factory machine. This tangible absence is to the class of manual workers and the proletarian revolution what the missing head of the state is to the democratic revolution and to intellectual authority. "Little did I dream the fateful part Jackson's arm was to play in my life," writes Avis, referring, however, not to the arm that is still there but to the missing one. Jackson's torn arm is the image of a concrete absence, a dark but powerful symbolic center of meaning: "The more I thought of Jackson's arm, the more shaken I was. I was confronted by the concrete . . . Jackson's arm was a fact of life."[11]

And so it is, if working-class "life" is Melville's "blankness" or Rebecca Harding Davis's "living death." Avis, like them, mirrors her subjectivity in the nocturnal outline of a negated subject. The symbolic centrality of the working class seems to stand in an inverse ratio to its perceived historical presence. Thus, London rewrites Karl Marx to suppress the positive: "The people of the abyss had nothing to lose but the misery and pain of living. And to gain?—nothing, save one final, awful glut of vengeance." There is no "world to win" for the people of the abyss.[12]

The impossibility of linguistic (self-)representation of the working class determines a shift to delegated political representation: workers can speak, or be spoken of, only through their *representatives*. Like the one-armed Jackson, Ernest—"social philosopher and ex-horseshoer"—is *no longer* a worker, but is nevertheless introduced as "a member of the working class," and speaks about, for, and to the working class. Avis's father discovers him as "a man on a soap-box addressing a crowd of working men." Avis perceives him, with an erotic shiver, as a working-class man with "bulging muscles and prize-fighter's throat" but also as a "natural aristocrat" and "a descendant of the old line of Everhards that for two hundred years had lived in America"—the American version of an aristocracy of the blood. Being "born in the working class" confers to Ernest his quarts of socialist nobility; but it is his "rise in society" and his being emphatically "born in the USA" in an age of foreign immigration that entitles him to the rights of speech, citizenship, and representation associated with ethnic purity and social mobility.[13]

"I am not a working man," Ernest tells a capitalist, "cap in hand, asking you to increase my wages." He can represent the workers, in other words, *because* he is no longer one of them. He is, however, already something else: "one of the leaders," "high in the councils" of his party. The dumb apathy attributed to the despised "wage slaves" authorizes Everhard to replace their missing voice with the "clarion-call" of his own, like the Voice from Calvary who spoke "for" Hugh Wolfe's "dumb soul."[14]

The negated subjectivity that makes the working class so powerful symbolically also makes it powerless politically. The delegation of representation to the revolutionary vanguard is an extreme form of the representation by substitution or "fiction," inaugurated by the bourgeois constitutional state. In fact, London insists on the reciprocal mirroring of the ever-hard *steel*-core vanguard of the revolutionary party and the *Iron* Heel of capitalist dictatorship. The most dramatic analogy, and the cause and ground for their fatal struggle, is their shared passion for power.

The war between these two identical and opposite fronts takes the form of an *exchange*: the mutual infiltration of underground agents and double-agents. "In the shadow-world of secret service identity was nebulous. Like ghosts, the agents came and went." The first change the revolutionaries experience by going underground is a loss of the body. Surgery changes the agents' features beyond recognition, and they internalize their disguises until they become second natures. The body offers no resistance to endless manipulation, indicating that matter cannot hinder the will and inert masses cannot interfere with the vanguard's design. The "people of the abyss" in revolt, therefore, are like a body breaking in pervasive, uncontrolled corruption: "bloated forms swollen with physical grossness and corruption, withered hags and death's heads bearded like patriarchs, festering youth and festering age, faces of fiends, crooked, twisted, misshapen monsters."[15]

"We could hear the rising roar of it"; the voice of the people of the abyss is the roar of the beast ("roaring for the blood of their masters . . . snarling and growing carnivorous") and the sound of the ocean ("an awful river that filled the street . . . concrete waves of wrath"). As in Whitman, these voices announce the inarticulate insurgency of nature and the body, but, as in Poe, they turn it into horror, decay, animal screams, and howling hordes. The people of the abyss are the ape of the rue Morgue, the mob that overthrows Monarch Thought, the decaying Red Death that invades Prince Prospero's palace. At this point, Avis faints.

When she first meets Ernest, Avis is both "delighted" and "terrified"; likewise, she later describes the people of the abyss as a "*fascinating* spectacle of *dread*" (italics mine). She had noted that the clothes seemed to burst on Ernest's uncontainable body; now the rags of the mob seem a horrid incarnation of that image. In both cases, the ambivalence of attraction and fear is generated by the arousal of repressed instincts. Her imagination sees Ernest "as a lover, a husband," and she exorcizes it by attempting to concentrate on his "delicate and sensitive spirit" rather than on his bulging muscles. But no such sublimation is possible when she is confronted with the "primitive strength" of the "abysmal beast." Her only escape is to blank out everything and vanish from consciousness.[16]

But it is only a temporary escape. When she emerges from "the monstrous flood that was sweeping" her, Avis is immediately confronted with a crude sexual metaphor, again in terms of clothes rent by the body: a man's coat, "slit along the centre seam," which "pulsed rhythmically, the slit opening and closing regularly with every leap of the wearer." She is lifted by the male arm of her comrade Garthwaite, who drags her along, hides her in a pile of corpses underneath a dying woman, and "with much squeezing and shoving, crawled in beside me and partly over me."[17] In this way, the body, sexuality, instincts, and death complete and fulfill the paradigm of repressed and denied forces signified by the working class.

When the screaming people of the abyss emerge from their indescribable darkness and dumb apathy, they foreshadow a generalized breakdown of controls. Leaders no longer control the masses, and hardly control themselves; intelligence and reason are swept away by the universal bestiality that fills the naturalistic imagination with fascination and dread. Narrative control is also dragged along in the general breakdown: the text can contain this invasion only in silences and blanks, and can represent it by no other form than the outlines of the night.

A VOICE FULL OF MONEY: FITZGERALD, STEINBECK, AND THE GREAT CRASH

At nine o'clock, one morning late in July, Gatsby's gorgeous car lurched up the rocky drive to my door and gave out a burst of melody from its three-noted horn.

—Francis Scott Fitzgerald, *The Great Gatsby*

Jay Gatsby's car is one of the great icons of the "roaring" twenties. It is less a means of transportation than a matrix of messages issued by its layers of transparent, sun-mirroring glass, melodious horn, bright radiating nickel. An automobile made of dawn, the fact that it carries people about is almost irrelevant; like the workers who built it, its silent engine is a mere material occurrence, not a meaningful fact.

Let us now look at another iconic automobile, from the following decade: the Joad family's jalopy in John Steinbeck's *The Grapes of Wrath.*

[Tom Joad] went directly to the Dodge and crawled under on his back. Al crawled under on his belly and directed the beam of the flashlight. "Not in my eyes. There, put her up." Tom worked the piston up into he cylinder, twisting and turning. The brass wire caught a little on the cylinder wall. With a quick push he forced it past the rings. "Lucky she's loose or the compression'd stop her. I think she's gonna work all right."[18]

As opposed to the "rich cream color" of Gatsby's, the Joads's automobile is opaque black. Far from irradiating light, it needs to be illuminated with a torch. Its sounds are not musical notes but symptoms of mechanical failures; it breaks down often, and its passengers must crawl underneath to fix it. While Gatsby's limousine is a means of communication, the Joads' jalopy is a means of transportation, one that carries the family to California. The most important part of the former is the body, of the latter, the engine.

The opposition of body and engine defines the before and after of the crisis of 1929. The years of Gatsby are those of a dizzy growth of mass communication and of the paper economy. That they are also the years of Fordism and of the assembly line is a less visible, less "roaring" fact. The jazz age rolls on silent wheels and does not care what keeps them turning; the assumption is that the industrial, productive basis of society will take care of itself. Thus Gatsby's car seems to have been made by no one. The only mechanic who appears in the novel ends up crushed underneath its wheels; the only workers are those whom Jordan, the "bad driver," almost runs over.

The years of the Joads, instead, come after an unexpected breakdown in the social and economic machinery. Like Tom Joad, artists and intellectuals now also feel the need to take a look underneath and inside, to lay their eyes and hands on the broken mechanism and get it going again. Thus, in *The Big Money*—a novel about the years of Gatsby written in the years of the Joads—Dos Passos reiterates the opposition between the technical "men bold enough to take charge of the magnificent machine" and the word-mongering "pigeyed speculators and yesmen at office desks."[19]

In fact, an awareness of the impending crisis is already implicit in *The Great Gatsby*. The inbalance between immaterial signs and material mechanisms, embodied in Gatsby's car, is a central thematic concern, reverberating in the unbalance between signs and referents, signifiers and signifieds, voice and body. Daisy's evocative, cryptic voice "full of money" is the vehicle of a language that is increasingly losing its hold on the world of things, amidst a paper economy that is increasingly losing sight of the production and use of material wealth.

When Nick Carraway moves to New York, he leaves his family's "hardware business" and takes a job in the "bond business." To the modern reader, the word "hardware" evokes an automatic association with "software," and, beyond the obvious anachronism, this is indeed what Nick's move is about. Bonds are a kind of software, further and further removed from its "hard" referents. Like Nick, Charley Anderson in *The Big Money* also leaves the hardware world of airplane engines to make money on the stock market. The passage from engines to stock, from metal to paper, signals the widening gap between the materiality of the world and the immateriality of its economic representations, between material wealth and monetary fiction—between automobiles as signs and automobiles as referents. No wonder that, as John K . Galbraith puts it, the stock of radio—the medium of swollen communication and nascent secondary orality—was "in many respects the speculative symbol of the time."[20]

On the other hand, the controversy over "hard" and "soft" money, and its linguistic implications, runs throughout the history of the United States: the redemption of revolutionary war bonds, for instance, was a monetary metaphor for the credibility of the new order. In the Jacksonian era, the expansion of paper money seems to endanger the very nature of signs and their relationship to objects. Poe alludes to the controversy between "paper men" and "gold bugs," and Irving plays heavily upon the relationship of paper and metal: his Dutch governor Wilhelm Kieft makes "war by proclamation" and causes an inflation of artificial "wampum" with "no more intrinsic value than those rags which form the paper currency of modern days."[21] Emerson preached:

> When . . . duplicity and falsehood take the place of simplicity and truth . . . new imagery ceases to be created, and old words are perverted to stand for things which are not; a paper currency is employed, when there is no bullion in the vaults. In due time the fraud is manifest, and words lose all power to stimulate the understanding and the affections.[22]

This inflated communication and exchange nullifies what Saussure and Barthes call the "value" of language—that is, the portion of the world with which language (and that specialized form of language that is money) can be "exchanged."[23] Thus, in the depths of the Depression, John Steinbeck pointedly abolished the "signicity" of money, to stress its humble material substance, that of a metallic coin that starts a juke-box, drawing sound and light out of a machine: "The nickel, unlike most money, has actually done a job of work, has been physically responsible for a reaction."[24] In *The Great Gatsby*, the dazzling expansion of signs dissolves what they are supposed to represent. Language is as inflated, falsified, valueless as money, and the vanishing of "value" (semiotic, economic, moral) lends a hollow ring to the "voice full of money."

"It was the kind of voice that the ear follows up and down, as if each speech was an arrangement of notes that will never be played again." The movement of Daisy's voice looks like the notes on a musical score, but also like the zigzag line of a financial chart. With an explicitly economic metaphor, Nick will later call it "fluctuating." Like money, this voice contains a promise (a bond?) of "exciting things" just happened and soon to happen, urging toward an endless accumulation, an ungraspable, irresistible elsewhere: "Her voice compelled me forward breathlessly."[25]

Like the bonds and titles whose commercial value has grown beyond proportion to the material goods they stand for, language becomes increasingly frantic and hyperbolic, out of proportion to experience and feelings (in this novel, one can really imagine that a billboard is God). Daisy's language is studded with figures of vertical and horizontal amplification, the correlative of an inflated monetary mass: hyperbole, emphasis, and "bantering irrelevance." Her favorite lexical mannerism is "absolute": "You remind me of a rose, of an absolute rose." Nick knows very well that a rose is a rose, and he is not one, but Daisy's rules of conversational exchange are dominated by a variant of Gresham's law, and he later repays her with the same bad money: " 'Do they miss me?' she cried ecstatically," and Nick replies: "The whole town is desolate."[26]

The gap between emphasis and sense increases the gap between the "promise" of Daisy's voice and the irrelevance (worse than the insincerity) of her conversation. The first chapter is a catalogue of the uses of the dash and its ambiguities. The number of suspended or interrupted sentences might just be realistic in a real conversation, but in this literary dialogue it signals a breakdown of manners, and therefore of ethics. Tom interrupts and prevaricates with everybody; Daisy and Jordan do not bother to finish their sentences or to clinch their exchanges because neither is really interested in concluding. In the market of words, what really counts is to keep the circulation up and increase the circulating mass. Rather than communicating meaning, conversation serves to remove it. What is on everybody's mind—Tom's affair with Myrtle—is rigorously unspoken. "Can't you talk about crops or something," asks Nick, not wholly in irony and nostalgic for hardware.[27]

Only Gatsby still believes that words ought to correspond to something. Rather than the words to the world, though, he believes that the world ought to correspond to the words. He therefore lies naively and furiously, as if his words had the power to reshape the world according to his wishes. His clichés , however, are "worn so threadbare" that they look like notes that have gone through too many hands. As if alluding to the controversy over metal and paper money, Gatsby concludes his invented autobiography by pulling out a "piece of metal," a medal. "To my astonishment, the thing had an authentic look," Nick says, still clinging to the belief that words *can* be authenticated. There's a medal, a photograph, a witness—who, however, only repeats what Gatsby told him. The proof of signs is more signs, equally threadbare.[28]

At last, signs and referents do come together, with tragic consequences. Gatsby's automobile turns from light and sound back into heavy metal, and crushes and kills. After the catastrophe, Daisy hardly speaks anymore: a voice full of money is as worthless as paper wealth after the great Crash.

In 1929, in fact, referents come back with a vengeance. America's warehouses overflow with them, but they are worthless because there is no medium of measurement or exchange. If the Crash results from "the pathological prevalence of paper economy over real economy,"[29] then the Depression is the pathological loneliness of "real" economy when paper no longer represents it. This is why Nick cannot be satisfied with just returning home to his "hardware business" but must begin to write, anxiously stirring the inescapable software of signs.

THE PEOPLE TALK: STEINBECK, CALDWELL, AND OTHER VOICES FROM THE DEPRESSION

For fear the hearts of men are failing
For these are latter days we know
The Great Depression now is spreading
God's word declared it would be so

The Carter Family, "No Depression in Heaven"

"Suddenly the lights went out": these are the first words of Robert Cantwell's *Land of Plenty* (1934), one the finest "proletarian novels" of the 1930s. The Crisis is a cultural apocalypse: "a rending of the earth in preparation for the Day of Judgment" (Edmund Wilson), a storm that "will hurl in midnight fear / and sweep lost millions to their doom" (the Carter Family). Machinery breaks down, power blacks out, the outlines of the night envelop the entire nation. The darkness, however, is not hushed in silence but vibrates with the hum of voices yet unheard: "They were silent for some time. There were no longer any voices near them but they could hear the low rustle of talk in the parts of the factory where the workers were close together, a hundred casual voices rising softly in the dark."[30]

In title after title, the books of the Depression years announce the discovery that the proletarian "dumb vacancy" is surprisingly full of sounds: Benjamin Appel's *The People Talk* (1940), Theodore Dreiser's *Harlan Miners Speak* (1933), Richard Wright's *Twelve Million Black Voices* (1941). Reportage, documentary, and interview are at the center of literary discourse. The speech of common people is recognized, collected, amplified, and reshaped by oral history and the folk revival, by the radio and the "talkies." The Federal Writers' Project collects the oral narratives of former slaves and Southern rural workers; John and Alan Lomax begin the systematic recording of American folk music for the sound archives of the Library of Congress; Constance Rourke reclaims the folk roots of national literature and character. And President Roosevelt elevates the radio fireside chat to the dignity of presidential discourse.[31]

The voice is supplemented by the body and the image as a sign of the presence of the common man. The Farm Security Administration photographers, and many others, document grassroots America, discovering that the common man can not only *be seen* (Erskine Caldwell and Margaret Bourke White's *You Have Seen Their Faces* [1937]), but can also *see*—indeed, that the common people are the only ones who retain a vision of some kind. Historic photographs—Dorothea Lange's "Migrant Mother," Arthur Rothstein's "Sharecropper Mother and Child," Margaret Bourke White's "Maiden Lane, Georgia," and countless others—focus on the eyes, on the gaze of their subjects directed beyond the frame of the picture and beyond contingent objects, in an abstract and cosmic act of vision. "They seemed to be staring at the dark"—Zora Neale Hurston's bean pickers in the hurricane—"but their eyes were watching God." Perhaps, through their eyes inured to the dark, we will also see God, and understand what is on His mind.[32]

These voices, eyes, and presences are a warning: "Gentlemen, but the people are talking," announces the radical Congressman Vito Marcantonio, "Can't you hear them?"[33] But they are also a resource. Used as the title of Ben Appel's book, Marcantonio's phrase is turned from threat to promise. John Steinbeck calls his 1938 pamphlet on migrant workers in California *Their Blood Is Strong*, as if to say that the crisis is but a transitory event that will be absorbed in the biological flow of blood and milk. The cover shows Dorothea Lange's "Okie Mother and Child," a sort of migrant Madonna of the Depression that also appears on many editions of Steinbeck's *The Grapes of Wrath.*

Also the industrial working class no longer seems a disturbing product of modernity but a new folk community, gathered around the workplace, the job traditions, the wisdom of manual work. It speaks in minimal dialogues, which allude to shared experience and knowledge, ritualizing emotions in self-control and silence. The characters of proletarian authors such as Jack Conroy or "tough-guy writers" of the James Cain school speak an "authentic Americanese" impregnated with professional jargons and colloquial vernacular, direct, salty, laconic. In the rustle of sounds rising from Cantwell's factory, one cannot tell the individual voice from that of the community and the nation.[34]

In this version of pastoral, the working class designates less the industrial present than a past rural community from which workers have been violently torn by industrialization. The conflict is no longer between the classes of industrial society but between the machine age and the pastoral ideal. The Depression is seen as the effect of the superimposition of an artificial system upon the natural integrity and simplicity of the people. Whether the characters are the independent, conservative yeomen of the Southern Agrarians or the exploited sharecroppers of the radical Left, the place is the South, the subjects are "peasants," the language is dialect.[35] Steinbeck writes in *The Grapes of Wrath:* "Listen to people a-talkin', an' purty soon I hear the way folks are feelin.' Goin' all the time. I hear'em an' feel'em; and they're beating their wings like a bird in a attic. Gonna bust their wings on a dusty winda tryin' ta get out." And:

> There in the Middle- and Southwest had lived a simple agrarian folk who had not changed with industry, who had not farmed with machines or known the power and danger of machines in private hands. They had not grown up in the paradoxes of industry. Their senses were still sharp to the ridiculousness of industrial life.
>
> And then suddenly the machines pushed them out.[36]

"The men in the fields looked up at the clouds and sniffed at them and held wet fingers up to sense the wind"; Steinbeck's Okies read nature's "writing" like Roland Barthes' primitive hunters, because they are part of it. They are links in the chain that goes from the turtle crossing the dusty road to the nomads of the Depression who cross the continent toward California; they carry in the memory of two or three generations all of the nation's history, from the expulsion of the Indians to the great Crash. They are the essence of "Manself," an Emersonian One Big Soul: "We was holy when we was one thing, an' mankind was holy when it was one thing."[37]

The expulsion of the farmers from the land, then, is not an episode in the class struggle but an aggression of the forces of inhumanity against those of humanity and nature, of the banks and the machines against the land and the people: "those creatures don't breathe air, don't eat side-meat. They breathe profits, they eat the interest on money"; "The man sitting in the iron seat did not look like a man; gloved, goggled, rubber dust over nose and mouth, he was a part of the monster." Uprooted from the earth, the defeated peasants lose their ability to read the signs of nature: "Back home we might get rain out of a wind like this," says Pa Joad, but so far from home he "can't tell" anymore.[38]

Writing and the body are battlegrounds in the struggle between the human and the inhuman. The farmers' thoughts and conversations are accompanied by the biblical gesture of drawing lines in the dust—a form of writing that is nonverbal, like the language of the body, and ephemeral, like the voice. The tractor, instead, draws permanent, straight lines on the earth , like those of print. "Got to keep the lines straight," the driver says, even if it means tearing down a house or burying a well. Tom Joad learns how to write in prison, and his only writing is buried in a grave. His father "always said what he couldn't tell a fella with his mouth wasn't worth leaning on no pencil about." To these illiterate peasants who never waste their words, writing is hard work, a pencil is like a spade. Familiar only with the writing of the Bible, they cannot conceive that words may be written easily and in vain. All writing—almanacs, novels, propaganda leaflets—is scripture, because "they wouldn't go to that trouble" otherwise. This nameless "they," like all the absent subjects of writing, can neither be traced nor questioned: "But where does it stop? Who can we shoot? . . . Maybe there's nobody to shoot. Maybe the thing isn't men at all."[39]

The absent subject of writing is related to a more general dissolution of tangible presences, including that of the body. The tractor driver buries his body underneath his mask, the rich ladies in the luxury cars cover theirs with cosmetics and fill them with pills "to make the bowels move" and "to make their sexual intercourse safe, odorless, and unproductive."[40] While these figures of modernity artificially manipulate and annihilate the body, farmers and peasants hold on to it: from diarrhoea to pregnancy, the body is a constant presence in the *The Grapes of Wrath.*

Because of their more intimate relation to the body, women can take over when men are overwhelmed by the crisis. In Steinbeck's rural world, men are *in touch* with nature, but women carry nature in them and can never be uprooted from it. The intensely, almost exclusively pregnant Rosasharn belongs to a dynasty of literary female figures who are powerful because they are ancestrally inarticulate, indifferent to everything but continuity and survival. Like Theodore Dreiser's Carrie Meeber in *Sister Carrie* or William Faulkner's Lena Grove in *Light in August,* Rosasharn is "inward," centripetal, mysteriously immune from history and language. "Woman got all her life in her arms. Man got it all in his head," Ma Joad explains: "Man, he lives in jerks . . . Woman, it's all one flow, like a stream." In women's lives, the discrete events that make up the lives of men are but "little eddies, little waterfalls" in an unterrupted flow.[41]

As power shifts from men to women, linear history fades in the circle of eternal return. The circular liquid images of rain and flood that open and close the novel outline, in Ernesto de Martino's terms, a "mythical dehistoricization of the crisis" in a reassuring cycle of life and death.[42] Connie and Rosasharn make love next to dying Grandma; later, Rosasharn, Okie mother who has lost her child, feeds a dying man with the milk destined for her unborn baby. As she restores life from death, so—Steinbeck implies—from the darkness and confusion of the crisis can we return to meaning and light. But first, like her, we must plunge out of history, into the atavistic depths below and before language. The silent exchange of gazes between mother and daughter at the end of *The Grapes of Wrath* mirrors the wise eyes of the "Migrant Mother" on the cover; and Rosasharn's final cosmic "yes" echoes the voice of Joyce's Molly Bloom.

Of course, it doesn't work. In *God's Little Acre* (1933), six years before *The Grapes of Wrath*, in the gloomiest phase of the Great Depression, Erskine Caldwell had stirred the same ingredients—the South, the family, the land, women, and machines—with very different results. Rather than a mythical reconstruction of meaning, Caldwell concocts a grotesque comedy of the elusiveness of signs. Under the land of the patriarch Ty Ty Walden lies an ungraspable signified: the gold vein for which the family, for fifteen years, has been digging holes instead of planting cotton. On the surface stands a shifting signifier: the cross that consecrates to God a portion of the land and is moved about here and there as the holes are dug underneath it, until it loses all relationship to what it ought to signify.[43]

Ty Ty claims that his search for gold is "scientific," and warns his son that he'll "never get rich" as long as he'd rather play than dig.[44] This grotesque mixture of rustic primitivism, scientist ideology, and work ethic illustrates the illusory nature of these modern myths but also suggests that it is vain to expect the peasants to save us from them. Digging, in fact, is both a figure of the search for roots and John Maynard Keynes's paradoxical recipe for bootstrapping the economy out of the Depression by digging holes and filling them up.[45] But in this case, it is the peasant family itself that destroys the land and undermines the house, without even the help of a bank or a tractor.

Alongside the gold and the cross, Caldwell deploys two other hauntingly passive signifiers: a body (Ty Ty's daughter-in-law, Griselda) and a factory (the locked-out textile mill where his son-in-law Will Thompson is employed). Griselda's resigned, ineluctable, silent sensuality puts her in the same category as Rosasharn and Lena Grove. Her body ("The first time I saw you," says Ty Ty, "I felt like getting right down there and licking something") is the unmoving motor of the Walden family, like Rosasharn's pregnant body is for the Joads. But rather than uniting the family, Griselda's body fragments it in a field of incestuous tensions: Ty Ty's "It's all in the family" is a before-the-fact parody of Ma Joad's "gotta keep the fambly together."[46]

The locked factory, closed and without electricity, is another metaphor of the Depression as "power failure." Caldwell, however, warns that turning the power back on will not suffice to set the world back in motion. At the end, Will Thompson succeeds both in possessing Griselda and turning the power back on. He believes that these actions will restore the meanings lost in the apocalypse of the crisis, nailing these two signifiers to stable signifieds. "When that power is turned on, nobody on God's earth is going to shut it off," he says; and, "I'm going to look at you [Griselda] like God intended for you to be seen."[47] But all he achieves is the breakup of the family and his own death. The way out of the crisis does not lead toward the light, toward nature and the body, but only further into chaos.

THE CRUEL RADIANCE OF WHAT IS: JAMES AGEE IN ALABAMA

In 1936, *Fortune* magazine asked Walker Evans and James Agee to prepare a "photographic and verbal record" of the life of a tenant farmer family in the South. Little did they expect that they would be handed not just another piece of reportage but a furious protest against the banality of reportage and the universal corruption of vision, a desperate attack on the limits of representation and language. It was five more years before *Let Us Now*

Praise Famous Men, "that documentary book written to end all documentary books," saw the light of print.[48]

"Actually, the effort is to recognize the stature of a portion of unimagined existence, and to contrive techniques proper to its recording, communication, analysis, and defence." In this book, Agee carries the guarantees inherent to the documentary genre—the object exists and the observer has seen it—to their extreme, ruinous consequences. No other documentary contains so much detailed information; no other documentary exposes so openly the observer's subjectivity; and no other documentary reveals so radically the impossibility of accounting for the elementary miracle of existence and experience.[49]

It is impossible, Agee insists, looking these people in the eyes, knowing that each of them is a creature like no other that ever existed and will exist, to speak of them either as representatives of a class ("sharecroppers") or as individuals ("my friends as I know you"). Both the generalizations of social science and the literary language of uniqueness and individuality are inadequate. These lives are too real to be used either for sociology or "for 'Art.' " Social sciences ignore the individuality of existence, while in literature objects and people exist "entirely through the writer." In life, however, each person derives meaning, dignity, and mystery from the fact that "he [or she] *exists*, in actual being" and "I too exist, not as a work of fiction but as a human being."[50]

The problem then is how to "contrive" ways of accounting for "the cruel radiance of what is." "The immediate instruments are two: the motionless camera, and the printed word. The governing instrument—which is also one of the centers of the subject—is individual, anti-authoritative human consciousness." The camera, like "the phonograph record and like scientific instruments," is a figure of tentative objectivity, while writing calls into question the author's own perception and expression, as well as the readers' conventions and assumptions. "Writing culture," as we know, is never a neutral action.[51]

"The text was written with reading aloud in mind," Agee explains. This, however, is not an operational prescription but an invitation to break through the impersonality of print by imagining the "authenticity" of orality and physical contact. Like Whitman, Agee insists that this is no book: "you should so far as possible forget that this is a book" but think of it as an experience, in which the reader is as "centrally involved" as the author and the subjects.

In order to explain what he means by the impact with experience, Agee uses a metaphor of sound. "Get a radio or phonograph capable of the most extreme loudness possible . . . Turn it on as loud as you can get it. Then get down on the floor and jam your ear as close into the loudspeaker as you can get it" and listen to a Beethoven or a Schubert symphony, "inside the music." "You won't hear it nicely. If it hurts you, be glad of it." The impossibility of transcribing sound is the logical metaphor for the inadequacy of representation: "But the music of what is happening is more richly scored than this; and much beyond what I can set down: I can only talk about it."[52]

Famous Men, then, explores all the formal solutions of the "oral" philosophy of composition. It is a book made of open and unclosed brackets, parentheses, and quotes; ill-fitting Chinese boxes and unmatching symmetries; episodes and sections ending with no final period; run-on periods knitted together by sequences of colons—marks of hypotaxis forced into parataxis; appeals to the readers and to the characters. It is even hard to define exactly where the book begins and ends. Walker Evans's photographs precede the title page, with no introduction or captions, as if to put us bluntly face-to-face with their subjects, again like Whitman's picture in the unsigned first edition of *Leaves of Grass*. But then, before we enter the text, we must cross pages and pages of notices, prefaces, digressions, challenges.

"I'm writing in a continuum," Agee says, stressing the nature of composition as performance. The frequent syncretisms between story and discourse, supported by the simultaneity of memory and the co-presence of all reality, call attention to the process of composition rather than to the finished text. Obsessive digressions indicate the programmatically unplanned nature of his discourse. "I shall digress," he writes, " and shall take my time over what may seem to be nonessentials." As always, Agee's digressions function both as a gesture toward total control and as total absence of control. The text expands in associative circles and contracts in closer and closer focalizations. Nothing can be omitted ("Ultimately, it is intended that this record and analysis be exhaustive"), but nothing can be finished either ("I am under no illusion that I am wringing this piece of experience dry").[53]

"All this while we are talking some: short of exact recording, which is beyond my memory, I can hardly say how." Lacking an instrument that will do for the voice what the camera does for images, Agee does not attempt exact mimesis of oral discourse. Speech appears mostly as sheer sound, mixed with other sounds, filtered by the listener's memory into free indirect discourse. "I heard her bare feet slow, the shuffling soles, and her voice, not whispering but stifled and gentle, Go to sleep now, git awn back to sleep, in that cadence of strength and sheltering comfort which anneals all fence of language and surpasses music."[54]

Transcription is at times acrobatic ("Rest vmd" for "The rest of them would"), but is always geared towards interpretation rather than imitation. Its occasional parodic excesses often designate a speech invaded by the arrogant clichés of writing, as in the landowner who objects to "nigrah education" in the name of "white syewpremcy." Perhaps Emma Woods, whose sexed presence pervades the first sections of the book, also sounds like this; but this is not how she is transcribed. Agee includes her voice in a free indirect speech that leaves her a recognizable but not overdone dialect: "we wisht you wasn't never going to go away." The interplay of this dignified speech with Agee's own embarassed formality documents less a linguistic difference than a type of relationship and recollection.[55]

The characters speak indirectly through Agee's text, but look us straight in the eye from Evans's photographs. The camera gazes openly and long upon persons and things, giving them time to gaze back, to arrange their own representation. The people in posed photographs, standing in bold relief against the houses' pine boards, in the porch's slanted light, are coauthors of the composition and leave a knowing trace of themselves in a fiction of their own making. The interaction of indirect speech and direct gaze, of text and photographs, finally indicates that the only possible objectivity is the recognition of subjectivity: Agee's in the written text; the families' in the apparent objectivity of the photographs; and the subjectivity shared and negotiated in the encounter of observer and observed, and of two different observers, in the extratextual experience in the field and in the textual experience of the book.

Camera and writing, Agee says, are the instruments of an "anti-authoritative human consciousness." Symmetric and inseparable from the observed reality, the observer's consciousness feels, however, guilty of a double betrayal toward the observed: violating the "human divinity" of existence in order to observe it, and then failing to report it adequately.

Entering those houses is both an act of love and a "spiritual burglary,"[56] a sacrament and a sacrilege. The sides of the Gudgers's house are "bone pine hung on its nails like an abandoned Christ." Agee's first meal with them repeats the induction ceremony of the Mass, and their bedroom wall is a work of art and an altar. But Agee recognizes their sacredness only after he has violated it, rummaging in the house like a "spy" in their absence. Facing the poor peasants of Lucania, the great Italian ethnologist Ernesto de Martino felt "an anxious guilt" for accepting the privilege of "not being like them," for being different from those "beings kept down at the level of beasts is spite of their yearning to become fully human."[57] But Agee's tenant farmers are already fully human. His guilt feelings do not derive so much from the awareness of inequality as from the wound he inflicts on their divine equality, as he violates it in order to know it and betrays it in order to represent it.

The only way of restoring their humanity is for the observer to give up the fiction of detached observation and openly step into the arena of representation. By exposing himself to our observation on the same plane as his subjects, Agee partly atones for the "obscene and terrifying" act of exposing the intimate lives of an "appallingly damaged group of human beings."[58] He can afford to describe the Gudgers' bed as an insult to human sexuality only because he has admitted his own sexual fantasies and recognized the unvoiced tensions in the glances, silences, touches between himself and Emma, Annie Mae, and Louise.

His own consciousness is also the only reality he knows firsthand. Since this is the filter through which he perceives and represents experience for us, by focusing on his own consciousness Agee allows us to know, if not the reality itself, at least some of the sources of distortion. This is why the book opens and closes on vocal metaphors of the failures and confusions of the observing consciousness. At the beginning he presents a sequence of broken dialogues and mutual misunderstandings between the observer and the observed; at the end he makes us listen to the mysterious nocturnal animal sounds calling after each other, of uncertain origin and meaning and suggestive not of the universal language of nature but of the "frightening joy of hearing the world talk to itself, and the grief of incommunicability."[59]

Another revelation of equality takes place in the discovery of beauty in the midst of poverty. It is a naked, classic beauty intrinsic to the materials, to the shape they receive from constant use, to the very artlessness of their makers—"irrelevant and undiscernible" for its creators but painfully revealed to those who see it from outside the circle. By claiming that the Alabama tenant farmers not only "thirst for" beauty like Wolfe's statue, but *are already* beautiful and surrounded by beauty for the mere fact that they exist, Agee daringly emancipates them from the reader's hypocritical pity.

The danger, of course, is that of turning the tenant families into "mere instances of a cosmic pattern" in which their lives are "lose their socio-material significance."[60] This risk, however, is tempered by the fact that their cosmic holiness is impervious to linguistic representation—"unimagined" and unspeakable—and that it has to be recognized and reaffirmed in the face of denial by class oppression and cultural blindness.

"Above all: in God's name don't think of it as Art," he implores. All the furies of the earth have been absorbed and silenced in the name of art, and the death blow consists in honoring them as such—using aesthetics as anesthetics, as it were—like the judge who declared that Beethoven cannot disturb the peace. The peace was not disturbed when *Famous Men* was finally published; ignored rather than attacked,[61] it became a cult book after Agee's death, harmless as a work of art—especially now that "sharecroppers"—living metaphor of the disappearance of referents in the solipsism of textuality—no longer *exist.* In his furious struggle against the limits of representation, Agee anticipated some of the ironic strategies of postmodern writing, from heterogeneity to fragmentation and pastiche. His intention, however, was not to widen the abyss between language and the material world but to drive us desperately back toward referents that, even if "unimagined," yet exist.[62]

"The one deeply exciting thing to me about Gudger is that he is actual, he is living, at this instant." The man whom Agee called "George Gudger" died in the early 1940s; his wife Annie Mae re-married and was still living in the mid-1970s. In 1976, at sixty-two, her only income a monthly Social Security check, "Emma Woods" mused on reading Agee's pages about her—"I didn't know Jimmy [Agee] felt that way.. if had known he felt the way he did . . . why, we'd have talked some more." "Now I feel kindly alone for a long time," she concludes: "I looked for something good to happen to me, like a little home, a pretty yard of flowers, and a garden, even some chickens . . . But I have give up my dream." "Margaret Ricketts" also never had "a beau, and strong land, and ladies nodding in the walks" as she dreamed. Instead, she had a retarded child from an incestuous union and lived in poverty, scorned by the polite members of her community.[63] Agee had attempted to be her equal, to share with her the scorn of educated, respectable people. Now that the polite members of society, like ourselves, are reading their book as " 'Art'," "Margaret Ricketts" is infinitely more alone.

A SONG AND A WALL: ON WOODY GUTHRIE

When the sun come shining and I was strolling
And the wheatfields waving and the dust clouds rolling
A voice was chanting and the fog was lifting
This land was made for you and me.

—Woody Guthrie, "This Land Is Your Land"

"This Land is Your Land," composed at the very end of the Depression by America's greatest oral poet, Woody Guthrie, is "an angry song" but also "one of the most beautiful songs ever written."[64] Part of its meaning lies in an articulate metaphor of the interaction between voice, writing, and social relationships:

Was a big high wall there that tried to stop me
A sign was painted, said Private Property
But on the back side it didn't say nothing[65]

The two sides of this wall, the writing of private property and the blankness of silence, are distinct and inseparable like the two sides of a sheet of paper in Saussure's famous image of signifier and signified. Woody Guthrie did not know Saussure, but he had been a painter of signs, and he knew very well that the back side of these signs of property was the silenced memory of an expropriation. And he tried to melt those walls of writing and silence into the movement of voice and light that, as in Hugh Wolfe's vision, can lift and dispel the fog. Woody Guthrie, however, does not posit an intrinsic, ahistorical "authenticity" as the source of the liberating power of the voice. Rather, he attributes the power of the voice to its dialogue and conflict with writing and property. The immaterial motion of voice and light grows into a metaphor of liberation only when it it must confront the material obstacle of a wall.

In the history of the song, however, the verse about the wall and the sign—less singable and more controversial than the rest—was partly forgotten. Besides, the optimistic climate of national antifascist unity of the war years also induced Woody Guthrie himself to underestimate, in his vision of freedom to come, the existence of the limits and obstacles symbolized by the wall. Consequently, the very meaning of the song, and the symbolism of the voice, were banalized and simplified. Once the wall of writing has been removed, the voice has no "other" against which to measure and define itself; it is reduced to a mere romantic and populist *flatus*, a presocial and classless utterance that can be shared by all. Even the builders of walls can appropriate the song, turn it into a folk national anthem of sorts—or into an advertising jingle—and appease the author with an ecological conservation award, as if he had been a lover of nature rather than a fighter in society.[66]

But Woody Guthrie knew very well that the voice detached from social conflict is ambivalent at best, and powerless always. One aspect of his struggle against the private property of language as well as of the land was the search for a voice that, like Frederick Douglass's, would appropriate writing without being silenced into it. Guthrie was an oral poet and a musician, but he was also a compulsive writer and a tempestuous typist, who struggled against both the writing of property and the property of writing:

> I have heard a storm of words in me, enough to write several hundred songs and that many books. I know that these words I hear are not my own private property.
>
> I borrowed them from you, the same as I walked through the high winds and borrowed enough air to keep me moving . .. I borrowed my life from the words of your life. I have felt your energy in me and seen mine move in you.[67]

In the years in which writers were ambiguously discovering the people's orality, the oral poet Woody Guthrie discovers literature (Robert Burns and Rabelais, of course, but also Pushkin, Whitman, and Joyce) and uses it, rejects it, changes it. In Steinbeck's *The Grapes of Wrath*, Tom Joad says that we are all part of "one big soul." When Woody Guthrie translated the novel into a ballad, he changed the phrase to: "everybody *might* be one big soul" (italics mine).[68] As Emerson knew, creation is not a finished text but an ongoing discourse. And Woody Guthrie reminds us that the unity of human kind is not a mythical past to be recovered but a future utopia to be built.

CHAPTER ELEVEN

TALKING HEADS

Who shall translate for us the language of the stones?

—Theodore Dreiser, *Sister Carrie*

At the very beginning of the century, Carrie Meeber, the "little shop-girl" of Theodore Dreiser's *Sister Carrie*, listened, helpless and inarticulate, to "the voice of the so-called inanimate." Things—clothes, jewels, commodities—speak to her "tenderly and Jesuitically for themselves" with a power of "vast persuasion." Four years later, Henry James heard things speaking all over the American scene: "Oh, come; don't look among us for what you won't, for what you shan't find . . . but only . . . the best value we allow you."[1] "The twentieth century heralded in the age of American advertising"; but there was more than an allegory of the fetishism of commodities in these sounds. In 1877 Thomas Alva Edison had spoken "Mary Had a Little Lamb" into his "talking machine"; in 1901 the creation of the Victor Talking Machine Company inaugurated the age of commercial phonography; by the end of the twenties "Another new medium—the radio—brought advertising billings to three and one-half billion dollars." At last objects and commodities had indeed learned to speak, and thus to "proclaim their right to exist independent of their relationship to people."[2]

With the advent of "secondary orality," in fact, humans are no longer exclusive depositaries of the voice. Commodity fetishism is supplemented by the synthetic voices that surround humankind with a swelling envelope of sound. These are the ancestors of Pedro Pietri's talking signs, Margaret Atwood's angelic answering services, and all the other mechanical voices of contemporary literature. In David Leavitt's story "Spouse Evening," a dog sits permanently by the radio, like the logo of His Master's Voice, "surrounded by a comforting haze of half-human noise." Meanwhile, a woman lies voiceless in a hospital bed, with a tape recorder on the night table bearing a note that says: "Hello, I'm Claire"—as if the machine had inhaled her very name—"Please turn over the tape in my tape deck."[3]

In the "word hospitals" of Gerald Vizenor's *Bearheart*, "the machines were humanized while the humans were mechanized." While machines learn to speak like humans, more and more people learn to speak like machines. If Carrie Meeber had not found a job in the shoe factory, she might have applied at the telephone company, where girls like her were hired as operators on the basis of their ability to speak in accentless and standardized intonation and phrases, as if imitating the voice of objects. Modern corporations and institutions, from banks to airlines, expect their employees to speak to the public in a formulaic, pretextualized language, as interfaces of an impersonal communication ("Thank you for using AT&T"). The formulaic quality of oral enunciation returns, in the modern world, not as an instrument to facilitate composition in performance and improvisation but as a barrier to prevent them. "Every day the same spiel from the same old man"; even the bouncers in the porn clubs on 42d Street, in Jay McInerney's *Bright Lights, Big City*, speak like machines, "The words and rhythm never vary." "I will not listen to you speaking as an institution," says Fourth Proud in *Bearheart*, to the federal officers who read out official messages with identical, unvarying tones and gestures.[4]

And yet we must not forget that the stones that speak so seductively to Carrie Meeber are jewels after all: the "persuasion" in the voice of commodities is powerful and real. Seduction, however, is accompanied by imperious command. As Paul Zumthor writes, "the voice, while it is compromised in the technological apparatus, yet benefits from the power inherent in it." The aural form of artificial voices, in fact, is supported by the power of a technology based on writing; most importantly, artificial voices are only capable of communicating in one direction. Like Edith Wharton's ghost butler, or Zora Neale Hurston's autocratic male, the machines speak but do not listen. To quote Zumthor again: "The common trait of these mediatic voices is that they do not admit of an answer."[5]

Carrie Meeber, however, does not remain inarticulate and speechless forever. She finds her voice when, working as a chorus girl, she improvises a line on stage and moves to a major speaking part. In the age of secondary orality, perhaps the expropriated voice can be recovered precisely in the secondary sphere of metadiscourse. The loss of the original voice is supplemented by voice represented, imitated, and reproduced. Carrie's improvised line, "Yours truly," is both a surrender and a signature: she has given up her real self, but her name is blazoned in advertising lights.

In the postmodern logic of late capitalism, Frederic Jameson has written, "aesthetic production today has become integrated into commodity production generally." Critical distance and the relative autonomy of aesthetics disappear, to the point that "even overtly political interventions, like those of *The Clash*, are all somehow secretly disarmed and reabsorbed by a system of which they themselves might as well be considered a part, since they can achieve no distance from it."[6] The Clash is a good example: it reminds us of how rock music, the highest form of technological orality and mass poetry in our time, is integrated into the machine—but also of how, in the process of integrating the voice, the machine is bound to incorporate some of its protest and resistance. Fewer and fewer antagonistic voices are allowed to speak from outside the system, but some of its contradictions are transferred inside. Following Carrie's hint, then, we will begin to listen for the dialectics of surrender and resistance still going on within the machine.

This chapter is concerned with aspects of the struggle for the control and definition of the voice and its technology in American mass culture, and of the tensions between hegemonic voice and popular audiences in its history—from the Puritan sermon to contemporary popular music and science fiction. A symbolic cluster links the bricolage and patchwork of traditional folk cultures with the modern forms of assembly and montage and the postmodern ones of fragment and pastiche. We will use this cluster as a map of the shifting shapes generated by the encounter between the discourse of power and of the machines on the one hand, and, on the other, the memory and vibrations of other voices that inhabit the machine and speak from within.

FROM UPLIFT TO ENTERTAINMENT.

—it is a great furnace of wrath, a wide and bottomless pit, that you are held over . . . and you have no interest in any Mediator and nothing to lay hold of to save yourself, nothing to keep off the flames of wrath, nothing of your own, nothing that you ever done, nothing that can induce God to spare you one moment.

—Jonathan Edwards, "Sinners In the Hands of an Angry God"

Down in the shadow of the penitentiary
Out by the gas of the refinery
I'm ten years burning down this road
Nowhere to run, ain't nowhere to go

—Bruce Springsteen, "Born in the U.S.A."

Let us return for a moment to Dimmesdale's sermon in *The Scarlet Letter*. The episode begins with the scene of writing: the study, lamp, books, manuscript, all indicate the relationship of the sermon as genre to writing. Voice and performance, however, soon take over: Dimmesdale rewrites the sermon in inspired, impulsive improvisation, and, when he delivers it in public, the voice becomes an independent vehicle of meaning. In this process, Hawthorne summarizes both the formal coexistence of writing and voice in the sermon and, most importantly, its historical evolution from textuality to performance, from syllogistic rationality to emotional enthusiasm, from liturgy to spectacle.

The voice is the very life of the Puritan sermon. Cotton Mather recalls that John Cotton, crossing the river from Boston to Cambridge, caught cold and lost his "clear, most audible voice." Unable to preach any longer, and unwilling to "outlive his work," Cotton slowly allowed himself to die.[7] In the Puritan tradition, however, the voice is primarily the vehicle of the text. The sermon is composed in writing and often intended for publication. It smells of the lamp and of booklore, and is constructed in carefully arranged, logical arguments. Emotion and improvisation are not banned; Mather remembers that John Wilson often preached "extempore . . . without any distinct propositions but chiefly in exhortations and admonitions." The textualized and ratiocinating form, however, remains the essence. John Cotton was, after all, both a voice and "a walking library."[8]

With the evangelical fervor that swept the land in the Great Awakening and the Great Revival, improvisation became dominant, and performance prevailed over text. Delivery was accompanied by an increasingly dramatic use of body and voice. "So many Ministers preach, not only without Book, but without Study," Charles Chauncy noted in the 1740s, "lest by previous Preparation, they should stint the spirit." Jonathan Edwards still maintained a balance between emotional intensity and theological doctrine, between sensational imagery and controlled delivery; but among his contemporaries preaching was already becoming increasingly theatrical.[9] The spirit of the Revolution, the impact of the frontier, the African-American example, the competition of mass culture, all these forces further shifted the balance from theological indoctrination to emotional release. The distance between the pulpit and the congregation was reduced. In camp-meetings and revivals, the event was as much in the collective emotions of the crowds and in their physical and musical expression as in the sermons that were preached. Indeed, the preachers' success began to be measured on their ability to excite these reactions.

The new evangelism of the early 1800s went a step further, and challenged mass culture on its own ground. "There are so many exciting subjects constantly brought before the public mind," noted Charles Grandison Finney, that the church cannot "get the public ear" without "sufficient novelty in measures." As "pulpit showmanship and verbal pyrotechnics" increased, sermons became "crowd-pleasingly theatrical," shifting the burden from argument to narrative, from logic to example. "Are there no amusements?" asked Charles Dickens, on his visit to New York: "Yes, there is a lecture room across the street . . . and there must be evening service for the ladies thrice a week, if not oftener."[10]

During his American visit, Dickens regularly took in famous preachers as a sort of tourist attraction. In Boston he visited the church of Father Edward Thompson Taylor, the seamen's preacher, admired by Emerson and praised by Whitman as the "one essential perfect orator." Both Dickens and Whitman describe Father Taylor's services in theatrical terms. Whitman likens him to the English actor Booth, while Dickens describes the pulpit "ornamented . . . with painted drapery of a lively and somewhat theatrical appearance," on which Father Taylor went back and forth rhythmically, as if on a stage or a ship's deck. Both Dickens and Whitman note Taylor's use of improvisation. Whitman remarks that "There was no sign of any MS, or reading from notes" and Dickens writes that the opening prayer was also "extemporary"—flawed with "frequent repetition" but "plain and comprehensive." According to Whitman, Father Taylor's logical arguments were also "brief and simple." His oratorical strategy, enriched by Biblical sonorities and images from life at sea, was aimed more at swaying the congregation's feelings than at awing it with eloquence and doctrine. "The mere words," Whitman writes, "seem'd altogether to disappear, and the *live feeling* advanced upon you and seiz'd you with a power before unknown."[11]

No wonder that Father Taylor should be one of the models of Melville's Father Mapple in *Moby-Dick*: "Father Mapple rose, and in a mild voice of unassuming authority ordered the scattered people to condense." The sermon's cohesive power *constitutes* the community, gathering the congregation in the communal circle of the preacher's voice. Father Mapple's voice rises from the colloquial register to "prolonged solemn tones, like the continued tolling of a bell in a ship that is foundering at sea in a fog," until it culminates in a burst of "pealing exultation and joy." As he "lines out" the hymn, in the time-honored folk fashion, even those members of the congregation who do not know or remember it are able to join in the singing, and the voices rise and swell "high above the howling of the storm." The preacher's sermon has grown into communal song: a cohesive effect that is repeated in black later, when Ahab's oratory molds the crew of the Pequod into one shout.[12]

Father Mapple's sermon is but one of the many brilliant literary representations of the folk sermon. One might also mention, among others, James Weldon Johnson's *God's Trombones*, or the sermons in William Faulkner's *The Sound and the Fury* and Zora Neale Hurston's *Jonah's Gourd Vine*. It was not Taylor's style, however, that became the norm in American preaching. Rather, what prevailed was a less imaginative and exciting, more soothing and sentimental style identified with another star of religious oratory, whose services Dickens also attended in Brooklyn—Henry Ward Beecher. Beecher's church was openly and purposely structured like a theater, with the circular platform of the pulpit in the center: "I want the audience to surround me," he said, referring to his listeners more as a theater-going public than a church congregation. Indeed, as Van Wyck Brooks writes, audiences attended Beecher's church "in the spirit in which they went to Barnum's Museum."[13]

Beecher's oratory was as alien as Taylor's from the theological rigors of Puritan preaching. His language, however, was more like a middle-class conversation than a folk epic. The sentimental tone and argument of Beecher's "middling style" of oratory provided a "soothing conciliation" to his mostly middle-class audience. Beecher combined the democratic principles of abolitionism with the spirit and practices of business enterprise, thus inaugurating a radical modernization of public discourse. "Since Beecher, and into the television age," writes Kenneth Cmiel, "the public colloquial has valued feeling over information, personality over character" and "sympathy over theology." This influence was to be felt also in political oratory, from Roosevelt's "fireside chats" to Ronald Reagan's "homiletics."[14]

The ambiguous greatness of later generations of mass preachers depends largely on their ability to combine the dramatic enthusiasm of camp-meetings and revivals with a personalized, conversational tone, an attenuated theology, and, more recently, the familiarizing yet distancing frame of the television screen. There was nothing dangerous in Billy Sunday's theology, yet his knowing use of music and the "acrobatic" theatricals of his ex-athlete performances conveyed a vivid sense of excitement: "He would leap about the platform like a tiger pouncing on an antelope, tear off his coat and hurl it into the audience, pick up a chair and smash it across the piano, crouch on the floor like a runner about to take off on a race"[15]—or like a rock musician in concert.

There is no need to go into detail to recognize in other forms of American public speech a parallel pattern of evolution from text to performance, from argument to emotion and sentiment, from "doctrine" to "sympathy," from uplift to entertainment. This is the case with the Lyceum lectures (which Dickens also listed among "entertainments") and, later, the Chautauqua Movement. In both cases, the goal was to spread knowledge and information, but they also provided occasion for entertainment and socializing, until the more spectacular themes and speakers gradually prevailed. Humorists and showmen rated over scholars and educators, and Artemus Ward and P. T. Barnum drew larger audiences than Ralph Waldo Emerson. In the open air lectures of the Chautauqua Movement, "lecturers found themselves competing with Swedish bell ringers, Scottish bagpipe players, magicians, jugglers, and trained dog acts."[16]

During and after the "golden age" of American oratory, public political speaking underwent a similar evolution. While the great orators were confined to increasingly celebrative and ritual, rather than deliberative, functions, a flaming and demagogic "stump oratory" was arising in the rural South and around the frontier. Its copious, bombastic tone and dramatic excitement were not unlike those of camp-meetings and revivals, and were to influence much Southern writing, including Faulkner's. "Life is very dull in the hill country," explained the notorious demagogue Theodore Bilbo (as late as the 1930s): "There are no movies, dances, night clubs, nothing of that sort. And even if there were, people would be too poor to pay for them. So they expect to get their entertainment from preachers and politicians."[17]

Political oratory, however, did not fail to develop its own version of Beecher's "middling style." The conversational, confidential approach of the so-called "spellbinders" dominated turn-of-the century political eloquence and culminated in Theodore Roosevelt. More concise and modern than their predecessors, these orators conversed with their audiences, in a language that came to sound increasingly like that of public relations and advertising.[18]

The timing and rhythm of modern oratory patterned themselves more and more upon that of entertainment and advertising. "Ours is an age of public speakers," the folklorist Richard Dorson notes, "and all of them, college presidents or ministers or politicians or conference leaders or professors rely on the apt anecdote," on "brief pointed stories, the emblem of our high-tempoed culture." Market research indicates that "adult Americans are not good listeners," and are "conditioned to enjoy being entertained rather than to weigh issues in a public debate."[19] The public figure's "sound bite" is modeled after the comedian's "one-liner." As Doc said in *Back to the Future*, no wonder the president was an actor.

Ronald Reagan's road from Hollywood to the White House, however, was also trod in the opposite direction. While religious, educational, and political discourse turned to entertainment, entertainers were turning to preaching and education. "I have always preached," declared the most successful stage humorist of the nineteenth century, Mark Twain: "If the humor came of its own accord and uninvited, I have allowed it a place in my sermon, but I was not writing the sermon for the sake of the humor."[20] The audience of the "literary comedians" of Mark Twain's generation wanted to be entertained rather than informed and uplifted; they also found less and less information and uplift in the "serious" genres of public discourse. Indeed, the parody of political and religious oratory was a popular device of stage comedians. Again, Melville recognized and used this fact, in Fleece's comic yet serious sermon to the sharks in *Moby-Dick*, one of his most biting attacks on conventional morality.

As they denounced the shallowness of official discourse, showmen and entertainers, in fact, increasingly took upon themselves the task of preaching to their audiences. Lenny Bruce, the prototypical modern standup comedian, was described as "really a wayward evangelist," a "shaman," "a moralist, a preacher." And one would not hesitate to apply some of the same terms to the work of Woody Allen.[21]

On November 6, 1988, at the Los Angeles Sports Arena, Prince "stepped to the mike and began preaching forcefully," as if shifting his concert's erotic charge to another plane. "You know, God isn't going to come down out of the sky and make things right for you. . . . Now, put your hand over your heart. Look inside yourself. God is in there." Then, "softly playing a guitar figure of almost unbearable beauty," Prince paused and said: "take your hand away. Let him out." And, whispering: "Cross the line, Los Angeles, cross the line."[22]

The line is crossed, erased, drawn, and crossed again in the blues, in rock and roll, in country music—that is, in all the forms of musical entertainment that have sprung from the dramatic religion and the excessive politics of the rural South, black and white. The sense of sin, removed from the sentimental decor of respectable churches and from the vulgarity of the electronic church, still haunts America's grassroots music, in the form of Robert Johnson's "hellhounds," or in white country music's dilemma of "beer-drinking Christians" caught "halfway from heaven and halfway from hell."[23] Bluesmen and preachers exchange roles frequently in African-American culture, but a great deal of rock and roll's self-destructive fury and transgression is rooted in the holiness and Pentecostal background of its founders, from Elvis Presley to Jerry Lee Lewis. If rock and roll and fundamentalist preaching are the essential radio sounds of contemporary America, this is because they are the only forms that have managed to combine the power of traditional orality with that of the "secondary" orality of the electronic age.[24]

At the Sun Studios at Memphis, Tennessee, in 1957, Jerry Lee Lewis is getting ready to record what will become his greatest hit, "Great Balls of Fire." But Lewis has attended a Baptist seminary, and recognizes in the mildly obscene double-entendre a Biblical metaphor, God's gift of the voice to His prophets. "Great Godamighty, great balls of fire!" he shouts. "It says, WAKE MAN! To the Joy of God! Only! But when it comes to *worldly music*—that's rock and roll . . . I have the devil in me! . . . JESUS! Heal this man!" Only after he is convinced that rock and roll is also part of God's gift of the voice does Jerry Lee resume his furious singing and playing, voicing God's gift of word in the devil's music.[25]

CREATION AND THE RECORD: RHETORICS OF THE VOICE IN INDUSTRIAL MUSIC

Yet hence arises a grave mischief. The sacredness which attaches to the act of creation . . . is transferred to the record.

Ralph Waldo Emerson, "The American Scholar"

During the performance of "Silver and Gold" at Denver's Temple Stadium (included live in *Rattle and Hum*), Bono, vocalist of the Irish group U2, interrupts his singing to speak to the audience: "This song was written in a hotel room in New York City, at the time that our friend Little Steven was putting together a record against apartheid." In this episode, three different technologies of the word are combined: the initial reference to writing, the "secondary orality" of the recording, and the memory of the oral tradition (Bono's phrase is a direct quote from Woody Guthrie). The sound shape of contemporary orality summarizes and incorporates the whole technological history of the word.[26]

Later, however, still in *Rattle and Hum*, a voice asks Bono about "the writing of the new album"; records are a key expression of the "aural" environment in the electronic age, but they are still perceived, under many aspects, as a form of *writing*. Walter J. Ong and Eric Havelock have correctly described the recorded voice as a modern form of orality. The electronic age, they argue, once again puts sound and hearing, rather than sight and writing, at the center of the stage.[27] If, however, we shift our attention from the sensory axis to the relationship of the word to time and matter, we recognize that the recorded word, a permanent, reproducible textualization of sound, is also a form of "writing." The combination of a sensory axis based on sound and a temporal axis based on textuality is the basis of the oxymoronic balance of media: writing the voice (phono*graphy*), capturing motion (cinemato*graphy*).

In fact, Bono's phrase also includes a further modality: montage. While he was *writing* in his hotel room, his friend Little Steven Van Zandt was *putting together* a record. Secondary orality is no longer an individual utterance, because the shift from the "act of creation" to the "record" also implies a decentralization of the creative process. The final product is the result of the combined efforts of many people, the assembly and montage of different talents and technologies, which only come together in the finished product. Under many aspects, this creative process recalls the combinatory bricolage of folklore and oral tradition, in which the individual voices become part of a social patchwork of discourse.

In Emerson's aphorism, the "record" is the after-the-fact transcription of an antecedent performance. The history of sound recording, however, is that of an evolution from the documentation of actual performances to the creation of sounds and images that only exist on the record. In the post-Beatles era, records are less the *reproduction* of a musical performance in real time than "studio events" made possible by technology (even though they may include also "bits of actual events").[28]

This process goes much farther than the absorption of creation into the record: the record *is* the creation. The event does not exist before the recording and cannot be reproduced outside of it. When the Beatles began to experiment with new studio techniques, in fact, they also put an end to their public appearances. The "presence" of the voice is transferred from the live performance to the sound writing of the record. In a way, phonography repeats the evolution of writing, from a technique to preserve speech to a distinct modality of linguistic creation and expression.

But hence arises another mischief. The more rock technology maximizes the separation between performance and recording, the more rock ideology insists on the value of presence, involvement, spontaneity, irreproducibility.[29] These values are actualized in rituals of authenticity and participation at concerts, tours, and "in person" appearances—which are in turn reproduced as "live" recordings, as is the case with U2's *Rattle and Hum*. Here, recording again functions as the document of an event's improvisational, interactive, and dialogic dimension. The audience's audible voice plays the part of the implied narratee in literature, and for much the same reasons. But, just as even the most "dialogic" novel is not a dialogue, so an "in concert" recording is not a concert.

A further step in the dialectics of recording, creation, and performance develops in the practice of generations that have grown up directly in the autonomy of recording, and are therefore immune from the nostalgia (and the memory) of the "real" event before the record. In genres such as "dub" or "scratch," the sound materialized on the record is manipulated and becomes the raw material of new performances that take place not before but after the recording. The advent of the sampler temporarily closes the circle. It is now possible to repeat "live" the "artificial event" created in the recording studio. From the record as document of the performance, we arrive at the performance as actualization of the record. "I never dreamed of doing '2000 Light Years from Home' on stage," says Keith Richards of the Rolling Stones: "It was a studio job with backward tapes and all kinds of effects. But now you can do that in concert because of today's technology."[30]

At the sources of traditional orality stand, as Gerald Vizenor reminds us, "the shamans who hummed and rattled."[31] In U2's *Rattle and Hum*, at the other end of the history of the voice, the rattle represents both the percussive beginning of music (ethnic instrument, children's musical toy), a threatening animal voice (the rattlesnake), and a deathly mechanical sound (the rattle of the machine gun). The hum, in turn, is both Whitman's continuous, prearticulate, organic voice and the mechanical noise of oncoming bomber planes (and of the machines in Melville's "Tartarus of Maids"). Beginning and end, birth and death, machine and nature, struggle over the meaning and possession of sound in the syncretic patchwork bricolage of folk orality and electronic mass culture that is rock and roll.

PICKING UP THE PIECES; QUILTMAKING AND POSTMODERNISM: BETWEEN ALICE WALKER, DOLLY PARTON, AND OTHERS

America is not a blanket, woven from one thread, one color, one cloth. When I was in South Carolina, and Momma couldn't afford a blanket, she didn't complain and we didn't freeze. Instead she took pieces of old cloth—patches—wool, silk, gabardine, crockersack—only patches, barely good enough to shine your shoes with. But they didn't stay that way very long. With sturdy hands and strong cord, she sewed them together into a quilt, a thing of power, beauty and culture. Now we must build a quilt together . . .

Jesse Jackson, "A Call to Common Ground"

"After dinner Dee (Wangero) went to the trunk at the foot of my bed and started rifling through it. Maggie hung back in the kitchen over the dishpan. Out came Wangero with two quilts." This is a story by Alice Walker, called "Everyday Use."[32] Dee (Wangero) is an educated black girl from the rural South, who has been up North, has taken an African name, and is now coming home to claim her roots incorporated in the old patchwork quilts.

> They had been pieced by Grandma Dee and then Big Dee and me had hung them on the quilt frames on the front porch and quilted them. One was in the Lone Star pattern. The other was Walk Around the Mountain. In both of them were scraps of dresses Grandma Dee had worn fifty and more years ago. Bits and pieces of Grandpa Jarrell's Paisley shirts. And one teeny faded blue piece, about the size of a penny matchbox, that was from Great Grandpa Ezra's uniform that he wore in the Civil War.[33]

The quilt, a patchwork of leftover, discarded pieces, is a symbol of folk culture and women's art: a useful thing of beauty, created out of fragments sewn into new, imaginative patterns. Dee, however, has learned from urban culture to separate the aesthetic from the useful. She does not intend to use the quilts to keep herself warm, she plans to hang them up to decorate her apartment. When her mother explains that she plans to give them to Dee's homey sister when she marries, Dee is outraged: "You just don't understand . . . your heritage," she tells them. Her sister, she insists, would "probably be backward enough to put them to everyday use."

Folk culture has always been a homemade heritage, torn to pieces and then pieced back together again for everyday use. In Antonio Gramsci's classic definition, folklore is "an undigested conglomeration of fragments of all the views of the world and of life which have succeeded one another in history. For most of them, indeed, only in folklore do we find the mutilated and contaminated remnants."[34] Beyond the surface of Gramsci's negative connotations, his image of folklore as cultural patchwork carries, like Alice Walker's old quilt, the memory of the violent fragmentation to which folk cultures have been subjected. What Gramsci neglects, and Walker recognizes, is that folk cultures, and the cultures of the oppressed in general, are also the product of resistance to this process, and of the constant effort to put the pieces back together. As the Chickasaw poet Linda Hogan says, "we make art out of our loss," by picking up, like Leslie Silko's Betonie, "the leftover things the whites didn't want" or, like Toni Morrison's Sethe, by making a wedding dress out of discarded or stolen old rags and curtains.[35]

In *Beloved*, the image of the quilt again evokes the painful experience of fragmentation and the painstaking work of healing. In the last scene, Sethe is lying on a quilt, and Paul D. washes her broken body one piece at a time. While she feels that she is about to fly to pieces and wonders "would the parts hold?," he muses: "She gathers me, man. The pieces I are she gather them and give them back to me all in the right order." This could also be a self-reflexive description of *Beloved* itself, or of Faulkner's *Absalom, Absalom!*: texts made of "rag-tags and bob-ends of old tales and talking," fragmented and pieced together in the associative processes of dialogue and recollection, quilting together the archaic roots of folk memory and contemporary literary experiment.[36]

In our time, the folk experience of fragmentation as pain and violence meets the postmodern vision of fragmentation as freedom, possibility, and multiplicity. Gramsci implicitly contrasted folklore's "undigested conglomerate" to the apparent consistency and rationality of modern cultures, but postmodern thought increasingly views this rationality and consistency as authoritarian delusion and violence. Thus the fragmentation that folk cultures suffer as a token of oppression and disruption acquires, in the postmodern imagination, the connotations of euphoric liberation. While folk cultures adapt to an aesthetic of repetition, second-hand and hand-me-down, because they have no access to original, permanent materials, postmodernism extols reuse, intertextuality, quotation, parody, and repetition because it does not believe that originals exist at all. The quilt, as Lance Olsen has noted, combines both meanings. It is the essence of folk tradition, "emblematic of community, of shared histories and myths and projects," and the essence of postmodernism, "of cultural fracture and pastiche, of personal fragmentation and disorientation."[37]

In *Mumbo Jumbo*, Ishmael Reed stitches together the folk and the postmodern implications of quilt and patchwork in the ambiguous, trickster-hustler character of Abdul. "I had no systematic way of learning," says Abdul, "but proceeded like a quilt maker, a patch of knowledge here a patch there but lovingly knitted." Like Frederick Douglass or Malcolm X, he "would hungrily devour the intellectual scraps and leftovers of the learned," to create "a "Griffin politics," a "chimerical art" suited for "eclectic" American reality: "a little bit of jive talk and a little bit of North Africa, a fez-wearing mulatto in a pinstriped suit."[38]

The mulatto, and mixed-blood characters in general, are in fact another literary figure of a patchwork of identities. Its Native American equivalent—the "breed" or the "crossblood"—is, according to Gerald Vizenor, the perfect trickster, living "on the seam," or, in Paula Gunn Allen's words, a "multicultural event" who also knows "the terrible pain of being a bridge."[39] The double perspective of possibility and pain, of postmodern multiplicity and ancient, violent fragmentation is often represented in a splitting of point of view, somewhat parallel to the opposition between the postmodern fascination with surfaces and the folk obsession with experience. "You mixed every which way, ain't you?," her husband tells the heroine in Gayl Jones's *Corregidora*: "You seem like you got a little bit of everything in you"; to which she answers, resentfully: "I didn't put it there."[40] The same dual perspective, between how it looks from outside and how it feels from inside, is enounced in an exchange between James Welch's Jim Loney and his white girlfriend: " 'Oh, you're so lucky to have two sets of ancestors. Just think, you can be Indian one day and white the next. Whichever suits you' . . . Loney thought, It would be nice to think that, but it would be nicer to be one or the other all the time."[41]

Mass culture is the crossroads where the rebellious and arrogant imagination that tears the straightjacket of conventional rationality and identities to pieces meets the humble and patient imagination that picks up the pieces in order to make a quilt or a coat for everyday use. "I recall a box of rags that someone gave us," sings Dolly Parton, unassuming and arrogant voice of popular culture, "and how my mama put those rags to use." Deeply rooted in its rural origins but fully at home in the glittering world of Nashville, country music is an ideal patchwork of modernized tradition and traditionalist modernity. Dolly Parton's "Coat of Many Colors," in fact, is both an autobiographical story of her Appalachian mountain roots and a metaphorical success story patterned on the biblical tale of Joseph and his many-colored garment. The coat that her mother, like Jesse Jackson's, sews together out of scraps and leftovers, is both a mawkish symbol of rural poverty and family love and a triumphant sign of election and success.[42]

"Although we had no money," sings Dolly Parton, " I was rich as I could be," because "one is only poor, only if they chose to be." Calvinism and the frontier ideology teach that poverty is neither a depository of moral values nor a hotbed of social rebellion (as Catholic or Socialist traditions would have it), but rather the consequence of some moral failure or weakness in the poor themselves. The "culture of poverty" is supposed to internalize "a strong feeling of marginality, of helplessness, of dependence and of inferiority"; and Dolly Parton, vulgar pop star and bitter

Appalachian voice, refuses to have anything to do with it, denying that she has ever been, in that sense, "poor."[43]

This preoccupation is not exclusive to the sentimental world of pop music. The poet Nikki Giovanni also warns her (white) critics not to talk about her "unhappy youth," because "Black love is black wealth" ("We were poor, but we had love," the Appalachian country singer Loretta Lynn would say), and "all the while I was quite happy." Both Dolly Parton and Nikki Giovanni respond to poverty by claiming the beauty of the everyday world of their poor, happy childhoods. The bricolage of folk culture, then, implies not only re-use, but also the aesthetic transformation that James Agee recognized in Alabama tenant homes. Dolly Parton's rags are charity, but it is her mother's folk and feminine culture that remakes them into a new, meaningful whole. Their many colors are a symbol of hope and life, like Alice Walker's color purple, the orange spots in Sethe's quilt, and Jesse Jackson's rainbow. Rightly and proudly, Emily Dickinson called her art the "humblest patchwork."[44]

Beauty, however, compensates psychological poverty but does not change material poverty. Refusing to *feel* poor may be a way of *staying* poor. The secret "endurance" that allows the poor and the outcast to bear their fate in pride and dignity—and do nothing to change it—is a theme dear both to country music and to William Faulkner.[45] In fact, if poverty is a personal, psychological matter, redemption is also personal and individual. "Coat of Many Colors" praises the quilt's collective culture, but—as Parton's other hit "Wildflower" makes clear—does so in order to escape from it.

Which brings back the original meaning of Joseph's coat as a symbol of election. Joseph recognizes as his brothers those who denied him, but he alone will become a mighty man in the kingdom of Egypt. "If you are ashamed of me," sings the Carter Family, "you ought not to be / If too much fault you find / You'll sure be left behind / when I'm sailing through the air." Dolly

Parton's classmates laugh at her patched-up rags, and she leaves them behind as she sails (on the wings of their shared culture) through the skies of success.[46]

ONE PIECE AT A TIME: JOHNNY CASH AND BRUCE SPRINGSTEEN ON THE ASSEMBLY LINE

I got a sixty-nine Chevy with a 3–96
Fuel head and a Hurst on the floor . . .
Me and my partner Sonny
Built it straight out of scratch

—Bruce Springsteen, "Racing in the Street"

The hot rod is to urban, male, youth culture what the quilt is to rural, female culture: a new idiosyncratic expressive whole created out of second-hand fragments and spare parts, by means of the shared knowledge of everyday labor. "One Piece at a Time," a 1976 Johnny Cash recording, tells the story of a Kentucky migrant who works on the Cadillac assembly line in Detroit and dreams of having a Cadillac of his own. For twenty years he smuggles parts out of the factory in his lunch box, but when at last he tries to assemble them he realizes that they don't fit: the '75 engine won't go with the '53 transmission, one tail fin is missing, and so on. But when he finally manages to put the parts together, he finds himself the proud owner of a Cadillac of many colors, an absolutely unique 1949, 1950, 1951, 1952 . . . model.[47] In this way, Johnny Cash transfers the memory of quilt making from folklore to industrial culture, implicitly changing its meaning. Appropriating automobile parts, in fact, is not so much a way of affirming one's roots as of claiming citizenship in the world of mass-manufactured machines and desires.

Indeed, while Dolly Parton's rags are a gift, the parts of Johnny Cash's Cadillac are stolen. The industrial environment does not allow workers the independent time and space available in rural society. The only way for industrial workers to piece back together toil and pleasure, work and expression, is to steal the time, knowledge, and materials they need—in the same way as Frederick Douglass or Rebecca Harding Davis's Hugh Wolfe. "I'd never consider myself a thief," pleads Johnny Cash, because "G. M. wouldn't miss just one little piece." In country music, working-class culture appears as a tricksterlike subculture of margins and interstices that survives thanks to its invisibility. As we move into Bruce Springsteen's working-class rock-and-roll world, however, these safe interstices are no longer available. Every action is conflict, every working-class property is theft: "I built that Challenger all by myself / But I needed money and so I stole."[48]

This song is called "The Promise." Like Johnny Cash's Cadillac (and Ellison's Dobbs hats), Springsteen's Challenger is the embodiment of a mass dream, of the elusive promise of the figures flitting on the drive-in screen. It is the "runaway American dream"[49] that can only be attained by violating the rules of reality, and (again, like Hugh Wolfe's) leads to jail.

Put together on the assembly line, the automobile is also a hybrid montage of put-together images: an assembly of promise and disappointment, everyday life and dreams, hope and defeat. "Working all day in my daddy's garage / Driving all night, chasing some mirage": the automobile is both day and night, work and evasion, the family of "descent" and the couple of "consent," the dead-end repetition of the hereditary "working life" and the individually unique, personal liberation. Like Huckleberry Finn, whose marginal point of view eludes the distinction between the passenger's aesthetic perception and the pilot's technical experience of the river, Springsteen's proletarian bricoleurs avoid the incompatibility between Gatsby's bodywork and the Joads' engine. The nocturnal "suicide machine" with which he runs through "mansions of glory" is perhaps the same "ramrod" he pieced together ("a roadrunner engine in a '32 Ford") working by day in his daddy's garage.[50]

"My dad, he sweats the same job from morning to morn, / Me, I walk home on the same dirty streets where I was born"; but "the day my number comes in, I ain't ever gonna ride in no used car no more." "Well, it ain't no secret, I've been around a time or two. / Well, I don't know baby, maybe you've been around too": Bruce Springsteen tells stories of second-hand cars and second-hand lives, who refuse to accept second-class status. His characters piece together their "Spare Parts and Broken Hearts" and jump-start their lives again, with no illusions ("Well 'round here baby, / I learned you get what you can get") and no surrender: "There's another dance / All you've got to do is say yes." This is what Springsteen's America, the America of immigrants and refugees, could or ought to be: another chance for lives already lived and discarded elsewhere. "Another dance"—this time, perhaps, with "a different drummer."[51]

MACHINE VOICES: ISAAC ASIMOV AND THE ORALITY OF ROBOTS

Can't you speak, you monstrosity?"
"I can speak," came the ready answer.

Isaac Asimov, "Liar!"

The literature of the industrial age begins with a hybrid figure of patchwork and assembly, a metaphor for the modern nightmares of the forced fragmentation of the working class and the failure of hegemonic recomposition: Frankenstein's monster. More than a century goes by before Isaac Asimov's democratic, technological optimism exorcises the "Frankenstein complex" by assembling a harmless mechanical monster whose First Law is the safety and well-being of its creators and masters: the robot.[52]

Asimov notes that, while Frankenstein's monster is "assembled by a student of anatomy," the robot is "designed by human engineers."[53] The shift from biology to engineering replaces the anarchic magma of living matter with the discrete rationality of machinery. The robot, however, shares a disturbing feature with Frankenstein's monster: it speaks. All the stories included in Asimov's *I, Robot* include descriptions of robotic voices, a metonymy of both the imagined technological evolution and the literary humanization of the machine. *I, Robot* can be seen as the composite *Bildungsroman* about a machine that learns to say "I." The robot's *Bildung* is the history of synthetic orality.

In the first story, "Robbie," the robot cannot yet speak but can trace alphabetic lines in the air (halfway between Chillingworth's theorems and Vonnegut's ghost narrator). The same story, however, includes the first appearance of a "Talking Robot," endowed with a syllabic staccato and a "booming mechanically timbred voice" with no "accent and intonation." The second generation still sounds "harsh, squawking," but the next batch is already capable of intonation, and in the following one the machine has learned to use the "cold timbre inseparable from a metallic diaphragm" as an expressive tool. Then, a new, improved diaphragm eliminates the "metallic flatness" by introducing overtones. Robots gradually learn to laugh, to scream, and to lie. The highest achievement, however, is the ability to "mumble inarticulately," which signals that the machine has evolved from the mechanical staccato to the continuum of inarticulation which Whitman and Poe's identified as the prerogative of living matter.[54] At this point, robotic voices can no longer be distinguished from human ones, and the final stories, which feature a robot "passing" for human, take the voice for granted.

The robotic cycle is, then, an ambiguous version of conquered speech as emancipation and of stolen speech as expropriation.

Since the very first story, the robot is variously associated with workers, blacks, women, animals. Ambiguously, it *stands for* all these subjects excluded from social discourse. It *represents* them, and the evolution of its speech is a metaphor of emancipation; it *replaces* them, and silences them as it learns to speak.

Early robotic voices sounded "like that of a medieval phonograph": the "Talking Robot" is also an extension of the Victor Talking Machine. But in the robot the *reproduction* of the human voice becomes its *imitation* and *substitution*. As "Robbie" listens in silence to the little girl's stories, he is probably storing them in his positronic memory toward the day when he will have the voice to tell them to her (in the same decade, David Riesman described mass media as "the new storytellers"). The reversal of the roles of narrator and narratee is sanctioned by the last story of the book, "Evidence." A scientist, who has lost his face and voice in an accident, builds a robot double of himself, which continues his career and becomes world legislator and ruler. In this science-fiction version of Poe's "William Wilson," once again the controller is voiceless and the voice of the entity that ought to be controlled becomes "law." The machines' control over the humans will be benevolent and rational, yet this is a surprising ending for a saga that started out to prove that humans could control the machines.

Ultimately the one mechanically toneless voice left is that of a human being, the robot psychologist Susan Calvin; once again, machines are humanized and humans mechanized. In fact, this process extends from the voice to the body. In Asimov's *The Bicentennial Man* (1976), humans acquire mechanical prostheses while robots are integrated with biological implants. The line between the organic and the inorganic is blurred in a continuous patchwork of heterogeneous parts.

Ostensibly this is a progressive metaphor for race integration, a general figure of the internalization of difference and the overcoming of barriers, including those between the biological and the mechanical, the human and the nonhuman. Robots are Asimov's often transparent metaphor for blacks, and the cyborg is a mulatto of sorts, a patchwork figure halfway between quilt and robot. Yet something disturbing remains: if Asimov's talking robot alludes to black integration, Ishmael Reed's "Talking Android" represents the "integrated" black as robot, the metaphor of a subordinate and manipulated identity. Behind both images, stands Philip K. Dick's *Do Androids Dream of Electric Sheep?*, in which the blurring of the threshold between humans and machines is an icon of metropolitan ambiguity and displacement. The first, disturbing failure that betrays the "electric sheep" who pass for organic is the breaking of the voice tape.[55]

TALKING HEADS: CYBERPUNK SF AND ITS PREDECESSORS

> So the Wizard unfastened his head.
>
> L. Frank Baum, *The Wizard of Oz*

> —he was in Singapore an hour after the explosion. Most of him, anyway . . . It took the Dutchman and his team three months to put Turner together again. They cloned a square meter of skin for him, grew it on slabs of collagen and shark-cartilage polysaccharides. They bought eyes and genitals on the open market. The eyes were green.
>
> William Gibson, *Count Zero*

William Gibson's "cyberpunk" novel, *Count Zero*, opens with the physical equivalent of Sethe's psychological experience in *Beloved*. Blown to pieces by a bomb, Turner is precariously put together again into an "angular patchwork." Later, like Sethe, he too is helped by love to rediscover "the unity of his body"—if only to go on to new fragmentations.

Gibson's postmodern universe is another stage in a long history. In America's most classic children's story, Frank L. Baum's *The Wizard of Oz*, written in the era between Frankenstein's monster and Asimov's robot, the Tin Woodsman loses his body one piece at a time and replaces it with metal parts like a precyborg of sorts. The Oz saga is tightly woven into the imagination of the age of mass industrial production, and it pullulates with figures of organic and inorganic mixtures: the Wheelers, half animals and half automobiles; Princess Langwidere, with her closetful of replaceable heads; Tiktok the talking Machine Man; a garrulous walking gramophone; and, of course, The Patchwork Girl, made out of an old quilt.[56] The Wizard of Oz, then, offers to children and to the age of the assembly line, steel, and early phonography, what Asimov's robots supply to an optimistic mass audience in the age of automation, aluminum, and high fidelity—and what William Gibson offers to disenchanted postmodern readers in the age of computer electronics, biotechnology, the sampler, and the synthetic voice: a glimpse beyond the boundary between the "natural" and the "artificial," life and nonlife, hand/brain and tool, the spoken word and its reproduction.

Gibson's world is filled with figures of assembly and hybridization between organic tissues, electronic implants, bio-mechanical prostheses, and direct plugs between the brain and computers that give access to fantastic virtual worlds. But these high-tech figures of patchwork are accompanied, in all of Gibson's books, by references to old-fashioned, archaic quilts. Characters wear quilted clothes and blankets, landscapes and art objects are patterned in "crazy-quilt" and "patchwork" style. The quilt reinforces the cyborg's image of fragmentation, but also expresses an underlying desire for unity. This double perspective is evident in the story "New Rose Hotel" in *Burning Chrome*. On the one hand, the quilt evokes community, tradition, and warmth ("all the soft weight of Europe pulled over us like a quilt"); on the other, it suggests fragmentation, fiction, and displacement (characters "shuffle" through and combine versions of their past like quilt pieces: "He'd lay the pieces out in different patterns, rearrange them, wait for a picture to form").[57]

Gibson has defined science-fiction writers as "folk poets of industrial society." The "folklore of console jockeys" and that of traditional orality—myths, legends, barroom tales, gossip, rumor—saturate his high-tech world.[58] Syncretic folk metropolitan cultures—voodoo, rasta—bridge the gap between the archaic and the postmodern. The quilt, then, may be Gibson's way of connecting his technological patchworks of "meat," hardware, and software to their traditional roots in the collective imagination.

By lowering the threshold between "natural" and "artificial" intelligence, Gibson creates a world of exhilaratingly expanded and vulnerably formless consciousness, boundless and defenseless. Bobby Newmark in *Count Zero* explores the exciting new worlds of cyberspace, but cyberspace, in turn, penetrates his mind and almost fries his brain. Simulated stimuli and brain sockets expand the mind at the price of blurring its outlines; the same gesture offers boundless power and boundless subjection. And sometimes the removed outer boundaries of the mind do not disappear but merely shift inside, as inner fragmentation. Both Angie (*Mona Lisa Overdrive*) and "Johnny Mnemonic" have no access to areas in their brains because they have been rented for the storage of other people's data.

Gibson thus rehearses the polarity between the ecstasy of possibility and the agony of formlessness and split identity that accompanies, throughout American literature, the expansion of democracy, of technology, of America itself. In his work, we again find the familiar constellation of voice, ghost, and headlessness that runs from Washington Irving's headless horseman to *Beloved*. "The ghost was her father's parting gift" are the first words in *Mona Lisa Overdrive*, a novel haunted by all sorts of bodiless minds and voices (the word *ghost* occurs no less than four times in the first page: "There were ghosts beyond the window, too, ghosts in the stratosphere of Europe's winter").

The most important source of ghosts is the computer, with its power to replicate intelligences, emit disembodied voices, and simulate immaterial apparitions, visions, and holograms. Computers create "constructs," synthetic personalities who obliterate the line between life and death, in ordinary repetitions of the strange case of M. Valdemar. For instance, Kumiko's father worships "ghosts" who are "the recorded personalities of former executives, corporate directors" in a new form of the Japanese cult of ancestors.[59]

The state has vanished as completely in Gibson's world as the monarchy has in Irving's. Therefore, he also represents as "ghosts" the new ungraspable sources of power: the pervasive, immortal, impersonal multinational corporations that have no more "head" and center than Baudelaire's America. But they do have brains—*ghost* brains, because the ultimate ghost is the computer itself (the first character who speaks of computers as "ghosts" is the rasta pilot in *Neuromancer*, a member of one of those syncretic cults who have no problems with robots, computers, and virtual worlds because they have always been familiar with ghosts, zombies, and afterlives). The ultimate computer, the "sylicon core" of *Neuromancer*, is a severed talking head: "a head, an intricately worked and cloisonné over platinum, studded with seedpearl and lapis . . . The thing was a computer terminal, he said. It could talk. And not in a synth-voice, but with a beautiful arrangement of gears and miniature organ pipes."[60]

The paradigm of ghosts and quilts melts into the figures of the voice, beheading, and bricolage. The figure that seems to summarize all the history and images of fragmentation and precarious, uncanny recomposition is the "Judge" in *Mona Lisa Overdrive*. A headless, homemade creature built from scratch, the

Judge is made of automobile parts like a hot rod, functions like a robot, and looks like a quilt: "Nearly four meters tall, half as broad at the shoulders, headless, the Judge stood trembling, in his patchwork carapace."[61]

The boy who built the "Judge" represented in it the impersonal powers of the law that punished his transgressions by erasing his memory. As in Hawthorne's "Custom House," headlessness designates not only the missing yet powerful identity and authority of the state but also the individual's missing self. Beheading is a figure of the radical separation of mind and body that takes place in a virtual universe. In *Neuromancer*'s technological brothels, women are transformed into "puppets" by detaching their bodies from their minds and sensory systems—just as, in a wholly different register, the narrator's wife in Jay McInerney's *Bright Lights Big City* is turned into a mindless mannikin by the fashion industry, with a "Space for Rent" sign on her forehead.[62] In another story, Johnny Mnemonic rents out brain space for data that he carries proudly and faithfully until his clients see it fit to extract them. In these mindless bodies and bodiless brains, Washington Irving's ghostly horseman finds not only his missing head but also several interchangeable ones.

And yet: who *is* Johnny Mnemonic? And, as Gore Vidal asks, is Princess Langwidere still herself when she puts on a new head?[63] When the Tin Woodsman encounters his original head, the new tin head and the old flesh and bone one hardly recognize each other, and are not interested anyway. Once cut off, the head remains just that—cut off.

The platinum computer in *Neuromancer* is routinely referred to as a "talking head." Angie is described as "a talking head . . . Like a puppet" when she appears on the simstim circuit (the sensory stimulation system that replaces television in Gibson's world). Bodiless talking heads with decentered, directionless, fragmented voices are at the cores of power in Asimov's robot world, in

The Wizard of Oz, and in the artificial planets of Gibson's universe: the musical platinum head stands in the sanctum of the Tessier-Ashpool clan; the Wizard is "an enormous Head, without body to support it or any arms or legs whatever"; and Asimov's ultimate computer, "The Brain," is a sphere hanging in the middle of a room. A character from Norman Rush's *Mating* rounds up the paradigm and clinches the metphor by designating the newly elected Ronald Reagan as "The Brazen Head," after "the hollowed metal idols" worshipped in Babylonia,"which were equipped with speaking tubes leading down into the bowels of the temple whence the priests would make the idol speak."[64]

Like the Brazen Head, all of these cut-off heads of power have a voice: the platinum head talks like music, the Wizard is a ventriloquist, the Brain speaks through a network of cables and peripherals. Each is related to power in a different form: the Wizard is a "humbug" supported by cheap vaudeville tricks; Gibson's talking head is the mouthpiece of the invisible economic power of a many-headed economic empire; Asimov's Brain controls all the power because it holds all the information; and Ronald Reagan, of course, is a movie actor, a talking head on TV, and a real president. Power as humbug, power as tool, power as reality—all have the same shape and sound: that of the bodiless Talking Heads, the ghosts who preside over the electronic, televised empires that surround our lives with the secondary orality of illusive, elusive, and terribly tangible power.

"And one day," says Johnny Mnemonic, "I'll have a surgeon dig all the silicon out of my amygdalae, and I'll live with my own memories and nobody else's, the way other people do."[65] The day his number comes in, Johnny Mnemonic ain't gonna ride no used brain no more. "But not for a while": in spite of their nostalgia for healing and recomposition, Gibson's heroes are reluctant to give up the elation and possibility implied in fragmentation. So they hold on to the margins, and Johnny Mnemonic keeps postponing his deathbed re-conversion. In the pathetic imagination, however, the hero always runs out of time. Johnny, unfortunate rake, dies before his number comes in, and the rampant Molly Million weeps for him beneath her impenetrable mirrorshades. With all her implants and sylicon, Molly Millions may be "tougher than the rest," but she is also "rough and ready for love," and an old broken heart throbs among all those spare parts. A scar runs across the length of her body, reminiscent of Ahab's—who, like her, is also part flesh and part replaceable implant.

In this ironic version of pastoral, the threat of the machine in the garden is reversed into the nostalgic hope of saving at least a piece of garden inside the machine. Though Gibson wears a double mask of postmodern neutrality and tough underworld stance, yet he too carries the same old pastoral yolk that is always sloshing around inside all those American hard-boiled eggs. In postmodern science fiction, as in country music and in most of mass culture, the eruption of the sentimental, pathetic voice expresses the nostalgia of the powerless for their lost wholeness, the prices paid for the euphoria of multiple identity and the creation of a new self. As Marly climbs through the core remnants of the old Tessier-Ashpool hive, she wonders why Jones is so keen on saving crazy old Wig's life. Then she understands: "Anything human, anything alive, might come to seem quite precious, here."[66]

NOTES

INTRODUCTION: THE TORN-UP LETTER AND THE HEADLESS GHOST

1. Washington Irving, "The Legend of Sleepy Hollow," in *The Sketch Book of Geoffrey Crayon, Gent.* (1820), in *The Works of Washington Irving*, Author's Revised Edition (New York: G. P. Putnam, 1867), 2: 418.

2. Irving, "Rip Van Winkle," *The Sketch Book*, p. 44.

3. Ernest Hemingway, *Green Hills of Africa* (1936; reprint, London: Jonathan Cape, 1954), p. 29.

4. Mark Twain, *The Adventures of Huckleberry Finn*, in *The Writings of Mark Twain* (Hartford, Conn.: The American Publishing Company, 1901), pp. 277–78.

5. Alba Gómez, Cherrie Moréga, Mariana Romo Carmona, with Myrtha Chabrán, "By Word of Mouth," introduction" to A. Gómez, Ch. Moréga, M. Romo Carmona, eds., *Cuentos: Stories by Latinas* (New York: Kitchen Table: Women of Color Press, 1983), pp. x–xi.

6. Paula Gunn Allen, "The Word Warriors," in *The Sacred Hoop: Recovering the Feminine in American Indian Traditions* (Boston: Beacon Press, 1986), pp. 93–94.

7. Etheridge Knight, "On the Oral Nature of Poetry," *The Black Scholar*, 19, no. 6 (Fall 1988): 92–95.

8. Eileen Julien, *African Novels and the Question of Orality* (Bloomington: Indiana University Press, 1992), p. 10ff.

9. Nathaniel Hawthorne, *The English Notebooks*, ed. Randall Stewart (New York: Russell and Russell, 1962), p. 433.

10. Herman Melville, letter to Evert A. Duyckink, April 5, 1849, *The Letters of Herman Melville*, ed. Merrel R. Davis and William H. Gilman (New Haven: Yale University Press, 1960), p. 83.

1. HOUSES OF DAWN

1. Harvey J. Graff, *The Legacies of Literacy: Continuities and Contradiction in Western Culture and Society* (Bloomington: Indiana University Press, 1987), p. 394.

2. Eric C. Havelock, *The Muse Learns to Write: Reflections on Orality and Literacy from Antiquity to the Present* (New Haven: Yale University Press, 1986), p. 64; Deborah Tannen, "Introduction," in Deborah Tannen, ed., *Analyzing Discourse: Text and Talk* (Washington, D.C.: Georgetown University Press, 1982), pp. ix–xiii.

3. Roman Jakobson and Linda Waugh, *The Sound Shape of Language* (Bloomington: Indiana University Press, 1979), p. 69 ff.

4. Jack Goody, *The Domestication of the Savage Mind* (Cambridge: Cambridge University Press, 1977), p. 37.

5. Jack Goody, *The Logic of Writing and the Organization of Society* (Cambridge: Cambridge University Press, 1986); Graff, *Legacies*, p. 5.

6. Walter J. Ong, *Orality and Literacy: The Technologizing of the Word* (London and New York: Methuen, 1982), pp. 35–57.

7. Ibid., p. 15; *The Presence of the Word* (New Haven and London: Yale University Press, 1967), pp. 88–89; Havelock, *The Muse Learns to Write*, p. 118. The Italian translation of Havelock's book, *La Musa impara a scrivere*, trans. Mario Carpitella (Bari: Laterza, 1987), p. 148, renders his "revived" with a more eloquent "resuscitata."

8. Sandra Cisneros, "Bien Pretty," in *Woman Hollering Creek* (New York: Vintage, 1991), pp. 149–50.

9. Robert Pattison, *On Literacy: The Politics of the Word from Homer to the Age of Rock* (New York and Oxford: Oxford University Press, 1982).

10. Eileen Julien, *African Novels and the Question of Orality* (Bloomington: Indiana University Press, 1992), pp. 13–15.

11. Jack Goody, "Alternate Paths to Knowledge in Oral and Literate Cultures," in Deborah Tannen, ed., *Spoken and Written Language: Exploring Orality and Literacy* (Norwood, N.J.: Ablex, 1986), pp. 201–16. On the role of literacy in the organization of the state, see Goody, *The Logic of Writing*; on literacy as a function of hegemony, see Graff, *Legacies*.

12. Plato, *Phaedrus*, trans. with introduction and commentary by R. Backfroth (Cambridge: Cambridge University Press 1952), sec. 59;

Claude Lévi-Strauss, *Anthropologie Structurale* (Paris: Plon, 1958), pp. 400–401.

13. Quoted in Dennis Tedlock, "On the Translation of Style in Oral Narrative," in *The Spoken Word and the Work of Interpretation* (Philadelphia: University of Pennsylvania Press, 1983), p. 55.

14. Jack Goody and Ian Watt, "The Consequences of Literacy," in Jack Goody, ed., *Literacy in Traditional Societies* (Cambridge: Cambridge University Press, 1968), p. 2.

15. Gianni Bosio, "Elogio del magnetofono" in *L'intellettuale rovesciato* (Milan: Edizioni Bella Ciao, 1985), pp. 169–83.

16. Ong, *Orality and Literacy*, p. 135 ff.; *The Presence of the Word.*

17. Roland Barthes, "Le grain de la voix," in *L'obvie e l'obtus* (Paris: Seuil, 1982,) pp. 236–45; Paul Zumthor, *Introduction à la poésie orale* (Paris: Seuil, 1983), pp. 9–17.

18. Barthes, "Aimer Schuman," in *L'obvie e l'obtus*, pp. 259–64; Roland Barthes and Eric Marty, "Orale/scritto," in *Enciclopedia Einaudi* (Torino: Einaudi, 1980), 10: 60–85; Jack London, "The League of the Old Men" in *Children of the Frost* (New York: Regent Press, 1902), p. 245; Thomas Bangs Thorpe, "The Big Bear of Arkansas" [1841], in Walter J. Blair and Raven L. McDavid, *The Mirth of a Nation* (Minneapolis: University of Minnesota Press, 1983), p. 55.

19. Jacques Derrida, *Of Grammatology*, trans. Gayatry Chakravorty Spivak (Baltimore and London: The Johns Hopkins University Press, 1976), p. 55.

20. "Derrida's own analyses," writes Frederic Jameson, "depend for their force on the isolation and valorization of script as a unique and privileged type of content: script has thus become the basic interpretive or explanatory code, one which is felt to have a priority over the other types of content": *The Prison-House of Language* (Princeton: Princeton University Press, 1974), p. 183. For a critique from the point of view of the study of oral culture, see Arnold Krupat, "Post-Structuralism and Oral Literature," in Brian Swann and Arnold Krupat, eds., *Recovering the Word: Essays on Native American Literature* (Berkeley: University of California Press, 1987), pp. 113–28; see also David Murray, *Forked Tongues: Speech, Writing, and Representation in North American Indian Texts* (Blomington: Indiana University Press, 1991), p. 24.

21. Derrida, *Of Grammatology*, p. 74.

22. Régis Durand, "The Anxiety of Performance," *New Literary History* 2, no. 1 (Autumn 1980): 167–76.

23. Henry Louis Gates, Jr., *The Signifying Monkey: A Theory of Afro-American Literary Criticism* (New York and Oxford: Oxford University Press, 1988), pp. 39, 21.

24. Ong, *Orality and Literacy*, p. 168; Eric C. Havelock, *Preface to Plato* (Cambridge: Harvard University Press, 1963).

25. Havelock, *The Muse Learns to Write*, p. 112; Jakobson and Waugh, *The Sound Shape of Language*, p. 73.

26. Dennis Tedlock, "Phonography and the Problem of Time in Oral Narrative Events," in *The Spoken Word and the Work of Interpretation* (Philadelphia: University of Pennsylvania Press, 1983), p. 198.

27. Jakobson and Waugh, *The Sound Shape of Language*, p. 72; Thomas Carlyle, "The Stump Orator," quoted in Barnet Baskerville, *The People's Voice: The Orator in American Society* (Lexington: University Press of Kentucky, 1979), p. 118.

28. Bessie Head, *Serowe: The Village of the Rain Wind* (London, Ibadan, and Nairobi: Heinemann, 1981), p. xii (italics mine); N. Scott Momaday, *House Made of Dawn* (1968; reprint, New York: Harper and Row, 1981), p. 90. On the horizon of extinction as a theme in Native American literature, see Kenneth Lincoln, *Native American Renaissance* (Berkeley: University of California Press, 1973), pp. 57–59.

29. Maxine Hong Kingston, *The Woman Warrior: Memories of a Childhood Among Ghosts* (1977; reprint, New York: Vintage, 1989), p. 11; Louise Erdrich, *Tracks* (New York: Harper and Row, 1988), p. 5; Leslie Marmon Silko, *Ceremony* (1977; reprint, New York: Penguin, 1986), p. 35.

30. N. Scott Momaday, "Twenty Years Ago on this Day," *Viva*, November 19, 1972, quoted in Mathias Schubnell, *N. Scott Momaday: The Cultural and Literary Background* (Norman, Ok. and London: University of Oklahoma Press, 1985), p. 5.

31. Silko, *Ceremony*, p. 1; Momaday, *House Made of Dawn*, p. 90.

32. Leslie Marmon Silko and James Wright, *The Fragility and Strength of Lace*, ed. Anne Wright (St. Paul, Minn.: Graywolf Press, 1985). Momaday's *House Made of Dawn* derives its title from a song included in the Navajo Night Chant ritual: see Washington Matthews, *The Night Chant: A Navaho Ceremonial, Memoirs of the American Museum of Natural History*, vol. 6 (1902); John Bierhorst, *Four Masterpieces of American Indian Literature* (New York: Farrar, Strauss and Giroux, 1974).

33. W. E. B. DuBois, "The Sorrow Songs," in *The Souls of Black Folk* [1903], in *Writings* (New York: The Library of America, 1986), p. 536.

34. James Still, *River of Earth* (1940; reprint, Lexington: University Press of Kentucky, 1970).

35. Tony Tanner, *City of Words* (New York and Evanston: Harper and Row, 1971).

36. J. D. Salinger, *The Catcher in the Rye* (1951; reprint, Harmondsworth, Midds.: Penguin, 1958), p. 220; Ernest Hemingway, *Fiesta* (1927; reprint, London: Granada, 1978), p. 204.

37. Frances Yates, *The Art of Memory* (London: Routledge and Kegan Paul, 1966).

38. Zora Neale Hurston, *Mules and Men* (1935; reprint, New York and Evanston: Harper and Row, 1965), p. 107; Silko, *Ceremony*, 34; Gertrude Stein, "Composition as Explanation," in *Selected Writings*, ed. Carl Van Vechten (New York: Vintage, 1972), pp. 518–21.

39. Tannen, "The Oral/Literate Continuum in Discourse," in *Spoken and Written Language*; William Bright, "Literature, Written and Oral," in Tannen ed., *Analyzing Discourse*, pp. 271–83; Dell Hymes, "Ways of Speaking," in Richard Baumann and Joel Sherzer, eds., *Explorations in the Ethnography of Speaking* (London and New York: Cambridge University Press, 1974), pp. 433–51.

40. Giorgio R. Cardona, "Oralità e scrittura," in Alberto Asor Rosa, ed., *Letteratura italiana* (Bari: Laterza, 1983), 2: 100–125.

41. Cardona, "Oralità e scrittura," pp. 26, 42

42. Ibid., p. 25; Derrida, *Of Grammatology*, p. 301.

43. Herman Melville, *Moby-Dick*, in *The Works of Herman Melville*, Standard Edition (New York: Russell & Russell, 1963), 7: 179.

44. Harold Bloom, *The Anxiety of Influence* (New York and Oxford: Oxford University Press, 1973), pp. 21, 10.

45. Grace Paley, "Friends," in *Later the Same Day* (1985; reprint, Harmondsworth, Midds.: Penguin, 1986), pp. 77–78. According to Arnold Krupat, a tendency to value "voice" over "text" prevails in both feminist and African-American literary theory: *The Voice in the Margin* (Berkeley: University of California Press, 1989), pp. 20, 45–46.

46. Walt Whitman, "Song of Myself," in *Complete Poetry and Collected Prose* (New York: The Library of America, 1982), sec. 24: 210 (all quotes from Whitman in this book come from this edition). For "Jesse James," see Alan Lomax, *Folk Songs of North America* (Garden City, N.J.: Doubleday, 1960), p. 352. Ludovica Koch discusses authorial identification and signatures in Scandinavian oral poetry in "Il corvo della Memoria e il corvo del Pensiero. Problemi dell'improvvisazione nella teoria

degli scaldi," in Giovanni Cerri, ed., *Scrivere e recitare: Modelli di trasmissione del testo poetico nell'antichitá e nel Medioevo* (Rome: Edizioni dell'Ateneo, 1986), pp. 143–61.

47. Ong, *Orality and Literacy*, p. 33.

48. Mikhail Bakhtin, "Discourse in the Novel," in *The Dialogic Imagination* (Austin: University of Texas Press, 1984), pp. 259–422; "The Problem of Speech Genres," in *Speech Genres, and Other Late Essays*, trans. Vern W. McGee (Austin: University of Texas Press, 1986), pp. 60–101.

49. Gerald Prince, "Introduction to the Study of the Narratee," *Poétique* 14 (1973): 177–96.

50. Erving C. Goffman, *Forms of Talk* (Philadelphia: University of Pennsylvania Press, 1981), p. 151.

51. Ong, "The Writer's Audience is Always a Fiction," in *Interfaces of the Word* (Ithaca and London: Cornell University Press, 1977), pp. 53–81.

52. D. Allen and R. Guy, *Conversation Analysis: The Sociology of Talk* (The Hague and Paris: Mouton, 1974), p. 26.

53. Stanley Fish, "Introduction, or How I Stopped Worrying and Learned to Love Interpretation," in *Is There a Text in this Class?* (Cambridge: Harvard University Press, 1980), p. 14.

54. See D. K. Wilgus, *Anglo-American Folk Song Scholarship since 1898* (New Brunswick: Rutgers University Press, 1959).

55. Roman Jakobson and Pëtr Bogatyrev, "Die Folklore als eine besondere Form des Schaffens," in Roman Jakobson, *Selected Writings* (The Hague and Paris: Mouton, 1967), 4: 1–15.

56. Krupat, "Post-Structuralism and Oral Literature"; Fish, "Interpreting the Variorum," in *Is there a Text*, p. 173.

57. Bakhtin, "The Problem of Speech Genres"; Dona J. Hickey, *Developing a Written Voice* (Mountain View, Cal., London, and Toronto: Mayfield, 1993), p. 1; Wayne Booth, *The Rhetoric of Fiction* (Harmondsworth, Midds.: Penguin, 1983), part 3, "The Author's Voice in Fiction," pp. 169–266; Stephen M. Ross, *Fiction's Inexhaustible Voice: Speech and Writing in Faulkner* (Athens: University of Georgia Press, 1989), p. 5 ff.; Gabriel Josipovici, *The World and the Book* (Stanford: Stanford University Press, 1971), p. 84; Cesare Segre, *Avviamento all'analisi del testo letterario* (Torino: Einaudi, 1985), p. 15 ff.; Malini Johar Schueller, *The Politics of Voice: Liberalism and Social Criticism from Franklin to Kingston* (Albany: State University of New York Press, 1992), p. 8.

58. Marie Maclean, *Narrative as Performance: The Baudelairean Experiment* (London and New York: Routledge, 1988), p. 10; Robert Scholes

and Robert Kellogg, *The Nature of Narrative* (London: Oxford University Press, 1988), p. 55.

59. Goody, *The Domestication of the Savage Mind*, p. 37; Agostino Lombardo, *Il testo e la sua performance* (Rome: Editori Riuniti, 1988); Richard Poirier, *The Performing Self: Compositions and Decompositions in the Language of Contemporary Life* (New York and Oxford: Oxford University Press, 1971), pp. 33, 66.

60. Dell Hymes, "Breakthrough into Performance," in *"In Vain I Tried to Tell You." Essays in Native American Ethnopoetics* (Philadelphia: University of Pennsylvania Press), pp. 79–141; Richard Bauman, ed., *Verbal Art as Performance* (Prospect Heights, Ill.: Waveland Press, 1984), p. 11.

61. Fish, "Literature in the Reader," in *Is There a Text*, p. 43.

62. Francis James Child, *The English and Scottish Popular Ballads* (1882–1898; reprint New York: Dover, 1965), 4: 65–74, n. 200.

63. Tedlock, "The Spoken Word and the Work of Interpretation in American Indian Religion," in *The Spoken Word and the Work of Interpretation*, p. 236.

64. Fish, "Introduction," in *Is There a Text*, p. 28.

65. Alberto Asor Rosa, "Tempo e nuovo nell'avanguardia, ovvero: l'infinita manipolabilità del tempo," in Ruggiero Romano, ed., *Le frontiere del tempo* (Milan: Il Saggiatore, 1981), pp. 77–96.

66. Mariantonia Liborio "Leggere l'oralità," in G. Cerri, ed., *Scrivere e recitare*, pp. 171–85.

67. Lincoln, *Native American Renaissance*, p. 62.

68. Black Elk, *Black Elk Speaks*, ed. John G. Neihardt (1932; reprint, Lincoln: University of Nebraska Press, 1979); Charles Olson, "Projective Verse," in Robert Creeley, ed., *Selected Writings of Charles Olson* (New York: New Directions, 1966), pp. 15–30 ; Momaday, "The Man Made of Words," in Rupert Costo, ed. *Indian Voices: The First Convocation of Native American Scholars* (San Francisco: The Indian Historian Press, 1970), pp. 49–62.

69. Brian Swann, *Song of the Sky: Versions of North American Songs and Poems* (Ashuelot, N.H.: Four Zoas Night House Press, 1988); Jerome Rothenberg, *Shaking the Pumpkin: Traditional Poetry of the Indian North Americans* (Garden City, N.J.: Doubleday, 1972); *Technicians of the Sacred* (New York: Doubleday, 1968); Fedora Giordano, *Etnopoetica: le avanguardie americane e la tradizione orale indiana* (Rome: Bulzoni, 1988); Michael Castro, "American Indian Influences on Modern Poetry," in

Laura Coltelli, ed., *Native American Literatures* (Pisa: SEU, 1989), pp. 101–13; George Quasha, "Dia-Logos: Between the Written and the Oral in Contemporary Poetry," *New Literary History* 8, no. 3 (Spring 1977): 408–506; Krupat, *The Voice in the Margin*, ch. 3; *Boundary 2*, no. 3 (Spring 1975), special issue on "The Oral Impulse in Contemporary American Poetry."

70. Dennis Tedlock, *Finding the Center: Narrative Poetry of the Zuni Indians* (Lincoln: University of Nebraska Press, 1972). Among contemporary works of criticism directly or indirectly influenced by an awareness of orality and oral cultures, are Krupat, "Post-Structuralism and Oral Literature"; Krupat, *The Voice in the Margin*; Gates, *The Signifying Monkey*; Henry Louis Gates, Jr., ed., *Black Literature and Literary Theory* (New York and London: Methuen, 1984); Henry Louis Gates, Jr., ed., *"Race," Writing, and Difference* (Chicago and London: University of Chicago Press, 1986); Michael J. Fisher, "Ethnicity and the Post-Modern Arts of Memory," in James Clifford and George E. Marcus, eds., *Writing Culture: The Poetics and Politics of Ethnography* (Berkeley: University of California Press, 1986), pp. 196–233; Werner Sollors, *Beyond Ethnicity: Consent and Descent in American Literature* (New York and Oxford: Oxford University Press, 1989).

71. The term *oral literature* is a contradiction in terms: Ong, *Orality and Literacy*, pp. 10–15 (for a contrary opinion, see Ruth Finnegan, *Oral Poetry* [Cambridge: Cambridge University Press, 1977]). Wallace L. Chafe seeks a common ground by defining as "oral literature" every oral discourse tending toward formalization: "Integration and Involvement in Speaking, Writing, and Oral Literature," in Tannen, ed., *Spoken and Written Language*, pp. 35–53.

2. FOUNDATIONS: ORALITY, ORIGINS AND THE DEMOCRATIC REVOLUTION

1. John Adams is quoted in Cathy N. Davidson, *Revolution and the Word: The Rise of the Novel in America* (New York and Oxford: Oxford University Press, 1986), p. 57. According to Graff, New England achieved universal literacy toward the end of the eighteenth century; two thirds of the population of Pennsylvania and Virginia were literate at the time. The 1840 census shows an illiteracy rate of 9 percent, a rate that decreases to 8.3 percent twenty years later. Differences caused by race, gender, and geography, however, remained high (*The Legacies of Literacy: Continuities and Contradiction in Western Culture and Society* [Bloomington:

Indiana University Press, 1987], pp. 251, 342–43). On the literacy of women and blacks, see Jennifer Monaghan, "Literacy, Instruction, and Gender in Colonial New England," in C. N. Davidson, ed., *Reading in America* (Baltimore and London: Johns Hopkins University Press, 1989), pp. 53–80; Dana Nelson Salvino, "The Word in Black and White," ibid., pp. 140–56.

2. Ralph Ellison, "Hidden Name and Complex Fate," in *Shadow and Act* (1964; reprint, New York: Vintage, 1972), pp. 163–64.

3. Giorgio R. Cardona, "Oralità e scrittura," in Alberto Asor Rosa, ed., *Letteratura italiana* (Bari: Laterza, 1983), 2: 82.

4. Sacvan Bercovitch, *The American Jeremiad* (Madison: University of Wisconsin Press, 1978), p. 123.

5. Richard Dorson, *American Folklore and the Historian* (Chicago and London: University of Chicago Press, 1971), pp. 174n., 28.

6. Alexis de Tocqueville, *L'amicizia e la democrazia: Lettere scelte 1824–1859*, ed. Massimo Terni (Rome: Edizioni Lavoro, 1987), pp. 78–79; *Democracy in America* (1835–40; reprint, New Rochelle, N.Y.: Arlington House, n. d.), 1: 307.

7. Charles Brockden Brown, *Clara Howard, or, The Enthusiasm of Love* (1801, reprint Kent, Ohio: Kent State University Press, 1986), p. 329. On the influence of Herder's concept of folklore and of German Romanticism, see Gene Bluestein, *The Voice of the Folk* (Amherst: The University of Massachusetts Press, 1972).

8. Arnold Krupat "Identity and Difference in the Criticism of Native American Literature," *Diacritics* 12, no. 3 (Summer 1983): 2–13; Richard Slotkin, *Regeneration through Violence: The Mythology of the American Frontier* (Middletown: Wesleyan University Press, 1973), p. 17; Washington Irving, "The Devil and Tom Walker," in *Tales of a Traveller* [1824], in *The Works of Washington Irving*, Author's Revised Edition (New York: Putnam, 1867), 7: 394.

9. David Hackett Fischer, *Albion's Seed: Four British Folkways in America* (New York and Oxford: Oxford University Press, 1989); Slotkin, *Regeneration through Violence*, p. 19, and all of chapter 12 ("Myth and Literature in a New World"); Constance Rourke, *American Humor* (New York: Harcourt, Brace, 1931).

10. Ernesto de Martino, "Intorno a una storia del mondo popolare subalterno," *Società* 5, no. 3 (September 1949): 411–35.

11. Washington Irving, *Salmagundi* [1807], in *Works*, 7: 210–11; Mark Twain and Charles Dudley Warner, *The Gilded Age* [1873], in *The Writings of*

Mark Twain (Hartford, Conn.: The American Publishing Company, 1901), 1: 251–52.

12. Nathaniel Hawthorne, "The Custom House," preface to *The Scarlet Letter* [1850], in *The Centenary Edition of the Works of Nathaniel Hawthorne* (Kent: Ohio State University Press, 1968), 1: 32.

13. Hawthorne "Howe's Masquerade" [1830], in *Twice-Told Tales* (Boston and New York: Houghton Mifflin & Co., 1879), p. 276.

14. Hawthorne, *The Scarlet Letter*, pp. 258, 259–60. The expression "multiple choice" is from Francis O. Matthiessen, *American Renaissance: Art and Expression in the Age of Emerson and Whitman* (New York and London: Oxford University Press, 1975), p. 276; "alternative possibilities" is from Yvor Winters, *In Defense of Reason* (New York: New Directions, 1947), p. 170.

15. Giorgio R. Cardona, *Antropologia della scrittura* (Torino: Loescher, 1981), p. 27.

16. Hawthorne, "The Custom House," pp. 30, 33, 42–43.

17. Hawthorne, "The Custom House," pp. 29, 27.

18. Hawthorne, *The Scarlet Letter*, p. 47.

19. See Alessandro Portelli, *Il re nascosto: Saggio su Washington Irving* (Rome: Bulzoni, 1981), pp. 25–48.

20. Rev. Isaac Skillman, "Oration on the Beauties of Liberty," quoted in Alice M. Baldwin, *The New England Clergy and the American Revolution* (Durham, N.C.: Duke University Press, 1928), p. 117. See also Peter Shaw, "Hawthorne's Ritual Typology of the American Revolution," in Jack Salzman, ed., *Prospects: An Annual of American Cultural Studies*, (New York: Burt Franklin & Co., 1977), 3: 483–98.

21. Hugh Henry Brackenridge, *Modern Chivalry* (1792–1815; reprint, New York: American Book Company, 1934), p. 358; James Fenimore Cooper, *The Pioneers* (1823; reprint, London: Dent, 1970), p. 147.

22. Bercovitch, *The American Jeremiad*, p. 134; Louis P. Simpson, "Federalism and the Crisis of the Literary Order," *American Literature* 32, no. 3 (November 1960): 254–66; Larzer Ziff, *Literary Democracy: The Declaration of Literary Independence in America* (New York: Penguin, 1982), p. ix; Edgar Allan Poe, "The System of Doctor Tarr and Professor Fether" [1844], in *Poetry and Tales* (New York: The Library of America, 1984), p. 715 (all references to Poe's tales and poems are to this edition).

23. Irving, "The Adventure of the German Student" [1824], in *Tales of a Traveller*, pp. 57–64.

24. Charles Baudelaire, "Notes Nouvelles sur Edgar Poe," in *Critique Littéraire et Musicale* (Paris: Armand Colin, 1961), p. 201; Henry James, *Hawthorne* (London: Macmillan, 1879), p. 26.

25. Karl Marx, *The Eighteenth Brumaire of Louis Bonaparte* (Moscow: Progress Publishers, 1977), pp. 18–19; Karl Marx and Friedrich Engels, "Manifesto of the Communist Party," in Robert C. Tucker, ed., *The Marx Engels Reader* (New York and London: Norton, 1978), p. 476. See Marshall Berman, *All That Is Solid Melts in the Air* (New York: Simon and Schuster, 1982).

26. Tocqueville, *L'amicizia e la democrazia*, p. 86.

27. Ellison, *Invisible Man* (1952; reprint, Harmondsworth, Midds.: Penguin, 1978), pp. 468, 7, 401–402.

28. David Riesman with Rewel Denney and Nathan Glazer, *The Lonely Crowd* (New Haven: Yale University Press, 1965), p. 223.

29. Tocqueville, *Democracy in America*, p. 259.

30. Arthur J. Schlesinger, *The Age of Jackson* (Boston and Toronto: Little, Brown, 1954), p. 95; James, *Hawthorne*, p. 32.

31. Thomas Paine, "The Crisis," in *The Essential Thomas Paine* (New York and Toronto: Mentor, 1969), p. 26; Bob Dylan, "A Hard Rain's a-Gonna Fall," in *The Freewheelin' Bob Dylan*, CBS BFG 62193, 1963.

32. Hawthorne, "My Kinsman, Major Molineux" [1831], in *Works*, 11: 231.

33. D. H. Lawrence, *Studies in Classic American Literature* (1924; reprint, London: Mercury, 1964), p. 8; Ralph Waldo Emerson, "Self-Reliance" [1841], in *Essays and Lectures*, ed. Joel Porte (New York: The Library of America, 1983), p. 261 (all quotations from Emerson in this book come from this edition); Sacvan Bercovitch, *The Puritan Origins of the American Self* (New Haven and London, Yale University Press, 1973), pp. 178–79.

34. Poe, "The Masque of the Red Death" [1842], p. 490

35. On volcano imagery in American literature see David S. Reynolds, *Beneath the American Renaissance* (New York: Knopf, 1988), pp. 414–16. Like that of the ghost, the image of the volcano and that of the earthquake combine violence and formlessness. Eruption and magma stand in the same symbolic relationship as beheading and ectoplasm: both pairs represent the eruption of passion into the realm of reason. The perception of the voice as an eruption of magmatic matter arising from the deep is not unknown to oral cultures, as Ludovica Koch has shown in "Il corvo della Memoria e il corvo del Pensiero: Problemi dell'improvvisazione

nella teoria degli scaldi," in Giovanni Cerri, ed., *Scrivere e recitare: Modelli di trasmissione del testo poetico nell'antichitá e nel Medioevo* (Rome: Edizioni dell'Ateneo, 1986).

36. Larry J. Reynolds, "*The Scarlet Letter* and Revolutions Abroad," *American Literature* 57, no. 1 (March 1985): 44–67; Eric J. Sundquist, "*Benito Cereno* and New World Slavery," in Sacvan Bercovitch, ed., *Reconstructing American Literary History* (Cambridge: Harvard University Press, 1986), pp. 93–122.

37. Royall Tyler, *The Algerine Captive; or, The Life and Adventures of Doctor Undike Underhill Six Years a Prisoner among the Algerines*, 2 vols. (1797; reprint, Gainesville, Fla.: Scholars' Facsimiles and Reprints, 1967), 2: 43.

38. Herman Melville, *Benito Cereno*, in *Piazza Tales* [1856], in *The Works of Herman Melville*, Standard Edition (New York: Russell & Russell, 1963), 10: 149.

39. Melville, *Benito Cereno*, pp. 98–99, 70–71, 98.

40. Brackenridge, *Modern Chivalry*, p. 419.

41. As in Irving's "Sleepy Hollow" [1820], Tyler's narrator will not vouch for the truthfulness of the dream but only claims to give the "facts." Once again, the "fact" is not what the legend or the dream says, but the fact of dreaming and storytelling. The authority of facts fades away in dreams like political authority fades in revolution.

42. Another "Indian deed" is hidden behind the portrait of the family's founder in Hawthorne's *The House of the Seven Gables* [1851], in *The Centenary Edition of the Works of Nathaniel Hawthorne* (Kent: Ohio State University Press, 1968); in a more recent text, Gerald Vizenor's *Bearheart* [1978], miles and miles of buried "Indian deeds" and "heirship records" surround the narrator of a postmodern Indian tale. On the controversial legality of Indian deeds see Francis Jennings, *The Invasion of America: Indians, Colonialism, and the Cant of Conquest* (Durham: University of North Carolina Press, 1975), ch. 8.

43. On the beheading of Philip of Pokanoket see the pamphlet *A Merchant of Boston, The Warr in New England Visibly Ended: King Philip That Barbarous Indian Now Beheaded*, etc. (1677; facsimile in *King Philip's War's Narratives*, Ann Arbor, Mich.: University Microfilm Inc., 1966). For a more detailed discussion see Portelli, *Il re nascosto*, pp. 273–84.

44. Irving, "The Devil and Tom Walker," pp. 393–94

45. Ibid., pp. 400, 407, 399. On the identification of Indians with the unconscious, see Michael Rogin, *Fathers and Children: Andrew Jackson and*

the Subjugation of the American Indian (New York: Knopf, 1975), pp. 116–18.

46. Poe, "The Gold Bug" [1843], pp. 591, 592.

47. Jack Goody, *The Domestication of the Savage Mind* (Cambridge: Cambridge University Press, 1977), ch. 5.

48. Melville, *Pierre; or, The Ambiguities* [1856], in *Works*, 10: 66.

49. Melville, *Moby-Dick*, in *Works*, 1: 7, 223–27, 236, 238, 243, 239, 204; 2: 34. The chapter on the whiteness of the whale is haunted by other images of legendary "ghosts" and "phantoms": the white shark, the albatross, the White Mountains of New Hampshire, and others.

50. Kurt Vonnegut, *Galapagos* (New York: Dell, 1985), p. 290.

51. Thomas Pynchon, *The Crying of Lot 49* (New York: Bantam, 1966), pp. 69, 72. Several cues link Pynchon to Hawthorne. The recipient of Lot 49 is named Pierce like the president whose electoral biography Hawthorne wrote. Pierce's term began in 1853, the same year in which the events described in the marker took place. Pynchon himself might be related to the Pyncheons of *The House of the Seven Gables*: see Roberto Cagliero, "Pynchon e le integrazioni segrete," afterword to Thomas Pynchon, *Un lungo apprendistato* [*Slow Learner*] (Rome: Edizioni EO, 1988), p. 184.

52. Don DeLillo, *Libra* (New York: Viking, Penguin, 1988), p. 181–82; Hawthorne, *The Scarlet Letter*, p. 48.

53. Gerald Vizenor, *Bearheart: The Heirship Chronicles* (Minneapolis: University of Minnesota Press, 1990), pp. vii–xiv (originally published in 1978 as *Darkness in Saint Louis Bearheart*).

54. Vizenor, *Bearheart*, pp. 217–18, 75, 230. On the myth of the founder hero's buried head (also relevant to the story of Philip of Pokanoket and Irving's "The Devil and Tom Walker"), see Nathan Wachtel, *La visione dei vinti* (Torino: Einaudi, 1985), p. 55.

55. Vizenor Bearheart, p. 167.

56. Ibid., p. 162.

57. Gerald Vizenor, *The Trickster of Liberty* (Minneapolis: University of Minnesota Press, 1988), p. x.

58. Poe, "The Imp of the Perverse" [1845], p. 284.

59. Nathaniel Hawthorne, "The Devil in Manuscript" [1852], in *Works*, 1: 177–78.

60. Irving, "The Legend of Sleepy Hollow," p. 424.

61. Cotton Mather, *Magnalia Christi Americana* (1702; reprint, New York: Russell & Russell, 1967), part 6, pp. 3–4 (2: 392, 393); part 6, pp.

1, 6 (2: 246); part 7, p. 1 (2: 529). On Mather's use of testimony, see Dorson, *American Folklore and the Historian*, pp. 228–29; on the story of the specter ship, ibid., 147–48; on Mather as story-teller, see Giorgio Spini, *Autobiografia della giovane America* (Torino: Einaudi, 1968), p. 133.

62. Richard Dorson, *America in Legend: Folklore from the Colonial Period to the Present* (New York: Pantheon, 1973), p. 18.

63. Michael T. Kammen, *A Season of Youth: The American Revolution and the Historical Imagination* (New York: Alfred A. Knopf, 1978), pp. 47, 52.

64. Richard Dorson, *America Rebels: Narratives of the Patriots* (Greenwich, Conn.: Fawcett Publications, 1962), pp. 28–29; John C. Dawn, ed., *The Revolution Remembered* (Chicago and London: University of Chicago Press, 1980), p. xx.

65. Rourke, *American Humor*, p. 19; David S. Reynolds, *George Lippard* (Boston: Twayne Publishers, 1982); Gay Wilson Allen, *The Solitary Singer: A Critical Biography of Walt Whitman* (New York: Macmillan, 1955), p. 13; Kammen, *A Season of Youth*, pp. 21, 44, 25.

66. Herbert T. Hoover "Oral History in the United States," in Michael T. Kammen, ed., *The Past Before Us: Contemporary Historical Writing in the United States* (Ithaca, N.Y.: Cornell University Press, 1980), pp. 391–407; Kammen, *A Season of Youth*, pp. 21, 44, 254; Charles T. Morrissey, "Why Call It 'Oral History'? Searching for the Early Usage of a Generic Term," *Oral History* (1980), pp. 20–48.

67. Walt Whitman, "Song of Myself," in *Complete Poetry and Collected Prose* (New York: The Library of America, 1982), p. 67; sect. 35, pp. 227–28 (all quotations from Whitman in this book come from this edition); "The Wound Dresser," sect. 1, pp. 442–43.

68. Melville, *Israel Potter*, in *Works*, 11: v–vi.

69. Bernard W. Bell, *The Afro-American Novel and Its Tradition* (Amherst: University of Massachusetts Press, 1987), pp. 285–95. Early African-American historians also used oral sources to document the role of black people in the revolution and their resistance to slavery: see William Cooper Nell, *Colored Patriots of the American Revolution* [1845]; William Still, *The Underground Railroad* [1872].

70. See Alessandro Portelli, *The Death of Luigi Trastulli: Form and Meaning in Oral History* (Albany: State of New York University Press, 1991) pp. viii-i, 1–26.

71. Ursula LeGuin, *The Left Hand of Darkness* (1969; reprint, New York: Ace Science-Fiction, 1976), p. 1.

72. Isaac Asimov, *Second Foundation* (1953; reprint, London: Panther, 1964), p. 22.

73. Ibid., pp. 174, 185.

74. Asimov *Prelude to Foundation* (1988; reprint, New York: Bantam, 1989), p. 150.

75. Asimov, *Foundation's Edge* (1982; reprint, New York: Ballantine, 1983), p. 357.

3. CHECKS AND BALANCES: THE STATE, THE MOB, AND THE VOICES OF THE HEART

1. Harvey J. Graff, *The Legacies of Literacy: Continuities and Contradiction in Western Culture and Society* (Bloomington: Indiana University Press, 1987), p. 252.

2. Hawthorne, "My Kinsman, Major Molineux" [1831], in *The Centenary Edition of the Works of Nathaniel Hawthorne* (Kent: Ohio State University Press, 1968), 11: 226; Alexander Hamilton, James Madison, John Jay, *The Federalist Papers* [1787–88], ed. Henry Cabot Lodge (New York and London: G. P. Putnam's Sons, 1888), pp. 79–80, n. 10 (written by James Madison).

3. Armando Petrucci, "Per la storia dell'alfabetismo e della cultura scritta: Metodi—materiali—quesiti," *Quaderni storici* 38 (May/August 1978): 452–65; Graff, *Legacies of Literacy*, pp. 341–42, 347.

4. Washington Irving, *Salmagundi* [1807], in *The Works of Washington Irving*, Author's Revised Edition (New York: Putnam, 1867), 7: 210.

5. Robert T. Oliver, *History of Public Speaking in America* (Boston: Allyn and Bacon, 1965), p. 48.

6. Barnet Baskerville, *The People's Voice: The Orator in American Society* (Lexington: University Press of Kentucky, 1979), p. 13.

7. Michael Warner, "Textuality and Legitimacy in the Printed Constitution," in *The Letters of the Republic: Publication and the Public Sphere in Eighteenth-Century America* (Cambridge, Mass., and London: Harvard University Press, 1990), pp. 97–117.

8. Francis Jameson, *The American Revolution Considered as a Social Movement* (Princeton: Princeton University Press, 1926); Jesse Lemisch, "The American Revolution from the Bottom Up," in Barton J. Bernstein, Jr., *Towards a New Past: Dissenting Essays in American History* (New York: Pantheon, 1968), pp. 3–45; Dirk Hoerder, *People and Mobs: Crowd Action in Massachusetts* (Berlin: Freie Universität, 1971); Warner, "Textuality and Legitimacy"; Robert A. Ferguson " 'We Hold These Truths': Strate-

gies of Control in the Literature of the Founders," in Sacvan Bercovitch, ed., *Reconstructing American Literary History*, pp. 1–28; Emory Elliott, *Revolutionary Writers: Literature and Authority in the New Republic, 1725–1810* (New York and Oxford, Oxford University Press, 1982), pp. 14, 10–11.

9. Hoerder, *People and Mobs*, p. 1.

10. Richard Hofstadter, *Anti-Intellectualism in American Life* (New York: Knopf, 1963); Graff, *Legacies of Literacy*, p. 253.

11. Moses Coit Tyler, *The Literary History of the American Revolution* [1879–1893] (New York: Frederic Ungar, 1957), pp. 6, 16, 26–27; Walter J. Ong, *Orality and Literacy: The Technologizing of the Word* (London and New York: Methuen, 1982), pp. 43–56; Richard Dorson, *America Rebels: Narratives of the Patriots* (Greenwich, Conn.: Fawcett Publications, 1962), p. 29.

12. Thomas Paine, "The Crisis," in *The Essential Thomas Paine* (New York and Toronto: Mentor, 1969) p. 75.

13. Dan Lacy, *The Meaning of the American Revolution* (New York: The New American Library, 1964), p. 274.

14. Warner, "Textuality and Legitimacy"; Mark R. Patterson, *Authority, Autonomy, and Representation in American Literature* (Princeton: Princeton University Press, 1988).

15. Warner, "Franklin and the Letters of the Republic," in *The Letters of the Republic* pp. 73–96.

16. Benjamin Franklin, *The Autobiography* [1791], in *Writings* (New York: The Library of America, 1987), p. 1318; Larzer Ziff, "Upon What Pretext? The Book and Literary History," *Proceedings of the American Antiquarian Society* 95 (1986), part 2, pp. 297–315.

17. Franklin, *Autobiography*, p. 1307.

18. Franklin, "Epitaph" [1728], in *Writings*, p. 91.

19. Franklin, *Autobiography*, p. 1386.

20. Warner, "Textuality and Legitimacy"; Ferguson, " 'We Hold these Truths.' "

21. Warner, "Textuality and Legitimacy."

22. Edmund S. Morgan, "Government by Fiction: The Idea of Representation," *Yale Review* 72, no. 3 (April 1982): 321–39. See also E. S. Morgan, *Inventing the People: The Rise of Popular Sovereignty in England and America* (New York and London: W. W. Norton, 1988); on the democratic and theatrical meanings of "representation" see Norberto Bobbio, "La democrazia e il potere visibile," in *Il futuro della democrazia* (Torino: Einaudi, 1974), pp. 75–100.

23. Madison, *The Federalist Papers*, p. 57, n. 10.

24. Hugh Henry Brackenridge, *Modern Chivalry* (1792–1815; reprint, New York: American Book Company, 1934), vol. 1, ch. 5, p. 20.

25. Robert A. Ferguson, *Law and Letters in American Culture* (Cambridge: Harvard University Press, 1984), p. 24.

26. Madison, *The Federalist Papers*, p. 220, n. 37.

27. Brackenridge, *Modern Chivalry*, p. 524.

28. Baskerville, *The People's Voice*, p. 34; Arthur J. Schlesinger, *The Age of Jackson* (Boston and Toronto: Little, Brown, 1954), p. 83.

29. Ferguson, *Law and Letters*, p. 78.

30. Gore Vidal, *Burr* (London: Heinemann, 1974), p. 336.

31. Henry Adams, *Democracy: An American Novel* (New York: Henry Holt & Co., 1880), p. 19.

32. Cathy N. Davidson, *Revolution and the Word: The Rise of the Novel in America* (New York and Oxford: Oxford University Press, 1986), p. 79; Ralph Waldo Emerson, "The American Scholar" [1837], in *Essays and Lectures*, ed. Joel Porte (New York: The Library of America, 1983), pp. 68–69 (all quotations from Emerson are from this edition).

33. Louis B. Simpson, "Federalism and the Crisis of the Literary Order," *American Literature* 32, no. 3 (November 1960): 254–56; Warner, "The *Res Publica* of Letters," in *The Letters of the Republic*, pp. 34–72; Elliott, *Revolutionary Writers*, p. 47 ff.; Ferguson, " 'We Hold These Truths.' "

34. Elliott, *Revolutionary Writers*, p. 16. On the multiplicity of languages in Brackenridge, see David Simpson, *The Politics of American English* (New York and Oxford: Oxford University Press, 1986), pp. 113–18; Patterson, *Authority, Autonomy, and Representation*, p. 50. For a critical discussion of Brackenridge's presentation of African-American speech, see Sylvia Holton, *Down Home and Uptown: The Representation of Black Speech in American Fiction* (Rutherford: Farleigh University Press, 1984), p. 32. Houston A. Baker, Jr. describes Brackenridge's representation of black speech as "*white dada* at its most obscene" in his *Modernism and the Harlem Renaissance* (Chicago and London: University of Chicago Press, 1987), p. 22.

35. Elliott, *Revolutionary Writers*, p. 185.

36. Charles Brockden Brown, *Wieland; or, The Transformation* (1798; reprint, New York: Anchor, 1972), pp. 216, 245.

37. Ibid., pp. 73, 8, 177.

38. Ibid., pp. 20, 227, 52, 186. On Cicero as a paragon of oratorical excellence and professional virtue for American lawyers, see Ferguson, *Law and Letters*, p. 142.

39. Ibid., pp. 88, 259.

40. Barbara Lanati, "Poe e la scrittura del corpo: Appunti sul corpo che diventa scrittura e la scrittura che diventa corpo," in Ruggero Bianchi, ed., *E. A. Poe dal gotico alla fantascienza* (Milan: Mursia, 1978), pp. 123–44.

41. Edgar Allan Poe, "The Haunted Palace" [1839], in *Poetry and Tales* (New York: The Library of America, 1984), pp. 76–77 (all references to Poe's tales and poems are to this edition).

42. Poe, "William Wilson" [1840], p. 328.

43. Ibid., pp. 341, 337. On the mob as emblem of unreason and despotism in Emerson, Poe, and Hawthorne, see Larzer Ziff, *Literary Democracy: The Declaration of Literary Independence in America* (New York: Penguin, 1982), pp. 70, 115.

44. Poe, "William Wilson," pp. 341, 345.

45. Nathaniel Hawthorne, *The Scarlet Letter* [1850], in *The Centenary Edition of the Works of Nathaniel Hawthorne* (Kent: Ohio State University Press, 1968), 1: 217.

46. Ibid., pp. 218, 195. Sacvan Bercovitch argues that the "office" of the scarlet letter is to turn conflict into process, absorbing transgression and multiplicity into an ever renewed unity of national ideology and identity; see *The Office of the Scarlet Letter* (Baltimore and London: The Johns Hopkins University Press, 1991).

47. Ibid., pp. 223–25.

48. Ibid., p. 249.

49. Ibid., p. 243. For a similar scene, see the episode in N. Scott Momaday's *House Made of Dawn* (1968; reprint, New York: Harper and Row, 1981), in which Abel, outside the *kiva*, listens to the voices of the praying elders: "He remembered the prayer and he knew what it meant—not the words, which he had never really heard, but the low sound itself, rising and falling away in his mind, unmistakable and unbroken" (p. 16).

50. Hawthorne, "The Custom House," p. 4.

51. Hawthorne, preface to *The House of the Seven Gables*, in *Works*, 2: 1, 3.

52. Hawthorne, *The Scarlet Letter*, pp. 74, 66, 58; Nina Baym, *The Scarlet Letter: A Reading* (Boston: Twayne Publishers, 1986), p. 61.

53. Hawthorne, *The Scarlet Letter*, pp. 58, 62, 75, 129.

54. Ibid., p. 91.

55. Ibid., pp. 68, 54.

56. John T. Irwin, *American Hieroglyphics* (Baltimore and London: The Johns Hopkins University Press, 1983), pp. 239–41. According to Larzer Ziff, the most desirable meaning of the A for Hester would be "Authority"; see his *Literary Democracy*, p. 137.

57. Hawthorne, *The Scarlet Letter*, p. 85; Daniel Hoffman, *Form and Fable in American Fiction* (New York and Oxford: Oxford University Press, 1961), p. 178; Edmund Leites, *The Puritan Conscience and Modern Sexuality* (New Haven: Yale University Press, 1986).

58. Hawthorne, *The Scarlet Letter*, p. 84.

4. PHILOSOPHIES OF COMPOSITION

1. Grace Paley, "Friends," in *Later the Same Day* (1985; reprint, Harmondsworth, Midds.: Penguin, 1986), p. 78.

2. Gertrude Stein, "Composition as Explanation," in *Selected Writings*, ed. Carl Van Vechten (New York: Vintage, 1972), p. 520.

3. Edgar Allan Poe, "Philosophy of Composition," in *Essays and Reviews* (New York: The Library of America, 1984), p. 13. All references to Poe's critical writings are from this edition.

4. Woody Guthrie, *Woody Sez*, ed. Marjorie Guthrie et al. (New York: Grosset & Dunlap, 1975), pp. 2–3.

5. Edgar Allan Poe, *Marginalia*, in *Essays and Reviews*, pp. 465–66. Nina Baym, in *Novels, Readers, and Reviewers: Responses to Fiction in Antebellum America* (Ithaca and London: Cornell University Press, 1987, p. 72), remarks on the prevalence of planned composition as critical principle. Thought doesn't always precede words in Poe: "Whenever, on account of its vagueness, I am dissatisfied with a conception of the brain, I resort forthwith to the pen, for the purpose of obtaining, through its aid, the necessary form, consequence, and precision" ("Thought and Words," *Marginalia*, p. 465).

6. William D. Howells, "Mark Twain: An Inquiry," in *My Mark Twain* (New York and London: Harper and Brothers, 1910), pp. 166–67; Neil Schmitz, *Of Huck and Alice: Humorous Writing in American Literature* (Minneapolis: University of Minnesota Press, 1983), p. 101.

7. Gertrude Stein, reported in John Hyde Preston, "A Conversation" (1935), quoted in N. Schmitz, *Of Huck and Alice*, pp. 190–91; "Composition as Explanation." On the concept of "limited horizon," see Wallace

L. Chafe, "Integration and Involvement in Speaking," in Deborah Tannen, ed., *Spoken and Written Language: Exploring Orality and Literacy* (Norwood, N.J.: Ablex, 1986), pp. 35–53.

8. Constance Rourke, *American Humor* (New York: Harcourt, Brace, 1931) p. 162. By "improvisation" I mean here all discourse composed in the course of enunciation, including the formulaic "oral composition" that Milman Parry and Albert Lord define as a separate category (Albert Lord, *The Singer of Tales*: Cambridge: Harvard University Press, 1960).

9. Nelson Algren, quoted in Malcolm Cowley, *The Flower and the Leaf* (New York: Viking, 1985), p. 352; Raymond Carver, "On Writing," in *Fires* (New York: Vintage, 1982), p. 26.

10. Ted Berrigan, "Jack Kerouac," *Paris Review* 11 (Summer 1968): 65; Paula Gunn Allen, interview in Laura Coltelli, ed., *Winged Words: Native American Writers Speak* (Norman: University of Oklahoma Press, 1990), p. 33.

11. Carver, *Fires*, p. 19; Henry Roth, *Mercy of a Rude Stream*. This work is still unpublished in English; I quote and backtranslate from the Italian translation by Mario Materassi, *Alla mercè di una crudele corrente* (Milan: Garzanti 1990), pp. 79–80.

12. Tillie Olsen, "I Stand Here Ironing," in *Tell Me a Riddle* (New York: Delta/Seymour Lawrence, 1989), pp. 1–2; Herman Melville, *Moby-Dick*, in *The Works of Herman Melville*, Standard Edition (New York: Russell & Russell, 1963), 7: 111.

13. Perry Miller, *The Raven and the Whale* (New York: Harcourt, Brace, 1956), p. 233; Cesare Pavese, "Poesia del far poesia," in *La letteratura americana e altri saggi* (Milan: Il Saggiatore, 1971), p. 157 (on Whitman); Paley, "A Conversation," in Anne Charters, ed., *The Story and Its Writer: An Introduction to Fiction* (New York: St. Martin's Press, 1987), pp. 313–17; Allen, in Coltelli, ed., *Winged Words*, p. 23.

14. George R. Stewart, "The Two *Moby-Dicks*," *American Literature* 25, no. 1 (January 1954), pp. 417–48; James Barbour, "The Composition of *Moby-Dick*," *American Literature* 48, no. 3 (November 1975): 343–60; Charles Olson, *Call Me Ishmael* (1947; reprint, London: Jonathan Cape, 1967), p. 35.

15. Hugh Henry Brackenridge, *Modern Chivalry* (1792–1815; reprint, New York: American Book Company, 1934), p. 668.

16. Compare the versions of "So Much Water So Close to Home" in Raymond Carver's *What We Talk About When We Talk About Love* (New York: Vintage: 1989), pp. 47–56, and in *Fires*, pp. 185–204. For a case of

variation as expansion, compare "A Small Good Thing" in *Cathedral* (New York: Vintage, 1984), pp. 58–89 and "The Bath," in *What Do We Talk About*, pp. 45–53. On Carver's "twice-told tales," see Paola Castellucci, *La letteratura dell'assenza* (Roma: Bulzoni, 1992), pp. 105–26.

17. Richard Sewall, *The Life of Emily Dickinson* (London: Faber and Faber, 1976), p. 701 ff.; Barton Levi St. Armand, *The Soul's Society: Emily Dickinson and Her Culture* (Cambridge: Cambridge University Press, 1983), p. 160 ff.; "Emily Dickinson's Babes in the Wood: A Ballad Reborn," *Journal of American Folklore* 90 (October/December 1970): 430–41. Dolores Dyer Lucas, *Emily Dickinson and Riddle* (DeKalb: Northern Illinois University Press, 1969); Suzanne Juhasz, *The Undiscovered Continent: Emily Dickinson and the Space of the Mind* (Bloomington: Indiana University Press, 1983), ch. 6.

18. Walter J. Ong, *Orality and Literacy: The Technologizing of the Word* (London and New York: Methuen, 1982) p. 96.

19. Joyce A. Rowe, *Equivocal Endings in Classic American Novels* (New York: Cambridge University Press, 1988).

20. There is an abundant critical literature concerning the final chapters of *Huckleberry Finn*. Among others, see Leo Marx, "Mr. Eliot, Mr. Trilling, and Huckleberry Finn," *American Scholar* 12, no. 4 (Autumn 1953): 423–40; Russell J. Reising, "Critics on the Phelps Farm," in *The Usable Past: Theory and the Study of American Literature* (New York and London: Methuen, 1986); David Kaufman, "Satiric Deceit in the Ending of *Adventures of Huckleberry Finn*," *Studies in the Novel* 19, no. 1 (Spring 1987): 66–87. On the ambiguous ending of "The Legend of Sleepy Hollow," see Alessandro Portelli, *Il re dormiente: Saggio su Washington Irving* (Rome: Bulzoni, 1981), ch. 3.

21. James Fenimore Cooper, *The Pioneers* (1823; reprint, London: Dent, 1970), p. 444; Washington Irving, "The Stout Gentleman," in *Bracebridge Hall* [1822], in *The Works of Washington Irving*, Author's Revised Edition (New York: G. P. Putnam, 1867), 6: 75–86.

22. Michael Gold, *Jews Without Money* (1930; reprint, New York: Avon, 1965), p. 224. Other "open" endings in "proletarian" novels are those of Clara Weatherwax's *Marching, Marching* (New York: John Day, 1935), which ends with workers and police facing each other on the brink of battle; and Jack Conroy's *The Disinherited* (1933; reprint, New York: Hill & Wang, 1963), which ends with the cinematic image of the characters headed down an open road. A more complex and interesting case is Henry Roth's *Call It Sleep* (1934; reprint, Harmondsworth,

Midds.: Penguin, 1976), which, as Marcus Klein has remarked, presents too complex a personal and social vision to allow a univocal ending (Marcus Klein, *Foreigners: The Making of American Literature 1900–1940* [Chicago and London: The University of Chicago Press, 1981], p. 194).

23. Henry James, preface to *Roderick Hudson*, in *The Art of the Novel* (New York: Scribner's, 1947), pp. 5–6; unsigned review in *Lippincott's Magazine*, February 1, 1882, pp. 213–15, excerpted in Alan Shelston, ed., *A Casebook on Henry James's* Washington Square *and* The Portrait of a Lady (London: Macmillan, 1984), p. 86; A. Robert Lee, " 'Impudent and ingenious fiction': Poe's *The Narrative of Arthur Gordon Pym of Nantucket*," in Lee, ed., *Edgar Allan Poe: The Design of Order* (London: Vision and Barnes and Noble, 1987), p. 113. Because of the novel's double ending, Lee describes *Gordon Pym* as "a body without a head."

24. John T. Irwin, *American Hieroglyphics* (Baltimore and London: The Johns Hopkins University Press, 1983), pp. 112–13.

25. Gerald Emanuel Stearn, *Gompers* (Englewood Cliff, N.J.: Prentice-Hall, 1971), p. 56.

26. Daniel Bell, *The End of Ideology* (New York: The Free Press, 1962); Leslie Fiedler, *An End to Innocence* (Boston: Beacon Press, 1955); Francis Fukuyama, "The End of History," *The National Interest* 16 (Summer 1989): 3–18; Mario Savio, "The End of History," in Massimo Teodori, *The New Left: A Documentary History* (Indianapolis and New York: Bobbs-Merrill, 1969), p. 159.

27. Isaac Asimov, *The End of Eternity* (1955; reprint, St. Albans, Herts.: Granada, 1973). See also Alessandro Portelli, "Il presente come utopia: la narrativa di Isaac Asimov," *Calibano* 2 (1978): 138–84.

28. Kurt Vonnegut, *Slaughterhouse-Five; or, The Children's Crusade* (1969; reprint, St. Albans, Herts.: Granada, 1972).

29. Walt Whitman, "Song of Myself," in *Complete Poetry and Collected Prose* (New York: The Library of America, 1982), sec. 3, 190 (all references to Whitman are from this edition); Claudio Guillén, "On the Use of Monistic Theories, " *New Literary History* 18, no. 3 (Spring 1987): 497–516; W. L. Chafe, "Integration and Involvement." On "incremental repetition" in popular ballads, see Gordon Hall Gerould, *The Ballad of Tradition* (New York and Oxford: Oxford University Press, 1957): 105–17.

30. Deborah Tannen, *Talking Voices* (Cambridge: Cambridge University Press, 1989), pp. 87, 48–51, 18–19; Paula Gunn Allen, *The Sacred Hoop: Recovering the Feminine in American Indian Traditions* (Boston: Bea-

con Press, 1986), pp. 63–64. Both Tannen and Allen downplay the role of repetition as a memory device.

31. On the relationship between syntactic subordination, narrativity, and evaluation, see William Labov, "The Transformation of Experience in Narrative Syntax," in *Language in the Inner City* (Philadelphia: University of Pennylvania Press, 1972), pp. 354–96; Livia Polanyi, *Telling the American Story: A Structural and Cultural Analyis of Contemporary Conversational Storytelling* (Cambridge and London, The MIT Press, 1989); Sandra A. Thompson, "Subordination and Narrative Event Structure," in Russell S. Tomlin, ed., *Coherence and Grounding in Discourse* (Amsterdam and Philadelphia: John Benjamins, 1987), pp. 435–54.

32. Ernest Hemingway, "After the Storm," in *The First Forty-Nine Stories* (London: Jonathan Cape, 1964), p. 304. On "fragmentation" as a feature of colloquial style, especially in Hemingway and Stein, see Richard Bridgman, *The Colloquial Style in America* (New York and Oxford: Oxford University Press, 1966).

33. W. L. Chafe, "Integration and Involvement"; D. Allen and R. Guy, *Conversation Analysis: The Sociology of Talk* (The Hague and Paris: Mouton, 1974), p. 170.

34. Leslie Marmon Silko, *Ceremony* (1977; reprint, New York: Penguin, 1986), p. 126.

35. Stein, "Melanctha," in *Selected Writings*, p. 385; "Portraits and Repetition," in *Lectures in America* (Boston: Beacon Press, 1957), p. 156.

36. Stein, "Melanctha," pp. 348–52; "Composition as Explanation," pp. 518 ff. On anaphora in oral and written discourse, see Barbara Fox, "Anaphora in Popular Written English Narratives," and Wallace L. Chafe, "Cognitive Constraints on Information Flow," in Tomlin, ed., *Coherence and Grounding in Discourse*, pp. 157–74, 21–51.

37. On "run-on sentences" in Stein, see Bridgman, *Colloquial Style*, p. 137; in Mark Twain, see Janet Holmgren McKay, " 'Tears and Flapdoodle': Point of View and Style in *Adventures of Huckleberry Finn*," *Style* 10 (Winter 1976): 41–50.

38. Mark Twain, *The Adventures of Huckleberry Finn*, in *The Writings or Mark Twain* (Hartford, Conn.: The American Publishing Company, 1901), pp. 161–62; E. Hemingway, "A Natural History of the Dead," in *The First Forty-Nine Stories* (London: Jonathan Cape, 1964), pp. 364–72.

39. William Faulkner, *As I Lay Dying* (1930; reprint, New York: Modern Library, 1967), p. 90.

40. Henry James, "The Patagonia" [1888] (New York Edition, 1909; reprint, New York: Charles Scribner's Sons, 1957), 18: 200.

41. James, *The Wings of the Dove* (1902; reprint, New York Edition), 20: 405; Bridgman, *Colloquial Style*, pp. 103–104.

42. Julian Hawthorne, "The American Element in Fiction" [1884], in Richard Ruland, ed., *A Storied Land: Theories of American Literature* (New York: E. P. Dutton, 1976), vol. 2, p. 184.

43. David S. Reynolds, *Beneath the American Renaissance* (New York: Knopf, 1988), p. 202.

44. Whitman, "Blue Ontario Shore," sec. 5, p. 471; "American National Literature," p. 1258; "Slang in America," p. 1165. On Whitman's "agglutinative" style, see Roger Asselineau, *The Evolution of Walt Whitman* (Cambridge: Harvard University Press, 1962), 2: 224. On Whitman's democratic concept of language, see also Gene Bluestein, *The Voice of the Folk* (Amherst: The University of Massachusetts Press, 1972), p. 62.

45. Cooper, *The Pioneers*, p. 28 ff.; Edwin Fussell, *Frontier: American Literature and the American West* (Princeton: Princeton University Press, 1965), p. 34; Nathanael West, *The Day of the Locust* [1939], in *The Collected Works of Nathanael West* (Harmondsworth, Midds.: Penguin, 1975), p. 11.

46. John T. Irwin, *Doubling and Incest/Repetition and Revenge* (Baltimore and London: The Johns Hopkins University Press, 1975), p. 157. On Quentin Compson's intertextual life (discrepancies between the two novels and the story "That Evening Sun"), see Dirk Kuyk, Jr., *Sutpen's Design: Interpreting* Absalom, Absalom! (Charlottesville and London: University Press of Virginia, 1990), pp. 110–12; Estella Schoenberg, *Old Tales and Talking: Quentin Compson in* William Faulkner's Absalom, Absalom! *and Related Works* (Jackson: University of Mississippi Press, 1977).

47. Allen, "Introduction" to Paula Gunn Allen, ed., *Spider Woman's Granddaughters* (Boston: Beacon Press, 1989), p. 12; Janice A. Radway, *Reading the Romance* (London: Verso, 1976), p. 198; Leslie Fiedler, *The Inadvertent Epic* (New York: Simon and Schuster, 1979).

48. Allen, *Spider Woman's Granddaughters*, pp. 4, 17, 18; Donald M. Bahro, quoted in Arnold Krupat, *The Voice in the Margin* (Berkeley: University of California Press, 1989), p. 223. Some Indian novels shaped like sagas are Mourning Dove's *Co-ge-wea the Half-Blood* (Boston: Four Seas, 1927), and Louise Erdrich's *Love Medicine* cycle (New York: Holt, 1984–88).

49. James Fenimore Cooper, *The Deerslayer* (1841; reprint, New York: Dodd, Mead, 1952), p. 107.

50. J. D. Salinger, *The Catcher in the Rye* (1951; reprint, Harmondsworth, Midds.: Penguin, 1958), pp. 190–91.

51. Mark Twain, *Roughing It* [1872], in *Writings*, 2: 121–27.

52. Silko, *Ceremony*, pp. 51–52.

53. Stein, "The Gradual Making of *The Making of Americans*,"in *Selected Writings*, pp. 255, 257.

54. Mark Twain, "How to Tell a Story" and "Fenimore Cooper's Literary Offenses," in *Writings*, 2: 7, 79.

55. Eudora Welty, *One Writer's Beginnings* (London: Faber and Faber, 1985), pp. 68–69.

56. Stein, "Composition as Explanation," p. 516.

57. Silko, *Ceremony*, p. 35; Faulkner, in Malcolm Cowley, *The Faulkner-Cowley File: Letters and Memories, 1944–1962* (London: Chatto & Windus, 1966), p. 16 (see also pp. 14, 112).

58. William Faulkner, *Light in August* (1933; reprint, Harmondsworth, Midds.: Penguin, 1960), p. 64.

5. CONVERSATIONS

1. Michael Morman, *Talking Culture: Ethnography and Conversation Analysis* (Philadelphia: University of Pennsylvania Press, 1988); Franco Moretti, *Signs Taken for Wonders*, revised edition (London and New York: Verso, 1988), pp. 257, 258.

2. Ralph Ellison, "Brave Words for a Startling Occasion," in *Shadow and Act*, (1964; reprint, New York: Vintage, 1972), p. 103.

3. Gérard Genette, "Frontières du récit," in *Figures II* (Paris: Seuil, 1969), pp. 55–56.

4. Deborah Tannen, *Talking Voices* (Cambridge: Cambridge University Press, 1989), pp. 98–101; Evan Eisenberg, *The Recording Angel: Explorations in Phonography* (New York: Academic Press, 1981), pp. 37–53.

5. Charles Goodwin, *Conversational Organization* (New York: Academic Press, 1981), pp. 37–53.

6. Erving C. Goffman, *Forms of Talk* (Philadelphia: University of Pennsylvania Press, 1981), p. 48; Goodwin, *Conversational Organization*, p. 8.

7. Michael Tolan, "Analysing Conversation in Fiction: An Example from Joyce's *Portrait*," in Ronald Carter and Paul Simpson, eds., *Language, Discourse, and Literature: An Introductory Reader in Discourse Stylistics*

(London: Unwin Hyman, 1989), p. 195. Cesare Segre defines direct discourse as "repetition" in *Avviamento all'analisi del testo letterario* (Torino: Einaudi, 1985), p. 16.

8. Henry James, *Daisy Miller: A Study* (1878; reprint, London: Macmillan, 1880), pp. 129, 102, 135. References are to this version of the story, rather than to the revised text included in the New York Edition of James's works, because in the later version the treatment of conversational traits is sacrificed to other aspects of discourse.

9. Goffman, *Forms of Talk*, p. 35.

10. Domenico Starnone, "La corte e la piazza: galateo dell'improvvisazione," *I Giorni Cantati* 2–3 (July/December 1981): 128–42; Henry James, *The Speech and Manners of American Women*, ed. E. S. Riggs (Lancaster, Penn.: Lancaster House Press, 1973), p. 43.

11. Richard Wright, *Native Son*, in *Early Works*, ed. Arnold Rampersad (New York: The Library of America, 1991), pp. 458–62. On African-American conversational style, see Roger Abrahams, "Black Talking in the Street," in Richard Bauman and Joel Sherzer, eds., *Explorations in the Ethnography of Speaking* (London and New York: Cambridge University Press, 1974), pp. 241–60; Thomas Kochman, ed., *Rappin' and Stylin' Out: Communication in Black America* (Urbana: University of Illinois Press, 1972). On patterns of call-and-response in black oral and written traditon, see John F. Callahan, *In the African-American Grain: Call-and-Response in Twentieth Century Black Fiction* (Middleton: Wesleyan University Press, 1989).

12. The imitation of whites is a form of African-American street folklore, in which speakers mockingly "converse with grave faces and in pompous language, selecting high-sounding words": Joseph Holt Ingraham, quoted in Roger Abrahams, "Introduction," to Abrahams, ed., *Afro-American Folk Tales* (New York: Pantheon, 1985), p. 11.

13. Ellison, "Brave Words for a Startling Occasion," p. 103.

14. Toni Morrison, interview, in Claudia Tate, ed., *Black Women Writers at Work* (New York: Continuum Press, 1983), p. 25; interview, in Tom Le Clair and Larry McCaffery, eds., *Anything Can Happen: Interviews with Contemporary American Novelists* (Urbana: University of Illinois Press, 1983), p. 257. On the coding of intonation, see Dwight Bolinger, *Intonation and Its Parts: Melody in Spoken English* (Stanford: Stanford University Press, 1986), ch. 1.

15. James, *Daisy Miller*, pp. 81, 13–14, 11; Donatella Izzo, " 'Daisy Miller' e il discorso dell'ideologia," *RSA Journal* 1 (1990): 45–68.

16. James, *Daisy Miller*, p. 44.

17. James, *Daisy Miller*, p. 70.

18. Henry James, *The Turn of the Screw* [1898], New York Edition (1909; reprint, New York: Charles Scribner, 1957), 12: 249.

19. James, *The Turn of the Screw*, pp. 223, 249.

20. Muriel Saville-Troike, "The Place of Silence in an Integrated Theory of Communication," in D. Tannen and M. Saville-Troike, eds., *Perspectives on Silence* (Norwood: Ablex Publishing Co., 1985), pp. 3–18. For an example of ellipses as a graphic indicator of mere continuity of sound, see Ernest Hemingway, *Fiesta* (1927; reprint, London: Granada, 1978), p. 56: some turns of dialogue consist only of dots in quotation marks, to signify a steady background of music and voices.

21. James, *Daisy Miller*, p. 46; J. Gerald Kennedy, *Poe, Death, and the Life of Writing* (New Haven and London: Yale University Press, 1987), p. 21; Paola Zaccaria, " 'Silence—A Fable' di Edgar Allan Poe: la lotta fra scrittura del visibile e scrittura dell'udibile," *RSA Journal* 1 (1990): 27–43.

22. Dennis Tedlock, "Learning to Listen: Oral History as Poetry," and "On the Translation of Style in Oral Narratives," in *The Spoken Word and the Work of Interpretation* (Philadelphia: University of Pennsylvania Press, 1983), pp. 115, 48.

23. James, *The Turn of the Screw*, pp. 228; R. W. B. Lewis, *The American Adam: Tragedy, Innocence and Tradition in the 19th Century* (Chicago: University of Chicago Press, 1955); Tillie Olsen, *Silences* (New York: Dell, 1978).

24. N. Scott Momaday, "The Native Voice," in Emory Elliott, ed., *Columbia Literary History of the United States* (New York: Columbia University Press, 1988), p. 7; *House Made of Dawn* (1968; reprint, New York: Harper and Row, 1981), p. 91; Leslie Marmon Silko, "A Geronimo Story," in *Storyteller* (New York: Little, Brown, 1981), p. 215. On silence in Indian cultures, see Ron Scholler, "The Machine Stops: Silence in the Metaphor of Malfunction," in Tannen and Saville-Troike, *Perspectives on Silence*, pp. 21–30; Keith Basso, "To Give Up on Words: Silence in Western Apache Culture," in Pier Paolo Gigliotti, ed., *Language and Social Context* (New York: Penguin, 1972), pp. 67–86; Marjorie Murphy, "Silence, the Word, and Indian Rhetoric," *College Composition and Communication* 21 (1970): 359–63. Of course, as Tannen and Saville-Troike's collection shows, silence is a form of communication in European and Euro-American cultures also; what is in question is the different awareness of this fact and the different sophistication in the uses of silences.

25. Momaday, *House Made of Dawn*, pp. 57, 191, 35–36, 57; Paula Gunn Allen, *The Sacred Hoop: Recovering the Feminine in American Indian Traditions* (Boston: Beacon Press, 1986), p. 138.

26. James, *The Turn of the Screw*, pp. 245–46.

27. Edith Wharton, "Mr. Jones," in *The Ghost Stories of Edith Wharton* (1937; reprint, New York: Charles Scribner, 1973), pp. 196–97; Ong, *Orality and Literacy: The Technologizing of the Word* (London and New York: Methuen, 1982), p. 79.

28. Ambrose Bierce defines "envelope" as "the coffin of a docment": *The Enlarged Devil's Dictionary* (1911; reprint, Harmondsworth, Midds.: Penguin, 1985), p. 110.

29. Wharton, "Pomegrenate Seed" [1937], *Ghost Stories*, p. 201.

30. Wharton, preface to *Ghost Stories*, pp. 1, 3.

31. Wharton, "Afterward" [1910] *Ghost Stories*, pp. 50, 59.

32. Hawthorne, *The Scarlet Letter*, in *The Centenary Edition of the Works of Nathaniel Hawthorne* (Kent: Ohio State University Press, 1968), 1: 51.

33. Jack London, *The Scarlet Plague*, 1915, in Dale L. Walker, ed., *Curious Fragments: Jack London's Tales of Fantasy Fiction* (Port Washington, N.Y.: Kennikat Press, 1975), p. 1.

34. Stephen Crane, *The Red Badge of Courage* (1895; reprint ed. S. Bradley et al., New York: W. W. Norton, 1976), p. 25.

35. James, *Daisy Miller*, p. 49.

36. Zora Neale Hurston, *Their Eyes Were Watching God* (1937; reprint, Urbana: University of Illinois Press, 1978), p. 10.

37. Saul Bellow, *Dangling Man*, (1944; reprint, Harmondsworth, Midds., Penguin, 1963), pp. 111–17.

38. Toni Morrison, *Beloved* (London: Chatto and Windus/Pan, 1987), pp. 215, 216.

39. Robert Scholes and Robert Kellogg, *The Nature of Narrative* (London: Oxford University Press, 1988), p. 51; Roland Bourneuf and Réal Ouellet, *L'univers du roman* (Paris: Presses Universitaires de France, 1981), p. 82.

40. For instance, in the telling of a folk tale the hero's departure from home can become a story of emigration, while in a life history the loss of a job can be told as a variant of "Snow White": see Aurora Milillo, *La vita e il suo racconto: tra favola e memoria storica* (Rome and Reggio Calabria: Casa del Libro, 1983); Alessandro Portelli, *The Death of Luigi Trastulli: Form and Meaning in Oral History* (Albany: State University of New York Press, 1991), pp. 104–105.

41. Scholes and Kellogg, *The Nature of Narrative*, p. 52.

42. Kenneth Lincoln, *Native American Renaissance* (Berkeley: University of California Press, 1973), p. 129; Hurston, *Mules and Men* (1935; reprint, New York and Evanston: Harper and Row, 1965), p. 23; Theodore Rosengarten, *All God's Dangers: The Life of Nate Shaw* (New York: Knopf, 1975), pp. 3–4 ("Nate Shaw" is a pseudonym for Ned Cobb).

43. Black Elk, *Black Elk Speaks*, ed. John G. Neihardt (1932; reprint, Lincoln: University of Nebraska Press, 1979), pp. 5, 66.

44. *Black Elk Speaks*, p. 8; Werner Berthoff, *The Example of Melville* (Princeton: Princeton University Press, 1962), p. 117.

45. Pretty Shield, "A Woman's Fight" [1932], in Paula Gunn Allen, ed., *Spider Woman's Granddaughters* (Boston: Beacon Press, 1989), p. 29.

46. *The Autobiography of Malcolm X*, with the assistance of Alex Haley (1965; reprint, Harmondsworth, Midds.: Penguin, 1968), p. 81.

47. Lucullus Virgil McWhorter, *Yellow Wolf: His Own Story* (1940, rev. and enlarged ed., Caldwell, Idaho: Caxton Printers, 1991), pp. 34, 193.

48. Ernest J. Gaines, *The Autobiography of Miss Jane Pittman* (Toronto and New York: Bantam, 1972), pp. vi–vii. Goffman's distinction between "speaker," "author," and "animator" is in *Forms of Talk*, pp. 131–33, 144–45. On the unity of author and narrator in autobiography, see Philippe Lejeune, *Le pacte autobiographique* (Paris: Seuil, 1975).

49. Melville, *Moby-Dick*, in *The Works of Herman Melville*, Standard Edition (New York: Russell & Russell, 1963), 7: 1; Hemingway, *Fiesta*, p. 7; Washington Irving, *A History of New York*, in *The Works of Washington Irving*, Author's Revised Edition (New York: G. P. Putnam, 1867), 7: 118.

50. Berthoff describes dialogic storytelling as a "model of free social intercourse in a libertarian democracy": *The Example of Melville*, p. 148.

51. Irving, "Adventure of the German Student," 7: 64.

52. Wayne Booth, *The Rhetoric of Fiction* (Harmondsworth, Midds.: Penguin, 1983), pp. 151–53; Scholes and Kellogg, *The Nature of Narrative*, pp. 268–70.

53. I have discussed this aspect of interviewing in "What Makes Oral History Different," in *The Death of Luigi Trastulli*, pp. 55–58.

54. Vito Amoruso, *Letteratura e società in America, 1890–1900* (Bari: De Donato, 1976), pp. 60.

55. Henry James, Preface to *The Golden Bowl*, in *The Art of the Novel* (New York: Charles Scribner, 1947), p. 346.

56. K. S. Valentine, " 'New Criticism' and the Emphasis on Literature in Interpretation," in David W. Thompson, ed., *Performance of Literature in Historical Perspective* (Lanham, N.Y., and London: University Press of America, 1983), pp. 549–65; James, *The Art of the Novel*, pp. 346–47.

57. James, "The Question of Our Speech," in *Two Lectures* (Boston and New York: Houghton Mifflin, 1905, p. 35.

58. James, *The Speech and Manners of American Women*, p. 43.

6. SYMBOLS: THE ORAL ORIGINS OF THE WORLD

1. Herman Melville, *Moby-Dick*, in *The Works of Herman Melville*, Standard Edition (New York: Russell and Russell, 1963), 7: ix; Walt Whitman, "Slang in America," in *Complete Poetry and Collected Prose* (New York: The Library of America, 1982), pp. 1165–66 (all quotes from Whitman in this book come from this edition). On orality and Spirit, word and Word, see Walter J. Ong, *The Presence of the Word* (New Haven and London: Yale University Press, 1967).

2. Kate Chopin, *The Awakening* (1899; reprint, London: W. W. Norton, 1976), p. 15.

3. Ralph Waldo Emerson, "The Poet"[1844], in *Essays and Lectures*, ed. Joel Porte (New York: The Library of America, 1983), p. 449 (all quotations from Emerson are from this edition).

4. Barbara Packer, "Origin and Authority: Emerson and the Higher Criticism," in Sacvan Bercovitch, ed., *Reconstructing American Literary History* (Cambridge: Harvard University Press, 1986), pp. 67–92.

5. Emerson, "Divinity School Address" [1838], in *Essays and Lectures*, p. 84; "The Poet," p. 458; Italo Calvino, *Six Memos for the Next Millennium* (Cambridge: Harvard University Press, 1988), p. 4.

6. Emerson, "The American Scholar" [1837], in *Essays and Lectures*, pp. 68–69; "The Poet," p. 466; "Divinity School Address," p. 91.

7. Emerson, "The Poet,"ˇ20p. 457; "Shakespeare; or, The Poet," *Representative Men* [1850], in *Essays and Lectures*,, p. 715; Whitman, "Slang in America," p. 1165.

8. Wolfgang Mieder, "The Proverb and Anglo-American Literature," *Southern Folklore Quarterly* 30 (Spring 1974): 49–62; Philip Charles La Rosa, "Invention and Imitation in Emerson's Early Lectures," *American Literature* 44 (March 1972): 13–30; Nelson F. Adkins, "Emerson and the

Bardic Tradition," *PMLA* 63 (1949): 662–77; Reaver J. Russell, "Emerson's Use of Proverbs," *Southern Folklore Quarterly* 27 (Spring 1963): 157–66; Charles Meister, "Franklin as a Proverb Stylist," *American Literature* 24, no. 2 (May 1952): 157–66.

9. Suzanne Juhasz, *The Undiscovered Continent*, pp. 33–34; Karl Keller, *The Only Kangaroo among the Beauty: Emily Dickinson and America* (Baltimore and London: The Johns Hopkins University Press, 1979), pp. 180–81.

10. Whitman, "Song of Myself," sec. 5, 192.

11. Whitman, "Sea-Shore Fancies," p. 796.

12. Whitman, "Song of Myself," sec. 5, 192.

13. John Berryman, "Song of Myself: Intention and Substance," in Jim Perlman *et al.*, eds., *Walt Whitman: The Measure of His Song* (Minneapolis: Holy Cow! Press, 1981), p. 155. According to Richard A. Spear's dictionary of *Slang and Euphemism*, Abridged Edition (New York: North American Library, 1972), the erotic meanings of *valve* (also as a synonym of *cock*) were already current in the 19th century. For a similar example and a parallel analysis, see the reading of the meanings of *tally* by Harold Bloom, "To the Tally of My Soul: Whitman's Image of the Voice," *Bennington Review* 10 (April 1971): 10–17.

14. Roman Jakobson, "Linguistics and Poetics," in Jakobson, *Selected Writings* (The Hague and Paris: Mouton, 1967), 3: 26 (discussing the electoral slogan "I like Ike").

15. Whitman, "Song of the Rolling Earth," sec. 3, 367.

16. Whitman, "Song of Myself," sec. 8, 195; on opera, Gay Wilson Allen, *The Solitary Singer: A Critical Biography of Walt Whitman* (New York: Macmillan, 1955), pp. 112–15; John T. Irwin, *American Hieroglyphics* (Baltimore and London: The Johns Hopkins University Press, 1983), p. 38.

17. Whitman, "When Lilacs Last in the Dooryard Bloom'd," sec. 5, 459; "Out of the Cradle Endlessly Rocking," pp. 388, 393; "Song of Myself," sec. 52, 247.

18. Whitman, "When Lilacs Last in the Dooryard Bloom'd," sec. 13, 463; "A Contralto Voice," p. 876; "Crossing Brooklyn Ferry," sec. 9, 312 and sec. 5, 310; "Out of the Rolling Ocean the Crowd," p. 263; "Song of Myself," sec. 24, 211.

19. Whitman,"Song of Myself," sec. 25, 213; Leslie Marmon Silko, *Ceremony* (1977; reprint, New York: Penguin, 1986), p. 68. An easily accessible version of "There'll Be No Distinction There" is on a Carter

Family CD reissue, *Clinch Mountain Treasures*, Floyd, Va., County Records CCS-CD-112, 1991.

20. Whitman, "Song of Myself," sec. 4, 211.

21. Richard Chase, *Walt Whitman Reconsidered* (New York: W. Sloane Associates, 1955), p. 86; Bruno Cartosio, "Whitman e le masse," *Contrasti* 1 , ed. Vito Amoruso (Bari: Adriatica Editrice, 1986): 61–81.

22. Régis Durand, "Whitman, le rhytme, le sujet de l'écriture," *Delta* 16 (May 1983): 63–78; Whitman, "A Song for Occupations," p. 89. The version published in 1855, which includes the line quoted here, was untitled.

23. Whitman, "Song of the Rolling Earth," sec. 1, 362–63.

24. Whitman, "So Long," p. 611; Allen Ginsberg, "A Supermarket in California," in *Howl and other Poems* (1955; reprint, San Francisco: City Lights, 1959), pp. 79–94.

25. Francis O. Matthiessen, *American Reinaissance: Art and Expression in the Age of Emerson and Whitman* (New York and London: Oxford University Press, 1975), p. 532; Calvin Bedient, "Orality and Power (Whitman's `Song of Myself'),'' *Delta* 16 (May 1983): 79–94.

26. Whitman, "Song of Myself," sec. 1, 188 and sec. 2, 189; Bedient, "Orality and Power."

27. Whitman, "Song of Myself," sec. 24, 211.

28. Régis Durand, "The Anxiety of Performance," *New Literary History* 2, no. 1 (Autumn 1980): 167–76.

29. Whitman, "Song of Myself," sec. 30, 217. The image of "oceanic crowds" was a recurrent cliché in the oratory of Benito Mussolini.

30. Henry Cary, quoted in Perry Miller, *The Raven and the Whale* (New York: Harcourt, Brace, 1956), p. 42; Henry James, *The Speech and Manners of American Women*, ed. E. S. Riggs (Lancaster, Penn.: Lancaster House Press, 1973).

31. James, *Speech and Manners*, pp. 31–32; Hawthorne, *The Scarlet Letter*, p. 51.

32. Paley, "The Loudest Voice," in *The Little Disturbances of Man* (1959; reprint, Harmondsworth, Midds.: Penguin, 1984), p. 55.

33. Nina Auerbach, *Communities of Women: An Idea in Fiction* (Cambridge: Harvard University Press, 1978), p. 123; Paley, "Faith in a Tree," in *Enormous Changes at the Last Minute* (1974; reprint, London: Virago Press, 1979), p. 81.

34. Tony Tanner, "*The Bostonians* and the Human Voice," in *Scenes of Nature, Signs of Men* (Cambridge: Cambridge University Press, 1987), pp.

148–75; Paley, "Friends," in *Later the Same Day* (1985; reprint, Harmondsworth, Midds.: Penguin, 1986), p. 78. The phonic and iconic association of pen and penis is explored in Sandra M. Gilbert and Susan Gubar, *The Madwoman in the Attic* (New Haven and London: Yale University Press, 1979), ch. 1. On the relationship of voice and women's identity, see also Carol Gilligan, *In a Different Voice* (Cambridge: Harvard University Press, 1982); Luce Irigaray, *Parler n'est jamais neutre* (Paris: Les éditions de Minuit, 1985), pp. 169–88, 281–92.

35. Paley, "The Loudest Voice," p. 55; Ellen Moers, *Literary Women* (London: The Women's Press, 1978), p. 55.

36. Paley, "It Is the Responsibility," in *Long Walks and Intimate Talks*, with paintings by Vera B. Williams (New York: The Feminist Press, 1991), no page number; Zora Neale Hurston, *Their Eyes Were Watching God* (1937; reprint, Urbana: University of Illinois Press, 1978), p. 17; Deborah Tannen, *You Just don't Understand: Women and Men in Conversation* (New York: William Morrow, 1990), p. 97 (on gossip in general, pp. 96–122); Eudora Welty, *One Writer's Beginnings* (London: Faber and Faber, 1985), pp. 13–14; Gertrude Stein, "The Gradual Making of *The Making of Americans*" in *Selected Writings*, ed. Carl Van Vechten (New York: Vintage, 1972), p. 135.

37. Paley, "At that Time, or The History of a Joke," in *Later the Same Day*, p. 95.

38. Margaret Atwood, *The Handmaid's Tale* (Toronto: McClellan and Stewart, 1985), p. 133. Atwood, of course, is from Canada; her novel, however, is set in the United States, and her work has been very influential there.

39. Julia Kristeva, *Revolution in Poetic Language*, trans. Margaret Waller (New York: Columbia University Press, 1984), pp. 26–27.

40. Lee Smith, *Fair and Tender Ladies* (New York: Ballantine, 1988), p. 144.

41. Toni Morrison, *Beloved* (London: Chatto and Windus/Pan, 1987), pp. 258–59.

42. Silko, *Ceremony*, pp. 94–95; Toni Morrison, *Song of Solomon* (New York: New American Library, 1977), p. 281.

43. Chopin, *The Awakening*, pp. 3–8.

44. Ibid.,, pp. 10, 20, 113.

45. Ibid., p. 113; Suzanne Wakenfeld, "Edna's Suicide: The problem of the One and the Many," appendix to the Norton edition of *The Awakening*, pp. 218–24.

46. William Faulkner, *The Sound and the Fury* (1929; reprint, New York and London: W. W. Norton, 1987), p. 177.

47. Don DeLillo, *Americana* (1971; reprint, Harmondsworth, Midds.: Penguin, 1989), p. 371; James Welch, *The Death of Jim Loney* (1979; reprint, New York: Penguin, 1987), p. 128. For David Leavitt and Jay McInerney, see in this book, the first section of chapter 11.

48. Margaret Atwood, *Cat's Eye* (New York: Doubleday, 1989), pp. 43–44.

49. Philippe Joutard, *Ces voix qui nous viennent du passé* (Paris: Hachette), p. 1983.

50. Lee Smith, *Oral History* (New York: Ballantine, 1983); Anne Rice, *Interview with the Vampire* (New York, Ballantine, 1976), p. 4.

51. Alice Walker, *The Temple of My Familiar* (New York and London: Simon and Schuster, 1989), pp. 359, 353.

52. Edgar Allan Poe, "The Murders of the rue Morgue" [1841], in *Poetry and Tales* (New York: The Library of America, 1984), p. 405 (all references to Poe's tales and poems are to this edition).

53. Poe, "The Power of Words" [1845], p. 825.

54. Poe, "The Facts in the Case of M. Valdemar" [1845], pp. 839, 840. On this story as "linguistic scandal," see Roland Barthes, "Textual Analysis of a Tale by Edgar Poe," trans. Donald G. Marshall, *Poe Studies* 10, no. 1 (June 1977).

55. Poe, "The Fall of the House of Usher" [1839], pp. 330, 336.

56. Poe, "Ligeia" [1838], pp. 272, 262, 263.

57. Poe, "The Philosophy of Composition" [1846], pp. 17, 18; "The Poetic Principle" [1850], p. 78; "The Domain of Arnheim" [1847], pp. 861–62. Guido Fink notes the symbolic implications of Poe's "sweetish abundance of liquid consonants" in *I testimoni dell'immaginario* (Rome: Edizioni di Storia e Letteratura, 1978), p. 254. On the relationship of music and the indefiniteness of poetic intuition in Poe, see Irwin, *American Hieroglyphics*, p. 115 ff. Edmund Wilson also notes that "Poe's poetry . . . does approach the indefiniteness of music" and is therefore "nonsensical in much the same way as, to the ordinary point of view, much of our best modern poetry appears": "Poe at Home and Abroad," in *The Shores of Light* (1952; reprint, New York: Farrar Strauss Giroux, 1979), pp. 188–89.

58. F. O. Matthiessen, *American Renaissance*, 267; D. S. Reynolds, *Beneath the American Renaissance* (New York: Knopf, 1988), pp. 229–31.

59. Robert Giddins, "Was the Chevalier Left-Handed? Poe's Dupin Stories," in A. Robert Lee, ed., *Edgar Allan Poe: The Design of Order* (London: Vision and Barnes and Noble, 1987), pp. 88–111; Walter J. Ong, *Orality and Literacy: The Technologizing of the Word* (London and New York: Methuen, 1982), pp. 149–51.

60. William Faulkner, *As I Lay Dying* (1930; reprint, New York: Modern Library, 1967), p. 19.

61. William Faulkner, *Absalom, Absalom!* (1936; reprint, New York: Vintage, 1987), pp. 271–72.

62. Calvino, *Six Memos*, p. 6.

63. Faulkner, *As I Lay Dying*, pp. 85–86.

64. Washington Irving, "The Legend of Sleepy Hollow," in *The Sketch Book of Geoffrey Crayon, Gent.*, in *The Works of Washington Irving*. Author's Revised Edition (New York: G. P. Putnam, 1867), 2: 442; Emily Dickinson, *The Complete Poems*, ed. Thomas H. Johnson (London: Faber and Faber, 1975), n. 258, p. 119; Faulkner, *As I Lay Dying*, pp. 91–92.

65. Faulkner, *Absalom, Absalom!*, pp. 4, 34.

66. Ibid., p. 379; Black Elk, *Black Elk Speaks*, ed. John G. Neihardt (1932; reprint, Lincoln: University of Nebraska Press, 1979), p. 4.

67. Faulkner, *As I Lay Dying*, p. 230.

68. Faulkner, *Light in August* (1933; reprint, Harmondsworth, Midds.: Penguin, 1960), pp. 87–88.

69. Whitman, "When Lilacs Last in the Dooryard Bloom'd," sec. 15, 465; "Song of Myself," sec. 24, 211; Dickinson, *Poems*, n. 1261, p. 553.

70. Faulkner, *Absalom, Absalom!*, p. 4; *As I Lay Dying*, p. 165.

71. Whitman, "Song of Myself," sec. 52, 247; Poe, "The Facts in the Case of M. Valdemar," p. 103; Faulkner, *As I Lay Dying* p. 165; *Light in August*, p. 113.

72. Faulkner, *Absalom, Absalom!*, pp. 5, 9.

73. Alessandro Portelli, *Biografia di una città* (Torino: Einaudi, 1985), pp. 174-78; for a more detailed analysis, see Alessandro Portelli, "Oral History and Literature: *Absalom, Absalom!*," in *The Death of Luigi Trastulli: Form and Meaning in Oral History* (Albany: State of New York University Press, 1991), pp. 270–82.

74. Rev. Hugh Cowans, interviewed by Alessandro Portelli and Cristina Mattiello, Lexington, Ky., October 3, 1983.

75. Faulkner, *Absalom, Absalom!*, pp. 470, 471.

7. LANGUAGES OF REALITY

1. Kenneth Cmiel, *Democratic Eloquence: The Fight over Popular Speech in Nineteenth-Century America* (New York: William Morrow, 1990), pp. 116–19.

2. Bruno Cartosio, *Lavoratori in America* (Milan: Arcipelago Edizioni, 1989), p. 87.

3. Werner Berthoff, *The Ferment of Realism: American Literature 1884–1919* (New York: The Free Press, 1965), p. 2.

4. Eric Sundquist, introduction to E. Sundquist, ed., *American Realism: New Essays* (Baltimore: Johns Hopkins University Press, 1982), pp. 3–24.

5. Ernest Hemingway, *Green Hills of Africa* (1936; reprint, London: Jonathan Cape, 1954), p. 29; Raymond Carver, *Fires* (New York: Vintage, 1982), p. 28; Walt Whitman, preface to the 1855 edition of *Leaves of Grass* in *Complete Poetry and Collected Prose* (New York: The Library of America, 1982), pp. 5–6 (all quotes from Whitman in this book come from this edition)., pp. 5–6; John Dos Passos, *U.S.A.* (1930–1938; reprint, Harmondsworth, Midds: Penguin, 1966), p. 7.

6. Whitman, "Slang in America," pp. 1165–66; David S. Reynolds, *Beneath the American Renaissance* (New York: Knopf, 1988), pp. 19 ff.

7. Woody Guthrie, "Ear Players," quoted in the booklet included in the album *Bound for Glory: The Songs and Stories of Woody Guthrie Sung by Woody Guthrie, Told by Will Geer,* ed. by Millard Lampell, Folkways Records FA 2481, 1961, p. 8; Hank Williams, quoted in Bill C. Malone, *Country Music U.S.A.* (Austin and London: University of Texas Press, 1968), pp. 236–37; Ralph Waldo Emerson, "The American Scholar" [1837], in *Essays and Lectures*, ed. Joel Porte (New York: The Library of America, 1983), p. 61 (all quotations from Emerson are from this edition).

8. Hugh Henry Brackenridge, *Modern Chivalry* (1792–1815; reprint, New York: American Book Company, 1934), vol. 1, p. 78; James Fenimore Cooper, *Notions of the Americans* (1828; reprint, New York: Hill and Wang, 1963), p. 108; Nathaniel Hawthorne, preface to *The Marble Faun* [1860], in *The Centenary Edition of the Works of Nathaniel Hawthorne* (Kent: Ohio State University Press, 1968), 4: 3; Henry James, *Hawthorne* (London: Macmillan, 1879), pp. 43–44; Emerson, "The Poet" [1844], p.465; Lafcadio Hearn, in "The Item," [1881], in Richard Ruland, ed., *A Storied Land: Theories of American Literature* (New York: E. P. Dutton, 1976) 2: 71; Joseph Freeman, quoted in Marcus Klein, *Foreigners: The Making of*

American Literature 1900–1940 (Chicago and London: The University of Chicago Press, 1981), p. 70.

9. Richard Dorson, *America in Legend: Folklore from the Colonial Period to the Present* (New York: Pantheon, 1973), pp. 76–77; Rupert Wilkinson, *American Tough* (Westport, Conn.: Greenwood Press, 1984), pp. 11 ff.; Klein, *Foreigners*, p. 116.

10. Ralph Ellison, "Change the Joke and Slip the Yoke," in *Shadow and Act* (1964; reprint, New York: Vintage, 1972), p. 52; Bruce Springsteen, "Tougher than the Rest," in *Tunnel of Love*, 1987, CBS 460270, 1988.

11. Dashiell Hammett, *The Maltese Falcon* (1930; reprint, San Francisco: North Point Press, 1987), p. 3. Even the hero's name, Spade, suggests a triangular, V-shaped object.

12. James Fenimore Cooper, *The Deerslayer* (1841; reprint, New York: Dodd, Mead, 1952), pp. 78, 150, 147, 159.

13. On Cooper's use of dialect, see Louise Pound, "The Dialect of Cooper's Leatherstocking," *American Speech* 2, no. 3 (September 1927): 479–88; and Mark Twain's "Fenimore Cooper's Literary Offenses"in *The Writings of Mark Twain* (Hartford, Conn.: The American Publishing Company, 1901), 2:78–80. On multilingualism in Cooper and Brackenridge, see David Simpson, *The Politics of American English* (New York and Oxford: Oxford University Press, 1986), pp. 117, 149, and passim; Mark R. Patterson, *Authority, Autonomy and Representation in American Literature* (Princeton: Princeton University Press, 1988), p. 50. On music and noise, see Thomas Philbrick, "*The Last of the Mohicans* and the Sounds of Discord," *American Literature* 43, no. 1 (March 1971): 25–41.

14. Mikhail Bakhtin, "Discourse in the Novel," in *The Dialogic Imagination* (Austin: University of Texas Press, 1984), p. 270; Thomas Jefferson, quoted in H. L. Mencken, *The American Language* (New York: Knopf, 1921), p. 11; Noah Webster, quoted in Richard Bridgman, *The Colloquial Style in America* (New York and Oxford: Oxford University Press, 1966), p. 8; Simpson, *The Politics of American English*, pp. 29–31.

15. Elijah H. Criswell, "Lewis and Clark, Linguistic Pioneers," *University of Missouri Studies* 15, no. 2 (April 1940); Frederick G. Cassidy, "Language on the American Frontier," in Walker D. Wyman and Clifton B. Kroeber, *The Frontier in Perspective* (Madison: University of Wisconsin Press, 1957); Michael T. Kammen, *Imagining Language in America: From the Revolution to the Civil War* (Princeton: Princeton University Press, 1990). The concept of "American koine" was formulated by Joey T. Dil-

lard, *All-American English* (New York: Random House, 1975), ch. 2 (English travelers to America at the turn of the century did report a feeling that language was more uniform there: see Robert T. Oliver, *History of Public Speaking in America* (Boston: Allyn and Bacon, 1965), pp. 43, 59–61). David Hackett Fischer, *Albion's Seed: Four British Folkways in America* (New York and Oxford: Oxford University Press, 1989), demonstrates the persistence of inherited cultural differences.

16. Brackenridge, *Modern Chivalry*, 1: 331; Henry James, "Preface" to "Daisy Miller," in *The Art of the Novel* (New York: Scribner's, 1947), p. 279.

17. James Russell Lowell, "Mr. Hosea Biglow's Speech in March Meeting," *The Biglow Papers*, Second Series, n. 11, in *The Works of James Russell Lowell* (Boston: Houghton Mifflin, 1894), p. 378; Neil Schmitz, *Of Huck and Alice: Humorous Writing in American Literature* (Minneapolis: University of Minnesota Press, 1983), p. 31; James M. Cox, "Humor of the Old Southwest," in Louis J. Rubin, ed., *The Comic Imagination in American Literature* (Washington, D.C.: Voice of America Forum Series, 1974), pp. 105–16. On Artemus Ward and the other literary comedians, see Brom Weber, "The Misspellers," *ibid.*, pp. 133–43; Jess Bier, *The Rise and Fall of American Humor* (New York: Holt, Rinehart and Winston, 1968), pp. 77–116.

18. Van Wyck Brooks, *The Times of Melville and Whitman* (New York: E. P. Dutton, 1947), p. 384; Roman Jakobson, "Six leçons sur le son et le sens," in *Selected Writings* (Berlin, New York, and Amsterdam: Mouton De Gruyter, 1988), p. 7. Stephen M. Ross, *Fiction's Inexhaustible Voice* (Athens: University of Georgia Press, 1989), pp. 109–10.

19. Karla F. C. Holloway, *The Character of the Word: The Texts of Zora Neale Hurston* (Westport, Conn.: Greenwood Press, 1987), p. 68; Cleanth Brooks, *The Language of the American South* (Athens: University of Georgia Press, 1975), pp. 37–38; Frederick L. Gwynn and Joseph L. Blotner, eds., *Faulkner in the University* (New York: Random House, 1965), p. 181.

20. William Faulkner, *The Sound and the Fury* (1929; reprint, New York and London: W. W. Norton, 1987), p. 73; Sumner Ives, "A Theory of Literary Dialect," *Tulane Studies in English* 2 (1950): 137–92; Ross, *Fiction's Inexhaustible Voice*, p. 104. The same convention applies to the author's own voice. Gwynn and Blotner note that in transcribing Faulkner's class conferences at the University of Virginia in 1957–1958, "we

have not attempted to render his striking regional dialect or individualized pronunciation" (*Faulkner in the University*, p. viii).

21. Shelley Fisher-Fishkin, *Was Huck Black? Mark Twain and African American Voices* (New York and Oxford: Oxford University Press, 1993); Toni Morrison, *Playing in the Dark: Whiteness and the Literary Imagination* (Cambridge: Harvard University Press, 1992); Charles Chesnutt, *The House Behind the Cedars* (1899; reprint, London: Collier, 1960), p. 10.

22. Charles W. Chesnutt, "The Wife of His Youth," in *The Wife of His Youth and other Stories* (1899; reprint, Ann Arbor: The University of Michigan Press, 1981), pp. 4, 20. For a more detailed discussion, see Alessandro Portelli, "La linea del colore: Introduzione a Charles Chesnutt," in Charles W. Chesnutt, *La sposa della giovinezza* , trans. Cristina Mattiello (Venezia: Marsilio, 1991).

23. Annalucia Accardo, "*Divine Right's Trip*: A Folk Tale or a Postmodern Novel?," *Appalachian Journal* 12 (Fall 1984): 38–43; Anna Scannavini, "Lingua e dialetto: James Still, poeta a Dead Mare," in A. Accardo et al., eds., *Un'altra America: Letteratura e cultura degli Appalachi meridionali* (Rome: Bulzoni, 1991), pp. 147–72.

24. Sylvia Holton, *Down Home and Uptown: The Representation of Black Speech in American Fiction* (Rutherford: Farleigh University Press, 1984), pp. 96–98, 199–200; Holloway, *The Character of the Word*, p. 80 ff.; Zora Neale Hurston, "Characteristics of Negro Expression" [1934], in *The Sanctified Church: The Folklore Writings of Zora Neale Hurston* (Berkeley, Cal.: Turtle Island, 1981), pp. 49–68; Robert Hemenway, *Zora Neale Hurston: A Literary Biography* (Urbana, University of Illinois Press, 1977), pp. 159–87; Barbara Johnson and Henry Louis Gates, Jr., "Black and Idiomatic Free Indirect Speech," in Harold Bloom, ed., *Zora Neale Hurston's Their Eyes Were Watching God* (Boston: Chelsea Publishers, 1987), pp. 83–85.

25. William Carlos Williams, *The Autobiography of William Carlos Williams* (New York: Random House, 1951), p. 311.

26. Mario Maffi, *Nel mosaico della città: Differenze etniche e nuove culture in un quartiere di New York* (Milan: Feltrinelli, 1992), p. 201.

27. Henry Roth, *Call it Sleep* (1934; reprint, Harmondsworth, Midds.: Penguin, 1976), p. 228.

28. Henry Adams, *The Education of Henry Adams* (1907; reprint, New York: Modern Library, 1967), p. 238; Henry James, *The American Scene* (1907; reprint ed. Leon Edel, Bloomington: Indiana University Press, 1968), p. 139.

29. Maffi, *Nel mosaico della città*, p. 188.

30. Werner Sollors, *Beyond Ethnicity: Consent and Descent in American Literature* (New York and Oxford: Oxford University Press, 1989), pp. 237–58; William Boelhover, ed., *The Future of American Modernism: Ethnic Writing between the Wars* (Amsterdam: V. U. University Press, 1990). By Abraham Cahan, see *Yekl: A Tale of the New York Ghetto* (New York: D. Appleton, 1986), and *The Rise of David Levinsky* (1917; reprint, New York: Harper and Row, 1960).

31. William Raiganal Benson, "The Stone and Kelsey 'Massacre,' first published in 1932 in the *California Historical Society Quarterly*, now in Donald McQuadre et al., eds., *The Harper American Literature* (New York: Harper and Row, 1987) 1: 742–48. See Michael Staub, "(Re)Collecting the Past: Writing Native American Speech," *American Quarterly* 43, no. 3 (September 1991): 425–56.

32. Alice Walker, *The Color Purple* (1982; reprint, New York: Washington Square Press, 1983), p. 11.

33. Mark Twain, *The Adventures of Huckleberry Finn* in *The Writings of Mark Twain* (Hartford, Conn.: The American Publishing Company, 1901), p. 15. On the interplay of vernacular and literary registers in *Huckleberry Finn*, see Bridgman, *The Colloquial Style in America*, p. 51; Richard Chase, *The American Novel and Its Tradition* (New York: Doubleday, 1957), pp. 139–42; Henry Nash Smith, *Mark Twain: The Development of a Writer* (Cambridge: Harvard University Press, 1962), pp. 1–22; Leo Marx, "The Vernacular Style in America," in B. Bottler and M. Light, eds., *The World of Words* (Boston: Houghton Mifflin, 1967), pp. 400–12. Robert J. Lowenherz, "The Beginning of Huckleberry Finn," *American Speech* 32, no. 3 (October 1963): 196–201, notes that this beginning achieves comic effect without relying on dialect. See also: David Carkeet, "The Dialects in *Huckleberry Finn*," *American Literature* 51, no. 3 (November 1979): 315–32; Curt Rulon, "Geographical Distribution of Dialect Areas in *The Adventures of Huckleberry Finn*," *Mark Twain Journal* 14 (1966): 9–12; and, most important, David R. Sewell, *Mark Twain's Languages: Discourse, Dialogue, and Linguistic Variety*, (Berkeley: University of California Press, 1987). The Italian translations of *Le avventure di Huckleberry Finn* referred to are those by Enzo Giachino (Torino: Einaudi, 1963) and by Maria Stella Sernas (Milan: Armando Curcio Editore, 1978). But the all-or-nothing alternative shapes all other translation efforts. Wallace L. Chafe discusses the ambiguity and fuzziness in oral discourse in "Inte-

gration and Involvement," in Deborah Tannen, ed., *Spoken and Written Language: Exploring Orality and Literacy* (Norwood, N.J.: Ablex, 1986).

34. Mark Twain, *Huckleberry Finn*, pp. 161–62.

35. Bakhtin, "Discourse in the Novel," pp. 262, 273.

36. Ibid., pp. 298, 292; Sewell, *Mark Twain's Languages*, p. 7; Maria Ornella Marotti, *The Duplicating Imagination* (University Park, Penn. and London: Pennsylvania University Press, 1990).

37. Mark Twain, *A Connecticut Yankee at King Arthur's Court*, in *Writings* 11: 144.

38. Pedro Pietri, "Beware of Signs," in *Puerto Rican Obituary* (New York: Waterfront Press, 1973), p. 17; on record, *Aquí se habla español* (New York, Discos Coqui LP 1203, 1973).

39. Nicolás Kanellos, "Oral and Hispanic Literature of the United States," in A. LaVonne Brown Ruoff and Jerry W. Ward, eds., *Redefining American Literary History* (New York: The Modern Language Association of America, 1990), pp. 115–23; Cordelia Candelaria, "Code-Switching as Metaphor in Chicano Poetry," in Geneviève Fabre, ed., *European Perspectives on Hispanic Literature of the United States* (Houston: Arte Público Press, 1988), pp. 91–97; Miguel Algarín, "Nuyorican Language," in M. Algarín and Miguel Piñero, *Nuyorican Poetry: An Anthology of Puerto Rican Words and Feelings* (New York: Morrow, 1975), pp. 9–27.

40. Tato Laviera, *Enclave* (Houston: Arte Público Press, 1981), p. 33.

41. Tomás Rivera, *And the Earth Did Not Part* (Berkeley: Quinto Sol, 1971; critical edition by Ricardo Hinojosa as *This Migrant Earth* [Houston: Arte Público Press, 1986]; reprinted as *y no se lo tragó la tierra . . . And the Earth Did Not Devour Him* [Houston: Arte Público Press, 1987], trans. Evangelina Vigil-Piñon); Carmen de Monteflores, *Cantando bajito / Singing Softly* (San Francisco: Spinster-Aunt Lute, 1989); Tato Laviera, *La Carreta Made a U-Turn* (Houston: Arte Público Press, 1981).

42. Frances R. Aparicio, "La vida es un Spanglish Disparatero: Bilingualism in Nuyorican Poetry," in Fabre, ed., *European Perspectives*, pp. 148–60.

43. Kanellos, "Orality and Hispanic Literature," p.117.

44. On the metaphor of the talking book, see Anita Seppilli, *La memoria e l'assenza* (Bologna: Cappelli, 1979), p. 30; Henry Louis Gates, Jr., *The Signifying Monkey: A Theory of Afro-American Literary Criticism* (New York and Oxford: Oxford University Press, 1988), pp. 127–69; Washington Irving, "The Mutability of Literature," in *The Sketch Book of*

Geoffrey Crayon, Gent. in *The Works of Washington Irving*, Author's Revised Edition (New York: G. P. Putnam, 1867), 2: 158–71.

45. Interview with Pedro Pietri, recorded by Alessandro Portelli, New York, November 23, 1983, in A. Portelli, "Come distinguere i vivi dai morti," in *Taccuini Americani* (Rome: Manifestolibri, 1991), pp. 58–65.

46. Pietri, *Puerto Rican Obituary*, pp. 24–26.

47. Pietri, "Do Not Observe the No Smoking Sign," in *Traffic Violations* (New York: Waterfront Press, 1983), p. 123.

48. Pietri, "The Broken English Dream," in *Puerto Rican Obituary*, p. 15.

49. Pietri, *Puerto Rican Obituary*, p. 3; "April 15th Until Further Notice," in *Traffic Violations*, p. 72.

50. Pietri, "1st Untitled Poem" and "13th Untitled Poem," in *Traffic Violations*, pp. 41, 60.

51. P. Pietri, "Purple Pedestrian," *in Traffic Violations*, p. 79.

52. Pietri, "Poem for My Daughter," in *Traffic Violations*, p. 85.

8. FRAMES

1. Herman Melville, *Moby-Dick*, in *The Works of Herman Melville*, Standard Edition (New York: Russell & Russell, 1963), 7: 152.

2. Melville, *Moby-Dick*, 7: 214. According to Harold Beaver's "Commentary" to the Penguin edition of *Moby-Dick* (Harmondsworth, Midds., 1972, p. 773), this is a verse from the song "Captain Beaver." The key lines, however, also occur in other sea songs.

3. "The Greenland Whale Fishery," in Ralph Vaughan Williams and A. L. Lloyd, eds., *The Penguin Book of English Folk Songs* (Harmondsworth, Midds.: Penguin, 1959), p. 50 (for an American variant, see Joanna Colcord, *Songs of American Sailormen* [New York: Oak Publications, 1964], pp. 37–39); Melville, *Moby-Dick*, 7: 154.

4. Alan Lomax, *Folk Songs of North America* (Garden City, N.J.: Doubleday, 1960), p. 61.

5. "The E-ri-ee was a-rising," in Russell Ames, *The Story of American Folk Song* (New York: Grosset and Dunlap, 1960), p. 179.

6. Daniel Hoffman, *Form and Fable in American Fiction* (New York and Oxford: Oxford University Press, 1961); Constance Rourke, *American Humor* (New York: Harcourt, Brace, 1931); Gene Bluestein, *The Voice of the Folk* (Amherst: The University of Massachusetts Press, 1972).

7. William Gilmore Simms, "The Sins of Typography," in *Martin Faber, The Story of a Criminal, and Other Tales* (New York: Harper and

Brothers, 1837), 2: 6–35 (I thank Paola Ludovici for drawing my attention to this story); Henry James, "Preface" to "Daisy Miller" in *The Art of the Novel* (New York: Scribner's, 1947), p. 279; Hoffman, *Form and Fable*, p. 49; Mark Twain, *Huckleberry Finn*, in *The Writings of Mark Twain* (Hartford, Conn.: The American Publishing Company, 1901), pp. 186–88.

8. Ray Bradbury, *Fahrenheit 451* (1951; reprint, New York: Ballantine, 1966), p. 103. The sentence is spoken, with negative intention, by a character; but the authorial voice throughout sees this function of books as their most positive property.

9. Rourke, *American Humor*, p. 161; Richard Dorson, "The Question of Folklore in a New Nation," in *American Folklore and the Historian* (Chicago and London: University of Chicago Press, 1971), p. 103.

10. Hoffman, *Form and Fable*, pp. 10–16; Richard Chase, *The American Novel and Its Tradition* (New York: Doubleday, 1957), pp. 243–46.

11. Richard Dorson articulates this approach in "The Identification of Folklore in American Literature," in *American Folklore and the Historian*, pp. 186–203. Daniel Hoffman criticizes him in "Folklore in Literature: Notes toward a Theory of Interpretation," *Journal of American Folklore* 79, no. 275 (January/March 1957), pp. 15–21, and Dorson replies (insisting on the importance of Rowland Robinson) in "Folklore in American Literature: A Postcript," also in *American Folklore and the Historian*, pp. 204–9. Dorson's two articles include valuable bibliographies. See also: Roger D. Abrahams, "Folklore and Literature as Performance," *Journal of the Folklore Institute* 8 (1972): 85–94; Theresa Meléndez, "The Oral Tradition and the Study of American Literature," in A. Lavonne Brown Ruoff and Jerry W. Ward, eds., *Redefining American Literary History* (New York: The Modern Language Association of America, 1990), pp. 75–82.

12. Marcus Klein, *Foreigners: The Making of American Literature, 1900–1940* (Chicago and London: University of Chicago Press, 1981), pp. 142, 99; Roak Bradford, *John Henry* (New York and London: Harper and Brothers, 1931).

13. Paula Gunn Allen, "Whose Dream is This Anyway?," in *The Sacred Hoop: Recovering the Feminine in American Indian Traditions* (Boston: Beacon Press, 1986), p. 81.

14. Ralph Ellison, "Hidden Name and Complex Fate," in *Shadow and Act* (1964; reprint, New York: Vintage, 1972), p. 157.

15. Melville, *Moby-Dick*, 7: 311; Bruce Jackson, *Get Your Ass in the Water and Swim Like Me: Narrative Poetry from the Black Oral Tradition*

(Cambridge: Harvard University Press, 1974); on record, see the album with the same title, Rounder Records 2014, Somerville, Mass., 1976. Another version is in Roger Abrahams, *Deep Down in the Jungle* (Chicago: Aldine Publishing Co., 1970), pp. 101 ff.

16. Augustus B. Longstreet, "Georgia Theatrics," in *Georgia Scenes* (1833; reprint, Gloucester, Mass.: Peter Smith, 1970), p. 1.

17. Thomas Bangs Thorpe, "The Big Bear of Arkansas," [1841], in Walter J. Blair and Raven L. McDavid, *The Mirth of a Nation* (Minneapolis: University of Minnesota Press, 1983), p. 30; Charles W. Chesnutt, *The Conjure Woman* (1899; reprint, Ann Arbor: The University of Michigan Press, 1972); Mark Twain, *Roughing It*, in *Writings*, 11: 62.

18. Nathaniel Hawthorne, *American Notebooks*, in *The Centenary Edition of the Works of Nathaniel Hawthorne* (Kent: Ohio State University Press, 1968), 8: 248–49; Leo Marx, *The Machine in the Garden: Technology and the Pastoral Ideal in America* (New York and Oxford, Oxford University Press, 1964), pp. 1–16.

19. Nathaniel Hawthorne, "My Kinsman, Major Molineux" [1831], in *Works*, 11: 230; David S. Reynolds, *Beneath the American Renaissance* (New York: Knopf, 1988), pp. 441–83; H. L. Mencken, *The American Language* (New York: Knopf, 1921), pp. 55–56; Constance Rourke, *The Roots of American Culture* (New York: Harcourt Brace, 1942), p. 128.

20. J. M. Cox, "Humor of the Old Southwest," in Louis J. Rubin, ed., *The Comic Imagination in American Literature* (Washington, D.C.: Voice of America Forum Series, 1974), pp. 105–16.

21. Jess Bier, *The Rise and Fall of American Humor* (New York: Holt, Rinehart and Winston, 1968), p. 57; Kenneth S. Lynn, *Mark Twain and Southwestern Humor* (Boston: Little, Brown, 1959), p. 64; John F. Callahan, *In the African-American Grain: Call-and-Response in Twentieth Century Black Fiction* (Middleton: Wesleyan University Press, 1989),p. 31.

22. Dell Hymes, "Breakthrough into Performance," in *"In Vain I Tried to Tell You." Essays in Native American Ethnopoetics* (Philadelphia: University of Pennsylvania Press); Erving Goffman, *Frame Analysis: An Essay on the Organization of Experience* (New York: Harper Colophon, 1974); Barbara A. Babcock, "The Story in the Story: Metanarration in Folk Narrative," in Richard Bauman, ed., *Verbal Art as Performance* (Prospect Heights, Ill.: Waveland Press, 1984), pp. 71–92.

23. Longstreet, "Georgia Theatrics," p. 3; Dennis Tedlock, "The Analogical Tradition and the Emergence of a Dialogical Anthropology," in *The Spoken Word and the Work of Interpretation* (Philadelphia:

University of Pennsylvania Press, 1983), pp. 321–38. We might conceive of the critical and bibliographic apparatuses surrounding folk texts in anthropological literature as an extreme form of the sanitary "frame." A more attenuated form of monologue is the one in which, as in Longstreet's "The Fight" in *Georgia Scenes*, vernacular characters talk to one another within the frame but not to the frame narrator.

24. James Clifford, "On Ethnographic Authority," in J. Clifford and George E. Marcus, eds., *Writing Culture: The Poetics and Politics of Ethnography* (Berkeley: University of California Press, 1986), pp. 88–121.

25. Hawthorne, "My Kinsman, Major Molineux," pp. 229–30.

26. Hugh Henry Brackenridge, *Incidents of the Insurrection* (1795; reprint, ed. Daniel Marder, New Haven, Conn.: College and University Press, 1972), pp. 80–89. Mark R. Patterson comments on this episode in *Authority, Autonomy, and Representation in American Literature* (Princeton: Princeton University Press, 1988), ch. 2.

27. Edmund S. Morgan, "Government by Fiction: The Idea of Representation," *Yale Review* 72, no. 3 (April 1982): 321–39; Simpson, *The Politics of American English* (New York and Oxford: Oxford University Press, 1986), p. 146; Brackenridge, *Incidents of the Insurrection*, p. 142.

28. Nathan I. Huggins, *Harlem Renaissance* (New York and Oxford: Oxford University Press, 1971), 252 ff.; Berndt Ostendorf, *Black Literature in White America* (Brighton, Sussex: The Harvester Press, 1983), pp. 92, 90 (and all of ch. 3).

29. Harris, "Preface" to *Sut Lovingood's Yarns* (New York: Fitzgerald Book Co., 1867), p. ix.

30. Edmund Wilson, *Patriotic Gore. Studies in the Literature of the American Civil War* (New York and Oxford, Oxford University Press, 1966), p. 509. See also Schmitz, *Of Huck and Alice*, pp. 157–69; Ziff, *Literary Democracy*, p. 191.

31. Arthur Asa Bergen, *Li'l Abner: A Study in American Satire* (New York: Twayne, 1970); James Dickey, *Deliverance* (Boston: Houghton Mifflin, 1970).

32. Chesnutt, *The Conjure Woman*, p. 10.

33. Werner Sollors, "The Gopher in Charles Chesnutt's Conjure Tales: Superstition and Ethnicity in America," *Letterature d'America*, 6, 27 (1985): 107–29.

34. Bret Harte, "Melons" [1870], in *The Works of Bret Harte* (Roslyn, N.Y.: Black's Reader Service, 1932), pp. 145–46.

35. Alfred Kazin, *On Native Grounds: An Interpretation of Modern American Prose Literature* (1942; reprint, New York: Reynal and Hitchcock, 1982), p. 29.

36. Benjamin T. Spencer, *The Quest for Nationality* (Syracuse: Syracuse University Press, 1957), p. 257; Twelve Southerners, *I'll Take My Stand* (1930; reprint, Baton Rouge and London: Louisiana University Press, 1980), p. xxxiv; J. M. Cox, "A Diminished Thing," in Emory Elliott, ed., *The Columbia Literary History of the United States* (New York: Columbia University Press, 1988), pp. 761–84.

37. Hamlin Garland, "Up the Coolly," in *Main Travelled Roads* (New York and London: Harper and Brothers, 1891), pp. 87, 117.

38. Garland, "Up the Coolly," p. 117; Edward Eggleston is quoted in Blair, *Native American Humor* (Scranton, Penn.: Chandler, 1960), p. 127; Kazin, *On Native Grounds*, p. 37.

39. Hamlin Garland, "New Fields" and "Local Color in Art," in *Crumbling Idols* (1894; reprint, Cambridge: Harvard University Press, 1960), pp. 21, 52; Donald Davidson, "Regionalism and Nationalism in American Literature," *American Review* 5, no. 1 (April 1935): 48–61; Davidson, "A Mirror for Artists," in *I'll Take My Stand*, p. 60; E. Eggleston, preface to the 1892 edition of *The Hoosier Schoolmaster*, in Richard Ruland, ed., *A Storied Land: Theories of American Literature* (New York: E. P. Dutton, 1976), 2: 122.

40. Garland, "Provincialism," in *Crumbling Idols*, pp. 8, 22; George Ella Lyon, "Literature in Its Place," *Hemlocks and Balsams* (Banner Elk, N.C.) vol. 9 (1989), pp. 4–8.

41. Henry David Thoreau, *Walden* (1854; reprint, Boston: Houghton Mifflin, 1964), p. 2; Lee Smith, *Oral History* (New York: Ballantine, 1983), p. 28; Garland, "Local Color in Art," p. 49.

42. Harte, "Melons," pp. 145–46; Henry James, preface to *The Portrait of a Lady*, in *The Art of the Novel* (New York: Scribner's, 1947), p. 46.

9. THE RED AND THE BLACK

1. N. Scott Momaday, "The Native Voice," in Emory Elliott, ed., *Columbia Literary History of the United States* (New York: Columbia University Press, 1988), p. 5; W. E. B. DuBois, "The Sorrow Songs,"in *The Souls of Black Folk* [1903], in *Writings* (New York: The Library of America, 1986), p. 537.

2. Thomas Jefferson, *Notes on the State of Virginia* (1787; reprint, New York: Harper & Row, 1964), Appendix 4, pp. 209–10; Edna C. Sorber,

"The Noble Eloquent Savage," *Ethnohistory* 19, no. 3 (Summer 1972): 227–35.

3. Jefferson, *Notes on the State of Virginia*, in *Writings* (New York: The Library of America, 1984), pp. 188–89; see also Myra Jehlen, *American Incarnation: The Individual, the Nation, and the Continent* (Cambridge: Harvard University Press, 1986), pp. 43–51. On the authenticity of Logan's speech, see Edward D. Seeber, "Critical Views on Logan's Speech," *Journal of American Folklore* 60 (1947): 130–46; Ron H. Sandefur, "Logan's Speech: How Authentic?," *Quarterly Journal of Speech* 43, no. 3 (October 1960): 289–96.

4. Werner Sollors, *Beyond Ethnicity: Consent and Descent in American Literature* (New York and Oxford: Oxford University Press, 1989), p. 102–30, mentions such titles as Augustus Stone, *The Last of the Wampanoags* [1829], or Joseph Daldrige, *The Last of the Race of Skillemus* ([1823], about Logan). Sollors also discusses the Indians' theatrical image as alternative fathers or ancestors; Michael Paul Rogin analyzes their complementary role as "children" of the "Great White Father" and "wards to the nation," in *Fathers and Children: Andrew Jackson and the Subjugation of the American Indian* (New York: Knopf, 1975). The phrase "improbable ghost ancestor" is from Constance Rourke, *American Humor* (New York: Harcourt, Brace, 1931), p. 115. An archetypical story of Indian adoption is James Fenimore Cooper's *The Pioneers*, in which the title to the land is legitimately passed on to white people when it turns out that the hero has been adopted by the Delaware. On Pocahontas, see Philip Young, "The Mother of Us All: Pocahontas Reconsidered," *The Kenyon Review* 14, no. 3 (Summer 1962): 391–415.

5. Constance Rourke, *The Roots of American Culture* (New York: Harcourt, Brace, 1942), ch. 1; Francis Jennings, *The Invasion of America: Indians, Colonialism, and the Cant of Conquest* (Chapel Hill: University of North Carolina Press, 1975).

6. Ken Kesey, *One Flew Over the Cuckoo's Nest* (New York: Viking, 1962).

7. N. Scott Momaday, "Man Made of Words," in Rupert Costo, ed., *Indian Voices: The First Convocation of Native American Scholars* (San Francisco: The Indian Historian Press, 1970) p. 51.

8. N. Scott Momaday, interview, in Laura Coltelli, ed., *Winged Words: Native American Writers Speak* (Norman: University of Oklahoma Press, 1990), p. 92; Kenneth Lincoln, *Native American Renaissance* (Berkeley:

University of California Press, 1973), p. 96; Momaday, *The Names* (Tucson: The University of Arizona Press, 1976).

9. Leslie Marmon Silko and James Wright, *The Delicacy and Strength of Lace*, ed. Anne Wright (St. Paul, Minn.: Graywolf Press, 1985), p. 28; Black Elk, *Black Elk Speaks*, ed. John G. Neihardt, (1932; reprint, Lincoln: University of Nebraska Press, 1979), p. 49.

10. James Welch, *Fools Crow* (New York: Penguin, 1986), pp. 334, 353.

11. Momaday, "Man Made of Words," p. 54.

12. Momaday, "Man Made of Words," pp. 55–57. For a critique of Momaday's approach, see Arnold Krupat, *The Voice in the Margin* (Berkeley: University of California Press, 1989), pp. 13–14.

13. Leslie Marmon Silko, *Ceremony* (1977; reprint, New York: Penguin, 1986), p. 122.

14. Silko, interview, in Coltelli, ed., *Winged Words*, p. 141; *Ceremony*, pp. 120–21.

15. Silko, *Ceremony*, p. 122; Simon Ortíz, interview, in Coltelli, ed., *Winged Words*, p. 105.

16. Silko, "I Always Called Her Aunt Susie" and "Lullaby," in *Storyteller* (New York: Little, Brown, 1981), pp. 3–7, 43–51. Gerald Vizenor describes the bureaucratic evil and deception that have destroyed the tribal trust in writing (*Crossbloods* [Minneapolis: University of Minnesota Press, 1990], p. 17); Paula Gunn Allen defines compulsory education as a form of "educational warfare" (Introduction to *Spider Woman's Granddaughters* [Boston: Beacon Press, 1989], pp. 15, 8.)

17. On translation and mediation, see Paula Gunn Allen, "Kochinnenako in Academe," in *The Sacred Hoop: Recovering the Feminine in American Indian Traditions* (Boston: Beacon Press, 1986), pp. 224–25; K. Lincoln, *Native American Renaissance*, pp. 24–40; Arnold Krupat, *For Those Who Come After* (Berkeley: University of California Press, 1985); David Murray, *Forked Tongues: Speech, Writing, and Representation in North American Indian Texts* (Blomington: Indiana University Press, 1991), pp. 5–14. On the impact of writing, see P. Gunn Allen, "Pushing Up the Sky," in *The Sacred Hoop*, p. 244; G. Vizenor, interview, in Coltelli, ed., *Winged Words*, p. 157.

18. On *Ceremony* as dialogic "hinge," see Krupat, *The Voice in the Margin*, pp. 161–70.

19. Jefferson, *Notes on the State of Virginia*, p. 267; Henry Louis Gates, Jr., "Editor's Introduction: Writing 'Race' and the Difference It Makes,"

in Gates, ed., *"Race," Writing, and Difference* (Chicago and London: University of Chicago Press, 1986), p. 11 .

20. Ishmael Reed, "Can a Metronome Know the Thunder or Summon a God?," in Addison Gayle, Jr., ed., *The Black Aesthetic* (Garden City, N.Y.: Doubleday, 1972), p. 381; Henry Louis Gates, Jr., *The Signifying Monkey: A Theory of Afro-American Literary Criticism* (New York and Oxford: Oxford University Press, 1988), pp. 44–102; Houston A. Baker, Jr., *Long Black Song: Essays in Black American Literature and Culture* (Charlottesville: University of Virginia Press, 1972), pp. 18, 20–21; H. A. Baker, *Blues, Ideology, and Afro-American Literature: A Vernacular Theory* (Chicago and London: University of Chicago Press, 1981); Bernard W. Bell, *The Folk Roots of Contemporary Afro-American Poetry* (Detroit: Broadside Press, 1974); Bell, *The Afro-American Novel and Its Traditon* (Amherst: University of Massachusetts Press, 1987), pp. 15–26.

21. Larry Neal, "And Shine Swam On," in Leroi Jones and Larry Neal, eds., *Black Fire: An Anthology of Afro-American Writing* (New York: William Morrow, 1968), p. 647; H. Rap Brown, *Die, Nigger, Die* (London: Allison and Busby, 1970), pp. 27–28.

22. Lawrence Levine, *Black Culture and Black Consciousness* (Oxford and New York: Oxford University Press, 1978), pp. 155–56; W. E. B. DuBois, "Of the Meaning of Progress," in *The Souls of Black Folk*, p. 408.

23. Ralph Ellison, "Change the Joke and Slip the Yoke," in *Shadow and Act* (1964; reprint, New York: Vintage, 1972), pp. 58–59; Zora Neale Hurston, *Mules and Men* (1935; reprint, New York and Evanston: Harper and Row, 1965), p. 17. Bell, in *The Afro-American Novel and Its Tradition,* writes of a "rediscovery" of "residual" folklore; according to Gayl Jones, until the end of the nineteenth century African-American authors tended to adhere to Western literary forms, and it was only later that "the literary uses of oral tradition actually started to flourish" (*Liberating Voices: Oral Tradition in African American Literature* [Cambridge and London: Harvard University Press, 1991], p. 2).

24. Robert B. Stepto, *From Behind the Veil* (Urbana: University of Illinois Press, 1979); William Bevis, "Native American Novels: Homing In," in Brian Swann and Arnold Krupat, eds., *Recovering the Word: Essays on Native American Literature* (Berkeley: University of California Press, 1987), pp. 580–620.

25. Frederick Douglass, *Narrative of the Life of Frederick Douglass, an American Slave. Written by Himself* (1845; reprint, Harmondsworth, Midds.: Penguin, 1986), pp. 23–24 (italics mine). On Douglass's begin-

ning, compared with that of Benjamin Franklin's *Autobiography*, see James Olney, " 'I Was Born': Slave Narratives: Their Status as Autobiography and as Literature," in Charles T. Davis and Henry Louis Gates, Jr., ed., *The Slave's Narrative* (Oxford and New York: Oxford University Press, 1985), 148–75.

26. Douglass, *Narrative*, pp. 58–59.

27. Douglass, *Narrative*, pp. 70–71.

28. Marion Wilson Sterling, *The Slave Narrative: Its Place in American History* (1946; reprint, Washington, D.C.: Howard University Press, 1988), p. 250.

29. Douglass, *Narrative*, p. 93.

30. Richard Wright, *Native Son* in *Early Works*, ed. Arnold Rampersad (New York: The Library of America, 1991), p. 517; Ralph Ellison, *Invisible Man* (1952; reprint, Harmondsworth, Midds.: Penguin, 1978), p. 252. On the refusal to sing for whites in order to avoid a stereotype, see L. Levine, *Black Culture and Black Consciousness*, pp. 164 ff.

31. Russell J. Reising, *The Unusable Past: Theory and the Study of American Literature* (New York and London: Methuen, 1986), p. 261; H. A. Baker, Jr., *The Journey Back* (Chicago: University of Chicago Press, 1980), pp. 38, 43.

32. Frederick Douglass, *My Bondage and My Freedom* (1855; reprint, New York: Dover Publications, 1969), pp. 147, 58.

33. Harriet Jacobs, *Incidents in the Life of a Slave Girl* (1861; reprint, ed. Jean Fagan Yellin, Cambridge: Harvard University Press, 1987), pp. 31, 128 ff.

34. F. Douglass, *My Bondage and My Freedom*, pp. 361, 392; on Captain Anthony, ibid., p. 81. On Douglass's relationship with the abolitionist movement, see Waldo Martin, Jr., *The Mind of Frederick Douglass* (Chapel Hill: University of North Carolina Press, 1985), pp. 35 ff.; on the reversal of authority and authentication from his abolitionist sponsors to Douglass himself in the *Narrative*, see Stepto, *From Behind the Veil*, pp. 17–26.

35. Stefania Piccinato, "Autobiografia e esemplarità: *Narrative of the Life of Frederick Douglass*," in A. Accardo et al., eds., *Identità e scrittura: Studi sull'autobiografia nord-americana* (Rome: Bulzoni, 1988), pp. 144–55; Robert G. O'Meally, "Frederick Douglass's 1845 *Narrative*: The Text was Meant to Be Preached," in Dexter Fisher and Robert B. Stepto, eds., *Afro-American Literature: The Reconstruction of Instruction* (New York: The Modern Language Association of America, 1979), pp. 192–211.

36. F. Douglass, *My Bondage and My Freedom*, pp. 97–98. Mrs. Carmela Luci, a former farm worker from Calabria and an excellent singer of traditional songs, told me in an interview that grape pickers were required to sing, lest they should eat the fruit (interviewed in Rome, October 28, 1973).

37. F. Douglass, *Narrative*, pp. 37–38.

38. F. Douglass, *My Bondage and My Freedom*, pp. 40, 233.

39. Frederick Douglass, *Life and Times of Frederick Douglass. Written by Himself* (1892; reprint, New York: Collier, 1962), p. 571. Albert E. Stone notes that only by *being* black and *becoming* free can Douglass "interpret" his culture: "Identity and Art in Frederick Douglass' *Narrative*," *College Language Association Journal* 17, no. 2 (June 1973): 192–213.

40. Douglass, *Narrative*, pp. 84, 107, 151.

41. Quoted in Sterling, *The Slave Narrative*, p. 250.

42. Ellison, *Invisible Man*, pp. 132, 437.

43. See the entries "Festa" and "Orgia," in Alfonso Di Nola, *Enciclopedia delle religioni* (Florence: Vallecchi, 1970). For a more detailed discussion of the anthropological background and the literary correspondances, see my "La rivolta e la festa: Per un'interpretazione di *Invisible Man*," in Alessandro Portelli, ed., *Saggi sulla cultura afro-americana* (Rome: Bulzoni, 1979), pp. 145–68.

44. Ellison, *Invisible Man*, pp. 430, 452, 433.

45. Ellison, *Invisible Man*, p. 438.

46. Ellison, *Invisible Man*, pp. 441, 440. For an application of this episode to an interpretation of the Los Angeles rebellion of 1992, see Alessandro Portelli, "Il linguaggio inascoltato della rivolta," in Andrea Colombo et al., *Los Angeles: No Justice, No Peace* (Rome: Manifestolibri, 1992), pp. 31–43.

47. In fact, it was Jack Johnson who defeated the "white hope" Jim Jeffries. By merging Johnson with Louis, the song creates a unified symbol of black identity and pride. According to oral tradition, Jeffries was saved from death by the referee, who stopped the match; in fact, he was KOed: see Levine, *Black Culture and Black Consciousness*, pp. 429–37.

48. Ellison, *Invisible Man*, pp. 445, 449. Throughout this episode, Ellison signifies intertextually upon the implications of folk rituals in Ernest Hemingway's *Fiesta* (1927; reprint, London: Granada, 1978, pp. 126 ff.). Both the fiesta and the riot start with an "explosion" of time ("time burst"; "At noon of Sunday July 6th, the fiesta exploded"). In Pamplona, as in Harlem, the ritual generates a "shifting of values." Thus, in the midst

of dancing and drinking, "Everything became quite unreal finally." Likewise, in the whisky-saturated air of Harlem ("all you got to do is breathe, and you drunk, man") reality blurs into a "blue dream." The main shift in values, in Hemingway as in Ellison, concerns the economy: "Late in the fiesta it would not matter what they paid"—"as though nothing could have any consequences" (both concepts reverberate on the Dupre/Scofield episode). An explicit parallel can be detected between Ellison's fat lady on the milk wagon and tipsy Brett Ashley sitting on a wine keg, surrounded by drunken dancers. The intertextual play is reinforced by Ellison's allusions to and parodies of Hemingway's favorite ritual of boxing (the Joe Louis fight) and, earlier in the novel, bullfight (*Invisible Man*, 288–89).

49. Robert O'Meally, *The Craft of Ralph Ellison* (Cambridge: Harvard University Press, 1980), ch. 5, pp. 78–104.

50. Ralph Ellison, "Garrulous Ghosts: The Literature of the American South," BBC radio program, 1982, quoted in H. A. Baker, Jr., *Blues, Ideology, and Afro-American Literature*, p. 174; "Change the Joke and Slip the Yoke," in R. Ellison, *Shadow and Act*, p. 58.

51. Berndt Ostendorf, "Ralph Waldo Ellison: Anthropology, Modernism, and Jazz," in Robert O'Meally, ed., *New Essays on Invisible Man* (Cambridge: Cambridge University Press, 1988), pp. 95–121. See also Baker, *Blues, Ideology, and Afro-American Literature*, pp. 174–75.

52. Ellison, "That Same Pain, That Same Pleasure," in *Shadow and Act*, p. 22.

53. Hurston, *Mules and Men*, pp. 89, 91.

54. Marianne Hirsch, "Maternal Narratives: Cruel Enough to Stop the Blood," in Henry Louis Gates, Jr., ed., *Reading Black, Reading Feminist* (New York: Meridian, 1990), pp. 415–30.

55. Alice Walker, "Zora Neale Hurston: A Cautionary Tale and a Partisan View," in *In Search of Our Mothers' Gardens* (San Diego, New York, London: Harcourt Brace Jovanovich, 1983), p. 85; Walker, "Dedication: On Refusing to Be Humbled by Second Place in a Contest You Did Not Design: A Tradition by Now," in Alice Walker, ed., *I Love Myself When I Am Laughing . . . And Then Again When I Am Looking Mean and Impressive: A Zora Neale Hurston Reader* (Old Westbury, N.Y.: The Feminist Press, 1979), pp. 1–5.

56. Zora Neale Hurston, *Their Eyes Were Watching God* (1937; reprint, Urbana: University of Illinois Press, 1978), p. 286.

57. Hurston, *Their Eyes*, pp. 138–39; Ralph Waldo Emerson, "The American Scholar" [1837], in *Essays and Lectures*, ed. Joel Porte (New York: The Library of America, 1983), p. 53 (all quotations from Emerson are from this edition); "The Poet" [1866], in *Essays and Lectures*, p. 458.

58. Z. N. Hurston, *Their Eyes*, p. 112; Emily Dickinson, *The Complete Poems*, ed. Thomas H. Johnson (London: Faber and Faber, 1975), p. 366, note 747. On this episode, see Barbara Johnson, "Metaphor, Metonymy, and the Voice in *Their Eyes Were Watching God*," in Harold Bloom, ed., *Zora Neale Hurston's Their Eyes Were Watching God* (Boston: Chelsea House Publishers, 1987), pp. 41–57.

59. According to Mary Helen Washington, Janie remains outside the folk community, excluded from the power of oral discourse: *Invented Lives: Narratives of Black Women, 1860–1960* (Garden City, N.Y.: Doubleday, 1987), p. 237; Stepto also judges that Janie's recovery of voice is only partial and incomplete (*From Behind the Veil*, p. 166). Henry Louis Gates, Jr., and Barbara Johnson, "Black and Idiomatic Free Indirect Discourse," in Bloom, ed., *Zora Neale Hurston's Their Eyes Were Watching God*, p. 75, describe free indirect speech as the dramatic expression of a divided self; H. L. Gates, *The Signifying Monkey*, p. 215, notes that free indirect speech can only be written.

60. Gates, *The Signifying Monkey*, p. 193; Molly Hite, "Romance, Marginality and Matrilineage," in Henry Louis Gates, ed., *Reading Black, Reading Feminist*, p. 443; Adam David Milner, "Some Observations on a Black Aesthetic," in A. Gayle, ed., *The Black Aesthetic*, p. 377.

61. Hurston, *Their Eyes*, pp. 270, 284, 286. One of the few critics who do not ignore the death of Tea Cake is Dianne Sadoff, "Black Matrilineage: The Case of Alice Walker and Zora Neale Hurston," *Signs* 11, no. 1 (1985): 4.

62. Toni Morrison, *Beloved* (London: Chatto and Windus/Pan, 1987), p. 5.

63. Ibid., 198.

64. Ibid., pp. 164, 210.

65. Ibid., pp. 200, 210.

66. M. Hirsch, "Maternal Narratives"; Elisabeth Boulot, "Rapports mère-fille dans *The Bluest Eye* et *Beloved* de Toni Morrison,"*Profils Américains* 2 (1992): 145–56, ed. Geneviève Fabre.

67. Morrison, *Beloved*, pp.104, 210. On white people as ghosts, see Olaudah Equiano, *The Life of Oulaudah Equiano; or, Gustavus Vassa the*

African—Written by Himself [1789], in Arna Bontemps, ed., *Great Slave Narratives* (Boston: Beacon Press, 1969), p. 27; Alice Walker, *The Temple of My Familiar* (New York and London: Simon and Schuster, 1989), p. 361.

68. Morrison, *Beloved*, pp. 104, 210. Sethe's act of splitting the contested baby in two bears a tragic echo of Solomon's story in the Bible (as we know, *Song of Solomon* is the title of another major work by Toni Morrison). See also Deborah Horvitz, "Nameless Ghosts: Possession and Dispossession in *Beloved*," *Studies in American Fiction* (Autumn 1989): 157–67.

69. Morrison, *Beloved*, p.172.

70. Ibid., p. 154.

71. Ibid., pp. 271, 274–75.

72. Ibid., p. 125.

73. Ibid., p. 95.

74. Eusebio L. Rodrigues, "The Telling of *Beloved*," *The Journal of Narrative Technique* 21, no. 2 (Spring 1991): 153–69.

75. Morrison, *Beloved*, p. 266.

10. THE SOUNDS OF SILENCE

1. Rebecca Harding Davis, *Life in the Iron Mills, or, The Korl Woman* (1861; reprint, New York: The Feminist Press, 1972), pp. 11, 20, 4.

2. Ibid., pp. 12, 22.

3. Ibid., p. 32.

4. Ibid., p. 12.

5. Ibid., p. 41. Tillie Olsen, *Silences* (New York: Dell, 1978) pp. 67–118; Ann Douglass, *The Feminization of American Culture* (New York: Knopf, 1977). A similar image, in another industrial novel written by a woman, is the portrait of Judas, which the heroine of Harret Arnow's *The Dollmaker* (1954) carves out of a log, as if liberating the face from the matter that imprisons it, only to finally break it into pieces.

6. Harding Davis, *Life in the Iron Mills*, pp. 41, 33; Ralph Waldo Emerson, "The Poet" [1844], in *Essays and Lectures*, ed. Joel Porte (New York: The Library of America, 1983) p. 460 (all quotations from Emerson come from this edition).

7. Harding Davis, *Life in the Iron Mills*, pp. 37, 38.

8. Harding Davis, *Life in the Iron Mills*, p. 47.

9. H. Bruce Franklin, *The Victim as Criminal and Artist* (New York: Alfred A. Knopf, 1977).

10. Jack London, *The Iron Heel* (1907; reprint, New Guildford, Surrey: Biddles Limited, 1974), p. 219. For a more detailed discussion of the matter of this subchapter in a broader context, see my "Jack London e la rivoluzione mancante: note sul *Tallone di ferro*," *Calibano* 5 (1980): 52–76, and "Jack London's Missing Revolution: Notes on *The Iron Heel*," *Science-Ficton Studies* 27, no. 9 (July 1982): 180–94.

11. London, *The Iron Heel*, pp. 31, 41. For a parallel symbol, see the metaphorically missing arm of the slave rebel Bras Coupé (brought to America on a ship named *Egalité*), whose story Aurora tells in George Washington Cable's *The Grandissimes*.

12. London, *The Iron Heel*. Compare with the celebrated final clause of Karl Marx and Friedrich Engels's *Communist Manifesto*: "The proletarians have nothing to lose but their chains. They have a world to win." ("Manifesto of the Communist Party," in Robert C. Tucker, ed., *The Marx-Engels Reader* [New York and London: Norton, 1978], p. 500.)

13. London pp. 7–8, 18–19, 53.

14. Ibid, pp. 59, 19, 18, 7.

15. Ibid, pp. 194, 207.

16. Ibid, pp. 20, 119, 99, 208 (italics mine).

17. Ibid, pp. 209–10.

18. John Steinbeck, *The Grapes of Wrath* (1939; reprint, Harmondsworth, Midds.: Penguin, 1976), p. 200.

19. Dos Passos, *The Big Money*, in *U.S.A.* (1930–1938; reprint, Harmondsworth, Midds: Penguin, 1966), p. 814.

20. John K. Galbraith, *The Great Crash: 1929* (1954; reprint London: Penguin with Hamish Hamilton, 1975), p. 40.

21. Marc Shell, *Money, Language, and Thought* (Berkeley: University of California Press, 1982), ch. 1; Washington Irving, *A History of New York* , in *The Works of Washington Irving*. Author's Revised Edition (New York: G. P. Putnam, 1867), pp. 213–19, 232–33.

22. Ralph Waldo Emerson, "Nature" [1836], in *Essays and Lectures*, p. 22.

23. Roland Barthes, "Elements of Semiology," in *Writing Degree Zero and Elements of Semiology*, trans. Annette Lavers and Colin Smith (London: Jonathan Cape, 1964), pp. 118–20; Ferdinand de Saussure, *Cours de linguistique générale*, ed. Tullio De Mauro (Paris: Payot, 1973), pp. 155–69. Marie Maclean defines money as a specialized form of language, adapting Mary Douglass's definition of ritual, in *Narrative as Performance: The Baudelairean Experiment* (London and New York: Routledge, 1988),

pp. 78–79. In fact, both Saussure and Barthes speak only of exchange between signifers and signifieds, or between signifiers. Money and words, however, are not signifiers but signs; as the signified of *horse* is the mental image of a horse rather than an actual horse, so the signified of money is the *possibility* of exchanging it with commodities rather than the commodities themselves. I think, therefore, that it would be best to speak in terms of exchange between signs and referents. The reluctance of early structural linguistics and semiotics to deal with referents, and the almost exclusive emphasis on the internal dynamics of the sign, served a purpose in establishing the scientific autonomy of these disciplines and their concepts; however, as Frederic Jameson has noted, "The emphasis on this relationship tended . . . to exclude any consideration of the thing itself, of the object of reference in the 'real world.' This declaration of independence of linguistics from any purely semantic concerns . . . has the effect . . . of encouraging the insulation of superstructure from reality" (*The Prison-House of Language* [Princeton: Princeton University Press, 1972], pp. 105–6).

24. Steinbeck, *The Grapes of Wrath*, pp. 171–72.

25. F. Scott Fitzgerald, *The Great Gatsby* (1925; reprint, Harmondsworth, Midds.: Penguin, 1976), pp. 15–16, 103, 20.

26. Fitzgerald, *The Great Gatsby*, pp. 21, 16.

27. Fitzgerald, *The Great Gatsby*, p. 19. On hyperbole, fragmentation, and irresponsibility toward referents in Daisy's conversation, see Louise K. Barnett, "Speech, Society, and Self-Image in *The Great Gatsby*," *R S A Rivista di Studi Americani* 5, no. 7 (1989): 303–14.

28. Fitzgerald, *The Great Gatsby*, pp. 72–73.

29. Mario Pirani, *La Repubblica*, October 21, 1987, discussing the 1987 stock-exchange crash. A similar concept is expressed in a front-page editorial of *Il Manifesto*, the same day, by Valentino Parlato.

30. Robert Cantwell, *Land of Plenty* (1934; reprint, Carbondale: Southern Illinois University Press, 1973), pp. 3, 26; Edmund Wilson, "The Literary Consequences of the Crash," in *The Shores of Light* (1952; reprint, New York: Farrar Strauss Giroux, 1979), p. 496; A. P. Carter, "No Depression in Heaven," in *More Favorites by the Carter Family*, London, Decca Ace of Hearts AH 112.

31. Jerre Mangione, *The Dream and the Deal: The Federal Writers' Project, 1935–1943* (1962; reprint, Philadelphia: University of Pennsylvania Press, 1983); John Lomax, *Adventures of a Ballad Hunter* (New York: Macmillan, 1947); Constance Rourke, *American Humor* (New York:

Harcourt, Brace, 1931) and *The Roots of American Culture* (New York: Harcourt, Brace, 1942).

32. Zora Neale Hurston, *Their Eyes Were Watching God* (1937; reprint, Urbana: University of Illinois Press, 1978), p. 236.

33. Benjamin Appel, *The People Talk: American Voices from the Great Depression* (1940; reprint, New York: Simon and Schuster, 1982), p. 502.

34. Marcus Klein, *Foreigners: The Making of American Literature, 1900–1940* (Chicago and London: University of Chicago Press, 1981), pp. 142–43; Daniel Aaron, Introduction to Jack Conroy, *The Disinherited* (1933; reprint, New York: Hill & Wang, 1963), p. xiii.

35. William Empson, *Some Versions of Pastoral* (1935; reprint, Harmondsworth, Herts.: Penguin with Chatto and Windus, 1966), pp. 11–25; Klein, *Foreigners*, p. 98; Walter B. Rideout, *The Radical Novel in the United States, 1900–1954* (1956; reprint, Cambridge: Harvard University Press, 1970), pp. 173–74; Twelve Southerners, *I'll Take My Stand* (1930; reprint, Baton Rouge and London: Louisiana State University Press, 1980).

36. Steinbeck, *The Grapes of Wrath*, pp. 275, 311.

37. Ibid., pp. 2, 88.

38. Ibid., pp. 33, 37, 473.

39. Ibid., pp. 40, 98–99.

40. Ibid., p. 166.

41. Ibid., p. 467.

42. Ernesto de Martino, *Morte e pianto rituale* (Torino: Boringhieri, 1975), p. 298.

43. In an otherwise rather bad film version, the point is reinforced by the fact that the cross is finally planted in midwater, in the river: a literally floating signifier.

44. Erskine Caldwell, *God's Little Acre* (1932; reprint, New York: New American Library, 1946), p. 2.

45. John Maynard Keynes, *The General Theory of Employment, Interest, and Money* (1936; reprint, London: Macmillan, 1964), pp. 128–31.

46. Caldwell, *God's Little Acre*, p. 26.

47. Ibid., pp. 52, 135.

48. James Agee and Walker Evans, *Les Us Now Praise Famous Men* (1941; reprint, Boston: Houghton Mifflin, 1980), p. xiii; Alfred Kazin, *On Native Grounds: An Interpretation of Modern American Prose Literature* (1942; reprint, New York: Reynal & Hitchcock, 1982), p. 495.

49. Agee and Evans, *Famous Men*, pp. xiv–xv; William Stott, *Documentary Expression in Thirties America* (New York and Oxford: Oxford University Press, 1973).

50. Agee and Evans, *Famous Men*, pp. 366, 100, 12.

51. Ibid., pp. 11, xiv–xv; James Clifford and George E. Marcus, *Writing Culture: The Poetics and Politics of Ethnography* (Berkeley: University of California Press, 1986).

52. Agee and Evans, *Famous Men*, pp. 15–16, 404; Walt Whitman, "So Long," in *Complete Poetry and Collected Prose* (New York: The Library of America, 1982) (all quotes from Whitman in this book come from this edition), p. 611; on the relationship between listening and experience, see Michael Staub, "As Close As You Can Get: Torment, Speech, and Listening in *Let Us Now Praise Famous Men*," *The Mississippi Quarterly* 61, no. 2 (Spring 1986): 147–60.

53. Agee and Evans, *Famous Men*, pp. 62, 242, xiv–xv.

54. Ibid., pp. 417, 58.

55. Ibid., pp. 297, 80, 64.

56. Agee, *The Letters of James Agee to Father Flye* (New York: Bantam, 1963), p. 105.

57. Ernesto de Martino, "Note lucane," in *Furore Simbolo Valore* (Milan: Il Saggiatore, 1962), pp. 107–21.

58. Agee and Evans, *Famous Men*, p. 7.

59. Ibid., p. 469.

60. Malini Johar Schueller, *The Politics of Voice: Liberalism and Social Criticism from Franklin to Kingston* (Albany: State University of New York Press, 1992), p. 114.

61. Peter Ohlin, *Agee* (New York: Ivan Obolesky, 1966), pp. 54–55, discusses contemporary reception.

62. T. V. Reed, "Unimagined Existence and the Fictions of the Real: Postmodernist Realism in *Let Us Now Praise Famous Men*," *Representations* 24 (Fall 1988): 175–76.

63. Agee and Evans, *Famous Men*, p. 240; Stott, *Documentary Expression*, p. 215; Bradford L. Jenkins, "Emma's Story: Two Versions," *Southern Exposure* 7, no. 1 (Spring 1979): 8–26.

64. Bruce Springsteen, spoken introduction to "This Land Is Your Land," in *Bruce Springsteen and the E Street Band Live, 1978–1985*, 1986, CBS 450227.

65. These lines are part of the original manuscript, dated February 23, 1940, reproduced as an illustration in Joe Klein, *Woody Guthrie: A Life*

(New York: Ballantine, 1980), and in Woody Guthrie, *Pastures of Plenty: A Self Portrait*, ed. Dave Marsh and Harold Leventhal (New York: HarperCollins, 1990), p. xxiv. Guthrie had initially written "God Blessed America for Me," as a response to Irving Berlin's "God Bless America." In the manuscript, however, this line is already crossed out and replaced by the present title.

66. Klein, *Woody Guthrie*, pp. 433–34; Alessandro Portelli, *Woody Guthrie e la cultura popolare americana* (Bari: De Donato, 1975), pp. 180–82.

67. Woody Guthrie, *Born to Win*, ed. Robert Shelton (New York: Collier, 1967), p.18.

68. Woody Guthrie, "Tom Joad," in *Dust Bowl Ballads*, Folkways FH 5212.

11. TALKING HEADS

1. Theodore Dreiser, *Sister Carrie* (1900; reprint, London: Constable, 1927), p. 98; Henry James, *The American Scene* (1907; reprint, ed. Leon Edel, Bloomington: Indiana University Press, 1968), p. 235.

2. Elizabeth Williamson, "Advertising," in M. Thomas Inge, ed., *Handbook of American Popular Culture* (Westport, Conn., and London: Greenwood Press, 1980), 2:3–29; James Von Schilling, "Records and the Recording Industry," ibid., 2: 3–29; Malini Johar Schueller, *The Politics of Voice: Liberalism and Social Criticism from Franklin to Kingston* (Albany: State University of New York Press, 1992), p. 52.

3. David Leavitt, "Spouse Night," in *A Place I've Never Been* (London: Penguin, 1990), pp. 18, 21.

4. Gerald Vizenor, *Bearheart: The Heirship Chronicles* (Minneapolis: University of Minnesota Press, 1990), pp. 167, 25–26; Lana F. Rakow, "Women and the Telephone (The Gendering of a Communication Technology)," in Chris Kramarae, ed., *Technology and Women's Voices* (London: Routledge and Kegan Paul, 1987), p. 214; Jay McInerney, *Bright Lights, Big City* (1984; reprint, New York: Random House, 1987), p. 19.

5. Paul Zumthor, *Introduction à la poésie orale* (Paris: Seuil, 1983), p. 28.

6. Frederic Jameson, *Postmodernism; or, The Cultural Logic of Late Capitalism* (Durham: Duke University Press, 1991), pp. 4, 49.

7. Cotton Mather, "Life of John Cotton," in *Magnalia Christi Americana* (1702; reprint, New York: Russell & Russell, 1967), 1: 271, 273.

8. Ibid., pp. 311–12, 254.

9. Robert T. Oliver, *History of Public Speaking in America* (Boston: Allyn and Bacon, 1965), pp. 34–35, 38. Charles Chauncy is quoted in Richard Hofstadter, *Anti-Intellectualism in American Life* (New York: Knopf, 1963), p. 64.

10. Charles Dickens, *American Notes* [1842], in *American Notes and Pictures from Italy* (London: Oxford University Press, 1966), p. 88; David S. Reynolds, *Beneath the American Renaissance* (New York: Knopf, 1988), pp. 24–25. Charles G. Finney is quoted in Frank Otto Gatell and John G. McPaul, *Jacksonian America, 1815–1840,* (Englewood Cliffs, N.J., Prentice-Hall, 1970), pp. 51–52.

11. Walt Whitman, "Father Taylor (and Oratory)," (New York: The Library of America, 1982), pp. 1143–46 (all quotes from Whitman in this book come from this edition); Dickens, *American Notes*, pp. 57–58; Reynolds, *Beneath the American Renaissance*, pp. 19–21.

12. Herman Melville, *Moby-Dick*, in *The Works of Herman Melville*, Standard Edition (New York: Russell and Russell, 1963), 7: 49–50.

13. Van Wyck Brooks, *The Times of Melville and Whitman* (New York: E. P. Dutton, 1947), p. 9; Oliver, *History of Public Speaking*, pp. 373 ff.; Constance Rourke, *Trumpets of Jubilee* (New York: Harcourt and Brace, 1927), pp. 17–80.

14. Kenneth Cmiel, *Democratic Eloquence: The Fight over Popular Speech in Nineteenth-Century America* (New York: William Morrow, 1990), pp. 190–99, 259.

15. Oliver, *History of Public Speaking*, p. 392; Sandra Sizer, *Gospel Hymns and Social Religion: The Rhetoric of Nineteenth-Century Revivalism* (Philadelphia: Temple University Press, 1978), pp. 119–20.

16. Barnet Baskerville, *The People's Voice: The Orator in American Society* (Lexington: University Press of Kentucky, 1979), pp. 101–2; Carl Bode, *The American Lyceum: Town Meeting of the Mind* (New York and Oxford: Oxford University Press, 1956); Joseph E. Gould, *The Chautauqua Movement: An Episode in the Continuing American Revolution* (New York: State of New York University Press, 1961).

17. Theodore Bilbo is quoted in Waldo W. Braden, *The Oral Tradition in the South* (Baton Rouge: Louisiana University Press, 1982), p. 88; on Faulkner and Southern oratory, see Stephen M. Ross, *Fiction's Inexhaustible Voice: Speech and Writing in Faulkner* (Athens: University of Georgia Press, 1989).

18. Cmiel, *Democratic Eloquence*, pp. 248–49, 259–60.

19. Richard Dorson, "A Theory for American Folklore," in *American Folklore and the Historian* (Chicago and London: University of Chicago Press, 1971), p. 47; Randall M. Fisher, *Rhetoric and American Democracy: Black Protest Through Vietnam Dissent* (Lanham, N.J.: University Press of America, 1985), p. 71.

20. Mark Twain, "Autobiography," in *Mark Twain in Eruption*, ed. Bernard DeVoto (New York: Harper and Brothers, 1922) (quoted in Janet Smith, ed., *Mark Twain and the Damned Human Race* [New York: Hill and Wang], 1962, p. 3).

21. Douglass Watts, "Musical Events," *The New Yorker* 93 (June 14, 1969); John Cohen, Foreword to John Cohen, ed., *The Essential Lenny Bruce* (St. Albans, Herts.: Granada, 1975), p. 9; Lawrence E. Mintz, "Standup Comedy as Social and Cultural Mediation," *American Quarterly* 37, no. 1 (Spring 1985): 71–80.

22. Lee Ballinger, "Dragging the Line," *Rock and Roll Confidential* 63 (December 1988): 7–8.

23. Robert Johnson, "Hellhounds on My Trail" [1937], in *The Complete Recordings*, Columbia Records C2K 46222, 1990; Lucy J. Dalton and B. Graham, "Beer Drinking Christians," sung by Lucy J. Dalton and Bobby Bare in *Take This Job and Shove It!*, Epic AL 37177, 1977; Alessandro Portelli, "Cristiani che bevono birra: la country music e le ambiguità della cultura operaia in America," *I Giorni Cantati* 5 (Spring 1984): 61–68.

24. Charles Keil, *Urban Blues* (Chicago and London: University of Chicago Press, 1966); Robert Pattison, *On Literacy: The Politics of the Word from Homer to the Age of Rock* (New York and Oxford: Oxford University Press, 1982), p. 203.

25. Greil Marcus, *Mystery Train: Images of America in Rock and Roll Music* (London and New York: Omnibus, 1986), pp. 286–90.

26. U2, *Rattle and Hum*, Island Records U27, 1988. The last verse of Woody Guthrie's "Jesus Christ" begins: "This song was written in New York City." U2 recorded this song in *A Vision Shared*, Folkways-CBS 460905, 1988. Though they are not from the United States, U2 (like the Beatles and the Rolling Stones, briefly discussed later in this chapter) belong in this analysis: *Rattle and Hum* is a report of their encounter with the United States, and—after all—the relationship of rock music with the United States goes beyond biographic details.

27. Walter J. Ong, *The Presence of the Word* (New Haven and London: Yale University Press, 1967), pp. 8–9; Eric C. Havelock, *The Muse Learns*

to Write: Reflections on Orality and Literacy from Antiquity to the Present (New Haven: Yale University Press, 1986), pp. 99–100.

28. Mark Lewisohn, *The Complete Beatles Recording Sessions* (London: The Hamlyn Publishing Group, 1988); Evan Eisenberg, *The Recording Angel: Explorations in Phonography* (New York: Academic Press, 1981), p. 109.

29. Felice Liperi and Vito Conteduca, "Aspettarsi l'inatteso: osservazioni e testimonianze sul ruolo dell'improvvisazione nel rock'n'roll," *I Giorni Cantati* 1, no. 2/3 (July/December 1981): 85–95.

30. Keith Richards, interviewed by Steve Morse, "The Stones are Showing Their High-Tech Style," *Boston Globe*, October 3, 1989, p. 28.

31. Gerald Vizenor, *The Trickster of Liberty* (Minneapolis: University of Minnesota Press, 1988), p. 142.

32. Alice Walker, "Everyday Use," in *In Love and Trouble* (San Diego and New York: Harcourt Brace Jovanovich, 1973), p. 56.

33. Walker, "Everyday Use," pp. 58–59; Alice Walker, *In Search of Our Mothers' Gardens* (San Diego, New York, and London: Harcourt Brace Jovanovich, 1983), pp. 238–39; Elaine Showalter, "Piecing and Writing," in Nancy K. Miller, ed., *The Poetics of Gender* (New York: Columbia University Press, 1986), pp. 222–45; Elaine Showalter, "Common Threads," in *Sister's Choice: Tradition and Change in American Women's Writing* (Oxford: Clarendon Press, 1991), pp. 145–75; Houston J. and Charlotte Baker, "Patches, Quilts, and Community in Alice Walker's 'Everyday Use,' " *Southern Review* 21 (July 1985): 710–16.

34. Antonio Gramsci, "Osservazioni sul folclore," in *Quaderni del carcere: Letteratura e vita nazionale* (Rome: Editori Riuniti, 1971), p. 268.

35. Linda Hogan, "Making Do," in Paula Gunn Allen, ed., *Spider Woman's Granddaughters* (Boston: Beacon Press, 1989), p. 195; Leslie Marmon Silko, *Ceremony* (1977; reprint, New York: Penguin, 1986), p. 127.

36. Toni Morrison, *Beloved* (London: Chatto and Windus/Pan, 1987), pp. 272–73; William Faulkner, *Absalom, Absalom!* (1936; reprint, New York: Vintage, 1987), pp. 378–79.

37. Lance Olsen, Foreword to Gurney Norman, "Book One from *Crazy Quilt*: A Novel in Progress" (Frankfort, Ky.: Frankfort Arts Foundation, 1990), p. xi; Jameson, *Postmodernism*, pp. 30–31.

38. Ishmael Reed, *Mumbo Jumbo* (1972; reprint, New York: Avon, 1978), pp. 41–42.

39. Gerald Vizenor, *Crossbloods* (Minneapolis: University of Minnesota Press, 1990), p. vii; Vizenor, interview, in Laura Coltelli, ed., *Winged Words: Native American Writers Speak* (Norman: University of Oklahoma Press, 1990), pp. 165, 174; Paula Gunn Allen, interview, ibid., p. 16.

40. Gayl Jones, *Corregidora* (1975; reprint, Boston: Beacon Press, 1986), p. 80.

41. James Welch, *The Death of Jim Loney* (1979; reprint, New York: Penguin, 1987), p. 14.

42. The song is quoted here as reported in Alanna Nash's authorized biography, *Dolly* (New York: Berkley Publishing Corporation, 1979), pp. 181–82.

43. Oscar Lewis, *La Vida: A Puerto Rican Family in the Culture of Poverty* (New York: Vintage, 1965), p. xlvii.

44. Nikki Giovanni, "Nikki Rosa," in *Black Feeling, Black Talk, Black Judgment* (New York: William Morrow, 1970), p. 59; Emily Dickinson, *The Complete Poems*, ed. Thomas H. Johnson (London: Faber and Faber, 1975), p. 305, n. 618. Incidentally, Nikki Giovanni, Dolly Parton, and James Agee all come from Knoxville, Tennessee, or its vicinity.

45. Alessandro Portelli, "Dai diamanti nella polvere all'angelo dei sotterranei," *Calibano* 6 (1981): 101–33; William Faulkner, "Appendix" [1946] to *The Sound and the Fury* (1929; reprint, New York and London: W. W. Norton, 1987), p. 236.

46. The Carter Family, "The Gospel Ship," in *The Famous Carter Family*, Harmony HS 113332.

47. Johnny Cash sings "One Piece at a Time" in the album by the same title, CBS 32016. See Yvonne Lockwood, "The Joy of Labor," *Western Folklore*, 43, no. 3 (July 1974): 202–11, for a study of workers' creative activities in the workplace.

48. Bruce Springsteen, "The Promise," in the bootleg album *All Those Years, All Those Miles*, no date.

49. Springsteen, "Born to Run," in *Born to Run*, CBS 80959, 1975.

50. Springsteen, "The Promised Land," in *Darkness at the Edge of Town*, Columbia 35318, 1978; "Born to Run"; "Ramrod," in *The River*, Columbia 36854, 1980; Leo Marx, "The Pilot and the Passenger: Landscape Conventions and the Style of *Huckleberry Finn*," *American Literature* 28 (May 1956): 129–46; on consent and descent, see Werner Sollors, *Beyond Ethnicity: Consent and Descent in American Literature* (New York and Oxford: Oxford University Press, 1989).

51. Springsteen, "Used Car," in *Nebraska*, CBS 100, 1982; "Spare Parts and Broken Hearts" and "Tougher than the Rest," in *Tunnel of Love*, CBS 460270, 1987; Henry David Thoreau, *Walden* (1854; reprint, Boston: Houghton Mifflin, 1964), p. 238.

52. Franco Moretti, "Dialectics of Fear," trans. David Forgacs, in Moretti, *Signs Taken for Wonders*, rev. edition (London and New York: Verso, 1988), pp. 83–108; Carole Beebe Tarantelli, "*Frankenstein*, ovvero la perdita del soggetto femminile," *Calibano* 6 (1981): 156–86; Alessandro Portelli, "La narrativa di Isaac Asimov: Il presente come utopia," *Calibano* 2 (1977): 138–84.

53. Isaac Asimov, Introduction to *The Rest of the Robots* (London: Granada, 1968), pp. 11, 14.

54. Isaac Asimov, in *I Robot* (1950; reprint, London: Granada, 1968): "Robbie," p. 27; "Reason," p. 60; "Liar!," p. 95.

55. Reed, *Mumbo Jumbo*, p. 79; Philip K. Dick, *Blade Runner (Do Androids Dream of Electric Sheep?* (1968; reprint, New York: Ballantine, 1982), p. 10.

56. Among Gibson's quilts are the blankets with which Tessier-Ashpool covers his daughter's corpse (*Neuromancer*) and the quilts used by Kumiko (*Mona Lisa Overdrive*) and Marly (*Count Zero*). Patchwork landscapes include Gaudy's "quilt-like ceramics" in the Parc Guell in Barcelona, London's "patchwork" of styles and eras, and the "patchwork of domes" of the Boston-Atlanta urban sprawl. In the final episode of *Count Zero*, the cosmic artist works like a quilt-making bricoleur: "They send me new things, but I prefer the old things"—including, like traditional quilts, scraps of Mary's clothes. William Gibson, *Count Zero* (New York: Ace, 1981), pp. 13, 99, 114, 226–27; *Neuromancer* (1984; reprint, New York: Ace, 1986), pp. 182, 185; *Mona Lisa Overdrive* (London: Grafton, 1988), pp. 38, 75; "New Rose Hotel," in *Burning Chrome* (1986; reprint, New York: Ace, 1987), pp. 107, 109.

57. Gibson, "Cyberspazio: Una trovata da 20.000 dollari," *Il Manifesto*, 27 November 1990, p. 10; on "folklore of console jockeys," see *Mona Lisa Overdrive*, p. 138.

58. L. Frank Baum, *The Patchwork Girl of Oz* (1913; reprint, New York: Ballantine, 1979), p. 15. On Oz and machine civilization, see Russell B. Nye, "An Appreciation," in Baum, *The Wizard of Oz*, ed. Michael P. Hearn (1900; reprint, New York: Schocken, 1983).

59. Gibson, *Mona Lisa Overdrive*, pp. 7, 133.

60. Gibson, *Neuromancer*, p. 74. For references to the computer as ghost, see *Neuromancer*, pp. 117, 166, 192, 229, 250–51. The image of the computer as ghost (as well as the speaking and singing robot) also appears in Thomas Pynchon, *Vineland* (New York: Viking Penguin, 1990), pp. 114, 193.

61. Gibson, *Mona Lisa Overdrive*, p. 84.

62. McInerney, *Bright Lights, Big City*, p. 151.

63. Gore Vidal, "On Rereading the Oz Books," in Baum, *The Wizard of Oz*, p. 263.

64. Baum, *The Wizard of Oz*, pp. 120, 172, 176–77. Norman Rush, *Mating* (1991; reprint, New York: Vintage, 1992), p. 89.

65. Gibson, "Johnny Mnemonic," in *Burning Chrome*, p. 22.

66. Gibson, *Count Zero*, p. 225.

INDEX OF NAMES AND WORKS

SUBJECT INDEX